$06

Canadian
Labour
and
Industrial
Relations:
public and private sectors

Suggested further reading from McGraw-Hill Ryerson:

The Practice of Industrial Relations

David A. Peach and David Kuechle

Canadian Labour
and

Industrial Relations:
public and private sectors
text and readings

Edited by H. C. Jain
Chairman, Division of Social Science and Administration
The University of New Brunswick in Saint John

McGRAW-HILL RYERSON LIMITED

Toronto   Montreal   New York   London
Sydney   Mexico   Panama   São Paulo
Johannesburg   Düsseldorf   New Delhi
Singapore   Kuala Lumpur   Auckland

CANADIAN LABOUR AND INDUSTRIAL RELATIONS: PUBLIC AND PRIVATE SEC-
TORS

ISBN 0-07-082259-X

1 2 3 4 5 6 7 8 9 10   AP   4 3 2 1 0 9 8 7 6 5

Printed and bound in Canada

iv

Table of Contents

PREFACE

In the last decade the volume of published research and unpublished studies on Canadian labour relations topics has increased considerably. Just a glance at the bibliography, given at the end of this book, will give the reader an idea of the output. The Prime Minister's Task Force alone has published more than two dozen monographs. These studies and publications reflect the growing interest among students, scholars and practitioners, their need for more information and their search for workable solutions to highly complex labour relations problems. Most Canadian universities, particularly Business faculties, offer courses in labour relations; some of them make such courses compulsory for all students. Because of the growing demand from community groups, as well as from other interested parties, for more knowledge and insights to help solve complex problems, many labour–management councils and institutes have sprung up across the country in recent years.

While there has been a great deal of research and writing on Canadian labour relations, most of these studies and publications are scattered and pertain to a specialized area of study. Having taught for more than eleven years at three Canadian universities as well as at the Labour College of Canada; having conducted numerous workshops and seminars for labour and management groups; and having acted as an arbitrator in labour disputes, I asked myself what kind of introduction to Canadian labour relations would best serve the needs of a public representing such a wide range of interests. This book embodies my answer. It is divided into five parts. The combination of this author's textual introduction to each part along with supporting readings is designed to serve as an introductory textbook in the field of Canadian labour relations. A synopsis precedes each article. At the end of each part a number of questions are listed for study and discussion.

The practice of industrial relations is a highly dynamic process. Developments, such as structural changes within the Canadian labour movement, legislation for dealing with the unique characteristics and problems of the construction industry, trends toward organization of professional workers and collective bargaining, legislation for dealing with dispute settlement in the public sector in various jurisdictions in Canada, have taken place at a such a fast pace that this author felt it imperative to request several Canadian scholars and practitioners to contribute special articles for this book giving up-to-date information on these developments.

While this book deals primarily with Canadian Issues it must be acknowledged that much original and excellent research in the area of collective bargaining in the private sector has been done in the United States. This research is directly relevant to the Canadian scene. Therefore several articles pertaining to the American environment have been included in this book. It has not been possible to include all relevant research and useful information in one book. However, I have tried to provide materials which should be adequate as a foundation for thinking and acting effectively with respect to contemporary Canadian labour relations issues.

Mere theoretical knowledge of the institutional and environmental factors which affect labour relations is not enough, a student also needs experience in interpreting facts and in making sound generalizations about them. If a student is interested in gaining practical insights into Canadian issues and problems he is advised to study and analyze real Canadian cases which are provided in my first book, *Canadian Cases in Labour Relations and Collective Bargaining*, published by Longman, Canada, in 1973; and in Peach and Kuechle, *The Practice of Industrial Relations*, 1975, McGraw-Hill Ryerson.

Acknowledgments and thanks are due: first to Professor Shirley Goldenberg, McGill University, and Professor Joseph Rose, University of New Brunswick, for writing articles specifically for this book; second to my colleagues and friends, Professors Alton Craig, University of Ottawa; Joseph Revell, University of Prince Edward Island; William Cunningham, Mount Allison University; George Newell, Canadian Union of Public Employees; to my students who provided helpful advice and suggestions; to John Roberts and Stan Skinner; and to Geoffrey Burn and the editorial staff of McGraw-Hill Ryerson for their assistance; and last, but not the least to my wife, Genevieve, for her understanding and her continuous encouragement and assistance in the completion of this project.

HEM C. JAIN

PART 1

CONCEPTUAL FRAMEWORK: FRAMEWORKS FOR THE ANALYSIS OF INDUSTRIAL RELATIONS

INTRODUCTION

No one can afford to be ignorant of the problems of industrial unrest. These problems are aptly highlighted in the communication media, television, radio and newspapers. Public statements of important officials from unions, management, government and universities have given the man on the street several basic solutions to many problems involving labour and management. Those proposals cover the entire spectrum of difficulties, from strike action to the need for compulsory arbitration. Not only do industrial conflicts affect labour and management but they also produce serious effects upon the public at large. Clearly there is a need for a scientific and systematic approach to the study of industrial relations problems as well as to the study of a variety of proposed solutions so that a logical and effective framework of principles may be constructed.

The articles in Part 1 have been selected to assist the reader in developing an overall view of industrial relations as a system. Many authors use the historical approach in introducing labour and industrial relations as a field of study. However, it has the disadvantage of frequently stirring up emotional responses which do not assist the readers in thinking systematically and objectively about industrial relations problems. While the value of human emotions is not to be denied, premature conditioning for or against the material to be presented subsequently can hinder to a great degree a reader's objectivity. Part 1, therefore, starts with two theoretical models of industrial relations. Covering these models are the articles by A.W. Craig and W.F. Whyte. Craig's model is more of a macro framework which applies to an industry or national system, whereas Whyte's model applies to a micro type of analysis, that is to a plant or a department within a plant. These frameworks are not mutually exclusive. They supplement each other.

The frameworks for analysis are set forth in the first part so that they will be available to students when they will come to analyze specific problems and cases involving relationships between union, management and government.

The third selection examines the external factors, unique to the Canadian setting, which affect the industrial relations system in Canada.

It is hoped that the questions at the end will be thought-provoking and will lead to fruitful discussion.

A MODEL FOR THE ANALYSIS
OF
INDUSTRIAL RELATIONS SYSTEMS*
Alton W. J. Craig

The conceptual model presented in this article brings together various partial theories of industrial relations and gives a schematic view of the industrial relations system in the abstract.

INTRODUCTION

In recent years the emerging discipline of industrial relations has been undergoing an agonizing appraisal both in terms of its subject matter and the methodology employed in its research. While studies in other social science disciplines such as economics, political science, and sociology have produced useful analytical research models and significant theoretical achievements, studies in industrial relations have been confined, with a few notable exceptions, to descriptive case studies, descriptive history, descriptions of collective agreement provisions, and formal analysis of statutory and common law developments. Where attempts have been made at some degree of generalization, these have been at the level of partial theory only. Unfortunately, the partial theories that have been developed have not yet been sufficiently integrated to provide even a minimum understanding of the totality of industrial relations behaviour.

The purpose of this paper is to articulate, however briefly, a conceptual model which, it is hoped, will be useful for conducting analytical studies and, eventually, for unifying the various partial theories into a general theory of industrial relations. The model presented here draws heavily on the works of a number of writers in various social science disciplines and, I hope, brings together a sufficient core of concepts for analyzing the totality of industrial relations behaviour.

INDUSTRIAL RELATIONS SYSTEMS DEFINED

Before proceeding to discuss the model itself, I would like to suggest that one of the reasons for the lack of any significant conceptual and theoretical developments in industrial relations is the fact that the discipline has never been defined in such a way as to give it some

---

* A paper presented at the annual meeting of the Canadian Political Science Association on June 7, 1967. Reprinted with permission.

degree of central focus. Dunlop, who probably comes closer than any-one else in defining the domain of industrial relations, defines it almost strictly in structural terms. Nowhere, except in his contrast with the economic system, does he touch on its functional character. However, an adequate definition of the discipline must comprise both its structural and functional components.

For our purpose, then, *industrial relations may be defined to include that complex of private and public activities, operating in an environment, which is concerned with the allocation of rewards to employees for their services.* By referring to the complex of private and public activities, this definition embraces the whole gamut of structural arrangements whereby employee rewards are allocated, ranging from unilaterial determination by the state or an employer to tripartite determination involving employers, unions, and public or private agencies. By referring to the rewards to employers for their services, this definition embraces not only material rewards, but also the psychological and social rewards which employees receive in the performance of their services.

THE MAIN COMPONENTS OF THE MODEL

Taking the allocation of rewards to employees as the central focus of industrial relations, let me now proceed to set forth the rudiments of our model. As some of you will no doubt observe, I have utilized an input-output model of the type used by David Easton for the analysis of political life.[1] (Our model is illustrated in graphic form in the diagram attached at the end of this paper.) Like any model, this one abstracts from empirical phenomena and attempts to capture in a nutshell the basic characteristics of industrial relations systems.

As you will observe, the model consists of four basic components: (1) inputs, summarized by the concepts of goals, values and power which are conditioned by the flow of effects from the environment sub-systems; (2) the mechanisms for converting the inputs into outputs; and (3) the outputs, comprising the financial, social and psychological rewards to employees; and (4) a feedback loop through which the outputs of the industrial relations system flow back into the environmental sub-systems. Let me now briefly discuss each of these components.

THE INPUTS OF AN INDUSTRIAL RELATIONS SYSTEM

As implied above, the inputs of an industrial relations system come from two sources. First, there are the inputs from within the system itself, which are summarized by the concepts of goals, values and power. Secondly, there is the flow of effects from the environmental sub-systems which becomes part of the inputs of the industrial relations system inasmuch as the environmental inputs condition the goals, values and power of the actors in the system. Let me now take a more detailed look at the nature of these two types of inputs.

INPUTS FROM WITHIN THE SYSTEM ITSELF

First, let us examine the inputs from within the system, or the within-puts. In order to discuss these we must first look at the actors in a system, i.e. those with whose activities we are concerned. The actors include individual workers in their role as workers, formal or informal organizations of workers, managers as individuals and as members of a management team, and government and private agencies and individuals. These are the actors whose goals, values and power constitute the inputs, and whose activities convert the inputs into outputs.

Goals refer to the objectives which an actor strives to achieve. *Values* refer to the norms or standards which an actor observes in establishing a hierarchy of objectives and the means of obtaining these objectives. *Power* refers to the ability of an actor to satisfy his needs or goals despite the resistance of others. Each actor in the system has his or its own particular set of goals and values. Speaking in a very general way, one might say that organized labour has a very pragmatic objective of obtaining more, more and more, as stated a long time ago by Samuel Gompers. However, labour may be concerned with obtaining more of (x) rather than more of (y) so that it becomes a matter of deciding what emphasis shall be placed on the various alternative objectives or goals that labour seeks. In determining its goals, labour is guided by the norm of egalitarianism. This is the basic value, or norm, behind those objectives which labour seeks to achieve.

Management is likewise motivated by the objective of obtaining more — basically more profits — and is guided by the competitive norm. Government and private agencies, at least in this country, have until quite recently been guided by the goal of assisting the two private parties, i.e. labour and management, to achieve settlement of their disputes without work stoppages and without damage to the public interest. In recent years, however, government agencies involved in the industrial relations system in a number of countries, including the United States and Great Britain, have had very positive substantive objectives, taking the form of wage freeze, wage guidelines, or incomes policies. Hence, all three actors in the system have their own goals. While there is general agreement among all the actors on some goals, to the extent that the actors come from different sub-goal and value groups in our society, they will have their own distinct objectives and values. It is where these different goals and values clash that we find conflict among the actors in the system.

The power of any one of the actors, as was stated above, may be defined as the ability of that actor to obtain its objectives despite the resistance of others. The power of any one of the three actors will vary according to conditions in the environment as well as conditions within the industrial relations system itself. For example, a very buoyant economy will give a good deal of power to labour, whereas a slack economy will add to management's power. Also, a very militant union membership will give a good deal of power to the labour leader when he meets with his counterpart in management, whereas an apathetic membership will not. Likewise the government, depending on the arsenal of weapons that it has at its control, may or may not have some degree of power. For example, the United States government had considerable power over the other two parties in a number of industries last year when it released stockpiles of basic materials.

In summary, then, the goals, values and power of the actors in the industrial relations system constitute, in summary form, the input variables. However, as we stated at the beginning of this section, the inputs are of two types, namely, those from within the system and those which flow from the environment. Let us now take a look at the flow of effects from the environment as it becomes a *conditioning input* into the industrial relations system.

FLOW OF EFFECTS FROM THE ENVIRONMENT AS CONDITIONAL INPUTS INTO THE INDUSTRIAL RELATIONS SYSTEM

In referring to the environmental inputs as conditioning inputs, I am suggesting that the environmental inputs act to impose a range within which the outputs of the system must fall. Specification of the outputs within that range, however, is determined by the goals, values and power of the actors within the system.

The environmental systems which have significant conditioning effects on the industrial relations system include the following: (a) the ecological system, (b) the economic system, (c) the political system, (d) the legal system, and (e) the social or cultural system. Let me now discuss each of these briefly, and in discussing each I will use only a few examples by way of illustration.

By *the ecological system*, I mean the physical surroundings in which man finds himself and the way in which he adjusts to these surroundings. For example, the natural resources of a country or region will have an impact on the inputs of the industrial relations system, inasmuch as they determine the structure of industry and the kinds of rewards that can be made. Also, climatic conditions will have an effect on the industrial relations system. For example, the climate in Canada is such that it closes our inland ports and slows down construction activities for a good part of the year. This, in turn, will lead the actors in these industrial relations systems to seek high rewards during the active season.

The economic system, comprising the product market, labour market, money market and technological innovation, also conditions the inputs of the industrial relations system. As mentioned previously, a period of high economic activity is a condition which gives rise to relatively substantial inputs and, consequently, outputs, whereas a period of slow economic activity will produce inputs and outputs of a somewhat smaller and probably somewhat different nature. As I see it, the labour market acts to establish the minimum inputs and outputs whereas the product market establishes a ceiling. Also, monetary and fiscal policies, inasmuch as they operate to speed up or slow down economic activity, will likewise act as factors affecting the inputs of the industrial relations system. Technological change, by determining the kind of job hierarchies, the skills required and productivity changes, has its impact on the inputs of the industrial relations system through its effect on manpower requirement and the power of the actors in the system and the goals they attempt to achieve. Ideally it would be desirable to have summary variables representing the impact of the economic system on the inputs — and consequently the outputs — of the industrial relations system. As you probably know, Eckstein and Wilson use unemployment and profit rates as summary variables of the labour market and product market respectively in their analysis of money wage changes in American industry.[2]

The *political system* operates to influence the inputs of the industrial relations system in a variety of ways. First of all, the executive branch of the political system may play a direct role by taking action to see that the public interest is protected. This has been used frequently in the United States and, as you know, in Canada as well. The political system also often operates through its legislative branch such as it did in Canada last summer when Parliament ordered the railway workers back to work with a minimum settlement which was subject to further negotiation or arbitration.

The *legal system*, comprising both common and statutory law, also has an effect on the inputs of the industrial relations system. First, by establishing procedural rules which the actors in the system must follow, the legal system prescribes or prohibits certain kinds of behaviour in converting the inputs into outputs. With the rash of illegal strikes during the past year, I need hardly remind you of the conflict that exists between the goals and values upon which so much of our common law rests and the goals and values of some of the actors in our Canadian industrial relations system. Secondly, labour standards legislation, including minimum wage laws, maximum hour laws, and so on, become conditioning inputs into the industrial relations system inasmuch as they establish a floor or a ceiling as the case may be.

The *social system* acts as a conditioning input into the industrial relations system in the very diffuse way. First, the actors in the industrial relations system are also part of the total social system, and consequently have assumed at least part of the main goal and value patterns of the broader social system.[3] It is this joint consensus on goals and values that keeps the system functioning smoothly. However, to the extent that there are sub-goal and value patterns within the general social system from which the actors in the industrial relations system come, to this extent the social system will have a divisive impact as a conditioning input into the industrial relations system. Furthermore, expectations within the social system may put pressure on the political system to take action with respect to some problem in the industrial relations system. For example, if it is felt strongly that a dispute in a particular industry is disruptive to the whole society or an important segment thereof, pressure will emerge from the social system for the political system to take some action to resolve that dispute or to establish some guidelines which the actors in the industrial relations system must follow.

In summing up this section on environmental influences, I would like to suggest that one of the major tasks for those of us who are engaged in the emerging discipline of industrial relations is that of defining the precise role of the inputs from within the system (the behavioural inputs) and the precise role of the environmental influences which condition these inputs: Ideally, we should be able to develop quantitative measures of each of these and combine them into some kind of composite index. A very suggestive approach to this problem has been made by Dr. Hameed, one of my colleagues in the Canada Department of Labour, in an article in the July 1967 issue of the British *Journal of Industrial Relations*.[4]

MECHANISMS FOR CONVERTING INPUTS INTO OUTPUTS

Let me now turn to another part of the model, that of the mechanisms for converting the inputs into outputs. These mechanisms may take various forms. First, the outputs may be determined unilaterally by one party alone, be it the employer or the state. This is true in our country, for example, in those firms or companies which are not yet unionized. Secondly, the inputs may be converted into outputs through bilateral negotiations between labour and management. Thirdly, the outputs may be determined by labour and management with the assistance of outside agencies, such as government or private mediators or arbitrators. This kind of three-way breakdown is a structural one. For our purposes, however, we will concentrate on the second and third structural types and discuss the various processes which organized labour and management may use for converting the inputs into outputs.

The most common process on the North American continent and most European countries is that of collective bargaining between labour and management, with government playing a mediatory role, at least most of the time. A great deal has been written about the collective bargaining process, about the mechanics of this process, the strategies which may be used by either of the parties, and the great emotional fanfare that accompanies the achievement of a contract settlement.[5] However, one of the most significant books written on this subject in recent years is that of Walton and McKersie entitled *A Behavioral Theory of Labor Negotiations*,[6] which breaks the labour negotiation process down into four sub-processes as follows:

(1) "distributive bargaining," which refers to those activities relating to the resolution of pure conflicts of interest;

(2) "integrative bargaining" which refers to those activities which are concerned with the resolution of problems common to both parties and which increase the gains;

(3) "intraorganizational bargaining" which functions to achieve consensus within each of the interacting groups;

(4) "attitudinal structuring" which refers to those activities which influence the attitudes of the participants towards each other.

This four-way breakdown is indeed a very useful way of looking at labour negotiations as one of the mechanisms for converting the inputs into outputs. It also has significant practical import for those concerned with the various forms of continuous bargaining.

In addition to the basic collective bargaining process between labour and management, there are various forms of third-party assistance which may be used as mechanisms for converting the inputs into outputs. In Canada, for example, we have the two-stage compulsory conciliation process in many of our political jurisdictions. I am sure that most, if not all of you in this audience, are familiar with the criticisms of this process. In some jurisdictions, this two-stage process is now giving way to a one-stage process in which the emphasis is placed on effective mediation. Finally, there is the process of compulsory arbitration. Since much has been said about this process during the past year, I will do no more than make reference to it here — which I must do as a social scientist who is interested in the various types of mechanisms for converting inputs into outputs.

If the various mechanisms mentioned above fail to convert the inputs into outputs, then the outputs are usually achieved as the result of a trial of strength. This may take the form of a strike by the workers or a lockout on the part of management. Eventually, however, one or more of the mechanisms mentioned above must be utilized during a strike or lockout in order to get the workers back on the job and to get an agreement with conditions which are satisfactory to them and to management. When a strike does result, however, it is important to recognize that this is an output of the industrial relations system and that it may have serious consequences for the other environmental subsystems as well as the industrial relations system itself. I will have more to say about this when I discuss the concept of the feedback loop.

Thus far, I have been speaking about the institutional or organizational mechanisms for converting inputs into outputs. However, I wish to point out that industrial relations consists not only of periodic negotiations — although those unfortunately seem to preoccupy our attention — but also of the day-to-day relationships among individuals at the work level. These constitute a complicated set of relationships involving those between managers, workers and managers, workers themselves, and workers and their union representatives. To a large extent, it is at this level that the participants satisfy their social and psychological needs. I should point out also that many of the individual and group needs are satisfied more through the informal structures which emerge rather than through the formal structures. And, as numerous studies of bureaucracy show, not only individual and group needs but also organizational needs are often best met through the informal structures.

THE OUTPUTS OF INDUSTRIAL RELATIONS SYSTEMS

Let me now look briefly at the outputs of industrial relations systems. As stated at the beginning of this paper, the main function of an industrial relations system is the allocation of rewards to employees for their services. Among the many types of substantive outputs of an industrial relations system, I would include wages, hours of work, statutory holidays, vacations with pay provisions, technological change provisions, training programs, pension plans, supplemental unemployment benefits, hospital and medical plans and the other types of fringe benefits which employees receive, as well as seniority provisions which determine, to some extent, who remains employed or gets promoted and consequently who receives rewards. Industrial relations research is concerned not only with changes in the level of rewards from one period to another, but also with the *levels of rewards* themselves. In order to provide a good understanding of the national industrial relations systems, one must make also comparisons among different industries and regions. Furthermore, when one examines the substantive outputs of an industrial relations system, one must also be concerned not only with the amount or rate of change in any one provision, but also with the emphasis that is placed on the different types of substantive outputs — i.e. the trade-off among the outputs. For example, during periods of high unemployment or rapid technological change, one will probably find a great deal of emphasis on various job and income security provisions, whereas during periods of high employment one will probably find a greater degree of emphasis on wages and more immediate and direct forms of benefits. The paper that I was to have presented today would have dealt predominantly with these types of subject matter. However, I do hope to complete a monograph during the summer covering these and other subjects for the period 1953 to 1966.

I should like to re-emphasize that the discipline of industrial relations must be concerned not only with the substantive or material rewards for employment, but also with the types of social relationships and rewards that exist between management and labour at any level of an industrial relations system, ranging from the national system down to the lowest unit of a plant. These social relationships and rewards are

often as critical in determining the degree of satisfaction which employees derive from employment as are the financial or material types of
rewards.[7]

Thus far I have been discussing the outputs of an industrial relations system in terms of rewards to employees for their services. However, I do not wish to leave the impression that one should look at the
outputs of an industrial relations system solely in these terms. One
must also look at the outputs in terms of their effect on the other
sub-systems of society. Hence, it is necessary that we have a feedback
loop linking the industrial relations system to the environmental sub-
systems within which an industrial relations system functions. It is to
this that we now turn.

THE CONCEPTS OF THE FEEDBACK LOOP

The feedback loop may be conceived of, then, as the linkage between the outputs of the industrial relations system and the environmental sub-systems within which the industrial relations system operates. Conceptually, then, the *outputs* of the industrial relations system
become *inputs* into the environmental sub-systems, and subsequently
through their effects on the environmental sub-systems flow back into
the industrial relations system as part of the conditioning inputs. I
should also point out that the outputs of an industrial relations system
feed back *directly* into the industrial relations system itself without any
intermediatory linkages. This is true, for example where satisfactory
wages and fringe benefits plus pleasant working conditions have a very
beneficial effect on the morale of employees in a work environment.

There are a number of reasons why the emerging discipline of industrial relations must be concerned with the feedback loop which is
part of our model. First, from a *scientific point of view*, it is necessary to
look at the feedbacks in order to see how the outputs of the industrial
relations system feed back into the environmental sub-systems and
through their effect of these systems subsequently come back to the
industrial relations system in the form of conditional inputs. This establishes a scientific basis for including the concept of the feedback
loop. Secondly, from a *public policy point of view*, it is essential that
we investigate the consequences of the outputs of the industrial relations system for the other sub-systems of society. For example, what is
the impact of strikes on the economic system, the legal system, the
political system and the social system? What is the impact of wage and
related changes on costs, prices, and employment? How do the outputs
of the industrial relations systems affect community attitudes to both
labour and management? While it may be difficult to establish objective measures with which to assess the impact of these outputs, it is
nevertheless incumbent on scholars interested in the discipline of industrial relations to develop measures which will enable us to ultimately assess what impact the outputs have.

CONCLUDING COMMENTS

With this discussion of the feedback loop, I have now come full circle since I am back to the environmental inputs again. I would like to make but one concluding comment. As you are well aware by now, I have made no substantive contribution to our knowledge of industrial relations today. This was not my purpose. My objective was to set forth, in a rudimentary way, a conceptual model which will help us better organize the knowledge we already possess and, more important, a model which should enable us to advance from the descriptive to the analytical or explanatory stage in the development of the emerging discipline in which many of us are engaged. I do not look upon the model that I have presented here today as the ideal model, nor do I expect all of you to agree with the approach suggested here. However, if my comments serve to stimulate thinking in an area that has been largely ignored by industrial relations scholars, then society, industrial relations practitioners, our emerging discipline and those of us who take it seriously will be the beneficiaries.

A FRAMEWORK FOR ANALYZING INDUSTRIAL RELATIONS SYSTEMS
(A STRUCTURAL-FUNCTIONAL APPROACH)

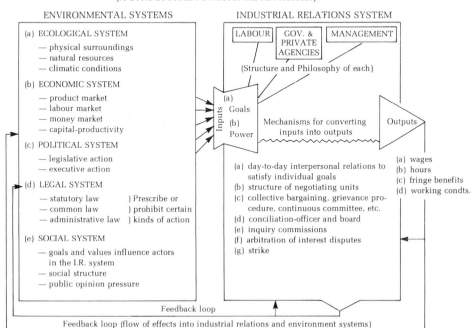

Feedback loop (flow of effects into industrial relations and environment systems)

FOOTNOTES

1. See David Easton, *A Framework for Political Analysis* (Englewood Cliffs, N.J.: Prentice-Hall, Inc. 1965), and *A Systems Analysis of Political Life* (New York: John Wiley & Sons, Inc., 1965).
2. See Otto Eckstein and Thomas A. Wilson, "The Determination of Money Wages in American Industry", *Quarterly Journal of Economics*, Vol. LXXBII, No. 3, August 1962, pp. 379-414.
3. For a brief discussion of the goal and value patterns in Canadian society, see John Porter, "Canadian Character in the Twentieth Century", *The Annals of the American Academy of Political and Social Science*, Vol. 370, March 1967, pp. 48-56.
4. See Syed M. A. Hameed, "Theory and Research in the Field of Industrial Relations," in the July 1967 issue of the *British Journal of Industrial Relations*.
5. See Carl M. Stevens, *Strategy and Collective Bargaining Negotiation* (New York: McGraw-Hill, 1963).
6. See R. E. Walton and R. B. McKersie, *A Behavioural Theory of Labor Negotiations* (New York: McGraw-Hill, 1963).
7. See Douglas McGregor, *The Human Side of Enterprise* (New York: McGraw-Hill, 1960).

SOCIAL SYSTEMS: A THEORETICAL STATEMENT*
William F. Whyte

A leading scholar presents the human relations approach in analyzing union-management relations. Professor Whyte suggests that a study of the system of communication within a management organization, or within a union, and the pattern of communication or human relations between union and management officials in a work environment can provide a fruitful analytical framework for examining union-management relations.

I look upon a company and the union with which it deals in a given plant as two interrelated and interdependent social systems. The parts

* From: John T. Dunlop and William F. Whyte, "Framework for the Analysis of Industrial Relations: Two Views", *Industrial and Labor Relations Review*, April 1950, pp. 393-401. Reprinted with permission from the *Industrial and Labor Relations Review*, Vol. 3, No. 3, April 1950. Copyright © 1950 by Cornell University. All rights reserved.

of the social system are the relations among the members of the organization. These parts are also interdependent.

Two propositions flow from that statement:

1. A change in one part of a social system affects all other parts. (Since the union and management systems interlock at several points, a change in one part of one system tends to affect not only other parts of that system but also the interlocking system.) Some changes will have such slight effects on other parts that they can be disregarded for most purposes, but there are cases in which an apparently small change in one part of a social system disrupts the equilibrium of that system and precipitates a crisis.

2. To determine how parts of a social system relate to each other, we need to study people with emphasis upon the *time* dimension.

What are the parts of these social systems that particularly require attention in studies of union-management relations? I would point to the following areas of human relations:

(a) Up and down the line of authority from top management to worker.

(b) Up and down the union hierarchy, from worker to top union officer. This area should also include what is generally known as informal organization among workers.

(c) Cross relations between union and management at every point of contact.

(d) Staff and control organizations in relation to the line of authority. Especially we need to observe the role of personnel or industrial relations, engineering, accounting and cost control, and industrial engineering.

(e) Work flow relations. The relations that arise among workers and among members of management in the flow of work from receiving the raw materials to shipping the finished products.

Research on such relationships involves the study of interaction, sentiments, and actions.

By *actions* I mean simply the things people do while participating in the social system. There are, of course, an endless variety of possible actions. For research purposes, it is well to concentrate upon those which can be most objectively observed and even measured; for example, productivity, absenteeism, labor turnover, presence or absence of work stoppages, and so on.

By *sentiments* I mean the way the people who are interacting express their feelings about each other, about their organizations, and about the jobs they are doing. Such data can be derived from personal interviews or, on a statistical basis, from questionnaires.

By *interaction* I am referring to *all* personal contacts between two individuals or among three or more individuals. There are these aspects of interaction that can be objectively observed: *Origination*: does A originate action for B, or does B originate for A? *Duration*: for how long a period do A and B interact with each other? *Frequency*: how often (in a given time period) do A and B interact? And how often does A originate for B compared with B's originations for A?

Further research may indicate a need to classify interaction into various types, but so far that definition has proved highly serviceable.

According to this approach, actions and sentiments are the items to be explained: Why do workers increase (or decrease) their productivity? Why do they stay on the job — or go out on strike? Why do they express hostile (or favorable) sentiments toward management? And the analysis of patterns of interaction seems to me the most effective means of explaining actions and sentiments. A number of studies have shown how quantitative changes in the pattern of interaction go together with changes in action and sentiments.[1]

APPLICATION OF THIS FRAMEWORK

Before going into further detail, I should make clear the claims that are being made for this framework. I feel that it has been useful for studies of the relationship between management and industrial unions. It has been used particularly to investigate such relations at the plant level. That does not mean that its utility is limited to small organizations; later I shall show how a study focused primarily at the plant level can add to our knowledge of large organizations.

I have made no attempt to apply the scheme to craft unions, such as the building trades, nor have I tested it out in industry-wide bargaining situations, such as we find in coal. I am not saying that the scheme has no value in such areas. I am simply saying that I make no claims beyond the area where I have done research.

This limitation is certainly in accord with the traditions of science. I feel that it is fruitless to seek a framework which will explain all industrial relations situations. If we begin that way, we will have such a vague, general theory that it will do us no good in specific instances. On the other hand, if we develop a theory which works reasonably well in a restricted area, we can then proceed step-by-step to modify and reshape that theory, so that it will be serviceable in broader areas.

WHY A HUMAN RELATIONS APPROACH TO INDUSTRIAL RELATIONS?

Since research in human relations arose partly in response to a presumed inadequacy of the work of economists in union-management relations, it may be well to spell out some of those criticisms before illustrating further the application of this particular human relations approach.

Most students have concentrated upon top level union-management relationships, arguing that this is where the key decisions are made. This sometimes leads to mistaking the formal policy statements of the parties for the actual motivations of people. It also leads to a gross over-simplification of organizational problems. We find a "tendency to personify such complex entities as the union and the business firm and to reason about group behavior on individualistic lines."[2]

Actually all of these "key people" have their specific places in this network of interdependent relations that we call a social system. Their behavior can only be understood as we develop and apply methods for analyzing such social systems. Neither classical nor institutional nor Keynesian economics supplies any of the tools necessary to cope with such a system of relationships. Consequently the economist cannot operate effectively in this area, unless he also acquires some of the tools of anthropology, sociology, or psychology. Since an increasing number of young economists are moving in this direction, we may hope that this particular criticism will lose its force as time goes on.

This top-level approach seems to assume that the formal agreements reached at this level set the pattern for the entire company in its relations with the union. The extent to which this is true varies greatly from organization to organization. Even in some very large companies top management allows a high degree of autonomy to the local plant managements. And even where top management centralizes its industrial relations policies, the actual working out of those policies will vary widely from plant to plant.

This is not to say that it is useless to study top level relationships. It is simply an argument against conclusions drawn about reactions of "management" or "the union" based largely, if not exclusively, upon study of the top officers. Social systems are just too complicated to submit to that approach.

Some union-management studies concentrate attention upon the so-called substantive issues (seniority, wages, management prerogatives, etc.). This approach yields significant conclusions on the relationship between certain contracts clauses and the economic and other environmental conditions of the industry.[3] However, if our problem is to explain the degree of harmony or conflict between union and management — and this is the popular problem today — then the substantive issue approach offers us very little.

We may have a number of different union-management relations, all equally harmonious, in which a particular substantive issue is handled quite differently. Therefore it does us little good to be told just what the agreement was on this point, and the logical arguments given by people on both sides for this agreement. On the other hand, it can be exceedingly valuable to us to get a play-by-play account of the relations developed among the various individuals in the solving of this problem. It is on the level of relationships that we will find uniformities from case to case. I am not suggesting that we throw the substantive issues out altogether. I am saying that we must develop means of showing the people in action in the process of solving their problems.

Some studies are particularly faulty in dealing with the relationship between economic conditions and human relations. We are told that "favorable economic conditions ... contribute to satisfactory labor relations"[4] and that economic crises tend to stimulate co-operation.[5] Why such a disagreement?

The most obvious answer is that the authors were simply studying cases at different periods of the business cycle. But that criticism in itself indicates that "economic conditions" were viewed as a broad, general factor, and no attempt was made to show how such conditions specifically affected the people involved in the cases.

If some of these studies fall down in relating economic factors to the union-management picture, they are even more grossly inadequate in dealing with the so-called psychological factors leading to or preventing union-management co-operation. We may be told that "personalities" play an important role in the process without being given any explanation of what the author means by "personalities" and how the role they play may be submitted to objective analysis. Or we may be told that "mutual trust" is important in achieving union-management cooperation. What we need to know is: How does this mutual trust come into being? Statements on the importance of mutual trust merely state the problem — in a vague way — and contribute nothing to its solution.

Many studies are inadequate because they present the picture in static terms. All of us recognize that the present has a past, but too often this is covered by a brief discussion of "past history" and a description of the present situation, with no convincing demonstration of how the present has evolved out of the past. People live through *time*. Our analysis must cope with this fundamental fact.

Finally, this concentration on "the big picture" prevents the researcher from testing his conclusions experimentally.

In industrial relations we should be able to predict the outcomes of certain actions, given a known set of conditions. The man who is able to get his own design of action acted upon, and then can follow through to determine the extent to which the results match the predictions, and study the factors which cause such conformity to or deviation from predictions, has a learning opportunity whose importance is hard to over-estimate. For the academic man accustomed to operate several levels of abstraction above the data of observation, the discipline of having to lay the theories on the line for the test of field experience can lead to very fruitful results.

If we seek to gain these advantages in a top level union–management study of a large corporation and an international union, we run into serious practical difficulties.

Even assuming that we were able to persuade such key management or union people to try out a new line of action — quite a large assumption indeed — the results of such action would extend in so many directions that it would be next to impossible to determine what results flowed from the planned action and what arose from quite different stimuli. To connect actions and outcomes firmly is a difficult enough problem in a single plant. The task of doing that job on a big business or big union basis staggers the imagination.

THE CASE FOR INTENSIVE HUMAN RELATIONS STUDIES

By contrast, human relations studies have tended to concentrate upon plant level relationships. While more attention may profitably be given to higher level relationships, there are good practical and scientific reasons for concentrating in this area at the present time.

To do an effective social science job, we must know where to draw the line. We cannot study everything significant at once. We can study all of the sets of relations making up the interdependent parts of the social systems of the plant and local union. We can examine them at first hand and at close range — as we never could if we sought to encompass a large-scale organization.

I say "we can," but I should add that it has not yet been fully done. Human relations studies in the past have concentrated upon some of the five areas listed above and have presented only fragmentary information about others; for example, the area of work flow relations was almost completely neglected until the recent Richardson and Walker study[6] showed how such data could be developed. But now the parts have been identified, the methods for their study have been developing, and we should be able to do an increasingly adequate job at analyzing such social systems.

Such studies can be and are being carried on through *time*, so that we can see how a change in one part of the social system is accompanied by changes in other parts. We have had field workers who have been able to observe and interview freely at all levels from workers to top plant management and from rank-and-file union members up to international representatives. In such studies, we have been able to sit in on union meetings, on management meetings, and on union–management meetings. While we have supplemented this by occasional interviews with higher management and higher union officials, we feel that this area of intensive work at the plant level provides opportunities for interviewing and observation that are difficult to match at higher levels.

Working at the plant level, we are able to test some of our conclusions experimentally. Perhaps "experimentally" is too big a word. We cannot carry on the closely controlled laboratory experiments characteristic of the natural sciences. Nevertheless, we can outline a course of action that should lead to certain results, persuade key people to embark on this course of action, and make careful observations of the results. If the results are as predicted the first time, we are encouraged but not convinced. If we observe similar results in similar situations several times, we are inclined to think that the theories on which we based our predictions are more or less sound. If the results do not meet our expectations, then we are forced to re-examine the data, question our assumptions, and reshape our theories. This sort of discipline is essential for establishing industrial relations on a scientific foundation.

These values of the in-plant study may perhaps be granted, and yet there will still be serious questions raised against it.

Recognizing that much behavior within the plant arises in response to actions of higher levels in union and management, will we not distort the picture if we study the plant as an isolated unit? Furthermore, since the plant is subject to the influences of the community social environment in which it is located and also to the pressures of the economic environment, will we not distort the picture if we treat the plant in isolation?

The answer, of course, is "yes" in both cases. We must have a means of dealing with influences from outside the plant. But at the same time, we are not dealing with influences in general. We must study them at the point of contact: where they actually enter the plant.

Suppose we are studying one plant of a large corporation. We concentrate on the relations we can observe in the plant and within the local union. We recognize that the plant manager is also part of a larger organization. Some managers have a high degree of autonomy; others are subjected to very tight controls. In either case, we must give close attention to these controls, so that we can understand the manager's behavior. We interview him concerning the policies that are passed down to him from top management and the personal influences upon him from above. We supplement this by interviewing one or more of the top management people having jurisdiction over activities in this plant, in order to get their perspective upon top management pressures on the plant.

In that way, we take into account the higher management influences that play upon the social system we have under observation. But — and this is the key point — we accept those influences as *given*. We do not seek to explain the motives of higher management people in exercising those influences. Suppose the plant manager has the primary responsibility for negotiating a contract with his local union. He will always act within certain limitations set from above; for example, it may be corporation policy that management will not arbitrate incentive rates. To understand how rate problems are handled, we must, of course, know of this policy, but we must go on to observe how all the parties involved react to this limitation in thrashing out their rate problems. For an analysis of the in-plant processes, it is not necessary to know why top management reached this particular decision.

The same point applies to the union. We cannot assume that the local president or international representative is completely free to make whatever agreement seems best to him. He is subject to certain policies and personal influences at higher levels in the union. To understand his behavior, we need to be fully aware of these policies and influences. But we do not need to explain them. We can accept them as *given* and go on to see how they are reflected in the behavior of the people in the local situation.

Of course, it would be interesting to know how top management reached its decision on incentive rates, but that is another study. The industrial relations field is so large and complex that we must rigorously cut our study areas down to manageable size. Only as we develop more systematic knowledge of these smaller units will it be profitable for us to tackle large organizations as a whole.

The relation of the plant to its social and economic environment can be dealt with in the same way. We need to examine how this environment comes to bear upon the behavior of people in the social system.

There have been case studies in which the researchers have checked off a number of points about the economic or community environment and have rested their case at that point without showing how that environment comes into the plant through the actual behavior of people in the observed situation. This is not to deny that these so-called environmental influences do come into the plant; of course, they do. The plant manager who finds the market for his product suddenly dropping away responds either to the reports of salesmen assigned to that plant or to directives from higher management, and makes decisions which may drastically alter the relations among people in the plant. But, if that is the case, then the effect of the environment must be noted in those terms rather than in the highly general discussion of the nature of the product market and of the effect of cyclical fluctuations upon management and union. In other words, we need to translate these so-called environmental influences into specific items of observed behavior.

The same can be said of the influence of the social environment. For example, if we were to study a plant having Negro and white workers in, e.g., Detroit, it is obvious that the race-relations situation in the community would have a bearing upon in-plant behavior. However, it is not obvious just what form such influences would take. We cannot assume that because the community race-relations pattern is so-and-so, it has contributed to such-and-such a situation within the plant. It is our task to fight shy of such assumptions and instead investigate carefully just how these community influences crop up in the in-plant behavior.

Whether we shall consider the environment, is not, I believe, the central issue. A man trained in sociology and anthropology would be the last one to deny the importance of the community environment. The problem is to discover the most effective ways of taking the environmental factors into account. I am simply proposing that we take the social systems of union and management as the central items for study. I am suggesting that we will make progress faster if we study small, manageable units, even when they are parts of large organizations. The influences flowing down from top management and top union can be noted as they are manifested in the behavior of the people under observation. Similarly, the community influences must be noted in exactly the same way: as they come out in specific items of behavior within the social system.

FOOTNOTES

[1] Many examples could be cited. See, for example, the author's "Who Goes Union and Why," *Personnel Journal*, Dec. 1944; or "From Conflict to Cooperation" by B.B. Gardner, A.H. Whiteford, and W.F. Whyte, special issue of *Applied Anthropology*, Fall 1916.

For an application of this theoretical scheme to a particular body of data, see my forthcoming article in *Human Organization* (formerly *Applied Anthropology*): "Structures of Union–Management Relations."

For a more thorough discussion of the interaction concept, see Eliot D. Chapple and Conrad M. Arensberg, "Measuring Human Relations," *Genetic Psychology Monographs*, Vol. 22, 1910, and Arensberg and A.B. Horsfall, "Teamwork and Productivity in a Shoe Factory," *Human Organization*, Winter 1919, pp. 13-25.

[2] Lloyd G. Reynolds, "Economics of Labor," in Howard S. Ellis, cd., *A Survey of Contemporary Economics*, p. 285.

[3] See particularly Sumner H. Slichter, *Union Policies and Industrial Management* (Washington: Brookings Institution, 1911).

[4] R.A. Lester and E.A. Robie, *Constructive Labor Relations* (Industrial Relations Section, Princeton University), p. 113.

[5] Slichter, *op. cit.*

[6] *Human Relations in an Expanding Company* (Labor–Management Center, Yale University).

THE CANADIAN SYSTEM OF INDUSTRIAL RELATIONS: ENVIRONMENTAL CONSIDERATIONS*

The Woods Task Force Report on industrial relations in Canada provides a set of environmental factors – political, economic, and social – unique to the Canadian setting.

A mixed enterprise economy, for example, is usually subject to cyclical fluctuations. The changing state of the economy can have a marked effect on the relative bargaining power of union and management on the level of industrial conflict. This makes the Canadian industrial relations system susceptible to a number of indirect influences from abroad, since the level of economic activity in this country is much affected by foreign developments.

The climate, physical proportions and natural resources of the country are important variables. Canada's harsh winters and the sea-

* From *Canadian Industrial Relations*, "Report of the Task Force on Labour Relations," Queen's Printer, December 1968; pp. 14-16. Reproduced by permission of Information Canada.

sonal nature of many of her industries lead to special labour relations problems because of the resulting irregular flows in incomes and associated characteristics. Canada's geographic spread and regional concentration of resources and production help explain why it took so long for unions to move across the country and to unite in any sort of coherent central body. In addition, these factors, together with Canada's heavy dependence on the international economy and her federal form of government, help explain why collective bargaining is so decentralized and fragmented. Regional differences affect industrial relations in other ways. For example, internal wage differentials, reflecting the varying degrees of industrial development by region, remain a contentious issue.

The role that natural resource booms have played in Canada's history is mirrored in the labour turbulence that has often accompanied these sectoral breakthroughs. Resource industries, especially lumbering and mining, have frequently proved a source of much industrial conflict. British Columbia's record of industrial relations shows that there is likely to be disproportionate unrest where a regional economy is based heavily on primary industries other than agriculture. Relationships between labour and management in such industries are often exacerbated by their isolated locations.

The pace of industrial conversion can be upsetting. It does not matter whether that conversion takes the form of technological change, exhaustion of raw materials or market shifts. The consequence can be a dramatically altered situation within which the parties must readjust their relationships.

Another feature which has had an impact on Canadian industrial relations is the number of foreign based, especially United States, unions and corporations which have extended their activities into this country. This is reflected in a long history of rivalry between national and international union groups, as well as in a number of other contentious areas. Although the significance of the international union presence can be exaggerated, particularly in the collective bargaining arena, it is not a factor to be minimized or ignored.[3]

Equally, if not more significant, has been the penetration of United States corporate enterprises into this country.[4] If there is a reason for concern about any United States influence on collective bargaining in Canada, that concern should be focused more on corporations than on trade unions; in most cases the former can wield much more authority over their Canadian offspring. In some cases, as in automobile manufacturing, both management and labour appear to have agreed to transfer effective decision making power in collective bargaining to the United States side of the border. Although the explanation seems to lie in unique circumstances relating to the Canada–United States Agreement on Automotive Products, there are a few isolated instances where the same thing has happened without any special inducement. The auto case in itself raises some fundamental questions about the sovereignty of the Canadian industrial relations system. If this major precedent sets a pattern for the future, the United States presence will become of overriding significance. In the meantime, similar problems can arise within some parts of Canada itself, especially when control on either or both sides of a bargaining relationship is found to lie in another political jurisdiction.

The fact that Canada is made up of two major linguistic and cultural groups is another important environmental consideration. French Canada has produced a distinctive labour movement which, although numerically weaker than its United States and English Canadian based rivals, is a force to be reckoned with in Quebec and within the federal jurisdiction. Another dimension of the same feature is the impact in many enterprises in Quebec of the continuing existence of unilingual English-speaking management dealing with a predominantly French-speaking work force.[5]

In other parts of the country a major problem has been presented from time to time by waves of non-English immigrants of low education and skill. At various stages in Canada's history some employers have used the resulting cleavages in their work forces to delay or forestall unionization. Because such tactics usually go hand-in-hand with attempts to exploit new-comers, the situation sometimes gives rise to explosive industrial relations consequences.[6]

FOOTNOTES

[3] For further reference see John Crispo, "International Unionism: A Study in Canadian–American Relations," (Toronto, McGraw-Hill, 1967).

[4] For a broader discussion of the role of United States subsidiaries in Canada see A.E. Safarian, "Foreign Ownership of Canadian Industry," (Toronto, McGraw-Hill, 1966); and Report of the Task Force on the Structure of Canadian Industry, "Foreign Ownership and the Structure of Canadian Industry," (Ottawa, Queen's Printer, 1968).

[5] See the special issue "Language at the Work Situation in Quebec" in *Relations industrielles/Industrial Relations*, Vol. 23 (1968), No. 3.

[6] For a recent example of such a sequence of events, see H. Carl Goldenberg, "Report of the Royal Commission on Labour–Management Relations in the Construction Industry" (Toronto: Queen's Printer, 1962).

QUESTIONS FOR DISCUSSION, PART 1

1. As bases for classifying the various factors at work in the operation of an industrial relations system, how do Craig's and Whyte's frameworks supplement each other?

2. Take an actual industrial relations case from the Canadian setting with which you are familiar and analyze the problems in it using the above-mentioned theoretical models.

3. Discuss the environmental factors (political, economic and social) unique to the Canadian setting, and their effect on labour-management relations.

PART 2

INSTITUTIONAL AND LEGAL FRAMEWORK

Section 1
Direction and Structure of the Canadian Labour Movement

INTRODUCTION

The selections in Part 2, Section 1, deal with the development of the Canadian labour movement and the factors which shaped its structure and direction.

Professor Kruger's essay examines the development of Canadian unionism within the context of environmental forces, such as population, growth and gross national product. Special features in the Canadian environment, for example, the impact of the United States on Canada; the French — English division in Canadian society and the constitutional divisions of responsibilities between the federal and provincial governments, have also influenced the structure of the Canadian labour movement.

McKendy's article describes the structure of the union movement as it exists today, and Crispo's and Kipling's essays analyze the role of international unions in the Canadian society.

The penetration of international unions in Canada was greatly influenced by increasing American ownership of Canadian industry. Cultural similarities between the U.S.A. and Canada also facilitated the presence of American based unions. The only exception is the province of Quebec, the predominantly French speaking province, which has followed a somewhat different course of union organization and legislation than other provinces.

In 1973, 56 per cent of total union membership in Canada belonged to international unions, with head office in the U.S.A. There is a great variation among international unions in the kind and in the degree of control that their executive councils exercize over their affiliates in Canada.

In Canada, there is a continuing debate over the extent to which the benefits of affiliation with American-based unions exceed the losses of a reduced autonomy of Canadian unions.

The Woods Task Force Report sets four important criteria as to how to judge whether full opportunity is being accorded the Canadian membership to handle its own problems.

1. There must be a central Canadian Office authorized to speak for the union in this country.
2. The Canadian membership must elect the top Canadian Officers.
3. There must be a Canadian policy conference empowered to deal effectively with the union's affairs in this country.
4. A competent staff must be available to serve the special needs of Canadian members.

In an examination of the present structure of the Canadian trade union movement, Professor Brian Williams contends that only a few of the Canadian unions affiliated with international unions meet all the four criteria. He concludes that "it is not that the freedom of Canadian locals is intentionally restricted, but rather national needs, aspirations and conditions are not sufficiently stressed in the formulations of collective bargaining policies to be followed by the branches of international unions operating in Canada."

In the next article "Deficiencies in Philosophy," Williams vehemently disagrees with the conclusions arrived at earlier by Kruger and Crispo.

Two essays in the second section deal with the development of public policy toward organized labour and collective bargaining in the various jurisdictions of Canada. The provincial jurisdictions are the most important ones since they cover almost ninety per cent of the organized labour in Canada. The federal jurisdiction extends to matters interprovincial in scope, such as interprovincial transportation and communications, as well as to federal government employees.

Jamieson in his essay on "Government Policy" traces the development of government industrial relations policy in Canada over a period of a hundred years and critically examines its objectives. While labour laws vary from one jurisdiction to another in a number of important matters, there is enough uniformity in the basic principles on which labour legislation is based in the eleven jurisdictions so as to permit us to speak of a Canadian system of industrial relations. The key common features are in the areas of (1) the right of employees for form and join unions, (2) certification of a union as bargaining agent and its right to bargain with employer, (3) mediation and conciliation services offered by government, (4) machinery for settlement of disputes during the life of a contract.

In recent years there have been numerous studies on the nature of collective bargaining and public policy in various jurisdictions of Canada. Despite wide-spread criticism of the existing collective bargaining system, most of these studies, particularly, the federal task force on labour relations, has supported the institution of collective bargaining because "there is no viable substitute in a free society."

Jamieson, in his essay, points out that as a result of these studies legislation in federal and provincial jurisdictions has been revised to strengthen the basic features of the system.

Special Legislation: The past history of collective bargaining in the construction industry in several jurisdictions had indicated that instability in labour management relations posed a serious threat to the completion of construction projects. Because of the short-term nature of construction employment in the industry, labour – management relations were, and still are, marred by jurisdictional disputes and wild-cat strikes.

The serious problems in the labour – management relations in the construction industry have been the subject of several inquiries and task force studies.

As a result of these studies many governments have enacted special legislation to deal with the unique problems of the construction industry. In the final essay Rose outlines the legislative provisions in various jurisdiction of Canada, which provide for accreditation of employers' organizations; faster certification and arbitration; special emphasis on area certification rather than site certification; and special measures for handling jurisdictional disputes.

Several provincial governments have enacted legislation to deal with the labour – management relationship for certain specific construction projects. For example, in Newfoundland, the government revised the existing legislation to establish a special collective bargaining relationship at the huge Churchill Falls, a project which employed 6000 people. The government of New Brunswick has established a Lornville Area Project Authority to deal with construction problems related to the establishment of a deep-water port for oil tankers on a specific site near Saint John. The Authority has the power to negotiate all agreements with unions covering the terms and conditions of employment on the site.

One of the external factors which seriously affect the collective bargaining area is the imposition by the government of wage and price controls. This measure removes from collective bargaining one of the most contentious issues and places severe restrictions on the discretionary power of the parties to set prices and wages. The last two readings deal wth controversial issues such as wage and price controls; the extent to which collective bargaining contributes to inflation; and the trade-off problem. Professor John Kenneth Galbraith said recently at a meeting of the American Economics Association in Toronto that the only way Canada could beat inflation without producing more unemployment was by wage- and price-control. The Canadian Chamber of Commerce at its forty-third Annual Meeting in Ottawa passed a resolution, which recommended that government should have a contingency plan ready which could be used if there was a serious outbreak of inflation. The plan could be applied equitably to all sectors of the economy "if a crisis and a consensus exist." This recommendation is similar to the one contained in the report of the Prices and Income

Commission, which suggested that Canada would be compelled to enforce controls in a time of emergency. The labour movement is less than enthusiastic about wage- and price-control and has adopted a "wait and see" attitude.

Consideration of the discussion questions at the end of Part 2 may help the student to gain insights into problems involved in current labour affairs.

LABOUR ORGANIZATIONS IN CANADA, 1973*

This article gives the latest up-to-date statistical data on union membership and labour organizations in Canada.

Statistics compiled by the federal Department of Labour show that union membership in Canada as of January 1973 totalled 2,556,236, an increase of 7.8 per cent from 1972. The 1973 figure represented 35.6 per cent of the total labour force; a year earlier these proportions were, respectively, 34.4 and 27.6 per cent.

Of all union members in Canada, 81 per cent were in unions affiliated with central labour organizations. Affiliates of the Canadian Labour Congress reported a membership of 1,847,064, representing 72.3 per cent of the Canadian total; Confederation of National Trade Union affiliates reported 164,492 members, or 6.4 per cent; *le Centrale des syndicats democratiques* reported 41,000 members, or 1.6 per cent; and Confederation of Canadian Union affiliates reported 17,455 members, representing 0.7 per cent. Unaffiliated unions, with a membership of 485,606, accounted for the other 19 per cent of total union membership in Canada.

The proportion of workers belonging to international unions in Canada was somewhat smaller than in the previous year. At the beginning of 1973, unions having their headquarters in the United States comprised 56.5 per cent of the total, compared with 59.6 per cent in 1972. Conversely, national unions made up 40.9 per cent of organized labour in 1973, compared with 37.7 per cent in 1972. The remaining 2.6 per cent (2.7 per cent in 1972) were members of local unions chartered directly by central labour bodies and independent local organizations.

At the beginning of 1973, 12 unions reported 50,000 or more members, compared with 10 unions in 1972. These 12 listed below accounted for 42.4 per cent of the total 1973 union membership in Canada; United Steelworkers of America (AFL-CIO/CLC), 173,662; Canadian Union of Public Employees (CLC), 167,470; Public Service Alliance of Canada (CLC), 133,503; International Union, United Au-

* "Unions Grow", *The Labour Gazette*, Oct, 1974, pp. 687-8. Reprinted with permission.

tomobile, Aerospace and Agricultural Implement Workers of America (CLC), 107,266; Quebec Teachers' Corporation (Ind.), 87,546; United Brotherhood of Carpenters and Joiners of America (AFL-CIO/CLC), 75,161; International Brotherhood of Teamsters, Chauffeurs, Warehousemen and Helpers of America (Ind.), 64,126; International Brotherhood of Electrical Workers (AFL-CIO/CLC), 59,700; Social Affairs Federation (CNTU), 58,378; International Woodworkers of America (AFL-CIO/CLC) 54,929; United Paperworkers International Union (AFL-CIO/CLC), 51,344; Canadian Food and Allied Workers, District 15 Council (AFL-CIO/CLC), 50,790.

THE
DIRECTION OF UNIONISM
IN CANADA*
Arthur M. Kruger

Professor Kruger reviews the nature of the environment, focusing on the elements that have conditioned the development of unionism in Canada. He also discussed the principal problems currently confronting organized labour and predicts the direction of Canadian trade union movement in the near future.

Frequently we speak of "organized labour" or "the labour movement" as if there were a cohesive institution with a clear-cut identity that was designated by these terms. Even a cursory look at our unions indicates that this concept is not true. Canadian labour is not a unified movement with a structured hierarchy and clearly defined goals. Rather, Canadian unions are decentralized and have diverse views of their objectives and methods. This is not to deny that unions have much in common, or to imply that no generalizations about unions are possible; however, the effort of any analysis usually focuses on common characteristics. In Canada the decentralization of labour demands that attention be given to the numerous exceptions to any generalization.

As this article will emphasize, the development of labour organization in Canada did not occur in a vacuum. A study of labour must embrace the context within which the unions developed. This context primarily includes the legal, market and institutional environment. In Canada, the study must embrace many special features of the environment, including the impact of the United States on Canada, the constitutional divisions of responsibilities between the federal and provincial governments, and the French-English division in Canadian society.

* This is an extract from an article in *Canadian Labour in Transition*, edited by Miller and Isbester, Prentice Hall, 1971, pp. 86-96 and pp. 104-7. Reprinted by permission of Prentice-Hall of Canada, Ltd.

Table 3-1

Percentage Distribution in Canada of Value Added or National Income Originating*, by Industry, Selected Years 1870-1955.

	Primary Industries					Secondary Industries						Tertiary Industries			
Year	Agriculture	Fishing and Trapping	Mining	Forest Operations	Total Primary	Manufacturing	Construction	Total Secondary	Public Utilities	Government	Other Service Industries	Total Tertiary	Total Industry	Adjustment**	Grand Total***
1870	33.3	1.1	0.9	9.6	44.9	19.0	3.0	22.0	—	—	—	20.9	87.8	12.2	100.0
1880	32.0	1.9	1.0	8.6	43.5	18.9	3.8	22.7	—	—	—	22.4	88.6	11.4	100.0
1890	27.0	1.6	1.4	6.6	36.6	23.5	4.6	28.1	—	—	—	26.7	91.4	8.6	100.0
1900	26.7	1.6	3.3	4.9	36.5	20.8	4.2	25.0	—	—	—	29.4	90.9	9.1	100.0
1910	22.8	0.9	2.6	3.9	30.2	22.7	5.1	27.8	—	—	—	33.6	91.6	8.4	100.0
1920	19.4	0.9	2.5	3.8	26.6	24.2	5.5	29.7	—	—	—	35.3	91.6	8.4	100.0
1929	12.1	0.6	3.9	1.7	18.3	24.5	6.1	30.6	12.8	8.0	35.8	56.6	105.5	-5.5	100.0
1930	11.3	0.4	3.5	1.4	16.6	22.6	5.6	28.2	12.7	9.6	39.6	61.9	106.7	-6.7	100.0
1933	7.6	0.3	4.7	1.3	13.9	22.8	2.8	25.6	14.1	15.1	40.5	69.7	109.2	-9.2	100.0
1939	11.7	0.3	6.8	1.6	20.4	26.6	3.4	30.0	11.6	10.5	33.1	55.2	105.6	-5.6	100.0
1945	11.8	0.6	2.8	1.6	16.8	27.5	3.5	31.0	11.0	18.0	24.9	53.9	101.7	-1.7	100.0
1950	11.7	0.5	3.9	1.8	17.9	30.7	5.6	36.3	10.2	8.1	30.1	48.4	102.6	-2.6	100.0
1951	13.4	0.5	4.0	2.2	20.1	30.1	5.0	35.1	10.2	8.2	28.4	46.8	102.0	-2.0	100.0
1952	11.4	0.4	3.6	2.0	17.4	29.4	5.6	35.0	10.7	9.0	29.4	49.1	101.5	-1.5	100.0
1953	9.9	0.3	3.2	1.7	15.1	29.7	6.4	36.1	10.8	9.5	29.8	50.1	101.3	-1.3	100.0
1954	7.3	0.3	3.4	1.9	12.9	28.8	6.6	35.4	10.9	10.7	31.5	53.1	101.4	-1.4	100.0
1955	7.8	0.3	3.8	1.9	13.8	28.7	7.0	35.7	10.7	10.6	30.7	52.0	101.5	-1.5	100.0

* For 1870 to 1920 inclusive, the figures represent value added by each industry. For 1929 to 1953, the data pertain to income originating in industry as given in the National Accounts.

** Adjustment item comprises rent, indirect taxes, less subsidies, plus net income for 1870 to 1920 inclusive, and national income of nonresidents for 1929 to 1953.

*** Covers gross national product for 1870 to 1920 inclusive, and net national income at factor cost for 1929 to 1953.

Source: O.J. Firestone, *Canada's Economic Development, 1867-1953, with Special Reference to Changes in the Country's National Product and National Wealth* (London: 1958), Table 68: DBS, *National Accounts, Income and Expenditure, 1950-1955,* Table 20. Reproduced by permission from Caves and Rolten, *The Canadian Economy,* Harvard Economic Studies, Harvard University Press, p. 604.

THE ENVIRONMENT

The factors in the environment that influence trade unions are developments in markets (both labour and product markets); the nature of legislation bearing on unions and collective bargaining, and the relative status of labour, management and government in the society. These subjects are treated at length elsewhere in this volume and in specialized works.[1] Here, we will merely indicate the highlights of these features of the environment.

The Growth of Canadian Industry[2]

A trade union movement is more likely to develop in urban societies where output and employment are concentrated in manufacturing, construction and transportation than in rural societies where agriculture, fishing and trapping predominate. Once a union movement does develop, its character is strongly influenced by the relative importance of the various sectors of the economy and by the nature of the predominant technology. Table 3-1 indicates how the relative importance of various sectors of the economy as measured by the value of output originating in these sectors has changed. Note the decline in the primary sectors and the growth in the position of the secondary and tertiary industries. You also will observe the significant rise in the relative position of the tertiary sectors in recent years.

These shifts have been accompanied by other changes in the nature of Canadian business that also have influenced the characteristics of the labour movement. The size of business firms in many sectors has increased enormously over the years, partly in response to technological change. There is some controversy concerning the degree to which selling markets have become more or less competitive. Numerous examples of both increased and reduced competition are readily available to support either contention. The development of our extractive and manufacturing sectors has been achieved through a vast influx of foreign capital, primarily from the United States, accompanied by foreign ownership and control over a very significant portion of these sectors.[3]

Shifts in the relative importance of the various sectors have changed the location of Canadian industry. Areas dependent on agriculture, fishing and forestry have become relatively less important as sources of output and employment than areas where manufacturing and services are concentrated. This will become more evident in the discussion of population and labour force changes.

Canadian Population and Labour Force Trends[4]

Industrial change and population change go hand in hand. The Canadian population has grown rapidly as a result of both natural increase and immigration. Within Canada, population has shifted geographically as industry and employment opportunities moved to certain regions.

Elsewhere in this volume, labour force trends are discussed at length. Here, we will merely point out the following important facts:[5]

a. the significant urbanization of the Canadian population and the growing concentration in certain parts of the country;

b. the rapid growth in the proportion of workers engaged in the service sectors in recent years and the long-term relative decline in employment in the primary sectors;

c. the growing proportion of workers employed in white-collar occupations. White-collar work has increased in importance in many sectors including some (e.g. manufacturing) that have traditionally been thought of as overwhelmingly blue-collar.

d. the rapid rise in female participation in the labour force and the concomitant growth in the female proportion of the labour force.

Canadian Labour Legislation[6]

The provincial governments, rather than the Federal Government, set the legal framework for labour organization and collective bargaining for most of the labour force. Although legislation differs among jurisdictions in a number of important matters, there is enough uniformity in the approach of the eleven governments to permit us to speak of a Canadian system. The Canadian system follows the American practice of letting workers in an "appropriate bargaining unit" decide which union, if any, will bargain for them. This is usually decided by majority vote of those in the unit. Once a union is designated as bargaining agent, no other union can act for those in the unit and the chosen union must represent everyone in the unit, members and non-members alike. Following a union's certification as exclusive bargaining agent for a given group of employees, both the union and management must negotiate "in good faith" with a view to drawing up the terms of a collective agreement. The law prohibits work stoppages during the term of a collective agreement.

Certain categories of employees are singled out for special treatment. Some are not permitted to belong to larger bargaining units (e.g. supervisory staff, foremen etc.); others are restricted to specified organizations (e.g. Ontario civil servants cannot choose any union other than the Civil Service Association of Ontario); and some employees are prohibited from striking (e.g. policemen).

The Status of the "Actors"

The final environmental determinant of union growth is the relative position of the "actors" (union leaders, employers and government officials) who participate in collective bargaining. Determination of status involves judgments which are difficult to document.

There is little doubt that the status of union leaders has improved greatly over the years. In the nineteenth and early twentieth centuries, these men were viewed as outlaws or at least dangerous radicals whose activities had to be controlled by legislation and the courts. On the other hand, property rights and the corresponding rights of management always have had strong support in our society. Managers tend to possess certain characteristics (wealth, income, education, family background and so on) that make them highly esteemed. A marked change in attitude began to take place during the 1930's when business leaders lost prestige in the face of economic collapse. World War II hastened the change. Legislation was enacted favouring union organization and collective bargaining. Union leaders were soon invited to participate as representatives of labour on numerous public bodies.

Nonetheless, suspicion of union leaders persists and the labour élite have not as yet arrived at a status comparable to that of either management or government leaders. This contention is supported by Canada's leading authority on Canadian élites, Professor John Porter, who concludes that the labour élite does not enjoy the prestige of other élites (business, government, religion, academic etc.) in this country.[7] Porter sums up his findings in the following comments:

Labour leaders rarely share in the informal aspects of the confraternity of power. They do not, as we have seen, have the range of honorific roles that the corporate élite does. Nor does the power of labour leaders extend beyond their institutional roles. They do not have the power, for example, to exploit non-economic areas of social life and harness them to the commercial principle as the corporate élite has with the world of sport.[8]

Labour leaders are, therefore, on the periphery of the over-all structure of power, called in by others when the "others" consider it necessary, or when the labour leaders demand a hearing from the political élite.[9]

The American Influence[10]

In addition to these forces, the United States has influenced Canadian trade unions. American unions followed the example of American corporations and extended their operations north of the border; in many cases, the firms involved were not American-owned. However, there is little doubt that the speed and extent of the penetration of international unions was influenced by the degree of American ownership of Canadian industry. In Canada, the American corporations and unions found an environment similar in many ways to that below the border and thus adapted readily to Canadian conditions. In turn, American ownership of industry and the presence of American based unions reinforced the Canadian tendency to follow American practices.

Even without these institutional links to the United States, the fact that Canada shares most of this continent with a large English-speaking neighbour would have exposed us to American patterns in any case.

The communications media have, of course, had a much stronger impact on the English-speaking than on the French-speaking parts of Canada. Quebec's tendency to follow a somewhat different course of union organization and legislation than the other provinces, has had its impact on the course of labour relations in that province.[11]

THE DEVELOPMENT OF THE CANADIAN LABOUR MOVEMENT

All of the environmental forces discussed above have operated to influence the development of unionism in this country. This section of the paper highlights the historical changes in the growth and the structure of Canadian unionism.

The Evolution of Canadian Unionism[12]

Labour organization in Canada began long before Confederation. The earliest recorded strike occurred among the voyageurs at Lac la Pluie in 1794.[13] Unions were important enough in Nova Scotia to provoke legislation to curb labour organization as early as 1816.[14] By the 1830's, there were a considerable number of union locals in Canada including the York Typographical Society, founded in 1832, which has had a continuous existence to this day. By the middle of the nineteenth century, British and American unions had entered Canada and established local branches of their unions. Foreign influence was also felt when British immigrants, with experience in unions in their native land, became active in labour organization in Canada.

However, most of these early unions were weak and very few of them survived for long. They were isolated from each other with little cooperation among locals in a given city or in a particular trade.

Some union leaders recognized the need to coordinate union activity to achieve labour's economic and political goals. As early as 1834, unions in Montreal combined to set up the Trades Union to coordinate their activities. This, and similar early efforts, failed. By the 1870's, some cities had established permanent and effective central bodies. Thereafter, municipal labour councils were established in many urban centres and today virtually every industrialized town or city in Canada has such a body.

By the 1870's, a growing number of Canadian locals had been organized by, or were affiliated with, American-based international unions. Although a few British affiliates carried on into the twentieth century, direct British influence was never significant. The role of the British immigrant leaders mentioned earlier persisted as a major influence in Canada and immigrant leadership is an important factor in some Canadian unions today.

National unions also have a long history in Canada. Among the unions that developed spontaneously in this country were the Provincial Workman's Association, the Quebec-based Catholic unions and the Canadian Brotherhood of Railway, Transport and General Workers Union. Other unions, such as the One Big Union (OBU) were offshoots of, or breakaway groups from, American unions. In 1873, the Canadian Labour Union was established to bring together organized workers from every craft in every part of the nation. It seems to have disappeared about 1878. In 1879, workers in Nova Scotia established the Provincial Workman's Association which included in its membership a variety of unions in that province. In 1886, the Canadian Trades and Labour Congress (TLC) was established, uniting workers in a variety of unions across Canada. The TLC, unlike its counterpart in the United States, the American Federation of Labour or AFL, embraced international craft unions; branches of the Knights of Labour, an American reformist union founded in 1869; affiliates of British unions; and purely Canadian unions. The TLC membership was concentrated at the outset in Ontario and Quebec and was quite small. As late as 1901, all Congress affiliates combined had a total membership of 8,381.[15]

Originally, the Knights had been in the majority in the TLC, but after 1894 the Knights declined in membership and the internationals soon dominated the TLC. Their parent unions in the United States had always been unhappy about the presence of the Knights and other unions in the TLC and pressed for a purge of "dual unions."[16] In 1902, the TLC finally succumbed to this pressure and expelled the Knights along with other unions. The purge was not complete and pressure from the AFL persisted. In 1913, the TLC expelled its last British-based affiliate, the Amalgamated Society of Carpenters, and in 1921, the Canadian Brotherhood of Railway Employees (CBRE) was forced out of the TLC on the charge of dual unionism.

The TLC began as an all-embracing house of labour; however, it soon faced the conflict between the exclusive jurisdiction principle that its international affiliates considered almost sacrosanct and the desire to accommodate national unions. This problem was exacerbated by the fact that the internationals were organized largely on craft lines and excluded the unskilled from membership, while the Knights and many national unions were based on the industrial union principal of organizing all workers, skilled and unskilled, irrespective of craft, in a given industry. Organized labour on this continent had long been divided on the issue of the appropriate form for union organization. Many bitter debates have been held on the subject. Furthermore, in practice, industrial unions frequently found themselves in conflict with one or more craft unions in their efforts to organize firms where skilled workers were employed. The purge of 1902 was only the first round in a long and continuing battle between proponents of these two forms of organization.

The TLC remained strong in spite of the members lost through these purges. Unions outside the TLC made several attempts to form rival central bodies which, in most instances, were composed of national unions hostile to international unions. In 1902, the expelled unions set up the National Trades and Labour Congress which was reorganized as the Canadian Federation of Labour (CFL) in 1908. By 1914, however, the CFL had very few affiliates. The next attempt to establish a rival congress occurred in 1919 when dissident locals of a number of internationals mostly in Western Canada, severed their ties with the internationals and established the One Big Union (OBU). The OBU emphasized both the need to break the ties with the American unions and the need to organize workers on a broader basis than by craft. The OBU remained a very small organization but continued to operate until the 1950's when most of its affiliates were absorbed by Internationals.

Of greater significance was the creation of the Federation of Catholic Workers of Canada in 1921. This body, confined to workers in Quebec, emphasized national unionism and multiple forms of organization, both craft and industrial, from the outset. Later, this group changed its name to the Canadian and Catholic Confederation of Labour (CCCL), and in 1960 it was reorganized under its present name — the Confederation of National Trade Unions.

Outside Quebec, attempts to establish a national body that would rival and replace the TLC continued. In 1927, the remnant of the old CFL combined with the Canadian Brotherhood of Railway Employees to form the All Canadian Congress of Labour (ACCL), a body that stressed the desirability of national unions. Left wing unions in the 1920's and 1930's grouped themselves in the Trade Union Unity League, later renamed the Workers Unity League. In the mid-1930's, new industrial unions were established in the United States to organize mass production industries such as automobiles, steel, rubber and so on. These unions soon set up branches in Canada as well. Before long, they found themselves in conflict with the craft unions. In 1937, the AFL expelled these new unions; the TLC, succumbing to pressure, followed suit in 1939. These new unions combined with the ACCL to form the Canadian Congress of Labour (CCL). National and international unions managed to coexist in the CCL largely because the new industrial-based internationals generally had granted greater autonomy to their Canadian districts than had been the case with the AFL affiliates and because all of the CCL unions accepted industrial unionism. The CCL grew rapidly and, while never as big as the older TLC, it was the only national labour centre ever to pose a serious challenge to the TLC. In 1956, the TLC and CCL merged to form the Canadian Labour Congress (CLC).

Today the CLC and the CNTU are the only union centres of any significance in Canada.[17]

The Changes in the Composition of the Canadian Union Movement

The earliest unions were organized on a craft basis with the unskilled worker largely outside the union fold. Skilled workers were more readily organized for a number of reasons. Some of them were immigrants with union experience in their native lands. They were better educated and, because they possessed scarce skills, they were more secure than the unskilled in conflicts with employers who opposed the unions. Skilled workers in such industries as construction, printing, and transportation, being among the first workers to be organized, are today among the most highly organized groups in Canada.

Once industrial unionism took hold, union organization followed more closely the growth and the pattern of distribution of the labour force discussed above. There are, however, some important exceptions:

a. Unions have been stronger in the urban centres than in small communities.
b. Blue-collar occupations have been more likely to organize than white-collar workers.
c. Unions have been much weaker in the service industries than in the goods-producing sectors.
d. Very small firms are less likely to be organized than larger ones.
e. A much smaller proportion of female workers than of male workers belong to unions.

Table 3-2 shows the change in the size of the labour movement over most of this century and compares this with changes in non-agricultural paid employment in the same period. The figures on non-agricultural paid employment provide the best available approximation of the potentially organizable. Many in this group, however, are not likely to join unions, e.g. management officials, doctors, or lawyers. The data in Table 3-2 illustrate the close relationship between union membership and growth in the non-agricultural labour force.

Union growth was also affected by periods of buoyant labour demand and favourable public policy during World War I and in the immediate postwar years. Employer hostility in the 1920's and the failure of the unions to reach the growing mass production industries, where industrial rather than craft organization was required, explains much of the union's decline in the decade. In the latter case, existing unions were mostly wedded to the craft base and legislation did not provide the support necessary for organizing the unskilled.

The onset of the depression in 1929 created heavy unemployment which, while it reduced the absolute number in the organized work force, did not affect the unionized share of the employed non-agricultural labour force. This was, in part, attributable to the advent of the new CIO industrial unions in the mid-1930's. By securing a measure of public support, these new unions began to penetrate the steel, automobile and other mass production industries. This campaign continued during and after World War II.

Union membership surged during World War II as labour demand rose rapidly and public policy shifted markedly in support of organization. Now that legislation and market forces favoured organization, the

Table 3-2

Union Membership 1911-1968, with Estimates of Total Paid Workers in Non-agricultural Industries in Canada, 1921-1968

Year	Union Membership* (Thousands)	Total Non-Agricultural Paid Workers (Thousands)	Union Membership as a Per Cent of Total Non-Agricultural Paid Workers**	Year	Union Membership (Thousands)	Total Non-Agricultural Paid Workers (Thousands)	Union Membership as a Per Cent of Total Non-Agricultural Paid Workers
1911	133	—	—	1940	362	2,197	16.5
1912	160	—	—	1941	462	2,566	18.0
1913	176	—	—	1942	578	2,801	20.6
1914	166	—	—	1943	665	2,934	22.7
1915	143	—	—	1944	724	2,976	24.3
1916	160	—	—	1945	711	2,937	24.2
1917	205	—	—	1946	832	2,986	27.9
1918	249	—	—	1947	912	3,139	29.1
1919	378	—	—	1948	978	3,225	30.3
1920	374	—	—	1949	1,006(a)	3,326	30.2
1921	313	1,956	16.0	—(b)	—(b)	—	
1922	277	2,038	13.6	1951	1,029	3,625(a)	28.4
1923	278	2,110	13.2	1952	1,146	3,795(c)	30.2
1924	261	2,138	12.2	1953	1,220	3,694	33.0
1925	271	2,203	12.3	1954	1,268	3,754	33.8
1926	275	2,299	12.0	1955	1,268	3,767	33.7
1927	290	2,406	12.1	1956	1,352	4,058	33.3
1928	301	2,491	12.1	1957	1,386	4,282	32.4
1929	319	2,541	12.6	1958	1,454	4,250	34.2
1930	322	2,451	13.1	1959	1,459	4,375	33.3
1931	311	2,028	15.3	1960	1,459	4,522	32.3
1932	283	1,848	15.3	1961	1,447	4,578	31.6
1933	286	1,717	16.7	1962	1,423	4,705	30.2
1934	281	1,931	14.6	1963	1,449	4,867	29.8
1935	281	1,941	14.5	1964	1,493	5,074	29.4
1936	323	1,994	16.2	1965	1,589	5,343	29.7
1937	383	2,108	18.2	1966	1,736	5,658	30.7
1938	382	2,075	18.4	1967	1,921	5,953	32.3
1939	359	2,079	17.3	1968	2,010	6,068	33.1

* Does not include members of professional associations, even where they engage in collective bargaining.
** Calculated from columns (2) and (3).
(a) Includes Newfoundland for the first time.
(b) Data on union membership for all years up to and including 1949 are as of December 31. In 1950, the reference date was moved ahead by one day to January 1, 1951. Thus, while no figure is shown for 1950, the annual series is, in effect, continued without interruption. The data on union membership for subsequent years are also as of January.
(c) Figures for all years up to and including 1952 are as of the first week in June. Data for subsequent years are as of January.

Source: *Labour Organizations in Canada* (Ottawa: The Queens Printer, 1911).

new CCL unions with their stress on industrial unionism were well suited to capture the large unorganized plants. During these years union membership doubled and the percentage of the paid labour force in unions rose sharply to over 25 per cent by the end of the war. In the years since World War II, the labour movement has continued to grow, but at a much slower pace than in the period 1936-46. Indeed, its growth has not been quite as rapid as that of the labour force, with the result that the percentage of organized workers in the labour force has slipped from above one-third to somewhat below one-third of the potentially organizable.

Although prosperity and favourable public policy served to promote union growth in the postwar period, other forces were working in the opposite direction. First, the most easily organized workers, the skilled craftsmen and those in large plants, were almost all organized by 1946. Unions then had to address themselves to workers who were more difficult to organize, including employees of small firms in small communities, professional workers and female labour. Furthermore, in the postwar years, the hard-to-organize white-collar, female and service sectors grew at the expense of the blue-collar, goods-producing sectors, which have been the traditional basis of support for unions. Consequently, growth of Canadian unions in the last two decades has been sluggish as compared with the dramatic gains in the late 1930's and the 1940's.

The above discussion indicates that the rate of growth of labour organization has largely followed the growth of the Canadian population and labour force. The composition of our union movement has reflected to a considerable degree the distribution of employment, which itself is largely determined by the composition of our Gross National Product. The relative facility with which different segments of the labour force are organized is itself the result both of market shifts in demand for commodities and services and of technological change. The shift in public attitudes in favour of unions during both World Wars and in the depression was a major factor in union success in these years. Only with public support were unions able to secure favourable legislation and obtain the support of the various agencies implementing and adjudicating the relevant legislation. Labour legislation since World War II has promoted both craft and industrial unions, especially the latter. Legislation does not permit the British pattern of multitude of unions in a single bargaining unit. Our unions tend to concentrate on more limited jurisdictions than many in Britain and elsewhere but within its jurisdiction each union seeks total control.

THE PROBLEMS AND PROSPECTS OF THE LABOUR MOVEMENT

In this section, we will examine the problems and shortcomings of the contemporary labour movement and its prospects for the future.

Several matters should first be clarified. Our focus on deficiencies does not in the least imply union failure or an inability to recognize the numerous achievements of organized labour. The previous two sections described the historical development of the labour movement and its present size, distribution and organization. Even in this brief survey, the significant achievement of union organization, particularly over the past thirty years, should be apparent. Union growth has been rapid; labour unions are now accepted by employers and by society as a permanent and even a positive force in our industrial community. Among many important gains, collective bargaining for workers has resulted most notably in replacing the absolute and often arbitrary authority of management with contractual provisions as well as creating a bilateral procedure for adjudicating grievances.

Any comment on union success and failure, must employ some standard. Over the years, there has been considerable conflict, both within the union movement and outside its ranks, concerning the appropriate role of unions.[18] Some have urged unions to concentrate on leading the working class to a revolution designed to overthrow capitalism and replace it with some variant of a worker controlled system. Others have suggested that unions focus on political action geared to the reform of the existing social system. For most union leaders and union members on this continent, collective bargaining designed to improve the lot of their membership at the work place, is the major goal of organized labour. Worker organization, higher wages and fringe benefits, and improved working conditions are what most unionists expect from unions. Although some also hope for effective political action, this is secondary, for the majority, to the union's function as an instrument of change at the work place. In appraising unions, the standard this discussion will employ is the standard set by most Canadian unionists themselves, namely success in organization and effectiveness in representing workers through collective bargaining.

Organizing the Unorganized

It was noted earlier that only about one-third of the non-agricultural labour force has been organized in trade unions. It is precisely in the most rapidly growing sectors (white-collar occupations, service industries, and female employees) that unions have had the least success in organizing. This has led some observers to predict a long term decline in the power and influence of the labour movement as its traditional areas of support become less significant. This would seem to imply that collective bargaining will also become less important as a device for setting terms and conditions of employment.

Others point to factors which indicate that this decline is not inevitable and that unions may well expand their organization and influence. In some countries, notably Sweden, a very high percentage of white-collar and professional workers belong to unions. Even in this country large numbers of white-collar workers in public service, transportation and manufacturing establishments are union members. Teachers have used their professional associations for bargaining for many years and have been highly effective. Some nurses, doctors and engineers are now following this same pattern and becoming more militant in the process. The traditional barriers to white-collar organization are disappearing. Women increasingly view paid employment as a more or less permanent feature in their lives. This should lead them to seek greater control over their work environment and remuneration than was the case when paid work was viewed by women as a temporary phenomenon. The militancy of some nursing associations and teacher groups dominated by women in recent years is a reflection of this new attitude.

Among professional employees, there is a distinct trend away from self-employment to salaried employment. This is true even among the traditionally independent practitioners of medicine, law and pharmacy. It is even more apparent among engineers, architects and accountants. Professionals are gradually adapting to the new situation and seeking effective means of influencing their working conditions. In many cases, where employment units are small and the practitioner feels he has considerable bargaining power, he is content to negotiate his own terms of employment. When the employment unit grows, management is often compelled to formalize salary schedules and working conditions. Individual bargaining is confined to narrow limits and professionals must then act collectively to share in the determination of the formal rules governing them. This is already apparent in hospitals where salaried doctors and nurses have moved toward collective bargaining as the requirements of the provincial government regulations increasingly limit the discretion of local hospital administrators.

This loss of face-to-face contact between employers and employees, applies with even greater force to the mass of non-professional white-collar workers employed in organizations of ever-increasing size. These workers (apart from those in public service) are still largely unorganized. Like the professionals, they resist joining unions, because they consider them organizations appropriate for lower status, blue-collar workers and beneath the dignity of the white-collar employee. Unlike the professionals, they do not have professional organizations which can be and have been adapted for purposes of bargaining. It seems unlikely that many Canadian white-collar workers will join existing unions. More likely is the development of associations of white-collar workers at the level of the firm which then may spread to industrial, regional and national groupings similar to what is already common among blue-collar workers.

If this appraisal is accurate, within a decade we may well see new national associations and a new confederation of associations called something other than unions, with no formal ties to existing unions. This is the pattern in Sweden where there are three national groupings of employees covering professional and non-professional white-collar workers, and blue-collar workers respectively. Our traditional unions will decline in importance, although not necessarily in absolute size; however, the collective bargaining process will be spread by these new forms of organization to groups which now are largely unorganized. The first prediction, then, is that unions will decline but that collective bargaining will be extended through new organizations to a majority of the employed labour force. For many of these workers, particularly those in public service and the professions, the strike probably will not be an acceptable procedure in the bargaining process. The parties will have to evolve some mode of arbitration that will be acceptable to all concerned.

FOOTNOTES

[1] For a further discussion of this approach, see S.M.A. Hameed's article in this volume. Also see J. Dunlop, *Industrial Relations Systems* (New York: H. Holt & Co., 1958).

[2] For further information see R. Caves and R. Holton, *The Canadian Economy* (Cambridge: Harvard University Press, 1961); G. W. Wilson et al, eds., *Canada: An Appraisal of Its Needs and Resources* (Toronto: University of Toronto Press, 1965); and W. T. Easterbrook and H. G. J. Aitken, *Canadian Economic History* (Toronto: Macmillan Co., 1956).

[3] See Canada, Privy Council Office, *Foreign Ownership and the Structure of Canadian Industry* (Ottawa: Queen's Printer, January 1968) for a well documented treatment of this subject.

[4] For further information, see H. D. Woods and S. Ostry, *Labour Policy and Labour Economics in Canada* (Toronto: Macmillan Co., 1962), Chapter X, XI and XI and XII; and Caves and Holton, *The Canadian Economy*.

[5] See S. Ostry's article in this volume.

[6] See also S. M. A. Hameed's article in this volume, and H. D. Woods and S. Ostry, *Labour Policy and Labour Economics in Canada* Part I (Toronto: Macmillan & Co., 1962), and E. Lorentsen "Fifty Years of Labour Legislation in Canada," *Labour Gazette*, September 1950.

[7] See John Porter, *The Vertical Mosaic: An Analysis of Social Class and Power in Canada* (Toronto: University of Toronto Press, 1965), Chapters XI and XVIII.

[8] *Ibid.*, p. 539.

[9] *Ibid.*, p. 540.

[10] See J. Crispo, *International Unionism* (Toronto: McGraw-Hill, 1967).

[11] See the article by A. F. Isbester in this volume.

[12] For a more complete treatment of the history of Canadian unions, see H. A. Logan, *Trade Unions in Canada* (Toronto: Macmillan Co. of Canada Ltd., 1948); S. Jamieson, *Industrial Relations in Canada* (Ithaca: Cornell University Press, 1957); J. T. Montague, "The Growth of Labour Organization in Canada 1900-1950," in *Labour Gazette*, September 1950.

[13] See H. A. Innis, *The Fur Trade in Canada* (New Haven: Yale University Press, 1930), p. 245.

[14] C. Lipton, *The Trade Union Movement of Canada 1827-1959* (Montreal: Canadian Social Publications Ltd., 1968), p. 7.

[15] E. Forsey, "History of the Labour Movement in Canada," *The Canada Year Book 1957-58*, (Ottawa: Queen's Printer, 1958).

[16] A dual union is defined as one that attempts to organize workers considered to be in the jurisdiction of some other union. On this continent, unions have long argued for exclusive jurisdiction over a given occupation or industry by a single union and have labelled dual unionism as undesirable. In other countries, dual unions are often accepted as part of the normal state of affairs.

[17] Apart from the CLC and the CNTU, there are two very small organizations claiming to be national union centres — the National Council of Canadian Labour and the recently formed Council of Canadian Unions. Both oppose international unions. Neither is large enough to warrant further discussion here.

[18] For various views on the purposes of trade unions see S. Perlman, *A Theory of the Labour Movement* (New York: Macmillan Co. 1928); R. F. Hoxie, *Trade Unionism in the United States* (New York: Appleton Century-Crofts, 1923); S. Webb and B. Webb, *Industrial Democracy* (London: Longmans, Green and Co. 1987); F. Tannenbaum, *A Philosophy of Labour* (New York: Alfred A. Knopf, 1951); K. Marx, *Selected Works* (New York: International Publishers, 1936); and C. Kerr and A. Siegel "The Structuring of the Labour Force in Industrial Society" *Industrial and Labour Relations Review*, January 1955 p. 155 ff.

THE STRUCTURE OF THE UNION MOVEMENT IN CANADA*

Francis J. McKendy

The labour movement is a hierarchy of units, each performing distinct functions within the overall organization. The units include local branches as well as international confederations of unions. McKendy examines these units in the Canadian context.

THE LOCAL

The basic unit of labour organization formed in a particular locality is the local — sometimes called "lodge," "branch," or in the case of CNTU (Confederation of National Trade Unions) affiliates, the *syndicat*. Locals, or their equivalents, have their own constitutions; and the members pay dues to and participate directly in the affairs of the local, including the election of officers, financial and business affairs and the relations between the local and the employer. Local un-

* A lecture delivered by F. J. McKendy, Chief, Labour Organizations and Labour Disputes Division, Economics and Research Branch; Canada Department of Labour to Dr. Hem C. Jain's graduate seminar at the University of Ottawa, 1972. Reproduced with permission. The views expressed in this paper are those of the author and are not necessarily those of the Canada Department of Labour by which he is employed.

ions normally have a good deal of autonomy, and in the Canadian industrial relations system most collective bargaining takes place between the local and the employer of its members. (There are certain exceptions to this practice where bargaining is carried on a national or regional scale and in some cases by combinations of unions or locals and associations representing employers.) Locals may vary in size, depending on the type of union to which they belong and the size of the establishments in which their members are employed. They may be one of three types: a local of a national or international union, one chartered directly by a central labour body, or an independent association not connected with any other labour organization. The locals of most national and international unions (outside the CNTU) are identified by the name of the union to which they belong and a local number. The equivalent of the local in the CNTU, the *Syndicat*, is normally identified by including in its name the industry and locality in which it operates.

THE UNION

The union is the unit of labour organization which organizes and charters locals in the industries and trades as defined in its constitution, sets general policies for its locals, assists them in the conduct of their affairs and coordinates their activities. It is financed by locals through per capita dues and assessments. Unions hold regular conventions of delegates from their locals at which general policies are set and at which officers are elected.

The equivalent of the union in the CNTU organization is the *fédération*. Federations are organized primarily along industry lines and in 1971 they were 12 in number.

Among the sub-structures of union organization are district councils — organizations of locals of a union in a particular area formed to coordinate the activities and administer to the needs of locals in a given area. District councils may hold meetings of delegates from each member local to deal with matters of mutual interest and to elect district officers. They are also known as "joint boards" or "conference boards".

Another part of the substructure, most frequently found among unions organized along craft lines, is the Allied Trades Federation. It is an organization of unions or of locals in a particular area functioning in the same industry to coordinate the activities of the members and to deal with jurisdictional questions. Policies are established and officers are elected at meetings attended by delegates from member organizations. Trades federations may be also known as union councils, union federations or joint councils.

Another part of the substructure is the local labour council. These are organizations formed by a labour central at the city level and they function in the same manner as a provincial federation but within the scope of a city. They are financed through per capita taxes on affiliates.

THE CENTRAL LABOUR BODY

The central labour bodies are really "organizations of unions" rather than unions in the sense that they do not normally perform union functions such as collective bargaining *per se*. They are concerned with coordinating at the national level the activities of their affiliated unions including the relations between the labour movement and government, and the establishment of relations with organized workers on an international (in this case meaning world-wide) scale. Their policies are developed in open conventions held each two years. Each year, they present briefs to the federal government in which they state their organizations' position on a wide range of economic, social and political issues as well as national and international affairs. They deal with such topics as labour legislation, human rights, housing, trade policy, etc.

The Canadian Labour Congress, being a national organization has in each province, a provincial federation. Provincial federations are made up of member unions of the Canadian Labour Congress in the respective provinces. They act, in the provinces, similar to the way the CLC acts on a national basis, presenting briefs to the government and coordinating the activities of member locals. Provincial federations do not, however, charter locals. All locals of CLC unions in the provinces are urged to affiliate with provincial federations, but it is not mandatory. Provincial federations of labour are financed by per capita fees from their member locals and as with other substructures, are entitled to send delegates to the Congress convention.

In the Confederation of National Trade Unions, in which the operation is not entirely but virtually all in Quebec, there are regional councils. These might be considered as equivalent, on a geographic basis, to the provincial federations of the Canadian Labour Congress.

The supreme governing body of both congresses is the Convention, held at two year intervals. In the CLC, the governing body between conventions is the Executive Council, comprising the President, Secretary-Treasurer, two Executive Vice Presidents, six General Vice Presidents, and nine Vice Presidents-at-large. The Executive Council meets at least four times a year.

In the Confederation of National Trade Unions, the governing body between conventions is the Confederal Council, comprised of the General President, the General Secretary, the General Treasurer, the General Vice President, the General Director of Services, one representative of each federation, eight representatives of central councils and one representing staff members of the Confederation. This body also meets at least four times a year.

In the CLC, the Executive Committee, comprised of the President, the Secretary-Treasurer, two Executive Vice Presidents, and the General Vice Presidents, are responsible for the administration of the affairs and activities of the congress, meeting at least six times a year.

The Confederal Bureau of the CNTU has a function similar to the Executive Council of the CLC.

The Canadian Labour Congress is affiliated with the International Confederation of Free Trade Unions, an international body composed of 121 affiliates in 94 countries in North, Central and South America, Europe, Asia, the Middle East, Africa and Australia. Canada has two members on the Executive Board and the total membership of the ICFTU is 48 million.

The Confederation of National Trade Unions speaks internationally through affiliation with World Confederation of Labour, with 81 affiliates in 72 countries in the Americas, Europe and Africa. The total membership of the World Confederation of Labour is 15 million. The CNTU is usually represented on the Executive of this organization by its President.

The structure of the Canadian labour movement as an operating concern is somewhat complex. Eighty-five per cent of all Canadian union members are in organizations affiliated with either of the two principal labour congresses, the CLC and the CNTU. Between these two congresses there has been much rivalry, arising out of jurisdictional matters and general philosophy. The CNTU has always been opposed to international unionism as espoused by the CLC and its predecessors, although the reason for this opposition has undergone some change throughout the years of the CNTU's existence. The CNTU has been less concerned than the CLC about such matters as raiding, believing that interunion competition is a desirable thing because it gives dissatisfied workers a choice. The CNTU has also believed in a more tightly controlled type of confederation, in contrast to the more loosely knit kind of organization that characterizes the CLC. In spite of their differences, there have been occasions where the Quebec Federation of Labour, the Quebec wing of the CLC, and the CNTU have cooperated in pursuit of jointly desired government action. A recent example of this was the "common front" made up of CNTU and QFL affiliates and the Quebec Teachers' Corporation, together representing 210,000 government employees seeking better conditions for hospital workers, civil servants, teachers, Hydro and Liquor Board employees, and taking joint strike action in support of their demands.

Following this strike action in April and May 1972, a rift occurred in the CNTU over the issue of political action. A breakaway of the more conservative elements under the leadership of the so-called Three-D's (Dion, Dalpe and Daigle, all former officials in the CNTU), followed, and the *Confédération des syndicats démocratiques* was formed, on a platform of independence from party politics. This new organization has been recruiting membership from erstwhile affiliates of the CNTU and, as of October this year, were reported in the press as having upwards of 30,000 members. There are some who interpret the joint action by the Quebec Federation of Labour and the other two Quebec-based organizations as indicative of a possible restructuring of the Quebec labour movement.

In any discussion of the structure of unions in Canada the very size of that part of the labour movement which is international, and the diverse relationships that result from this fact, make the international aspect of union structure the most interesting and unique feature of our union movement.

There are 99 international unions in Canada whose membership is deployed among 5,000 local unions; this is about half the total number of locals in the country. Many people are inclined to regard the Canadian labour movement as merely a part of the United States movement. In support of this thesis they cite the fact that Canadian locals operate under the same union constitutions, are represented at international conventions on the same basis as American locals, pay the same per capita dues to international headquarters and are entitled to the same strike pay and other benefits for their members as American locals. There are, of course, differences among international unions in policies respecting such matters as strike authorization, contract authorization, etc. However, in collective bargaining matters, Canadian locals or sections of internationals enjoy a large degree of autonomy, particularly in those unions formerly in the CLO before the 1955 merger and in construction unions formerly affiliated with the American Federation of Labour. Most international unions with locals in Canada have Canadian representatives on their executives — either as vice presidents or as board members.

There are many differences in the *de facto* relationships between Canadian locals belonging to internationals and United States locals of the same union. Canada is a sovereign power, with a different form of government and different industrial relations legislation but with largely similar economic problems. However, the Canadian Labour Congress is a separate and autonomous Canadian central labour body. Most executives of international unions recognize these political and legal differences and acknowledge that Canadian problems can best be handled by Canadian officers. This is reflected in the sometimes greater degree of autonomy and control enjoyed by the Canadian sections of internationals in Canada than is the case with their counterparts in the United States. The Canadian portions of a good many internationals are organized as separate Canadian districts. This is especially true of the internationals with large Canadian memberships. (A good example is the Steelworkers, and even in a declining union such as the United Mineworkers there have been for many years two separate districts in Canada, one in the East and one in the West).

The trend toward separate Canadian districts is likely to continue, as a result of the guidelines put forward by the Task Force on Labour

Relations and subsequent declarations by the Canadian Labour Congress.

The indications are that unions in Canada are here to stay for a long while and will continue to play a significant part in the economic affairs of our country. The structure of the union movement will depend to a large extent on the kind of political, economic and legislative environment in which it will have to operate. It is generally conceded that a free union movement is an essential part of a democratic society; and free collective bargaining is, on the whole, a pretty good system of allocating the output of our resources and efforts.

It is fair to speculate that unions will become larger; mergers are being encouraged within the movement, so that unions will be in a better position to provide the kind of services demanded by their members in a modern industrial society. The problem of international unionism in Canada, if indeed it is a problem, is likely to be left to the unions themselves to solve. Workers are generally pragmatic and they will, given the choice, join the union that services them best.

It is also fair to say that pressure to make corporations more socially conscious, whether it be in terms of industrial relations policies or environmental control, or in other fields, will have an effect on unions and their attitudes. And unions will be responsive to initiatives, wherever they originate, to promote the common good of all Canadian citizens as well as of the citizens of other parts of the world that are less fortunate, economically, than we are.

THE ROLE OF INTERNATIONAL UNIONISM IN CANADA*

John H. G. Crispo

Professor Crispo outlines the advantages and disadvantages of international unionism to Canadian workers, employers and public, and to international unions themselves. Misgivings and fear about the potential political or other influence that international unions might exert on Canada are critically examined.

THE ADVANTAGES OF INTERNATIONAL UNIONISM TO CANADIAN WORKERS

International unions have brought many benefits to Canadian workers. In the first place they helped establish a labour movement in Canada

* John H. G. Crispo, *The Role of International Unionism in Canada*, (Montreal and Washington: Canadian-American Committee, 1967) pp. 29-49. Reprinted with permission.

earlier and on a firmer basis than would otherwise have been the case. By doing what a few British unions and numerous local indigenous groups could not do, they provided the foundation for a viable trade union movement. This would doubtless have come in time anyway, but it might have been delayed for decades, and this would clearly have been to the detriment of Canadian workers.

A more intriguing way in which international unions have bene-fited Canadian workers is by reinforcing the American "demonstration effect." The presence of international unions has caused Canadian workers to become more aware of American collective bargaining breakthroughs and made them more eager to strive for the same goals themselves. On the wage front, international union gains in the United States invariably set targets for their Canadian members. On other fronts, such as the area of fringe benefits, they have established prece-dents which have also attracted much attention. To the extent that they have helped to satisfy the appetites thus created, they have usually enhanced the position of Canadian workers, even those outside the union ranks.

International unions have noticeably augmented the bargaining power of their Canadian Members, especially where they have put up substantial strike funds in times of crisis. They have had similar, if less tangible, effects in numerous other cases. The very fact that there is an international union behind a local sometimes adds immensely to a feeling of confidence among its leaders and members. Moreover, the power behind international unions has sometimes been exaggerated in the minds of employers and thereby contributed to their willingness to make concessions they might otherwise have withheld. The extent to which international unions bolster the bargaining power of their Cana-dian members varies considerably, but it is rarely inconsequential.

The Canadian members of international unions have also taken ad-vantage of the experience and expertise available to them through the American link. Some international unions maintain well-staffed re-search, industrial engineering and actuarial departments, which are just as readily available to their Canadian as to their American com-panies. It is often extremely useful for the Canadian membership to be able to draw on American union personnel who are familiar with a firm's industrial relations policies and practices south of the border. Even where the experience and expertise available through an interna-tional union is not geared to Canadian circumstances, the benefits are sometimes noteworthy.

Other advantages accruing to Canadian workers should be cited. In certain fields, such as the entertainment and building trades, access to American work opportunities remains an important consideration of benefit to Canadian workers. Without membership in the appropriate international unions such opportunities would be more restricted than they are at present. These and other similar benefits are easily over-looked.

ADVANTAGES TO CANADIAN EMPLOYERS

While some management spokesmen would be inclined to argue that the presence of international unions offers no advantages to Canadian employers, the evidence suggests that this is far from being the case. Such advantages are exemplified by the moderating role which international unions have played in collective bargaining in Canada. Although there are cases where these unions tend to aggravate labour-management relationships in Canada, such cases are outweighed by others where international unions act to restrain the bargaining demands or tactics of their Canadian membership. Where this moderating influence is exercised, it may reflect a variety of considerations. It may simply be that in a given setting an international union feels that there is nothing to be gained by a militant stand. In any case there are numerous instances where Canadian employers have requested, or have at least welcomed, the intervention of an international union headquarters in disputes.

Canadian employers also benefit occasionally from the experience and expertise available through international unions. Related to the moderating role that these unions sometimes play in collective bargaining is the sobering effect that their advice and counsel may have during the term of a collective agreement. An example is provided by the occasions when industrial engineers from international headquarters have convinced local union representatives of the untenability of positions they have taken. Equally important in the odd case are the technical services supplied to employers who are able to show that they cannot comply with a wage demand because of inability to pay. At least one union, the Amalgamated Clothing Workers, has professional advisors on styles and production techniques to assist firms that are in difficulty.

A number of other advantages can accrue to Canadian employers who bargain with international unions. In a few of the building trades, for example, it is sometimes important for large contractors to be able to draw upon workers on both sides of the border. In these settings international unions often serve as recruitment agencies able to draw on a much broader labour market than would otherwise be possible.

Another advantage may be found in industries that depend heavily on exports to the United States. Where use of an international union label is helpful, as in newsprint, Canadian firms often prefer to deal with an international union. This is because American members of international unions are felt to be less likely to resist imports from Canada if they are being produced by fellow members, or by members of other international unions. In a few cases, in fact, international unions have publicly gone on record against curbing imports from Canada, even where there were signs that these imports were doing some injury to their American members. (Since the advantages afforded by this feature of the situation benefit the public at large, as well as Canadian employers, it will be dealt with in more detail in the next section.)

International unions may also be more sympathetic to complaints about the dumping of American goods in Canada than they would be if they had no Canadian members. While it is difficult to provide direct evidence in this regard, the Canadian leadership of the Textile Workers' Union of America, for one, claims that there have been occasions when the international union has assisted them in investigating and curbing alleged dumping of American goods in Canada.

ADVANTAGES TO THE PUBLIC AT LARGE

Some of the advantages that international unions bring to the public at large are rather nebulous, but some are very real indeed. In the former category is the belief that international unions "helped to bring industrial democracy to Canada." If it can be assumed that Canadians support the intent of their present legislation in the labour relations field, this factor must be recorded as an advantage. Moreover, international unions have often contributed to this end while at the same time successfully curbing the more militant and irresponsible elements in their ranks. As indicated in the previous section, this moderating influence has tended to lessen industrial conflict.

There is another way in which international unions might be said to benefit the public at large. This advantage concerns the part that international unions have played in imbuing Canadians with the mass-consumption psychology which serves so effectively to spur on both the Canadian and the American economies. While it can be argued that national unions have had the same effect, international unions have probably had an incremental impact. A former Canadian trade union official credits them with even more:

> "American" unions in both Canada and the United States have translated a theory of mass production into a reality, through the demand for conspicuous mass consumption, without which mass production would be merely something to talk about . . .
>
> . . . mass production cannot live in a vacuum, or without mass consumption. Without the economic militance of "American" unions in demanding a maximum share of production, enterprise would have remained comparatively stagnant, invention at least delayed and, with it, mass production and distribution dammed up.
>
> International unions, therefore, brought to Canada one thing which, more than any single factor, influenced the lives and patterns of all Canadians. What they brought can be seen as a good or bad thing but, in projecting the highest possible wage levels, and with it mass consumption, they have revolutionized the patterns of living standards and living for all Canadians.

While this would appear to overstate the case, it is doubtless true that international unions, with their emphasis on Gompers' "more, more, more," have added to the pressures on Canadian employers to "deliver the goods." To this extent they have acted as a goad and forced these employers to strive for ever higher levels of efficiency. In one way or another this phenomenon (viewed purely in terms of its constructive effects) has redounded to the benefit of all Canadians.

Among the more important benefits of international unionism to the public at large, one is outstanding: the access to American markets. Three noteworthy examples show how international unions can act to protect and/or enhance Canada's trade position with the United States.

The first example is a long-standing one: the periodic attempts by American interests to discriminate against Canadian imports of iron and other base metal products. Speaking on this point, the Steelworkers' Canadian Director has said:

> Even more important in the long run have been cases where, because Canadian and U.S. workers both belong to the same union, we have seen U.S. working men oppose their fellow-countrymen's attempts to discriminate against Canadian exports to the United States. On several occasions there have been attempts to have Canadian iron and other base metal sales blocked or curtailed by discriminatory legislation. In each such case, the lobbyists' moves were offset by delegations of the U.S. workers whose jobs were involved, requesting that nothing be done to harm the jobs of Canadian workers.

Important as this example is, it must be qualified to some extent. While the Steelworkers have consistently defended imports of Canadian iron ore and base metals, they have not done so with respect to imports of finished steel products.

The second example grew out of a situation in 1962, when Canadian imports were being blamed for the shutdown of hundreds of softwood lumber mills in the American Northwest. Despite the growing pressure of American industrial interests to curb the Canadian imports, the International Woodworkers of America strongly opposed such a move. In defence of the interests of its Canadian membership it prepared an elaborate series of briefs to show that imports from Canada were not the major cause of the problem. Armed with its research findings, the IWA appeared before a special congressional committee, at which occasion it stated:

> During the past several months, there has been a great deal of publicity about the 100 mills which have gone out of business in the past year, all allegedly because of Canadian competition. We suggest that there is no evidence to support this conclusion. In fact, the available evidence suggests entirely different forces are at work. From 1948 through 1959, approximately 1,000 mills have

closed their doors, and if another 100 have closed their doors in the past year, it suggests further the trend which has been clearly established in the industry: the capacity of the industry has been maintained among fewer producers: that is, large mills have replaced smaller ones, and older mills have expanded. . . .

Thus, we think the situation is not as desperate as has been suggested. We do not believe the answer lies in imposing quotas on Canadian imports. We think the answers lie in other directions.

This conclusion flew in the face of almost all the testimony then being heard by the Congressmen. But, interestingly enough, it anticipated the U.S. Tariff Commission's findings of almost a year later, which effectively quenched this militant campaign to curtail softwood lumber imports from Canada.

The third and most recent example of an international union's action taken to protect or enhance Canadian interests is also the most noteworthy: the stand taken by the United Automobile Workers (UAW) during the negotiation and ratification of the recently signed Canada-U.S. Automotive Agreement of 1965. While many of the implications of this pact remain to be seen, it does seem clear that it will mean a relative shift of some production and employment from the United States to Canada. Despite what was felt by many to be a potential threat to its American members, the UAW supported the plan in congressional hearings. Its only public reservations were about the adequacy of the scheme's provisions for manpower adjustment in the two countries. The union maintained its general support for the plan against opposition among its American members and in spite of misgivings expressed by a number of American legislators and auto parts manufacturers.

One can only assume that the UAW persevered in this position out of consideration for its Canadian membership. Otherwise there is every reason to suppose that the union would not have supported the pact, for it held little evident advantage for U.S. workers. Assuming that the pact is in the interest of the Canadian public (there are some who have grave doubts), this support by American labour provides an outstanding illustration of the way in which the international union link can serve the interests of the Canadian people as a whole. It should be added that the UAW was the only body among those appearing before the American congressional committee that made an issue of Canadian prices. The union was conviced that the ultimate value of the pact to all concerned would be jeopardized unless car prices in Canada are quickly brought down to American levels.

The significance of these three cases should not be minimized. In each instance the position taken by the international union may have been a decisive factor. Had these unions chosen to join with others in the United States pressing for policies narrowly protecting U.S. economic interests at the expense of Canadian interests, the U.S. Administration might have been compelled to bow to domestic pressures. While it cannot be argued that the unions involved took the position they did solely out of concern for the interests of their Canadian membership, this concern seems to have been uppermost in each case. Thus the presence of international unions in these situations apparently benefited the Canadian workers involved and, more significantly, their employers and the Canadian economy as a whole.

ADVANTAGES TO THE INTERNATIONAL UNIONS THEMSELVES

The presence of international unions in this country has advantages for the international unions themselves. While a few of them have misgivings about their Canadian link, most continue to cherish it, for both idealistic and practical reasons. These unions value international solidarity and feel an obligation towards their Canadian membership. In addition, there is pride and prestige associated with being an international union.

There are also practical benefits in being an international union. In the first place, it provides a broader base of operations and thereby sometimes contributes to the overall effectiveness of the organization. In some unions this is an extremely important consideration since the Canadian section not only pays for itself but also helps pay for the rest of the international.

The Canadian link is also important in many internationals because it enhances their ability to "protect their flanks." This consideration is particularly important with respect to wage levels, but also applies, to a lesser extent, to work rules. Where American productivity and/or tariff protection are not high enough to exclude goods produced by lower-wage Canadian workers, an international union obviously improves its position in the United States by narrowing the wage gap between the two countries. Similarly, where there is a possibility of work rules in one country affecting those in the other, international unions must of necessity try to avoid adverse Canadian precedents.

THE DISADVANTAGES OF INTERNATIONAL UNIONISM TO CANADIAN WORKERS

The costs to Canadian workers of belonging to international unions are difficult to evaluate, because most of them derive from the lack of Canadian "colouration" in most international unions. This inadequacy is especially obvious in those unions that refuse to allow their Canadian members to elect their own officers and determine their own policies. When the senior Canadian officers owe their positions to the international administration, and there is no separate Canadian policy-making forum, there is a tendency to neglect purely Canadian considerations and points of view. This factor does not usually apply in collective bargaining, because international unions normally grant their Canadian sections very substantial autonomy in this area. But it does apply in others, some of which are of vital concern to the Canadian labour movement as a whole. Take such considerations as the unity and structure of the Canadian labour movement, for example, where the international union link clearly reduces the ability of the movement to chart its own course.

International unionism has played a very disruptive role at various critical moments, particularly in 1902 and in the thirties, as noted earlier. Aside from these examples, however, it is easy to exaggerate the significance of international unionism as a disruptive element. Very often it has been assumed that a particular split was associated with the international union issue, when in fact it was not. Few of the early western breakaway movements, for example, were motivated by anti-international union sentiments alone, for most of them had American ties themselves.

It has been argued that between 1939 and 1956 "the chief obstacle to labour unity in Canada lay in the United States in the failure of the AFL and CIO to come to terms." While this is a defensible thesis, it should be added that, having held up the cause of unity (which is assumed here to be a good thing) in Canada for some time, the American labour movement gave the cause something of a push after the AFL-CIO was formed, and since then has occasionally taken action to help maintain labour unity in Canada. Recently, for example, the American headquarters of the United Automobile Workers and the International Association of Machinists worked out a solution to an impasse between their respective sections in Canada that was threatening to result in open war between the two.

This latter example is only one illustration of the evidence that sometimes the causes of labour disunity in Canada are domestic. An interesting slant on the problem is provided by the fact that the various groups most openly hostile to international unionism have never been very unified themselves. Even today they are anything but united. They range from the powerful and well organized Confederation of National Trade Unions in Quebec to small independent associations scattered all over the country. This suggests another possibility; given the variations in Canadian culture, geography, economics, and politics, it could be argued that the resources that various international unions have been prepared to expend in Canada have been among the mainstays of whatever labour unity there has been.

All in all, one is led to the conclusion that while international unionism has indeed been a primary source of labour disunity at particular times, and has aggravated the problem on numerous other occasions, the significance of this factor should not be exaggerated. Considerable disunity would doubtless have characterized the movement even in the absence of international unionism.

Related to the unity any labour movement displays is the structure it adopts. It is generally recognized that the structure of the Canadian labour movement needs rationalizing, and it is obvious that international unionism has been an obstacle of some significance. Evidence of this difficulty is to be found in the experience of the CNTU in Quebec which has made a number of significant changes in its structure since the war. If the CLC were interested in making similar changes, it could not do so without jeopardizing the American link. In effect this means that mergers between international unions cannot be consummated in Canada before they take place in the United States.

While the most effective solution to the problems posed by the multiplicity of unions would involve a reduction in their number through mergers, there are other possible solutions or partial solutions. Effective use of inter-union councils could do much. The fact that little advantage has been taken of this possibility in Canada shows that it is not international unions alone that stand in the way of rationalization of the Canadian labour movement. For one thing, there are those in Canada who have just as vested an interest in the status quo as their American counterparts. Nonetheless, there is understandably greater interest in mergers in the Canadian than in the American labour movement, because of the smaller size of the units Canadians have to contend with. But, despite the fact that many trade unionists in Canada recognize this problem they obviously feel that the advantages of international unionism more than outweigh this disadvantage.

The American trade union link may also have affected the philosophy of the Canadian labour movement in a way that could be construed to be detrimental to the interests of Canadian workers. While it would be difficult to document this assertion many international unions appear to have served to make the Canadian labour movement somewhat more wage conscious and somewhat less class conscious than it otherwise would have been. To this extent they have helped tto bolster Canadian workers' faith in what is still called the free enterprise system and to lessen the appeal of those who would make any radical change in it. This has doubtless affected both the economic and the political posture of the Canadian movement.

In the private memorandum referred to earlier this matter was dealt with at some length:

> A good way to assess the economic impact of International Unions in Canada might be in projecting a situation where International Unions would have no members in Canada, and where Canadian workers would be members of a "pure" Canadian Union.

> Under such a condition Canadian workers would, undoubtedly, have more closely adhered to European concepts and practices. In the process the Canadian worker would have, because of living next door to the impact of the United States, acquired a split economic personality. But the adherence to European ways of doing things would have predominated. The chief effect would

have probably been greater emphasis on partisan and class party politics, with less emphasis on immediate gains.

Wages would have been lower, and living standards would also have been lower, not only for Canadian workers but for all of the Canadian population. Out of this would probably have come a greater dependence on political solutions for workers' problems.

... The merits of trades union adherence to free enterprise in the United States is not, of course, a matter for discussion in this memorandum. The effect of the adherence to free enterprise by International Unions in both Canada and the United States is, however, important within the present context. By support of free enterprise, the International Unions have managed to lay a seed bed of thinking among Canadian workers in stressing immediate needs, or wants and gains, much more than they emphasize the overall need for a basic change in economic and political systems.

The effect in Canada has been, by and large, for Canadian branches and members of International Unions to "work within the system" rather than seek to abolish it. The end product of this type of "American" union penetration and indoctrination has been, not the development of a generally class-minded Canadian worker, but rather the Canadian version of his United States fellow union member, a weird hybrid type of middle-class proletarian. He is militant, not in seeking a "new society" but with a penchant for a heaven offering continually rising consumption.

Whether this is a valid conclusion is debatable. Even if it is, it is questionable whether such an effect upon Canadian workers and their movement should be considered beneficial or detrimental to their long-run interests. This is a speculative question to which there is no easy answer.

Another related point is equally difficult to evaluate. No matter how they attain office, the top officers of international unions in Canada still hold subordinate positions. Such men may be disinclined to take decisive action when it is called for — especially where they owe their positions to the international union administration. Although there is usually less tendency to move with caution where the Canadian officers are elected by the Canadian membership, there may still be hesitancy, if only because the financial constraints. The danger in all cases is that the general mentality of the senior Canadian officers may be affected by their secondary status. The author's analysis suggests that this problem is not serious in the few unions that have gone a long way towards recognizing the "Canadian fact" but indicates that it is in some others. Where the subordinate position of the Canadian leadership results in undue procrastination and indecision, it clearly can work to the disadvantage of the Canadian workers involved.

Finally, it has to be recognized that some international unions do not take their Canadian operation very seriously. It is not seen as essential to the union's overall welfare and is sometimes treated as little more than a holding operation. This attitude invariably means that when funds are short, activities in Canada are the first to suffer. The consequent failure to organize new workers and give adequate service to those already organized is patently detrimental to the workers affected. However, the problem is less common among the major international unions and its significance should not be exaggerated. In many international unions there is, as was noted earlier a tendency to spend proportionately more on organizing and servicing in Canada than in the United States.

It should be added here that where international unions spend proportionately as much in Canada as in the United States they may get less return than national unions because of the general international union policy of paying their Canadian staff American salaries. The rates in national unions are often 25 per cent lower, which means that the members of these unions frequently get service at less cost than their counterparts in international unions. But here again, there is little evidence of complaint among Canadian workers on this score, and this may be because the international unions are able to recruit higher calibre personnel because of their higher salaries.

DISADVANTAGES TO CANADIAN EMPLOYERS

Except for relatively small employers, especially those located in rural and semi-urban areas, most Canadian employers tend to favour the presence of international unions. Almost unanimously however, they share one major set of reservations. These concern the framing of demands by the Canadian sections of international unions based on the objective of wage parity with the United States and the enhanced bargaining power they may be able to bring to bear to attain that objective. Canadian employers are convinced that the Canadian economy cannot afford wage parity until its overall productivity rises correspondingly. They believe that a premature movement in this direction would not only be disadvantageous to themselves but also to Canadian workers and to the Canadian people.

Employers in Canada are sometimes critical of international unions on at least three other scores. First, although they usually welcome the participation of American union officers in Canadian negotiations, occasionally they object very strenuously. In some instances it has also been alleged that labour leaders in the United States can order strikes in Canada. And finally, there are some employers who believe that international unions can, and often do, veto collective agreements arrived at in Canadian settlements.

Participation by American union officers in Canadian negotiations is a declining practice in almost all unions. Moreover, when such officers participate, they normally do so only if invited and even then in an advisory capacity. Where present, moreover, they usually have a restraining effect. Even more significant is the fact that American subsidiaries are more disposed than international unions to utilize American personnel in Canadian negotiations. This is particularly true of American corporations that have relatively small branch plant operations. Rather than go to the expense of maintaining full-time industrial relations specialists in Canada, they often find it more economical to draw upon their home personnel. Compared with the American officers of international unions who participate in Canadian negotiations, American corporate personnel usually have far more power to act.

There is a great deal of misunderstanding as to the power of international unions to call strikes and veto settlements in Canada. While international unions are often empowered under their constitutions to refuse to sanction strikes or provide strike assistance, there are only one or two cases where international unions are empowered constitutionally to order strike action. This does not mean that they cannot endeavor to persuade their members to go on strike in a particular situation, but it does mean that they cannot force them to do so.

There are a few exceptions to this general rule besides the one or two cases where international unions have the power to call local strikes under their constitutions. The first occurs where Canadian and American negotiations are fully integrated, and conducted on a continent-wide basis. In this kind of setting Canadian unionists could conceivably find themselves embroiled in a strike not of their own calling. Even then, however, they could not be forced out either against the law or against their will.

There is a second and perhaps more serious way in which international unions can virtually force a strike upon their Canadian membership. Such is often the case when an international union has, and chooses to use, the power to veto a collective agreement arrived at by one or more of its local unions. Only one international union, the International Typographical Union, appears to resort to this veto power very often, and it has attracted much attention. In the protracted newspaper strike in Toronto, for example, there is no doubt that the international used its constitutional power to force the continuation of a strike on an unwilling local membership. It has done this by threatening to expel any members voting to return to work, thus making it impossible for them to do so without forfeiting their rights under the union's generous pension plan.

It takes only one such case to give international unions in general a black eye in Canada. To avoid misinterpretation, therefore, one must stress that it is exceptional for an international union to be empowered to call a strike in Canada, either directly or indirectly, and even more unusual for it to utilize such power. For the most part, international unions are more likely to urge restraint than to counsel strike action.

DISADVANTAGES TO THE PUBLIC AT LARGE

Possible disadvantages to the Canadian public resulting from the presence of international unions are easy to identify but hard to assess. Most of these disadvantages relate in one way or another to the main problem employers associate with international unionism — the pressure for wage parity. Growing out of this concern, it could be argued that by forcing up wages in Canada, international unions have reduced the country's competitiveness at home and in export markets. In considering whether this criticism is justified, one can only speculate as to the behaviour of national unions, if international unions had not existed. However, it is also possible to argue that union wage pressures have the effect of rousing managements to new efforts in improving efficiency and productivity, so that Canadian competitive ability is improved rather than reduced.

There have been occasions, nonetheless, when Canadian employers have raised the possibility that international unions were trying to price Canadian firms out of the market. An example is the following account of one such charge in Nova Scotia:

> Cosmos Imperial Mills Limited suggests that it is wrong that foreign labour organizers should conduct negotiations with Nova Scotia companies on behalf of the union concerned. It is alleged that this is particularly true in the textile industry as it would be to the advantage of the American textile industry, and presumably the workers in it, if our labour rates were to be pushed so high that our textile industry would lose the markets it enjoys at the present time.

Almost without exception no hard and fast evidence is offered to back up this kind of assertion. If Canadian workers were offered conclusive proof that international unions were employing such a strategy, they would doubtless abandon them very quickly.

One international union that has in the past sought measures contrary to the interests of the Canadian economy is the Papermakers. Particularly during the 1930's this union took action designed to curb Canadian imports into the United States on the grounds that they were being produced under sub-standard conditions. The same union also took strong exception to the eventually successful efforts by the Ontario and Quebec governments to have paper processed more fully in Canada before being exported to the United States. This position was consistent with the union's earlier unsuccessful fight against the attempts of U.S. publishers to have the American tariff on newsprint removed. Had the union met with success in any of these campaigns, it would have been interesting to see the reaction of the Canadian membership.

DISADVANTAGES TO THE INTERNATIONAL UNIONS THEMSELVES

For the most part, international unions are not conscious of any major disadvantages stemming from the extension of their activities into Canada. The one exception is in unions that find they still have to subsidize their Canadian operations. Only in the event of a major strike in Canada, however, are these subsidies likely to prove very burdensome. Even then they are likely to be taken for granted, much as would a subsidy to any other segment of the union that was undergoing a critical test of strength.

More aggravating, in the case of some international unions, is the internal trouble their Canadian members may seem to cause. Some international union officials feel that their Canadian members are always complaining about lack of service of one kind or another or demanding more autonomy. In these situations the Canadians tend to be seen as troublemakers by the international administration.

INTERNATIONAL UNIONISM AND CANADIAN SOVEREIGNTY

National sovereignty is an elusive concept. It might be defined as the ability of a country to determine its own destiny, free of external constraints. In a shrinking world, however, this may no longer be a reasonable interpretation. Today, a country's sovereignty within the world at large may perhaps be compared most appropriately with the position of the individual citizen within the nation. In this context the following citation is of interest:

> First let us take a quick look at the concept of sovereignty itself, a term which we usually apply to national governments and which commonly brings to mind Thomas Hobbes' belief in a final and absolute political power. But most people now recognize that no authority is absolute. Even the state must admit that it lacks the power to compel certain kinds of behaviour but must often bargain to secure the performance that it wants, holding out inducements and threatening sanctions which are sometimes effective and sometimes not.
>
> In western society, where we tend to think of certain inviolable civil liberties, not only of the individual but of organizations, soviegnty becomes a fragmented thing, distributed throughout a society. So, obviously when we talk about sovereignty we are not talking about Hobbes' absolutism but about degrees and kinds of discretion. Nevertheless, if the term sovereignty is to retain any meaning it must relate to degrees and kinds of discretion — authority — within a hierachical framework; where people at one level

within an organized society recognize and respond to an authority which is lodged over them, right on up to some peak authority.

While no country is completely sovereign in today's world, nations enjoy differing degrees of sovereignty in their relations with one another. It is clear that Canada and the United States do not enjoy equal degrees of sovereignty. Unless one assumes that the United States feels just as constrained to consider the Canadian ramifications of its policies and practices as does Canada with regard to the United States, no other conclusion can follow. This is not to deny that Canada is a relatively sovereign state, as these matters go in the modern world, but to assert that it is less sovereign than its neighbor, at least in the relationship between the two. This state of affairs exists not only because of the vast power of the United States and its relatively advanced economic development, but also because of the degree of penetration of American institutions into Canada.

This institutional penetration applies particularly in the corporate field, where a growing number of American subsidiaries are subject to a form of dual sovereignty:

> The nub of the problem which we are examining today lies in the fact that certain components of Canadian society important in function and number, must respond to two peak authorities, while sometimes the same, are sometimes different and conflicting. The components in question are of course the Canadian-domiciled subsidiaries of American corporations. As institutional citizens, or at least residents of Canada, they are units of a larger organized society of which the Canadian government is the peak authority. When it asserts its sovereign powers — which as we have seen are hierarchical even though not absolute — these business units recognize and accept its discretion and authority. They may complain of particular governmental actions, they may seek to change government policies, but they admit its powers in its constitutional areas of competence. They know that they are lesser units within a system of organized activity where terminal authority lies with the federal government.

> But these same business units are also part of another larger organized society of which the corporate headquarters, off somewhere in the United States, is the peak authority. When it asserts its sovereign powers — which are hierarchical even though not absolute — these Canadian business units recognize and accept its discretion and authority. They may complain of particular headquarters actions, they may seek to change corporate policies, but they admit the power of corporate headquarters within its areas of competence. They know they are lesser units within a system of organized activity where terminal authority lies with an American corporation.

The author of this quotation goes on to suggest a number of ways in which allegiance to these two authorities can result in conflicting loyalties. Under the circumstances there are bound to be times when the result is to diminish the sovereignty of the Canadian government in one way or another. Only if this diminution is considered a serious threat by the Canadian government is it likely to protest. While Canadian discretion in this respect might appear untenable to the dedicated nationalist, it is a fact of life which most Canadians have learned to accept without giving it a second, if indeed a first, thought.

The same problem grows out of the international union link. The Canadian sections of international unions also have a dual allegiance. As part of the Canadian nation, they feel obliged to abide by its laws, practices, and customs. As integral parts of international unions, they must work within their constitutional frameworks. As in the Canadian subsidiaries of American corporations, this dual loyalty can give rise to conflicting, and sometimes irreconcilable, pressures. Two examples will serve to illustrate how the inability to satisfy the requirements of both systems can lead to decisions and activities which impinge either directly or indirectly upon the sovereignty of the Canadian nation.

The first grew out of the Seafarers' International Union (SIU) crisis, which began in the early 1960's. This affair resulted in a frontal challenge to the sovereignty of the Canadian government. Even after the government reluctantly decided to impose a trusteeship, the SIU did not rescind a boycott it had begun much earlier of Canadian Great Lakes ships in American ports. In the case of the one shipping company, this boycott lasted for several months despite the fact that it appeared to be illegal under U.S. law. Although the Canadian government persisted, the trusteeship eventually made a deal with the SIU, the terms of which were doubtless influenced in large measure by the pressure that this organization was able to bring to bear.

The critical point is that the Canadian government's jurisdiction over a problem arising in Canada and primarily involving Canadian interests was endangered because it threatened the interest of an international union that had AFL-CIO support and was also able to defy the American government, at least for a time. Although the Canadian government persevered in pushing through its legislation, it soon thereafter permitted the trusteeship to make a deal with the SIU to smooth the troubled waters. In this instance, therefore, it might be said that while Canadian sovereignty was upheld legislatively, it was later compromised administratively.

The manner in which another aspect of Canadian sovereignty can be jeopardized by the international union (and corporate) link is suggested by the probable collective bargaining ramifications of the recently negotiated Canada-U.S. Automotive Agreement. While the initiative in this matter is likely to be taken by the United Automobile Workers, the end result will ultimately depend upon the extent and form of the parallel corporate and trade union links between the two countries. In the opinion of some observers the outcome is almost certain:

> Now the United Auto Workers propose another natural extension of the free trade principle in the area. The leaders of the union have decided to achieve parity between Canadian and U.S. wages in the industry, if necessary by striking the entire industry on both sides of the border. The decision must still be ratified by the union's constitutional convention next May and later by UAW councils at each auto company. But it would be useless to say that the development is unexpected, however unpleasant to Canadians who value national sovereignty, and equally useless to say that no other infringements of sovereignty lie ahead.
>
> The automotive industry is a key one in the United States. If the union were actually to strike it, the impact on the U.S. economy would be enormous. The U.S. Government would almost inevitably become involved either in preventing or abbreviating the strike; and in the ensuing battle of huge Government, huge industry, huge union, the Canadian Government, subsidiaries, and union locals would be unconsidered pigmies. However diplomatically the orders might be worded, they would be orders; and the pigmies would find it difficult not to obey them.
>
> When all the results of the free trade pact become apparent, it will be evident that Canada has lost sovereignty over its automotive industry and the companies and people involved in it.
>
> There will, of course, be compensations. Canada's share of the international auto market will have increased. Canadian auto workers will enjoy a higher standard of living, some of this enhanced prosperity will be passed on to other Canadians. But to a measurable degree Canadians will have ceased fully to command their own destiny.

There are doubtless other, less significant, ways in which international unions contribute to a loss of Canadian sovereignty vis-à-vis the United States. Take the question of political activity on the part of Canadian local unions, for example, where there are still some international unions that impose restrictions despite the absence of Canadian legal prohibitions or restrictions on this practice, except in British Columbia.

INTERNATIONAL UNIONISM AND CANADIAN – AMERICAN RELATIONS

For the most part, international unions have had a very positive effect on Canadian-American relations. They have served to strengthen the ties between the two countries and in doing so normally have helped to resolve problems that might have given rise to a good deal of difficulty. As already noted, international unions have on occasion raised their voice against those who would have restricted important Canadian exports to the United States. In addition, unions have served to facilitate an interchange of skilled workers and have thus helped to eliminate problems that could have arisen in this respect. The only case in recent years when international unionism has had a marked negative effect on Canadian-American relations was the SIU affair. Had there been no international union involved, it is inconceivable that this issue could have so complicated relations between the two countries. It was an exceptional case, however, and should be recognized as such.

IS CANADIAN – AMERICAN LABOUR SOLIDARITY FOREVER?*

Bogdan Kipling

Mr. Kipling, a noted journalist, discusses the pros and cons of the link that binds Canadian unions with their American counterparts in the light of recent economic developments. He argues that the only valid and lasting basis for Canadian-American cooperation will be found in enlightened economic self-interest.

"Solidarity Forever" has been the labour movement's theme song for as long as any one can remember. Unionists sang it while fighting management goons in and out of uniform. Strikers invoke it to hold the ranks. Sympathy pickets chant it to stiffen the back of the underdog in an uneven contest. And it's the marching song at Labour Day parades.

Solidarity means different things at different times. On the broader stage, it is supposed to unite working people and their organizations across international boundaries. For obvious reasons of history, culture and geography, these bonds of solidarity are supposed to be particularly strong between the Canadian and American labour movements.

In practical terms, solidarity meant that established organizations such as the American Federation of Labor helped to unionize Canadian workers by extending financial, technical and moral assistance. The Congress of Industrial Organizations fought many of its battles simultaneously on both sides of the border. Several AFL unions have been in Canada for decades. The ties among some of the old warriors and unions are still strong, though now the accent is mainly on economic power, decidedly less on solidarity in the fraternal meaning of the word.

* Bogdan Kipling, "Is Canadian – American Labour Solidarity Forever?" *The Labour Gazette*, March, 1974, pp. 184-90. Reprinted with permission.

Judging by recent developments in Canada and in the United States, however, solidarity of any kind between the two countries' labour organizations is wearing awfully thin. So thin, in fact, that there is a serious question whether any of it survives at all. Like it or not, Canada and the U.S. are growing apart; and what may have been the right thing when relations between both countries were usually described in terms of "undefended frontiers" and "hands across the border" is not necessarily the right thing now.

Does Canada need international unions? Does it need the link that no longer binds? Are some Canadian unions holding on to American apron strings long after they should have let go? Are Americans all that eager to have Canadian affiliates — and if so, why?

In my view, Canadian unions ought to start operating on their own steam. I am not anti-American or intellectually opposed to international unions. Nor do I believe the frequently paraded propaganda of super-Canadians that American unions are bleeding Canada white by way of per capita payments. If anything, the balance over the years probably favours Canadian locals of international unions. But, in most cases, Canadian unions are now strong enough to ensure their own financial basis. They are perfectly capable of electing their own officers and running their own affairs. The overwhelming reason why the international ties ought to be dissolved, however, is that the economic interests of both countries are diverging.

Some American unions are probably holding on to their Canadian locals for the same reasons most organizations protect their integrity: they don't like letting go of any part of their empires. But down-to-earth reasons also enter the picture. In some cases, American union leaders could count on solid electoral support in Canada. This was true of Tony Boyle, the deposed president of the United Mine Workers, now facing trial for triple murder in the killing of his rival for power, Joseph Yablonski, and his wife and daughter. United Steelworkers of America President I. W. Abel won his post with the decisive help of Canadian members. But these local and personal loyalties come and go. It is doubtful that Boyle would command much support in Canada now; and the next Steelworkers president may neither have nor seek votes in Canada.

The main argument advanced in favour of international unions by the CLC and many of its affiliates is that the emergence of multinational corporations calls for an international labour counterforce. Union leaders say it is easier to deal with powerful corporations that operate in many countries when the employers know they can be hit in any one of them. This is said to be particularly true of companies operating in the U.S. and Canada. Taken to its logical conclusion, this means that Canadian union branches would have to abdicate all important decision making in favour of their big American parents, for smaller units seldom dominate bigger ones.

I don't think this is what Canadian unionists want or even think about. At any rate, a move toward that kind of internationalism would be sadly out of step with developments in both countries. Canada is moving toward a more conscious nationalism, and the U.S. seems to be turning toward neo-isolationism. Canadian workers are already rebelling against even some of the best run international unions such as the USWA. In the U.S., judging by the recent AFL-CIO convention, the only thing unions are interested in is protecting their jobs and jurisdictions. There is no evidence of concern about Canada or its international unions' locals.

Canada's recent steps toward greater economic autonomy may be highly dissappointing to those nationalists impatient for instant change. The New Democrats barely brought themselves to vote for the foreign takeover legislation. Many of the younger Liberals were disappointed with their own Government. Among the Tories, there are several in Parliament who would have gone much farther.

The Canada Development Corporation took nine years and several federal elections to hatch, and many persons are skeptical that it will ensure Canadian ownership of resources and industries. The CDC's mandate to be profitable, critics argue, condemns it to timidity. Nevertheless, the CDC made a successful bid for Texasgulf Inc., and thereby retrieved one of the richest base metal mines in Canada. The new national oil policy forced on the Trudeau Government by the energy crisis is based on the need for Canada's self-sufficiency. Oil now exported to the U.S. will have to be diverted to feed the pipeline to Montreal. The so-called "third option" for Canada's foreign policy is predicated on a gradual lessening of dependence on American markets. Rightly or wrongly, Ottawa decided that Canada must find more baskets for its export eggs — and Parliament acquiesced in that decision.

None of these policies is anti-American. They are merely designed to foster a greater degree of Canadian economic independence. But, even if some of these policies seem timid and belated to Canadians, that is not how they look to Americans. Seen from Washington or New York, Canada is audaciously nationalistic. The Texasgulf takeover dismayed investment dealers because a "government-owned outfit," as one commentator put it, dared to bid for a "free enterprise company." The takeover act puzzles Americans, as any Canadian diplomat or journalist working in the States will readily attest. They are bewildered by what they think are "prohibition" on foreign ownership in Canada. Even when it is explained that Canada is not trying to "prohibit" but merely to control foreign ownership, Americans find it difficult to take. They point out that foreigners are free to invest in the U.S. The "third option" has everybody puzzled except the international trade experts. Most other Americans are incredulous that anybody would want to look far afield when the best and most reliable trade partner is right next door — and speaks English to boot. They do not realize that after

Nixonomics, in August 1971, Canada was forced to re-think its policy, and re-examine its overwhelming dependence on one market.

John Connally, the former U.S. Secretary of the Treasury, gave Canada a jolt few Ottawa policymakers and few labour leaders are likely to forget. He imposed a 10 per cent surtax on all imports, including those from its closest neighbours, Canada and Mexico. He tried to extort unilateral trade concessions (on the auto pact, for one) that would have cost thousands of Canadian jobs. And he did it with the enthusiastic backing of the American labour movement. The USWA's Abel commented at the time that the surcharges should have been twice as high, and should have been imposed ages ago.

What it boils down to is that Canadian economic policies are poorly understood in the U.S., and that there is no solidarity when it comes to jobs. As Jean Beaudry, the CLC's fraternal delegate to the AFL-CIO convention last October in Bal Harbour, Florida, put it: "The intended victim" of American protectionist measures, as exemplified by the Connally-Abel axis, was "the jobs of Canadian workers." And I have not yet mentioned the Burke-Hartke bill. That particular piece of legislation, not yet dead in Washington, would impose permanent import quotas on foreign goods. If ever enacted, it would cost the Canadian economy billions of dollars, and "the cost in jobs could be astronomical," as Beaudry told the same convention. The estimates of economic losses, he said, were made by CLC economists. What the CLC executive vice-president did not rub in was the fact that the Burke-Hartke bill was drafted at the AFL-CIO headquarters in Washington. Beaudry called it "this infamous bill," but no one at the convention raised an eyebrow.

The Connally surcharges were temporary; the AFL-CIO's Burke-Hartke would make the quotas stick for good. American labour leaders defend the bill as one promoting "fair trade." They say American unions cannot stand by and watch American jobs disappear; only the quotas, they say, will protect American jobs. The other part of the bill would curb American exports of capital and technology. The big corporations would be restricted to keeping their plants at home.

How all this protectionism squares with international labour solidarity is one of the nastiest questions for Canadian union leaders to ponder. They know better than most Ottawa policymakers what is at stake when plants start shutting down because the products they make have been excluded from the export market. They see their own members thrown out of work. This is far more concrete evidence of what protectionism means than dozens of academic or bureaucratic abstracts on the subject.

President Nixon presented a trade bill to Congress last spring. It is a tough piece of legislation, but its basic outlook is one of free trade — expanded world trade that would benefit all. It is tough because it gives the President powers to retaliate against unfair trade practices by foreign countries. It would make it possible for the White House to raise or lower duties during a five-year period while the international conference under the General Agreement on Tariffs and Trade tries to work out new deals to regulate commercial transactions between nations. The purpose of the GATT negotiations is to lower tariffs and eliminate non-tariff barriers that hinder the exchange of goods.

The AFL-CIO is the leading lobbyist against the Nixon bill. Just before Christmas, it wrote every congressman that the bill must be defeated. The CLC, although quiet on the Nixon bill, lost no time in telling the AFL-CIO what it thought of Burke-Hartke. The bill was unacceptable to Canadians, and it ran against the CLC's often-stated preference for free trade. Canadian labour leaders lobbied against Burke-Hartke in private meetings with AFL-CIO brass. They got nowhere.

Canadian unions are seeking more autonomy, Beaudry told the AFL-CIO convention, because they have been forced to "by the divergence in policies being advocated by our two trade union movements." He could not have said more plainly that what pains Canadian labour is American protectionism, and Burke-Hartke in particular. "The Canadian labour movement, as represented by the Canadian Labour Congress," he added, "feels most strongly that the economic interests of Canadian and United States workers, and many other Canadians, could be seriously undermined if this bill were passed. The relations between our two movements in North America," he warned, "could also be seriously undermined, if not irreparably strained, if you shut the door in the faces of your Canadian members of international unions."

Pleading for some understanding, Beaudry told the American labour élite: "Try to place yourselves in the position of a Canadian elected officer, international representative, or shop steward of an international union whose international executive board is actively supporting the bill." He got no response. But the ALF-CIO likes to cover all bets. Until it can have suitable protectionist laws, the organization's executive council passed the following resolution, as printed on page 156 of the executive council's report: "Congress should deny the granting of preferential entry (duty free or special tariff status), either partially or wholly, from any country that subsidizes exports, grants tax subsidies to foreign investors, or requires production or investment within its country."

Canada stands guilty on all counts. Workers at Douglas Aircraft in Toronto would not be collecting their pay cheques if Canada had not insisted on "production" in return for jet airliner orders a decade ago. The auto workers would be distressed to know that Canadian Government tax breaks played an important role in negotiating the auto pact which created thousands of new jobs. Fishermen on the east coast might not have a market for their catch if the processing plants had not been propped up with money from the Department of Regional Economic Expansion.

But if the AFL-CIO had its way, none of the products could be sold in the U.S. Of course, the AFL-CIO would be reluctant to acknowledge that American exports also are heavily subsidized. Most of the sophisticated industrial products that Canada buys from the States were developed with government money. The range includes electronics, modern plastics, telecommunications equipment, fuels and lubricants, and whatever else one cares to mention. The research and development was paid for by American taxpayers, mainly in the form of defence on space appropriations. As Prime Minister Trudeau said of Mr. Connally: "With friends like that, who needs enemies?"

Canadian workers are probably not spending sleepless nights worrying whether the international unions they may happen to belong to advocate protectionist policies, or how those policies may affect their livelihoods. Most people do not go about their daily lives consciously pondering such questions. But Canadian labour leaders had nevertheless better prepare themselves to counter the charges that they are aiding and abetting policies harmful to Canada by keeping silent, or by remaining within organizations that advocate policies incompatible with the best interests of Canada. And they can hardly be doing it in the name of solidarity. Not that it is a trade-off, but I have no doubt that the AFL-CIO would gladly shed its Canadian affiliates if it could get the protectionist legislation it wants.

The pre-Christmas issue of the AFL-CIO News bemoans the fact that, under the Nixon bill, tariffs on products from developing countries could be eliminated altogether. The "emerging nations," the News says, are "emerging as sources for low-wage labour for multinational companies that have closed down plants in the United States." That sort of thing really feels like a punch below the belt.

The other intended crime Nixon is accused of is that "he could eliminate completely a tariff of 5 per cent, reduce a 25 per cent tariff to 10 per cent, and slash tariffs over 60 per cent to as low as 15 per cent."

Smoot-Hawley! Where are you, now that the AFL-CIO needs you? In 1929-30, ultra-reactionary forces in the House of Representatives and the Senate combined to pass the Smoot-Hawley trade act, which raised tariffs to virtually insurmountable heights. That disastrous exercise in protectionism contributed its fair share to the deepening of the Great Depression. It is distressing to see the AFL-CIO heading in the same direction today. It is even more distressing to see that, indirectly, Canadians are marching along.

The last thing the world needs now is a return to narrow nationalism and protectionism. The leading world economies are facing a most difficult transition period from free availability of resources to periodic or prolonged scarcities. Raw materials and industrial commodities are in increasingly short supply, and there is no reason to look for dramatic improvements.

This year, it is the shortage of oil; next year, it could be copper; and the year after, nickel, bauxite, or even iron ore that could produce a squeeze on industrialized countries. Before long, pressures will become irresistible for the international sharing of dwindling resources. Considering this trend, it is sheer madness for the AFL-CIO to be pushing for a highly protectionist trade bill.

Rogers C. B. Morton, U.S. Secretary of the Interior, said last December that the U.S. should be getting concerned lest it become subject to "blackmail" with respect to bauxite and iron ore. Most of its bauxite comes from Jamaica, and half of the iron ore it imports from abroad comes from Canada. It would not be surprising if, before long, the AFL-CIO starts appealing for "solidarity" in sharing these and other vital raw materials so that American industries and American workers can keep operating. How are Canadian unions going to react to such appeals? Are they going to go to bat on behalf of their American "brothers and sisters" in the trade union movement? Or will someone remember Abel's statement on surcharges and throw it right back across that "undefended frontier"?

The only valid and lasting basis for Canadian – American cooperation will be found in enlightened economic self-interest. Canada will have to use its natural resources as a bargaining lever to ensure that it is not left out in the cold or taken for granted when the U.S. works out new economic accommodations with western Europe and Japan. Regardless of which party is in power in Ottawa, it will have to bargain hard to protect Canada's national interests.

Canadian unions affiliated with American unions should start gearing up to do the same. They may have to lay it on the line that the price of retaining international links is a show of sanity on present and future trade legislation. The AFL-CIO, and specifically its member unions, will have to understand that they cannot advocate policies detrimental to Canada, and at the same time expect to retain "fraternal" and international links with Canadian unions. It goes without saying that this kind of a quid pro quo would apply also to Canadian unions and policies they advocate.

Failing accommodation along such lines, Canadian unions had better prepare for the day when the links are cut, and each of them starts going its separate way. Meanwhile, a thorough debate on the role and future of international unions in Canada is long overdue.

SOME VIEWS ON DEFICIENCIES IN PHILOSOPHY*

C. Brian Williams

Professor Williams argues that continued adherence to the international trade union philosophy will make it increasingly difficult for Canadian labour to find its much needed accommodative role in contemporary Canadian society and to meet the challenges as they arise.

It is difficult to separate Canadian trade union structure from Canadian trade union philosophy. The structure of the movement is the organizational manifestation of its philosophy; consequently, a change in one affects the other. International trade unionism not only has molded the structure of the Canadian movement, but also has shaped its philosophy; an international trade union structure means an international trade union philosophy.

The philosophy of class collaboration is the philosophy of international trade unionism. It was this philosophy that was manifested in the Dominion Trades and Labour Congress of 1886 and in the international trade unions, and it is the current philosophy of the Canadian Labour Congress. The philosophy of class conscious trade unionism was the philosophy of organizations that were set up in opposition to the philosophy of international trade unionism. Organizations such as the National Trades and Labour Congress, the All Canadian Congress of Labour, the Canadian Federation of Labour, the One Big Union and, to some extent, the Canadian Congress of Labour are the best examples.

The essential elements of these two opposing schools of trade union philosophy are not difficult to identify and are well documented in the platforms, proceedings and records of each organization. In broad terms, differences focus on: a. the role of trade unionism in society, b. the means or methods whereby the trade union movement is to advance the cause of the working class and, as a corollary, c. the structure to be adopted in order to effectively advance this role and method.

The philosophy of international trade unionism was the philosophy of class collaboration. It was this philosophy that emerged after great debate in the platform of the American Federation of Labour in 1886, and by the turn of the century was the predominant philosophy of the American labour movement. It was the philosophy of "pure and simple business unionism" and of "Gomperism." It was a philosophy that was arrived at after an examination of alternative positions.

* This is an extract from an article in *Canadian Labour in Transition*, edited by Miller & Isbester, Prentice Hall, 1971; pp. 161-72. Reprinted by permission of Prentice-Hall of Canada Ltd.

The philosophy of class collaboration accepted not only the existing system, but also the form of government that went along with it. The role of the trade union movement was one of wringing improvements in wages, hours and working conditions from reluctant American employers. A pragmatic philosophy, it cast government's role in secondary terms. Its method was collective bargaining and its weapon was the work stoppage. Its structure in turn was shaped to maximize its chosen method — organization within exclusive jurisdictions by crafts, surrender of local autonomy to the central body of the craft, the international trade union, internal government by constitution and bylaws, and the development of a "defense" or strike fund. It sought to organize workers wherever non-union labour or products met the competition of union labour or products. Emphasizing solidarity of the craft or trade, the central organization of the craft or trade was given complete autonomy in matters of collective bargaining and the strike. To the national federation, The American Federation of Labour, fell the responsibilities for acting as the spokesman for all of organized labour and for advancing labour's legislative cause within the established political framework. It adopted an independent political stance. The cornerstone of this philosophy was self-centred — self-help and sole reliance on the resources within the "House of Labour."

The philosophy of class consciousness was diametrically opposed to the philosophy of class collaboration. The following words, drawn from a recently published class-conscious interpretation of Canadian labour history, illustrate:

> In the period under review, trade union progress demanded a fighting wage policy, organization of the unorganized, unity, industrial and Canadian unionism, political action. Yet the dominant trade union officialdom in Canada, and its ally, U.S. international headquarters, resisted. Why? One reason was class collaboration. Not the word or ideological trend, although it was a word and ideological trend. Not collective bargaining or legislative representations to governments. But something distinct: Subordinating the movement's interest to reconciliation with the employers, settling for less than it was possible realistically to get.[1]

The philosophy of class conscious trade unionism rejected the existing economic and political systems. As replacements, it advocated various degrees of reform, ranging from direct worker control of the means of production to direct worker representation in the existing economic and political system. In answer to the dictum of organization by crafts, with a central union having exclusive jurisdiction, the philosophy called for a loose organization of all workers in an industry, whether skilled or unskilled, into one organization. This philosophy placed great emphasis on the unity and solidarity of labour regardless of one's trade or calling. It de-emphasized collective bargaining and the strike as the method of protest against an employer, in favour of political action and the demonstration of labour solidarity through the general or industrial strike.

The philosophy of class collaboration trade unionism was introduced in Canada with the establishment of the Dominion Trades and Labour Congress of Canada in 1886. Through the years, with the rise of the CIO in the United States and the CCL here in Canada, its organization by craft theory was broadened to include organization by industry, semi-skilled and unskilled workers, although still within the context of the notion of exclusive jurisdiction. Today, the class collaboration philosophy represents the philosophy of all but a very small section of the Canadian trade union movement. It is a philosophy that is subscribed to by national unions as well as international unions.

Although there have been several attempts to introduce various degrees of class consciousness into the Canadian trade union movement, these attempts have been repeatedly rebuffed by Canadian trade unionists. On this point, it is sufficient to say that the philosophy of class collaboration has worked well in the past, yet one wonders whether it can continue to do so when confronted by the requirements of the next decade. As a meaningful trade union philosophy, it may be obsolete. The role assigned to national and international unions is too narrow and the emphasis placed on self-centred selfhelp is too great. In short, and this is the second of the two main propositions advanced in this essay, the two major philosophical cornerstones of business unionism — the limited role of national and international unions and the emphasis on self-centred self-help through the employer – employee collective bargaining relationship — will make it difficult for the Canadian trade union movement to find the accommodative role it urgently needs in contemporary Canada.

There are those who will say that some of the above charges represent failings on the part of collective bargaining and not Canadian trade unionism. They will say that it is collective bargaining that is ill-equipped to handle the issues arising in contemporary labour — management relations. It is not collective bargaining that is obsolete, however, but the philosophical setting within which it is asked to work by Canadian labour — a setting that in turn makes it difficult for collective bargaining to continue to do the job that we have asked of it.

There is nothing inherently wrong with the class collaboration philosophy itself, but recognizing the present transformations in our social and economic system, it is a philosophy that runs counter to the values held in contemporary Canadian society. It is a philosophy that unduly restricts the role of national and international trade unions, and places far too much reliance on a narrowly conceived self-centred self-help collective bargaining method.

THE ROLE OF NATIONAL AND INTERNATIONAL TRADE UNIONS IN THE CLASS COLLABORATION PHILOSOPHY

Within the philosophy of business unionism, national and international unions are encouraged to play a relatively limited role in extending trade union organization and influence throughout all levels of the economic system. The philosophy supports the exclusive character of a union's area of influence, with the result that it is deeply committed to jealously protected and well defined occupational or industrial jurisdictions. This area of interest and of influence extends only to the craft or industry, not to the economic system as a whole. Because of this acceptance of and emphasis on protecting and working within established occupational or industrial jurisdictions, the labour movement ostensibly has little interest in either extending its jurisdiction to new occupational classes or industries or in changing established occupational classes and industries, even though occupational and industrial definitions are rapidly changing. It shows little concern with national issues and seems indifferent to the impact of decisions in their craft or industry on the national scene. In terms of what the national and international unions *should* be concerned about and who they should be concerned about, this philosophy grants an extremely limited role to these organizations.

Many of the new occupations such as school teachers, nurses, and public servants, which have extended the labour management area, are represented by organizations that are not part of the traditional trade union movement. That is, they are not within the jurisdiction of established trade union organizations. In most cases these occupations are most reluctant not only to affiliate but even to be associated with the traditional trade union organizations. They find the image of the traditional trade unions quite repulsive.

If the trade union movement of Canada is to re-establish its role in Canadian social and economic affairs, it must adopt a philosophy that not only encourages extending organization beyond established occupational and industrial jurisdiction, but also quickens the interest and concern of national and international trade unions on the impact of developments within the craft or industry on the national scene. It must replace rigidity with flexibility and self-centred interest with national interest. It must actively work to extend its concern to the labour force as a whole, and to organize and assist all persons seeking improvement in their position within Canadian society, through collective bargaining or otherwise. In order to do this, it must adopt a philosophy that grants national and international trade unions a much more active and participative role. Specicically, it must confront and solve problems of jurisdictional disputes, raiding, extension of trade union organization to new occupations and industries, and the impact of trade union activities within a craft or industry on the national economy.

Like the matter of structure, some members of the Canadian trade union movement are equally concerned over the restrictive character of international trade union philosophy. In January 1964, an editorial in *Canadian Labour* spoke on the role of the Canadian trade union movement.

> The whole labour movement is today critically appraising its role in society. Inevitably, as society changes and develops, the labour movement will adapt to meet those changes and developments. The Canadian Labour Congress, as the focus of the labour movement on the national scene, will undoubtedly be called upon to reflect sharply those changes in the service of its members across Canada.[2]

Earlier in 1962, Wilfred List, labour reporter for the Toronto *Globe and Mail* and a friend of labour wrote:

> Organized labour in Canada is groping toward an uncertain future, clouded by the rapid changes taking place in the composition of the work force and the emergence of a universal middle class no longer attracted by traditional union slogans.
>
> • • •
>
> Imaginative new approaches are needed if labor is to continue as an influential force and bargaining instrument in the future. The challenge is only now being given serious recognition, but the response is still one of groping for a solution.
>
> • • •
>
> The warning signs are plain enough, but organized labor is still basically tradition-rooted and difficult to arouse to the challenge of the changing times. Here and there, as gadflies on the body politic of organized labour, some union leaders are raising their voices in a warning of the crisis ahead.
>
> • • •
>
> Pure and simple business unionism divorced from any philosophy or ultimate goals still dominates much of the union movement, particularly in the building trades. Unions will have to demonstrate that their vision goes beyond the immediate wage goal.
>
> • • •
>
> The solution to many of the labor movement's difficulties may lie in the area of greater central direction of union affairs, as is the case in Sweden. But jealously guarded jurisdictions and rivalries, as well as the fact that some of the larger unions are outside the Canadian Labour Congress makes any approach toward a more central form of authority difficult indeed.[3]

coming under the jurisdiction of the federal government. The amendment also provided that the I.D.I. Act could extend to operations within
the jurisdiction of any province that passed enabling legislation. Provincial governments acted accordingly. Between 1925 and 1932 all
provinces except Prince Edward Island passed new laws allowing the
I.D.I. Act to be brought into force within their respective jurisdictions.
Subsequently the provinces of Alberta and British Columbia repealed
their enabling acts and passed similar provincial laws of their own.[3]

The almost revolutionary change in government attitude and policy
toward organized labour in the United States during the 1930s had a
delayed impact in Canada. The Wagner Act of 1935 firmly established
the by now well-known principles of guaranteeing workers the freedom to organize into unions of their own choosing, free from employer
interference or attack; of establishing labour relations boards to investigate complaints of unfair labour practices, to prosecute offenders, and
to conduct supervised elections to decide certification of unions representing the majority of workers in appropriate bargaining units; and
of requiring recognition and bargaining by employers with properly
certified unions. Notably absent from the act were measures to aid
unions and employers to negotiate agreements, to regulate the contents
of agreements, or to restrict the use of strikes or lockouts. Through the
device of certification, however, it did have the effect of sharply reducing the issues of recognition and jurisdiction as major causes of strikes.

Government industrial relations policy in Canada, under pressure
from organized labour and its supporters, followed slowly and reluctantly along the path charted in the United States. The legislatures of
most provinces during the latter thirties passed new labour statutes
which varied widely in content and application. Most of them retained
in modified form the restrictions of the I.D.I. Act and a few added some
provisions of the Wagner Act, such as freedom of association and collective bargaining on the majority principle. Various gaps and am-
biguities in such legislation, however, and lack of proper machinery to
enforce it, rendered most provincial labour statutes relatively
ineffective.[4] The federal government limited itself to amending the
Criminal Code to prohibit employers from discharging workers solely
for reason of union activity.

That such measures were far from adequate was brought out in an
official survey by A. E. Grauer in 1939.

> The hostile attitude of many employers to collective bargaining has
> defeated the chief purpose of unions in organizing to bring about
> greater equality in bargaining power ... Analysis of strikes and
> lockouts in Canada for six years ... shows that a considerable
> number of strikes and a substantial loss of working time has been
> occasioned by disputes over recognition of unions or dismissals for
> union activity; and that industrial disputes resulting from these
> causes have increased rather than diminished in recent years.[5]

Canada's participation in World War II brought a new crisis in industrial relations. As in World War I, the government at first attempted to meet the crisis by using the I.D.I. Act as the "chosen instrument." In effect, this temporarily annulled a number of new provincial statutes. Clothed with emergency wartime powers that widened its jurisdiction, the federal government extended the I.D.I. Act, with its compulsory conciliation and "cooling-off" provisions, to cover all industries deemed essential to the war effort. This was followed by special measures to impose wage ceilings, job freezes, and compulsory transfer or allocation of labour in essential industries. They were accompanied by a number of supplementary wartime orders in council which were designed to overcome various deficiencies in existing legislation and to meet new crises as they developed. In this rather piecemeal fashion a labour code of sorts had developed on a nationwide basis in Canada by 1942. Its principal features were recognition of the right to join unions, encouragement of collective bargaining and compulsory conciliation of disputes. Conciliation procedure now required two votes to be taken of workers in disputes before direct action could be taken: first, to get a conciliation board established; and second, to authorize a strike. Notably lacking were provisions for certifying unions or requiring employers to recognize and bargain with certified organizations.[6]

These provisions were wholly inadequate to stem the tide of mounting labour unrest. The unprecedented wartime expansion in output and employment, and the vigorous campaign by trade unions to unionize hitherto unorganized industries in the face of strong employer opposition, brought industrial conflict to a new peak of intensity and bitterness during 1943. The new emergency orders in council passed to meet the wartime crisis tended if anything to aggravate the problem, for they put additional curbs and delays on unions' freedom of action without giving them effective protection from employers. By far the majority of disputes and strikes during this period arose out of unions' attempts to force employers to recognize and negotiate with them.[7] Testimony from employers, at hearings conducted by the National War Labour Board to investigate the industrial relations crisis, brought out divergent viewpoints. Some groups were in favour of legislation modelled mainly on the Wagner Act. Others, including representatives of the most strategic sectors of Canadian industry, were opposed. A spokesman for the Ontario Mining Association, for instance, supported the principle of company unionism, and a spokesman for the highly influential Canadian Manufacturers' Association expressed strong opposition to the principles of compulsory union recognition and compulsory collective bargaining.[8]

Finally, after an exhaustive public inquiry by the National War Labour Board during 1943, a new "blanket" order in council, P.C. 1003, was passed. This measure superseded previous legislation during the war emergency and brought the national labour code more into line with the American pattern. It included the main principles of the

Wagner Act and established much the same type of machinery to enforce it: guarantees of labour's right to organize; selection of units appropriate for collective bargaining; certification of bargaining agents; compulsory collective bargaining; and labour relations boards to investigate and correct unfair labour practices. At the same time it retained, in amended form, the procedures derived from the I.D.I. Act for preventing or settling disputes: compulsory conciliation of disputes and compulsory delay of strikes or lockouts pending investigation; intervention of a conciliation officer at the first stage of a dispute; and, failing settlement, the establishment of a tripartite conciliation board. It also provided for compulsory arbitration of disputes that were not otherwise settled where agreements were in force. The vote previously required to apply for conciliation boards, as well as the vote required to strike, were both abolished.[9]

The provisions of P.C. 1003 became the basis for most postwar industrial relations legislation in Canada. Parliament in 1948, after official termination of the wartime emergency, passed a new statute, the Industrial Relations and Disputes Investigation Act, that retained most of the principles and procedures of P.C. 1003 as outlined above. It had, however, the much more restricted jurisdiction over labour matters accorded the federal government in peacetime. The provinces, therefore, with the exception of Prince Edward Island, passed new labour relations acts likewise modelled largely on P.C. 1003.

Government industrial relations policy in Canada since 1948 has thus been represented by eleven different authorities. The federal government's jurisdiction covers a little over 5 per cent of the non-agricultural labour force, and the ten provincial governments are responsible for almost 95 per cent. The various statutes, incorporating the basic principles of the Wagner Act and the I.D.I. Act, by the mid-1950s were sufficiently similar to constitute a fairly uniform national labour code. All of the provinces, with the exception of Prince Edward Island, had much the same type of administrative machinery as that established in the United States in the 1930s and in Canada during World War II to determine bargaining units, select bargaining agents, and investigate unfair labour practices. With the notable exception of Saskatchewan, whose legislation provided for voluntary rather than compulsory conciliation, they likewise retained essentially the same types of procedure as during wartime for settling industrial disputes. Among them,, however, there was a considerable variety in details regarding such matters as the definition and legal status of "bona fide" as against "company" unions, "unfair" labour practices of unions and employers, the bases for determining appropriate bargaining units, restrictions upon strikes and lockouts, the sequence and duration of conciliation proceedings, and the functions and powers allotted to labour relations boards in the interpretation and enforcement of legislation.

A new wave of strikes in the immediate postwar period created a more hostile public reaction and demands for new legislative curbs upon unions. While retaining the basic principles outlined above, a number of the new postwar provincial labour relations statutes, particularly in the more highly industrialized and urbanized provinces, were revised to place new restrictions on unions' freedom of action. Some of these may have been inspired, in part, by the Labour – Management Relations (or Taft-Hartley) Act of 1947. Nothing as drastic as the Taft-Hartley Act or the "right-to-work" laws of several states applied in Canada, however, except perhaps in the provinces of Quebec and Prince Edward Island. Only in these, for instance, were there any restrictions on unions' freedom to negotiate closed shop agreements. Prince Edward Island is a small, predominantly agricultural region with a total population of hardly more than 100,000, so that its labour legislation was of relatively minor significance. Quebec, however, is an industrial province of major importance. Its industrial relations policy was represented by four main statutes: the Trades Disputes Act, the Public Service Employees Act, the Labour Relations Act, and the Collective Agreements Act. In the aggregate, until replaced by a new labour code in 1964, they imposed greater restrictions on unions than did the statutes of other provinces, or of the Dominion, with regard to such matters as strikes, union security, communist sympathies or affiliations, certification of unions and elections of officers.

Criticism of Government Policy

It is a safe generalization to state that the degree of government intervention in industrial disputes has been, and continues to be, much greater in Canada than in the United States. Two principles of major importance distinguish Canadian labour disputes legislation in this regard. These are: (1) compulsory delay and one-stage or two-stage conciliation of "interest" disputes arising out of the negotiation of new or revised agreements; and (2) compulsory arbitration of unsettled "rights" disputes and prohibition of strikes while agreements are still in force.

Compulsory two-stage conciliation that provides for settlements recommended by tripartite boards, as described above, has been a particularly distinctive feature of Canadian legislation, dating back to the I.D.I. Act of 1907. The main weakness in most Canadian labour statutes seems to lie in their compulsory provisions. These have been widely criticized for a number of reasons.[10] As H. D. Woods has pointed out, most of the compulsory measures were adopted originally in response to threatened crises.[11] But procedures suitable for meeting temporary crises, particularly in wartime, are often irritating and ineffectual when carried over to more or less normal peacetime conditions. The long-drawn-out conciliation procedures and inevitable delays in handling disputes, for one thing, often have the effect of exacerbating rather than reducing conflict. As Canada's two main trade union congresses stated in their joint report to a special Royal Commission in 1956:

> The "cooling off" period often turns out to be a "hotting up" period, and the longer it lasts the hotter the dispute gets, and the greater the likelihood of a strike by workers who have lost all patience with "the law's delay."
> ... Nothing is so corrosive of good relations, or potentially good relations, as delay and procrastination. And, we might add, no part of the existing labour relations legislation is so heavily weighted against the trade unions as the built-in delays. [12]

The most widely criticized provision in most Canadian labour statutes during the 1950s was the requirement that conciliation boards submit their own recommendations for settling disputes. For this involved a conflict of principles and a confusion of roles, or of "accommodative" and "normative" procedures, to use Woods' terminology. Conciliation, in principle, is supposed to mean using every legitimate means of persuasion to encourage the parties to a dispute to continue bargaining, to make concessions and to reach agreement on their own terms if at all possible. Most conciliation board chairmen and members probably conceive their function in these terms. But many chairmen, faced with the necessity for submitting recommendations in an official majority report, tend to act as *arbitrators* rather than conciliators. They conceive their role as being that of neutral representatives of the public, who sit in judgment on the contending parties and, with the support of the labour or employer board nominees as the case may be, recommend settlements which they consider closest to the "public interest." Where unions and employers are compelled by law to submit their disputes to such procedure, the effect has often been to circumvent or distort the process of collective bargaining. In many cases the representatives of the parties to a dispute take rigid positions beforehand, refuse to make any substantial concessions necessary to reach agreement, and then depend upon the conciliation board to get them "off the hook." More frequently, perhaps, collective bargaining does not really begin until after the lengthy and complicated conciliation procedures required by law have been completed. Each party saves its main ammunition for the conciliation board, in the hope of getting a majority recommendation that will support its case against the other party. For to the extent that board recommendations *do* influence public opinion, they may be an important element in bargaining power. The frustrations and delays involved may in themselves make bargaining less effective when it is undertaken because, in the process of formal conciliation, the demands of each party have been made public and their positions have become relatively fixed. As Woods points out:

> The conception that the parties are assisted out of a deadlock by the conciliation agencies overlooks the fact that in many cases the

deadlock has been reached because of the compulsory steps ahead, and at the expense of collective bargaining.[13]

For such reasons as these, many observers maintain that compulsory measures for settling labour disputes can be effective only if they are used sparingly.[14] Specifically, it is argued, they should be reserved for use only in industries of major importance, in which strikes or lockouts would jeopardize the welfare and livelihood of large sections of the population. Where legislation applies standard formulae of compulsory delay and conciliation to each and every dispute, large or small, significant or insignificant, it tends to be discounted beforehand, adjusted to, or manipulated by, the contending parties. It thus tends to discourage or undermine collective bargaining and reduces the effectiveness of compulsory measures in those instances where they really are required as the only alternative in case of serious deadlock.

Changes in Disputes Settlement Procedure

In view of these obvious limitations in Canada's traditional two-stage system of conciliation and the mounting criticism from several quarters, governments in most provinces undertook various experiments during the later fifties and sixties in search of greater flexibility and, hopefully, effectiveness in disputes settlement procedure. In some provinces, notable British Columbia, Quebec and Nova Scotia, these were brought about by passing new legislation. Others, such as Ontario, Manitoba and New Brunswick, relied mainly upon changing administrative rulings and procedures under the aegis of prevailing legislation.[15] In all, the results were substantially the same, namely a sharp reduction, or outright elimination in some cases, of tripartite conciliation boards.

British Columbia was the first to undertake significant steps in this direction, and its example to varying degrees was followed by most other provinces. The British Columbia Industrial Conciliation and Arbitration Act of 1947 had provided for the familiar compulsory delay and automatic two-stage conciliation procedure. It was revoked and superseded, in 1954, by the Labour Relations Act. This statute, and subsequent amendments in 1959 and 1961, provided a wide list of options regarding means for attempting final settlement of disputes. Under their provisions a conciliation officer, as before, was empowered to intervene when requested to do so by either party to a dispute. Failing settlement by this official, however, the Minister of Labour was given discretionary power as to appointment of a conciliation board. Other alternatives available to him included: accepting the conciliation officer's report and recommendations as final; referring the dispute back to the contending parties for further negotiations; or referring the dispute to an Industrial Inquiry Commissioner or to an outside mediator acceptable to both parties.

The legislature of British Columbia launched a new and far more controversial experiment in 1968, when it revoked and replaced the Labour Relations Act with the Mediation Commission Act. This new statute provided for even more flexible arrangements for handling most industrial disputes, but more drastic provisions for government intervention and control in cases officially interpreted as having a special "public interest." Conciliation officers were replaced by "Mediation Officers," and ad hoc conciliation boards by a full-time tripartite Mediation Commission. This body was given the power of deciding whether or not to appoint mediation officers to intervene in disputes even if requested to do so by one or both of the contending parties. In disputes involving a special public interest, by contrast, the commission was empowered to intervene unilaterally without prior request and, if agreement could not be reached by the parties in dispute, to impose the final terms of settlement upon them. This involved, in effect, compulsory arbitration in potentially any industry or trade. While generally supported by major business representatives in the province, the new act aroused intense and virtually unanimous opposition from the trade union movement. Indeed, the British Columbia Federation of Labour proclaimed a policy of boycotting hearings of the Mediation Commission, which affiliated as well as unaffiliated unions overwhelmingly supported. This has tended to emasculate the commission. In a number of major disputes the provincial government circumvented that body by appointing special mediators.

The federal government, in the face of what appeared to be a crisis in the mid sixties, appointed a special Task Force on Labour Relations to carry out a comprehensive series of research studies. In its final *Report* the Task Force strongly endorsed collective bargaining rather than legal regulation as the main principle underlying labour-management relations, and on balance, recommended reducing the scale and frequency of governmental intervention in, and restriction of, collective bargaining activities.[16]

The federal government did not take steps to adopt such recommendations until 1971, when a bill was introduced in Parliament to provide for a comprehensiive revision of the Industrial Relations and Disputes Investigation Act of 1948. The new proposed act is designed to give the Minister of Labour a wider list of options for disputes settlement, similar to those provided in most new provincial legislation. The most controversial proposal, however, is one that would require an employer to give a union a minimum 90 days' notice of intention to introduce any technological change likely to affect the working conditions or job security of any significant number of employees. And, while an agreement is still in force, the union would have the right, if authorized by the Labour Relations Board, to serve notice to the employer to bargain and, in case of a stalemate, to strike for, provisions to assist employees to adjust to such technological change.

Legislation for the Public Service

One unintended result of compulsory conciliation procedures, particularly when combined with government-supervised strike votes, as in British Columbia, was to give an aura of official sanction to strikes and dispute settlements in the private sector. These often provided for large increases in wages and fringe benefits. This fact, combined with the tendency for rates of pay in the public sector to lag behind those for comparable jobs in the private sector during periods of inflationary expansion, imbued various groups of public service employees with a new and growing incentive to unionize and, occasionally, strike for their demands, even if illegally. There was growing agitation and pressure on governments at all levels during the later 1950s and 1960s to pass new legislation granting recognition and bargaining rights, including the right to strike, to organizations of employees in the public service.

Among provinces, Saskatchewan had been the first to move in this direction, in its Trade Union Act of 1944. By the 1970s all provinces with the exception of British Columbia had extended formal recognition to, and collective bargaining relations with, provincial government employees' unions. Quebec, in its comprehensive labour code of 1964, went furthest in granting the right to strike to such workers. Most provinces applied restrictions in their legislation, ranging up to outright prohibition and compulsory arbitration.

A particularly interesting experiment was the federal government's Public Service Staff Relations Act of 1967. Under its provisions certified organizations of federal government employees, with the exception of a few designated categories, were given two choices of disputes settlement procedure in negotiating agreements with their employer: they could opt for binding arbitration, and for the time being thereby forfeit the right to strike for their demands; or they could opt for prescribed conciliation procedures, with the right to strike if in disagreement with the recommended terms for settlement.

New Restrictions on Strikes

Accompanying or closely following the new legislative and administrative experiments was a rising incidence of strikes and lockouts in Canada during the late fifties and sixties, as described earlier. This in turn generated further experiments in legislation that were designed to place additional restrictions on unions' freedom of action and impose stiffer penalties for infractions of the law. British Columbia again took the lead in this direction. The Industrial Conciliation and Arbitration Act, as amended in 1948, had required a government supervised vote among workers and employers alike before a strike or lockout could be undertaken, and another supervised vote when a strike or lockout was already under way if either party to the dispute made a new offer.

Unions and members judged guilty of participating in illegal strikes were made liable to substantial fines. The Labour Relations Act of 1954, while retaining these clauses, imposed new restrictions on the freedom to strike and more severe penalties on unions for illegal strikes. It was supplemented by the Trades Union Act of 1959, which authorized the issuance of *ex parte* injunctions against strikes, picketing or boycotting activities in violation of the Labour Relations Act, and for the first time rendered unions liable to damage suits by employers. And finally, as noted earlier, the Mediation Commission Act provided for compulsory arbitration of any dispute deemed to be threatening to the public interest.

Legislation in several other provinces adopted similar provisions, and a number of new and more restrictive statutes were enacted during the 1960s. The Saskatchewan legislature in 1966, for instance, passed an "Act Respecting the Continuation of Services Essential to the Public." Initially it prohibited strikes or slowdowns in hospitals and public utilities. Subsequently it was extended to apply to construction workers.[17] Along similar lines, the Alberta Labour Act of 1960 was amended in 1969 to provide for establishment of special "public emergency tribunals" to deal with "public interest disputes." The Quebec Assembly, again, on three different occasions during 1967-70 passed emergency legislation ordering strikers to return to work pending final settlement of their disputes by arbitration. These measures were applied to strikes of police and firemen, school teachers and construction workers.[18]

The construction industry came in for special attention in the new wave of legislative restrictions during the 1960s. More than any other industry, to quote Crispo, it had been "plagued by jurisdictional disputes, short illegal strikes, protracted legal stoppages and runaway settlements."[19] On the assumption that many of such difficulties arise from the fragmented employer structure and the superior bargaining power of unions in the industry, a number of provinces, including British Columbia, Saskatchewan and Ontario, passed special legislation to accredit employers' associations as more-or-less exclusive bargaining agents on a basis similar to that of workers in certified unions. Quebec has gone much further in this direction because of the special difficulties presented by rival unionism. The legislative assembly in that province in 1969 decreed, by statute, that there be multi-employer bargaining in the construction industry on a regional basis between the two main labour federations, the QFL and the CNTU, and three designated contractor associations. Subsequently, as noted, in the course of a large and protracted strike, the legislature passed special legislation ordering a return to work and imposing a series of settlements upon the contending parties.[20]

A number of other provinces, including British Columbia, Saskatchewan and Nova Scotia, also passed new legislation, or utilized existing legislation, to apply compulsory arbitration procedures to disputes in the construction industry that were deemed to constitute a threat to the public interest.[21]

Impact of Government Policy

Any attempt to assess the impact of postwar labour disputes legislation upon industrial relations in Canada must, of course, be made with reference to the major objectives that such legislation was designed to achieve. These were, broadly, twofold: (1) encouragement of, or at least protection of the right to establish, trade unionism and collective bargaining; and (2) settlement of disputes and prevention of strikes.

There can be little doubt about the effectiveness of Canadian labour legislation as regards the first objective. Union membership in Canada grew at a substantial rate under its aegis during and after the war. The basic principles of the Wagner Act that were incorporated in most postwar Canadian labour statutes have more than compensated for any new restrictions that have been placed on unions' freedom of action. As noted earlier, union membership in Canada by 1955 was more than 80 per cent above the 1945 level, and as a proportion of total non-agricultural workers it had achieved virtual parity with the United States. Its declining rate of growth during the latter 1950s and early 1960s, however, has been blamed, to some extent at least, on various legislative restrictions. In terms of bargaining power and cohesiveness of organization, moreover, the Canadian trade union movement and most of its constituent organizations continued to fall considerably short of their American counterparts. Divisions of jurisdiction between the federal and provincial governments, and the many differences in legislative content and administrative policy from one province to another, coupled with the absence of anything approaching nation-wide uniformity in government-enforced wage and hour standards, have all been contributing factors. Canadian unions often face extreme difficulty attempting to coordinate the policies of their local and regional branches, let alone to bargain collectively with employers on a nationwide scale.

The second major objective — that of settling disputes and preventing strikes by compulsory means — is more questionable in terms both of the validity of its premises and of the degree to which it has been achieved. Legislation that attempts to reduce or eliminate strikes by compulsory means has been widely criticized on a number of counts, mainly on the grounds that it is based on misleading assumptions. The frequency or size of strikes in an economy is not necessarily an indication of economic inefficiency or unhealthy industrial relations, nor can an absence of strikes be taken as evidence of labour-management harmony. Industrial conflict can take many forms, convert as well as overt, such as: anxiety and tension; frustration and apathy; absenteeism, tardiness or carelessness at work; slowdowns and outright sabotage; high turnover; and so on. Strikes and lockouts represent only one overt manifestation of conflict that has become highly institutionalized through trade unionism and collective bargaining. And, as several authors have stressed, strikes in many cases play a positive role in temporarily settling conflicts and bringing about voluntary agreement between unions and employers.[22]

The frequency or magnitude of strikes in Canada, therefore, does not in itself provide an adequate picture of industrial relations in this country. It is one sort of index, however, that does throw some light on the effectiveness, or otherwise, of Canadian labour disputes legislation in terms of its own objectives, and it brings out some interesting comparisons with the United States.

To the degree that the effects of Canadian legislation can be measured at all by strike statistics, the record seems to be one of mixed success and failure. Strikes during the later 1940s and the 1950s were well above prewar levels in size, frequency and duration, despite the elaborate machinery which post-war Canadian labour statutes provided for settling disputes. To a great extent, of course, these increases merely reflected the change from depression to relatively full employment and the great expansion in non-agricultural employment and union membership that had occurred in Canada during and after the war. In relative terms, indeed, the overall incidence of strikes during this period declined in Canada, in common with the United States and most comparably industrialized nations.[23] This apparent trend was reversed during the sixties, when strikes and lockouts reached a new peak in numbers and magnitude.

Some interesting findings were brought out on these points in a broad comparative survey of strike experience in fifteen countries, including the United States and Canada, by Arthur M. Ross and Paul T. Hartman.[24] In order to measure the relative incidence of strikes while allowing for variations in employment and union membership, the authors presented a series of detailed statistical tables showing workers involved in strikes as a percentage of all non-agricultural workers and union members, and working days lost in strikes as a multiple of total non-agricultural employment and union membership, from 1927 to 1956 inclusive.[25] It was found that, while strikes in absolute terms had greatly increased in size and frequency in most countries since the 1930s, particularly in Canada and the United States, in relation to total employment and union membership they showed a downward trend. As noted earlier the general incidence of strikes in Canada came second only to that in the United States, and the authors concluded that the two nations have essentially the same industrial relations system. The various strike indices for Canada ranged from one-quarter to two-thirds of those for the United States in most of the years covered. The relative impact of strikes in Canada after the war remained below that of the United States in most respects. It rose slightly according to some indices, and decreased according to others, from 1948 and on throughout the 1950s.

Canada's strike experience, however, diverged from this general pattern in some important respects. First, during World War II, particularly the years 1942 and 1943, the impact of strikes in Canada as measured by all four indices rose well above that in the United States. This could be accounted for primarily by the special stresses and strains imposed on industrial relations in Canada during the war, coupled with serious inadequacies in legislation and government policies for dealing with them. Second, a reversal of the trend towards a declining incidence of strikes occurred in the mounting wave of industrial unrest during the 1960s. In 1966 and 1968, the impact of strikes in Canada, as measured by all four indices, again exceeded that in the United States. As suggested earlier, this could probably be explained by numerous special strains and maladjustments that the Canadian economy, and society generally, experienced during the decade. Third, strikes in Canada have diverged sharply from those in the United States and the other three countries studied by Ross and Hartman with regard to *average duration*. As with the other indices, average duration of strikes in Canada was well below that in the United States prior to World War II — less than one-half, in fact. But, where the trend in the United States and the other countries was almost consistently downward after the 1930s toward strikes of shorter duration, the trend in Canada was upward. The average duration of strikes in Canada was higher than in the United States during nine of the twelve years from 1945 to 1956 inclusive, Ross and Hartman found, and the average for the period as a whole was about 20 per cent higher. [26] It continued to be well above the American level in nine out of the thirteen years from 1957 to 1969 inclusive. [27]

These facts taken together lead to some interesting hypotheses regarding the impact of unionism and labour legislation upon overt conflict in the two countries. Prior to World War II, strikes in Canada, even in proportion to total employment and union membership, were far smaller, fewer in number, and of shorter duration than were strikes in the United States. Apart from differences in national temperament discussed before, the lower strike rate in Canada could be attributed mainly to the fact that labour in this country, as compared to the United States, was poorly organized and badly divided, while employers were in a comparatively stronger bargaining position. Furthermore, organized labour in Canada at that time did not have protection from employer opposition and attack comparable to that enjoyed by unions in the United States under the Wagner Act. A much larger proportion of walkouts in Canada, therefore, consisted of recognition or protest strikes to force employers to bargain with unions, to reinstate workers discharged for union activity, and the like. Strikes of this kind are generally of shorter duration than those that arise over the negotiation of new agreements between unions and managements that have long-established bargaining relations.

The new industrial relations statutes passed by the federal and provincial governments during and after the war greatly reduced these sources of conflict in Canada, and strikes arising from them. Similarly, the legal prohibition of walkouts, slowdowns or other concerted work interruptions while agreements are in force — a feature common to all federal and provincial statutes — probably reduced or limited the relative frequency and scope of wildcat strikes. By far the majority of strikes during the fifties arose over the negotiation of new agreements. The elaborate conciliation procedures required under most of the new legislation undoubtedly were of some effect in this latter type of dispute too, in preventing a number of strikes that might otherwise have occurred. To this extent, therefore, the new postwar labour legislation could claim at least some credit for the fact that the number of strikes, and of man-days of employment lost in strikes, did not increase in proportion to total union membership and non-agricultural employment after the war, despite the unprecedented boom-time conditions, the rapid industrialization, and the great increase in numbers, size and bargaining power of trade unions.

But the very features of Canadian legislation that were effective in preventing numerous strikes from occurring may also have rendered strikes more difficult to settle once they did develop. This may be one of the major reasons that, in contrast to trends in the United States and elsewhere, the average duration of strikes in Canada rose above the prewar level and remained considerably above that in the United States.

It is difficult again, as in the 1950s, to assess the impact of various experiments in new legislation or administrative procedures upon the magnitude and intensity of industrial conflict in Canada over the past decade. On the face of it, the more flexible disputes settlement procedures did not seem to reduce the incidence of strikes. On the contrary, strikes and lockouts, as noted before rose in frequency and magnitude to new peaks during the 1960s, on a level far above the preceding decade. The various new pieces of restrictive legislation were passed largely in response to this mounting wave of unrest.

It would be oversimplifying and misleading, however, to attribute this disturbed industrial relations climate primarily to mistakes or limitations in new legislative and administrative experiments during the late 1950s and 1960s. It arose, rather, from the much more unstable economic, social and political environment in the latter decade. From what limited evidence is available, a case could be made for the argument that changes in conciliation procedure had an insignificant, if any, effect upon the level of industrial conflict. W. Cunningham carried out a detailed statistical analysis of strikes and dispute settlement experience in Ontario, Nova Scotia and New Brunswick, covering a period of several years before and after the virtual abandonment of conciliation boards in those provinces. His findings indicate that the change had "no evident effect on the proportion of disputes that were settled without resort to strikes." Indeed, Ontario's proportion of all strikes in Canada, in terms of man days of employment lost, declined after the new policy was adopted.[28] On the other hand, new legislative restrictions by various provincial governments likewise appear to have had limited effect, as evidenced by the unprecedented magnitude of the strikes that occurred during the later 1960s and into the 1970s.

Canada's system of regulation and disputes settlement legislation as a whole, however, viewed over a period of several decades, does appear to have been one important factor contributing to instability in industrial relations. The pattern of industrial conflict during the 1960s, as described earlier, was characterized not only by the frequency and magnitude of strikes, but also by the frequency of such incidents as wildcat strikes, issuance of court injunctions, violence and illegality, with consequent arrests and imprisonment of many union leaders and members.

A recurring theme throughout the 1960s, as well as in earlier decades, has been the apparent inability of the Canadian industrial relations "system" (if such it may be called) to adjust easily to major changes in the economic and social structure and to deal effectively with issues and maladjustments generating widespread unrest. It thus recurrently builds up to an explosive point, leading to waves of strikes, usually accompanied by illegality and legal suppression. The prevailing system of laws periodically finds itself unable to contain or control new forces of change and widespread flouting of the results.

In the face of each crisis new and more or less drastic changes are undertaken in labour legislation, union and employer policies and the like. These lead to a new period of stability, followed by a gradually rising new wave of unrest that again reaches a climax in a new wave of strikes. And so on.

In previous decades, the main issue underlying the most intense conflict was a basic inequity in the laws and in employer policy. The law, as stressed earlier, went to great lengths to protect employers' property and their freedom to use it pretty much as they saw fit, while providing little or no protection of workers' freedom to organize in defence of their jobs and livelihoods.

That source of inequity or injustice has been largely corrected, in principle at least, by legislation passed during and since World War II. But a basic inconsistency in ideology and policy remains, and it is one that seems to go far towards explaining the scope and frequency of industrial conflict in Canada. In no country, other than the United States, do employer and union spokesmen proclaim so strongly the virtues of freedom, of "free enterprise," "free" unions and "free" collective bargaining, including freedom to engage in strikes and lockouts. But each party, in seeking such freedom, has come to depend upon government to protect it against the actions of the other. The result has been the evolution of such a complex, pervasive and in some ways rigid system of laws and administrative procedures governing organized labour-employer relations that violations of the law and resort to illegal actions have become frequent and perhaps unavoidable.

Weaknesses in organization on both sides further contribute to excessive dependence upon legal prescriptions and procedures, particularly the frequent issuance of court injunctions against unions. Organizational weaknesses on both sides lead, further, to ineffectiveness in bargaining and therefore to frustration and unrest. These in turn are conducive to a relatively high frequency of conflict and illegality.

There is another apparently basic inconsistency in Canada, between legislation governing industrial relations on the one hand, and economic reality on the other. This, likewise, seems provocative of labour unrest and conflict. Government intervention via compulsory conciliation, mediation or arbitration is designed to settle disputes and prevent strikes, presumably on the assumption that the "innocent public" should be protected from interruptions in the production and distribution of goods and services. Yet under the prevailing ideology of free enterprise, employers in principle have a free hand to reduce or cease production, displace workers from their jobs by introducing technological changes, and lay them off temporarily or discharge them permanently, whenever it is economical or profitable to do so. During recessions particularly, losses from unemployment and reduced output far exceed those caused by strikes, even in the peak years of labour unrest. How, then, can extensive government intervention be justified in attempting to achieve stability in the industrial relations sector alone, and not be extended to the economy as a whole, through comprehensive and detailed planning, to achieve overall economic stability? Economic instability, as noted earlier, appears to have been an important factor contributing to a high incidence of industrial conflict in Canada. Presumably, then, a combination of "free" collective bargaining and a relative absence of strikes or other manifestations of conflict would be feasible and workable in the system of "free enterprise" only if it could achieve and maintain a state of economic stability and full (or nearly full) employment. The record to date has not been reassuring in this regard.

Barring major changes in organizational structure and in the ideologies and attitudes of employers, unions and the general public itself, therefore, the possibilities of attempting to reduce the scope, range and intensity of industrial conflict in Canada merely through changes in legislation and administrative procedures, would seem limited.

FOOTNOTES

[1] The brief outline of legislation and policy in Canada up to the 1950s has been based mainly on: Edith Lorentzen and Evelyn Woolner, "Fifty Years of Labour Legislation in Canada," and Ronald Hooper, "Conciliation Law and Practice in Canada," in *Labour Gazette*, 50th anniversary edition, Vol. 50, No. 9 (September 1950).

[2] Logan, Ware and Innis, *Labour in Canadian – American Relations*, pp. 66-7.

[3] J. T. Montague, "International Unions and the Canadian Trade Union Movement," *Canadian Journal of Economics*, XXIII (February 1957), 77.

[4] See, e.g., George Rose, "The Relationship of the Local Union to the International Organization," *Labour Law Journal*, IV (March 1953), 334-51.

[5] Philip Taft, "The Constitutional Power of the Chief Officer in American Labor Unions," *Quarterly Journal of Economics*, LXII (August 1948), 459-71.

[6] Montague, *Canadian Journal of Economics*, XXIII (February 1957), 78.

[7] *Ibid.*

[8] H. J. Lahne, "The Intermediate Union Body in Collective Bargaining," *Industrial and Labor Relations Review*, VI (February 1953), 163-7.

[9] Lorentzen and Woolner, *op. cit.*, p. 1450.

[10] See, e.g., Milton F. Gregg, "Social Responsibilities and the Conciliation Process"; J. C. Adams, "The Conciliation Process: A Management Viewpoint"; and Eamon Park, "The Conciliation Process: A Union Viewpoint"; in H. D. Woods, ed., *Industrial Conflict and Dispute Settlement*, 7th annual conference, Industrial Relations Centre, McGill University, April 18 and 19, 1955 (Montreal: Quality Press, 1955).

[11] H. D. Woods, "Canadian Collective Bargaining and Dispute Settlement Policy: an Appraisal," *Canadian Journal of Economics*, XXI (November 1955); also his "A Critical Appraisal of Compulsory Conciliation in Canada," in *Industrial Conflict and Dispute Settlement*, pp. 96-111.

[12] *Joint Submission*, Trades and Labour Congress of Canada and Canadian Congress of Labour to the Royal Commission on Canada's Economic Prospects (Ottawa: Mutual Press, 1956), p. 38.

[13] H. D. Woods, *Canadian Journal of Economics*, XXI (November 1955), 464.

[14] See, e.g., Edgar L. Warren, "Mediation and Fact Finding," in Kornhauser, Dubin and Ross, eds. *Industrial Conflict* (New York: McGraw-Hill, 1954), pp. 292-300; and Sumner Slichter, "Trade Unions in a Free Society," in E. Wight Bakke and Clark Kerr, eds., *Unions, Management and the Public* (New York: Harcourt, Brace, 1948), p. 915.

[15] *Labour Gazette*, Vol. 71, No. 3, March 1971.

[16] Canadian Industrial Relations," *Report*, Prime Minister's Task Force on Labour Relations (Ottawa: Queen's Printer, 1968).

[17] *Canadian Labour* (Ottawa: CLC), Vol. 15, No. 11 (November 1970), p. 19.

[18] *Labour Gazette*, March 1971.

[19] John Crispo, "Industrial Relations in Western Europe and Canada," in *A Review of Industrial Relations Research*, Vol. 2 (Madison Wisc.: Industrial Relations Research Association, 1971), p. 197.

[20] *Ibid.*, pp. 183-229; also *Labour Gazette*, Vol. 69, No. 6, June, 1969, p. 335.

[21] Crispo, *op. cit.*

[22] See, e.g., Edgar L. Warren, "Mediation and Fact Finding," in Kornhauser, Dubin and Ross, eds. *Industrial Conflict* (New York: McGraw-Hill, 1954), pp. 292-300; and Sumner Slichter, "Trade Unions in a Free Society," in Bakke and Kerr, *op. cit.*, p. 915.

[23] Ross and Hartman, *Changing Patterns of Industrial Conflict*, chapter 3, pp. 15-32.

[24] *Ibid.*

[25] *Ibid.*, pp. 208-09.

[26] *Ibid.*

[27] *Report*, Task Force, *op. cit.*, Table 17, p. 126.

[28] W. B. Cunningham, "Conciliation: The End of Compulsory Boards," *Paper*, 6th annual meeting of Canadian Industrial Relations Research Institute, Montreal, June 18-19, 1969.

ACCREDITATION: A REPRESENTATION PLAN FOR EMPLOYERS IN THE CONSTRUCTION INDUSTRY*

Joseph B. Rose

Professor Rose discusses the objectives of special legislation which deals with the unique characteristics of the construction industry and examines strengths and weaknesses of various aspects of this legislation.

One of the arguments advanced by the labour movement for granting employees the right to organize was the inequality of bargaining power between employees and employers. The passage of the National Labor Relations Act (1935) in the United States and subsequent legislation in Canada guarantees employees the right to organize and bargain collectively with a view toward advancing the cause of industrial peace.

The denial by employers of the right of employees to organize and the refusal of employers to accept the procedure of collective bargaining lead to strikes and other forms of industrial strife or unrest which have the intent or the necessary effect of burdening or obstructing commerce . . .

It is hereby declared to be the policy of the United States to eliminate the causes of certain substantial obstructions to the free flow of commerce and to mitigate and eliminate these obstructions when they have occurred by encouraging the practice and procedures of collective bargaining and by protecting the exercise by workers of freedom of association, self-organization, and designation of representatives of their own choosing, for the purpose of determining the terms and conditions of their employment or other mutual aid.[1]

The belief in collective bargaining as a vehicle for industrial peace is expressed in the Canada Labour Code which acknowledges the "long tradition in Canada of labour legislation and policy designed for the promotion of the common well-being through the encouragement of

*Dr. Rose is an Assistant Professor of Business Administration, University of New Brunswick. The author wishes to acknowledge research support from the New Brunswick Department of Labour. Mimeographed.

free collective bargaining and the constructive settlement of disputes."[2]

Arthurs and Crispo have noted that labour relations legislation in Canada is based on the "assumption that countervailing power in employee-employer relations is a desirable public objective."[3] Both federal and provincial statutes provide certification procedures for employees to exercise their right to organize. The certification process has had two desirable results. First, it has virtually eliminated union strikes to gain representation rights and second, collective bargaining itself has reduced industrial conflict by "substituting what may be called industrial democracy for the arbitrary power of the employer."[4]

Historically, labour relations legislation has aided employee organization. Conversely, employer efforts to organize into employer associations for collective bargaining purposes have not been similarly protected and promoted.[5]

The purpose of the present article is to examine the concept of accreditation, an employer representation scheme which has been incorporated into several provincial legislative frameworks. The analysis will examine the problem of instability in labour relations in the construction industry, present an overview of accreditation legislation, and assess the strengths and weaknesses of accreditation legislation.

LEGISLATIVE CHANGE IN THE CONSTRUCTION INDUSTRY

Since World War II, there has been growing concern over the apparent inadequacy of general labour legislation for the conduct of labour relations in the construction industry. This stems from the failure of existing labour legislation to accommodate the unique characteristics of the construction industry, e.g., mobile work sites and irregular employment.[6] Moreover, the structure of collective bargaining in the construction industry is different.

> In most industries a relatively small number of firms confront only one major union in each of their plants, if not throughout their entire enterprise. In the construction industry, by contrast, a large number of small independent contractors often confront one or more of the building trades unions. In such a setting there exists a real risk of a power imbalance in favour of labour.[7]

In most jurisdictions, collective bargaining takes place on a trade-by-trade basis. A major problem with single-trade bargaining is the ability of unions to employ divide-and-conquer tactics, e.g. whipsawing and leapfrogging, which are a threat to the stability of the industry's labour relations system. Such tactics have had an unsettling effect on employer unity, particularly during critical periods in negotiations. The ability of individual contractors to abandon their associations has rendered such organizations ineffective in collective bargaining. The rapid rise in wage inflation and disruptions to industrial peace are in many respects symptomatic of the economic vulnerability of employers' organizations.

One recommendation for the resolution of the imbalance of power in the construction industry is the accreditation of employers' organizations. Accreditation, which is analogous to union certification, gives an employers' organization exclusive bargaining rights for a unit of employers. Such a scheme is designed to insure greater employer solidarity since association members would be prevented from withdrawing from negotiations and resorting to individual bargaining, a traditional structural impediment which has hampered bargaining.

> It will make for better structured management groups and perhaps a reduction in the number of cases where marginal employers run the risk of destroying by their individual action well established policies of the association and a majority of the contractors concerned.[8]

By promoting greater employer unity in collective bargaining, accreditation should help restore bargaining parity in the industry. A greater equalization of bargaining power might encourage more centralized collective bargaining and stimulate multi-trade bargaining. This in turn would tend to lessen the economic impact of successive inter-trade settlements, and might reduce the likelihood of economic conflict. The latter could be achieved if a diminution in the use of the whipsaw tactic led to a reduction in the number of negotiating rounds required to produce a peaceful settlement.[9] Labour boards could also play a significant role in reducing union leverage by promoting multi-trade, multi-party bargaining across broad geographic areas.[10] The impact of accreditation on bargaining structure is discussed below.

AN OVERVIEW OF ACCREDITATION LEGISLATION

Accreditation legislation is of recent origin and has been adopted by six provinces: British Columbia (1970), Alberta (1970), Ontario (1971), New Brunswick (1972), Nova Scotia (1972), and Prince Edward Island (1973). There are two basic types of accreditation systems, the "conservative" and the "realistic." The conservative approach encompasses those contractors who belong to an existing employer organization which has a collective bargaining relationship with a trade union in a particular trade, sector and geographic area. Under the realistic model, an accredited employers' organization would be the exclusive bargaining agent for all unionized contractors (regardless of membership in the employers' organization) organized by a trade union in a particular trade, sector and geographic area. With the exception of

British Columbia, the realistic approach has been adopted in all provinces.

The remainder of this article will present an in-depth review of various aspects of accreditation legislation. Specifically, the analysis will focus on: (1) the process of accrediting an employers' organization; (2) the extent to which accreditation promotes greater employer unity; and (3) the influence of accreditation on bargaining structure.

The Accreditation Process

Applications for accreditation must specify the unit the employers' organization seeks to represent. While different criteria may be used to determine an appropriate unit, the major focus of attention is on the sector[11] and geographic area applied for. In most jurisdictions labour boards have the power to combine sectors[12] or geographic areas and the right to add or exclude employers from the unit.

Accreditation can be granted on a trade or sector basis. Trade accreditation, which has been adopted in Ontario, New Brunswick and Alberta, specifies that accreditation orders depend on existing bargaining rights between an employers' organization and a trade union or unions. For example, the Ontario Labour Relations Act states:

> Where a trade union or council of trade unions has been certified or has been granted voluntary recognition . . . as the bargaining agent for a unit of employees of more than one employer in the construction industry or where a trade union or council of trade unions has entered into collective agreements with more than one employer covering a unit of employees in the construction industry, an employers' organization may apply to the Board to be accredited as the bargaining agent for all employers in [the unit] described in the said certification, voluntary recognition documents or collective agreements, as the case may be.[13]

Under sector accreditation (adopted in Nova Scotia and Prince Edward Island), an employers' organization is not bound by existing bargaining rights; instead it can apply for accreditation in any sector and geographic area for which it claims support.[14] The impact of these provisions on bargaining structure will be discussed below.

To be accredited, most provinces have gone beyond the simple majority support test applicable in certification cases.[15] In Ontario and New Brunswick a double-majority is required. Thus, an employers' organization must obtain the support of a majority of the unionized employers in the unit who, in turn, employ a majority of the employees in the designated unit. A variation of this approach is found in Nova Scotia and Prince Edward Island, where an employers' organization must either have the support of a majority of the unionized employers in the unit or represent not less than 35 per cent of the employers who employ a majority of the employees in the designated geographic area and sector. Both of these standards of majority support are designed to balance the representational interests of small and large contractors, although the double-majority requirement is clearly more stringent.[16]

Under the conservative scheme of accreditation, the British Columbia Labour Relations Board does not have as elaborate an administrative role to play as do other provincial labour boards. This is made possible by a system which is restricted to association members and operates on a voluntary basis.[17] The British Columbia Board must be satisfied that the employers named in the application:

> (a) constitute a group appropriate for collective bargaining; and (b) are members of the organization making application ... and (c) have agreed to the accreditation of the applicant as the bargaining agent.[18]

In addition, the accreditation process is simplified by the fact that two province-wide organizations, the B.C. Road Builders Association (representing the road building sector) and the Construction Labour Relations Association (representing all other phases of construction) represent most unionized construction firms in British Columbia.

Employer Unity

One way of testing the effectiveness of accreditation is to determine how well it promotes employer unity. This can be measured, in part, by examining the degree to which the legislative framework enables employers' organizations to exercise direction and control over their members. In addition to granting exclusive bargaining status to an employers' organization, accreditation legislation prohibits individual contractors from engaging in collective bargaining[19] and bans any agreements or understandings for the supply of employees during a legal strike or lockout.[20] Alberta's legislation further enhances employer unity by banning selective strikes and requiring all employers represented by an accredited employers' organization to participate in a lockout which has been endorsed by a majority of the employers.[21] Despite these provisions to bolster employer unity and reduce fragmentation, there are a number of weaknesses in accreditation legislation which must be examined.

The "Saving" Clause. Both Ontario and New Brunswick have adopted a "saving" clause which would allow an employer to operate during a strike or lockout even if an accredited employers' organization has instructed the employer to do otherwise.[22] Such a provision would appear to contradict the very intent of accreditation legislation — to enable employers' associations to regulate the behaviour of their members. Moreover, if employers' organizations are unable to direct their members during the most crucial phases in negotiations, then surely the bargaining position of the accredited group will be undermined. This would also have the effect of reducing the bargaining strength of employers' associations to their pre-accreditation level and do little to promote greater bargaining parity in the industry.

Some critics have charged that the "saving" clause is the antithesis of the prohibition on individual bargaining and may lead to a breakdown in the accreditation system.[23] Other critics point to how unions could obtain manpower during a work stoppage.

> During a lock-out it will permit any employer to continue his normal activities and employ the locked-out workers. Although the [Ontario Act] prevents the supply of manpower through union sources during a legal strike or lock-out, this could easily be circumvented by any employer through a newspaper advertisement. Through this medium, employers would also be able to advertise proposed wage rates and this would have the same effect upon negotiations as an interim agreement.

> It is considered to be essential that no work should be performed in the trade concerned during any legal strike or lock-out, excepting emergency work related to public health or safety which would be authorized by the accredited association.[24]

The 60-day Work Stoppage. In Alberta, the prohibition on individual bargaining is applicable except where a work stoppage extends for more than 60 days. In other words, where an accredited employers' organization and a trade union reach a bargaining impasse and a legal strike or lockout lasts for more than 60 days, individual contractors will be free to bargain and conclude a collective agreement.[25] While such agreements would become void upon the conclusion of a collective agreement between an accredited employers' organization and a trade union,[26] the question arises whether an accredited association could successfully negotiate a collective agreement once a significant number of individual contracts were in force.

Although not as open an invitation to circumvent the ban on individual bargaining as the "saving" clause, misgivings over this aspect of the Alberta Act have increased in light of the recent history of prolonged work stoppages in British Columbia. Another problem is that an application to terminate an accreditation order can be filed "after a strike or lockout has been in effect for a period of 60 days."[27] This provision is in marked contrast to de-accreditation provisions in other statutes and indicates that an accredited employers' organization could have a very short "insulated" period in which its exclusive bargaining agent status is secure.[28]

In Nova Scotia and Prince Edward Island, neither a "saving clause" nor a 60-day provision exists. Individual contractor bargaining is banned except when an accreditation order has been terminated.

National–International Contractors. Another problem for employers' organizations is national – international contractors. Only in Alberta have accredited employers' organizations been given exclusive bargaining rights to negotiate on behalf of national – international contractors who employ employees in the geographic area and trade jurisdiction.[29] The inclusion of these contractors within the accreditation system promotes employer unity by prohibiting these contractors from signing "free-ride" agreements, i.e., contracts in which they agree to pick up local collective agreements in exchange for a pledge of labour peace. Such agreements tend to jeopardize the bargaining position of local employer associations because union members have been able to obtain employment with national – international contractors during strikes and lockouts. These actions also heighten the insecurity of local contractor associations and perpetuate the imbalance of bargaining power in the industry.

Inclusiveness of Accreditation. The major threat to employer unity in British Columbia is the failure of accreditation to be all-inclusive.[30] The voluntary nature of accreditation is troublesome because non-association members can continue to operate during labour disputes and national – international contractors can negotiate free-ride agreements. Failure to shut down all unionized construction represents a strain on accredited employers' organizations to maintain solidarity.

Despite the inability to control non-association members, the Construction Labour Relations Association (CLRA) has significantly reduced employer fragmentation. CLRA was able to stand united during two lengthy lockouts which lasted more than three months in 1970 and 1972.[31] A major reason for CLRA's success can be attributed to their alliance with the Employers' Council of B.C., a group concerned with industrial, community and government relations and composed of most major companies in the province. One commentator suggested that "one of the reasons the B.C. legislation has achieved a degree of success, even in construction, is because the major purchasers of construction have supported the contractors through the Employers' Council of B.C."[32] The ability to reduce the pressures of construction users on contractors to complete projects overcomes one of the traditional sources of strain on employer unity. From the British Columbia experience it is evident that accreditation can be aided by the development of strong employer organizations and alliances.

Unifying Contractor Associations. The preceding review has focused on a number of weaknesses in legislation to promote greater employer harmony in collective bargaining. While the British Columbia experience demonstrates that employers can do a great deal to help themselves, several other approaches can be taken to ensure employer unity. One step would be to have potentially harmful statutory provisions repealed and to seek amendments to existing legislation where accreditation can be strengthened.[33] Another possibility would be to require compulsory membership in an accredited employers' organization. This could be achieved through legislation or through employer security clauses negotiated between an accredited association and a trade union.

Bargaining Structure

Accreditation has not significantly altered bargaining structure. Legislation in Ontario and New Brunswick does not actively promote more centralized bargaining patterns because accreditation is linked to existing bargaining rights.[34] While both the Ontario and New Brunswick Acts provide for the certification of councils of trade unions, a step which could stimulate multi-trade bargaining, there is no evidence of unions moving in this direction.[35] In British Columbia, accreditation has for the most part formalized in law the bargaining pattern which existed prior to its inception.[36]

Two developments suggest that accreditation may ultimately promote more centralized collective bargaining. These include the move toward sector accreditation and Alberta's scheme of transferring accreditation rights. The prospects for reducing the existing trade fragmentation in collective bargaining will be greater under sector accreditation since employers' organizations need not be bound by prevailing bargaining relationships. Labour boards in Nova Scotia and Prince Edward Island will be able to influence bargaining patterns to a greater extent than labour boards in other provinces.

Alberta's legislation overcomes the limitations of trade accreditation by permitting the assignment of bargaining rights. This transfer may take place when an accredited employers' organization "(a) is merged or amalgamated into another employers' organization, or (b) agrees to transfer its rights . . . to another employers' organization."[37] Such a provision could have a significant effect on the coordination and centralization of collective bargaining since it would enable various employer associations to transfer their bargaining rights to the Alberta Construction Labour Relations Association (ACLRA). While ACLRA hopes to move toward multi-trade bargaining in the long run, it sees a need to first negotiate a single collective agreement for each trade on a province-wide basis.

SUMMARY AND CONCLUSIONS

Accreditation legislation has been adopted on the assumption that there was a need for countervailing employer power in the construction industry. In addition, it was felt that existing labour legislation could not adequately deal with the industry's unique characteristics. The objective of accreditation is to reduce contractor fragmentation and provide employers' organizations with a greater measure of direction and control over their members. Proponents of such legislation argue that more unified employer groups will help reduce the imbalance of power in the industry and promote more stable labour – management relations.

Three aspects of the accreditation legislation have been examined. These include the accreditation process and the impact of accreditation on employer unity and bargaining structure. While accreditation is still in its early stages, a preliminary analysis of collective bargaining under this system suggests that employer unity has been enhanced. In British Columbia, where our experience is greatest, CLRA has significantly reduced employer fragmentation. On the other hand, accreditation has not had a measurable impact on bargaining structure, although the recent legislative developments in Nova Scotia, Prince Edward Island and Alberta bear watching.

There are weaknesses in several accreditation systems which could undermine the ability of employer associations to effectively control their members, e.g. the "saving" clause. The determination of how serious an obstacle these provisions will be to employer unity must await further bargaining experience under accreditation. Other avenues are available to ensure stable contractor associations, including changes in legislation and voluntary efforts to build stronger employer associations and bolster alliances with construction users.

The ultimate test of the efficacy of accreditation to stabilize labour-management relations will depend on how much employers are willing to do for themselves. Accreditation, like union certification, represents no more than a framework for contractors to designate representatives of their own choosing. It remains to be seen if employers will learn the lesson the labour movement has learned: through organization there is unity and strength.

FOOTNOTES

[1] National Labor Relations Act, Section 1, 49 Stat. 449 (1935).

[2] Bill C-183, An Act to amend the Canada Labour Code (1972), Preamble.

[3] H. W. Arthurs and John H. G. Crispo, "Countervailing Employer Power: Accreditation of Contractor Associations," in *Construction Labour Relations*, eds. H. Carl Goldenberg and John H. G. Crispo (Ottawa: Canadian Construction Association, 1968), p. 376. For a criticism of the theory of countervailing power, see Sanford Cohen, "An Analytical Framework For Labor Relations Law," *Industrial and Labor Relations Review*, XIV (April, 1961), pp. 350-62.

[4] Archibald Cox and Derek C. Bok, *Cases and Materials on Labor Law* (6th ed.; Brooklyn, New York: The Foundation Press, Inc., 1965), pp. 121-2.

[5] Arthurs and Crispo, loc. cit.

[6] For a discussion of the economic features of the construction industry, see *Report of the Royal Commission on Labour-Management Relations in the Construction Industry*, H. Carl Goldenberg, Commissioner (Ontario, 1962), pp. 1-7 and Joseph B. Rose, *Report on Accreditation and the Construction Industry* (Fredericton: New Brunswick Department of Labour, 1972), pp. 1-88.

[7] Arthurs and Crispo, loc. cit.

[8] Gerard Hébert, S.J., "Industry-wide Bargaining by Legislation, The Case of the Construction Industry," Ottawa, June 19, 1970, p. 22. (Mimeographed.)

[9] Arthurs and Crispo, op.cit., pp. 410, 412.

[10] Union reaction to multi-trade bargaining patterns will most likely be negative.

> . . . union officials would be loath to see a contractor association accreditation scheme that embraced more than one trade in its bargaining unit . . . Powerful unions fear the loss of intertrade leverage because it might lead to across-the-board improvements, thus undercutting their preferred status, while weaker unions fear the loss because in the absence of whipsawing they might never be able to catch up.

Arthurs and Crispo, op. cit., p. 412.

[11] Sector represents a division of the construction industry, e.g. the industrial, commercial and institutional sector, the residential sector and so forth. Ontario has specified eight sectors in its legislation, New Brunswick seven, and Nova Scotia and Prince Edward Island have four sectors plus any other sector(s) determined by either labour board to be appropriate. Alberta does not define trade jurisdiction (sector).

[12] Concern has been expressed that explicit definitions of sector restrict labour board discretion in defining the appropriate unit and does not permit the degree of latitude which exists in certification cases. Moreover, where bargaining patterns either cut across sectors or take place within a sector, such determinations become more troublesome. This is less of a problem in Nova Scotia and Prince Edward Island where sector is broadly defined. However, the failure to define sector in Alberta's legislation is no panacea. Without adequate guidance from the Alberta Labour Act, the Alberta Industrial Relations Board has experienced numerous difficulties in designating the trade jurisdiction. See Joseph B. Rose, op. cit., pp. 201-3.

[13] Ontario Labour Relations Act (1971), Section 113.

[14] Nova Scotia Trade Union Act (1972), Section 94 (1); Prince Edward Island Labour Act (1973), Section 48D (1).

[15] Alberta is the exception. The possibility of a representation vote to assess employer support is contemplated in three provinces: Alberta, Nova Scotia and Prince Edward Island.

[16] Other prerequisites for accreditation are commonly required. For example, in Alberta the Industrial Relations Board must be satisfied that the employers' organization is a proper organization for the purpose of collective bargaining. Furthermore, the Alberta Board must be satisfied that proper authority has been vested in the association by individual members and that there has been no union interference in the formation of the employers' organization.

[17] In British Columbia, accreditation is applicable to other industries besides the construction industry. This is largely a result of a more prevalent pattern of association bargaining in the province.

> . . . We have a labour force of 750,000 workers; 42 per cent of those workers are union members, some 316,000 employees. One half of that 316,000, a total of 157,000 workers, reach agreements with their employers through association bargaining.

Testimony of Mr. R. M. Bibbs, Vice President of MacMillan Bloedel Ltd., *Minutes of Proceedings and Evidence of the Standing Committee on Labour, Manpower and Immigration*, Issue No. 14, May 18, 1972, p. 16.

[18] British Columbia Labour Relations Act (1972), Section 9A (4).

[19] It should be noted that the certification procedure does not *necessarily* preclude individual bargaining, but specifies that individual bargains cannot *conflict* with the collective bargain. However, under accreditation there can be *no* individual bargains, conflicting or otherwise, at all.

[20] Ontario Labour Relations Act (1971), Section 119 (1)-(2); New Brunswick Industrial Relations Act (1972), Section 51 (1)-(2).

[21] The Alberta Labour Act (1970), Section 98 (8)-(9).

[22] For example, Section 119 (3) of the Ontario Labour Relations Act (1971) states:

> Nothing in this Act prohibits an employer, represented by an accredited employers' organization, from continuing or attempting to continue his operations during a strike or lock-out involving employees represented by the accredited employers' organization.

[23] See John Crispo, "Ontario's Bill 167: Reform of the Status Quo," *Relations Industrielles*, XXVI (January, 1972), p. 861 and Joseph B. Rose, op. cit., pp. 221-3.

[24] Peter M. Allen and Michael H. Eayrs, *Labour Relations For Construction Employers In Ontario* (Waterloo, Ontario: Department of Civil Engineering, University of Waterloo, 1972), pp. 38-9.

[25] The Alberta Labour Act (1970), Section 75 (6).

[26] The Alberta Labour Act (1970), Section 75 (7).

[27] The Alberta Labour Act (1970), Section 76 (1). The cancellation of an accreditation order is similar to the decertification of a trade union.

[28] Applications for terminating accreditation are normally associated with the termination date of a collective agreement or fixed time intervals. In general, applications will not be entertained until an accreditation order has been in effect for twelve months.

[29] The Alberta Labour Act (1970), Section 75 (4)(a)(iii).

[30] Section 9A(6) of the British Columbia Labour Relations Act does not appear to promote employer unity since it would enable an employer to divorce himself from an accredited employers' organization during the fourth and fifth months following the execution of a collective agreement. While this provision would appear to do little to solidify employer representation, the B.C. Board has imposed strict standards for withdrawal which have made it very difficult for contractors to opt out of accreditation, e.g. a change in the nature of the business.

[31] During the 1970 and 1972 lockouts CLRA experienced three employer defections; one firm is now out of business and the other two were sued for breach of contract. Under the CLRA's constitution, members are required to sign a contract which prohibits them from making sweetheart deals while CLRA is engaged in negotiations. This degree of control is made possible because as an accredited group, CLRA represents only its own members. In other provinces, accredited employers' organizations represent non-members as well as their own members, and association bylaws are not binding on non-members.

[32] Letter from A. J. K. Keylock, Industrial Relations Director for the Employers' Council of B.C., March 9, 1972.

[33] A number of changes in New Brunswick's accreditation system have been recommended, e.g., the repeal of the "saving" clause and a ban on selective strikes. Joseph B. Rose, op. cit., pp. 221-6.

[34] The accreditation orders have brought some individual employers who normally bargain independently within the employers' organization and this has resulted in a single negotiating round with a trade union in a particular geographic area and sector.

[35] J. H. Brown, Q.C., "The New Labour Relations Act in Ontario With Special Reference to the Construction Industry," *Address to the Canadian Industrial*

Relations Research Institute (Montreal, Quebec), June 22, 1972, p. 18.
(Mimeographed.)

[36] In 1972, six unions requested bargaining on a multi-trade basis. Such a
development may represent the beginning of more centralized collective
bargaining.

[37] The Alberta Labour Act (1970), Section 75.1.

INFLATION, UNEMPLOYMENT AND INCOMES POLICY*

John H. Young
and
Donald F. Gordon

*The authors discuss the nature of economic and political problems
in Canada, such as the regional disparities in unemployment rates
and income and the difficulties of enforcement of wage and price
controls. They also discuss the interaction of inflation, unemployment and income policy in the Canadian context. At the end
Professor Kruger presents an interesting and lively critique of their
paper.*

Any paper with the words inflation, unemployment and incomes policy in the title invites a question about the nature of the trade-off among
the three. For example, can the sustainable level of employment be
raised by accepting a higher rate of inflation, or can this be accomplished more effectively with the occasional use of incomes policy?
Readers of the report of the Prices and Incomes Commission will know
that the answer given there was that incomes policy held out more
promise than a higher rate of inflation for reducing the average level of
unemployment over the years. It was argued in the report, however,
that the conditions for the successful use of incomes policy are more
stringent than is often recognized.

Before considering the interaction of the three *dramatis personae*
they should each be briefly introduced. It is true that inflation, unemployment and incomes policy have a good deal in common from country
to country but there are differences which need to be recognized.

Thus it is important to know that there has been less inflation in
both Canada and the United States during the post-war period than in
most other countries. For this reason and perhaps because of other
factors at work, there has been a tendency for Europeans to develop a
different explanation of inflation than many North Americans. For ex-

* Industrial Relations Research Association Series. Edited by G. G. Somers,
December, 28-29, 1972; pp. 33-42. Reprinted with permission.

ample, among European economists and economic advisers many have held that there is only a weak connection between changes in the level of wage increases and the variations in the state of the labour market which are politically feasible, and thus the rate of inflation is largely determined by institutional and political forces. For many North Americans the experience of the early 1960's has been recent enough to suggest that our economic and political institutions have not made our economies generally unmanageable without fundamental changes or some permanent form of direct controls.

While relative price stability is more a part of the life experience of North Americans than of that of most people in other parts of the world, it is worth remembering that even in Canada and the United States the age groups now playing a central role in governments, corporations and unions have experienced something like a tripling of the price level during their working lives and are thus not insensitive to the possibility of a further decline in the value of money. If one thinks of Canadian economic history extending back into the European countries from which most of us came, it is necessary to retrace steps to the sixteenth century to find a comparable experience of irreversible price increases.

While by international standards, post-war price increases have been relatively low in Canada, the opposite has been the case with unemployment. It is of course true that the raw percentage rate of Canadian unemployment needs adjustment before meaningful comparisons can be made with countries other than the United States, but attempts have been made to recalculate unemployment rates for a number of European countries using U.S. concepts. While differences between the Canadian rate and adjusted European rates are less striking than thos between the raw estimates, the average Canadian unemployment rate is still high.

How high the rate of unemployment needs to be in order to avoid a rise in the rate of increase of prices and wages would appear to have been a highly controversial question in Canada over the last decade. Eight years ago the Banking and Finance Commission spoke of 4-5 per cent; a few months later the Economic Council of Canada suggested an objective of 3 per cent; two years later the Royal Commission on Taxation talked of 3½ per cent; five years after that the Senate Committee on National Finances recommended 4-4½ per cent; and in 1972 the Prices and Incomes Commission suggested that in the last two economic expansions the conditions for accelerating price and wage increases had developed where the national rate of unemployment was 4½-5 per cent. While there have been real differences in interpreting the evidence and even wider differences among these groups on the weight to be accorded various objectives of policy, the range of opinion is not as great as appears.

The Economic Council, while on occasion using the 3 per cent to evaluate current policy, has held this out as a hope for the future.

Indeed, the original staff study by Frank Denton and Sylvia Ostry which yielded the figure of 3 per cent pointed out that the estimation of a minimum unemployment rate had been made without reference to associated price effects. Similarly, the 3½ per cent estimate of the Taxation Commission was hedged with such a variety of qualifications that it is not comparable with the others. It is probably safe to conclude that taking conditions as they are, not as they might be, most people have thought that the range of unemployment consistent with a stable rate of increase of prices and wages was 4-5 per cent, with some hoping that the lower end of the range was possible while others feared that problems would arise close to the top end of the range. In its Ninth Annual Review in November 1972, the Economic Council accepted a 4½ per cent unemployment rate as an interim target for 1975.

Why has the "normal" level of unemployment been so high in Canada? Many of the generalizations which hold for other countries apply here, with higher rates for the young, the unmarried, the unskilled and those employed in industries with sharp swings in demand of a temporary or seasonal nature. One characteristic of Canadian unemployment which stands out more clearly from the record than in most other countries is the sharp regional differentials. Over the course of the last two decades the national average rate of unemployment has been just over 5 per cent. During the same period the rate in Ontario has been something over 3½ per cent, in Quebec over 6½, in the West around 4 per cent, and in the Atlantic provinces about 8 per cent. In the years 1968 and 1969 when the national average rate of unemployment was about 4¾ per cent, the rate for just over 60 per cent of the Canadian labour force west of the Ottawa River was about 3½ per cent, and for just under 40 per cent to the east of the Ottawa valley was roughly 7 per cent.

As for the third element, incomes policy, Canada was late comer to the field. When the White Paper on the subject was issued in 1968 and the Prices and Incomes Commission established in 1969 there was little direct experience on which to draw. It is true that some work had been done on preparing a program of controls during the Korean War, but the last occasion on which any use had been made of direct intervention in wage and price decisions was during World War II. In many respects the lessons of this experience were a misleading guide to the results of applying incomes policy during a period of economic slack when prices and incomes were failing to respond to current market conditions. Thus it was easy for people to identify the use of controls with the imposition of a constraint on wages and prices below levels which would equilibrate supply and demand curves. Effective controls had earlier led to shortages and rationing and it was easy to envisage the need for an army of bureaucrats to administer a program of controls which would frustrate the play of the market with resulting economic waste and limitations on personal freedom.

Moveover, it could readily be argued that such controls would not prevent a fall in the value of money. Money declines in value as surely when one cannot purchase the desired quantities of goods and services at going prices as when those prices rise. On the other hand, those who thought in terms of less comprehensive and less mandatory forms of intervention had no difficulty in pointing out the problems which would arise from the nature of the Canadian economy, with its openness to external influences and the decentralized character of its governmental, business and labor union institutions.

With the more modest forms of incomes policy widely regarded as likely to be ineffective but with a typical Canadian reluctance to deal with issues of this kind by legal compulsion before other avenues had been explored, the right prescription was not obvious. We, on the Prices and Incomes Commission, had fewer illusions than most on the necessity of a measure of compulsion to ensure adherence to norms of income policy, but it seemed clear that an effort must be made to secure agreement on a set of criteria. There will remain differences of view on what was accomplished, first by the attempt to reach a general agreement, second by the price restraint program of 1970, and third by the wage and salary guideline introduced later as a supplement to the limitation on profit margins. What did happen is that many questions were taken out of the realm of speculation and a good deal was learned about how a workable system of controls could be devised. Thus well before the American initiative of August 1971, there was a fairly well developed set of ideas in Canada on how to set up a system quite similar to that finally adopted in Phase II.

With this brief background, we are now in a position to consider the interaction of inflation, unemployment and incomes policy in the Canadian context. To do this one can begin with the economy at a normal level of unemployment, i.e. a level at which there is no tendency for price and wage increases to accelerate or decelerate. This is not a precise magnitude and was described in the Prices and Incomes Commission Report as the "critical range of unemployment" or the "full employment" level, and estimated to have been in the area of 4½-5 per cent during the economic expansions of the mid-fifties and mid-sixties. This range does not appear to have been shifted in recent years by the changing structure of the Canadian labour force, the low unemployment rates of the rising share of women offsetting the higher rates of the rising share of young people. On the other hand, other factors including the more generous unemployment insurance provisions introduced a year ago appear to have raised the critical range significantly.

We have found it convenient to classify the circumstances producing measurable unemployment at the "full employment" level into a set of categories related to the traditional economic concepts of demand and supply. Thus unemployment can arise from problems on the demand side or the supply side of the market, or from difficulties and delays in bringing demanders and suppliers together.

Unemployment arising on the supply side exists when there are jobs or potential jobs available for which unemployed people are qualified but they do not choose to take these jobs at the wage levels offered. Many of these individuals can show up in the unemployment statistics since they are looking for work in the sense that they would accept a job if the pay exceeded their reservation price.

Search unemployment arises when there exist demanders and suppliers who are willing to complete negotiations at mutually acceptable wages but there are difficulties and delays in bringing them together. These adjustment problems arise primarily from the heterogeneity in labour markets on both sides. The typical job seeker, rather than taking the first job that comes along, will find it to his advantage to take some time to find a reasonably suitable opening. Similarly, the maximizing employer will find it advantageous to wait some time to find qualified employees rather than to raise the going wage immediately to equate demand and supply.

Both of the foregoing types of unemployment have been discussed in the literature on the trade-off. Somewhat less discussed is the phenomenon of "job rationing", that is, a situation in which both employer and employees recognize an observed excess of supply over demand at the going wage, but the employers do not lower the wage, or, more typically today, lower the rate of increase in wages in order to reduce the rate of increase in their costs. In some cases this results from legal or union imposed minima, but in many labour markets these are not crucial.

Such sticky wage policies have important implications for both the level of, and changes in, aggregate employment, output and inflation and for the kinds of policies which are suitable for dealing with them. We believe that this aspect of the labour market has been underemphasized in the past, and that this stickiness goes far towards making more plausible the role of expectations in determining the nature of the trade-off between unemployment and inflation and the change in such trade-offs and time lags that we appear to observe.

In the labour field we would suppose that expectations would affect union wage bargaining in a fairly clear-cut manner, and their importance would depend upon (and influence) the length of the union contract. But hitherto the role of expectations in the non-union field has had empirical and logical difficulties. Thus it has been argued that both of the first two kinds of unemployment noted above — reservation price unemployment and search unemployment — can be expected to increase when demand is restrained after an inflationary period. This is because employees expect wages and prices will continue to increase, and when they find that wages cease to increase as rapidly, they believe incorrectly, that they are being offered relatively low real wages. Hence they drop out of the labour force or continue to search. This account implies that the onset of a recession is characterized by declining wages (or rates of increase) and higher quit rates, which are contrary to the facts. Moreover, in modern economies where the state of the economy is subject to so much intense and continuous comment, it does not seem plausible to suppose that workers cannot adjust their expectations to the existence of a recession fairly quickly. But if they did so they would adjust their demands and the recession would cease.

The major features of our analysis of the interrelated questions of inflation, unemployment and incomes policy that differ from many other commentaries is that we believe that in the non-union labour markets employer expectations are particularly important, and that the expectations that are relevant are not expectations about the current or short term state of the labour market but about a considerably longer term. These expectations will increase job rationing unemployment when aggregate demand is restrained after a substantial period of inflation.

If the employer, as part of a long run maximizing policy, wishes to offer wage and job security to a substantial fraction of his labour force, he cannot when demand is restrained cut the rate of wage increase, let alone cut wages. He could only do so if he believed that the current slack is not merely a temporary pause but an historic turning point ushering in a new era of price stability. But the employer (or his employee) is most likely to judge the future by past long run trends, and possibly by observing other wage increases. In this case wages will continue to rise, in part feeding on each other for a long and, in terms of output and employment, very costly period if inflation is to be halted by demand tools alone.

In short, we believe that it is the long term nature of employment relationships based on employee security which require predictions of long term future trends. At one time this created sticky wages and now creates sticky wage increases.

In some respects this is an optimistic view of our recent difficulties. It fully accepts the view that excessive demand is the basic driving force behind inflation. While recognizing that there are many imperfections in the markets for both factors and final goods and services, and while recognizing that in some important areas institutional changes in recent years have exacerbated our difficulties, it is not our view that fundamental institutional changes are a *sine qua non* for the achievement of a reasonably stable economy. We take some comfort from the fact that both Professors Tobin and Friedman, who differ sharply on many policy questions, can agree on the logical inadequacy of explanations of inflation which are based on the monopoly power of unions or corporations or both.

On the other hand, we are not as optimistic as those who think that the problem will go away or that it is enough for Canadians to sit quietly and wait for the effects of the stabilization efforts of the United States to flow across the border and solve the problem for us. Nor are we optimistic enough to think that acquiescing in increasingly rapid rates of inflation will provide more than a temporary increase in the level of output and employment.

What then is to be done? Writing over six months ago, the Prices and Incomes Commission pointed out that before long the march of events might well bring serious consideration of a temporary program of controls. It was pointed out, however, that two essential conditions must be satisfied if such a program was to work effectively and be phased out with a minimum risk of a renewed outburst of inflation. The first was that the public must be convinced that such measures were necessary and that there existed on the part of governments a determination to make the controls operate as effectively and as equitably as possible. Second, that price and income controls should only be used as part of a longer term policy aimed at maintaining underlying demand conditions both during and after the control period consistent with the target rates of increase in average price and income levels.

Events have now moved on and some of the uncertainties have been resolved. In particular, the decision to seek an extension of the control system in the United States and the indication of the steps likely to be taken to avoid an overshoot of demand have helped to clarify the external framework within which Canadian economic policy will be formed. The likelihood of a significant and perhaps widening divergence between the rates of increase of costs and prices in the two countries is becoming more apparent and this may soon be reflected in a deepening sense of disquiet among Canadians. It is easy to say that the exchange rate can adjust to a divergence of this kind but the relative stability of the ratio between the two currencies over a period of more than a century indicates that this has not been a course which has had much appeal in the past.

There is some danger that a variety of factors will combine to delay action. The difficulty of interpreting current unemployment statistics may continue to focus attention on the unemployment problem, and this combined with existing political uncertainties may delay the public recognition of the neef for action. What cannot be ruled out is that the present economic expansion will in due course bring enough pressure to bear on enough markets to pose a serious threat to a system of controls which has been introduced too late. If this should happen, we shall not only fail to deal with our current problem but leave behind a performance record which will discourage the use of incomes policy in the future.

These comments strike a negative note but if one compares the Canadian inflationary problem with that of most other countries of the world there are clearly no grounds for despair. Thus while one cannot envy those responsible for dealing with our current difficulties, this country has a better chance than most to establish a reasonably stable framework for future economic growth.

DISCUSSION

Arthur Kruger

I would like to comment at a somewhat greater length on the paper by Professors John Young and Donald Gordon since it involves the Canadian experience in the last few years. In this paper they point out the limited success with a jaw-bone attack in Canada. A year ago in the land of the Bible I reminded Professor Young that the only known successful experience with a jaw-bone attack occurs in the biblical story of Sampson where the hero is reputed to have killed a thousand Philistines with a jaw-bone of an ass. I would like to think that the reason for Professor Young's failure at the time that he led the Canadian Government attack on inflationary pressures through the use of jaw-boning can be ascribed to the fact that he has the wrong sort of jaw-bone for this task.

In their paper, Gordon and Young indicate that the most serious economic problem in Canada revolves around the enormous regional disparities in unemployment rates and in income in this country. I could not agree more with their view on this question. Nowhere in the paper, however, do they show in what way a successful application of price and wage controls could significantly alleviate the serious regional disparities in unemployment rates of income in this country. The emphasis that they and others have given to the problem of inflation and to wage and price controls as the central issue of economic policy has, if anything, detracted from the consideration of the more serious regional disparities problem.

In examining the Canadian inflationary experience in recent years, they conclude that the problem results from excess demand and has little to do with monopoly power in product or labour markets. If this is the case, then we are entitled to ask why their proposed solution focuses on wage and price controls rather than on changes in policies affecting aggregate demand.

The discussion in the paper of the rate of downward rigidity in the rate of wage increases is interesting and I would hope the authors explore this further. They might bear in mind the fact that the quality of workers is responsibe to market forces and, that if this is considered, the market may be more effective than appears from an examination limited to wage rates or changes in wage rates.

The authors discuss the likelihood of adjusting exchange rates in order to rectify problems created when Canadian price increases exceed those in the United States. They correctly point to the resistance to devaluation. However, in proposing wage and price controls as the alternative. I believe they fail to recognize the extent to which this would prove distateful to Canadians. They have not made a case for the assumption that devaluation would be less popular than controls.

One of my colleagues once remarked that in a country with the sort of regional problems Canada has, the problems to which wage and price controls address themselves are not terribly significant. He went on to suggest that John Young and the Prices and Incomes Commission were attempting to apply a sledge-hammer to a bed bug. My own metaphor was somewhat different on this matter. I would suggest that those who favour wage and price controls in the Canadian context are attempting to drown the bed bug in urine. Professor Young and others have reminded us that for success you have to move quickly and aim with great accuracy. But even if you succeed in drowning the bed bug, one must remember that you are left with a wet bed and long after this problem has been alleviated, the stench remains.

QUESTIONS FOR DISCUSSION, PART 2

(1)   Total union membership in Canada in 1973 increased by 7.2 per cent in one year, that is over the 1972 total. Explain the reasons for recent growth and other changes in union membership.

(2)   Discuss the factors in the Canadian environment which have influenced the development and structure of the trade union movement in Canada.

(3)   What is the impact of the rivalry between the two major federations (C.L.C. and C.N.T.U.) on the growth of the labour movement?

(4)   Comment critically on the following statement:
"Trade unions will, however reluctantly, have to come to terms with the fact that they are in many ways structurally out of keeping with the times. They will have to become larger and fewer, more streamlined in their operations, and more flexible in their institutional response to technological and other socio-economic changes".

(5)   Do you agree with Professor Kruger's prediction that traditional unions will decline but that collective bargaining will be extended through new organizations to a majority of the employed labour force?

(6)   Several writers have expressed conflicting arguments concerning the advantages and disadvantages of international unions to Canadian workers and employers. What are these advantages and disadvantages? What, in your opinion, are viable alternatives to international unions?

(7)   To what extent have the international unions met the four criteria set by the Woods Task Force Report in judging whether full op-

portunity is being accorded the Canadian membership to handle its own problems?

(8) Is Professor Williams justified in his criticism that adherence to international union philosophy has contributed to many of the problems that the trade union movement in Canada faces today?

(9) Why is it that Canadian governments seem to be preoccupied with attempts to prevent strikes or lockouts?

(10) What were the major objectives of the post-war labour disputes legislation? How effective has this legislation been in accomplishing these objectives?

(11) What are the major criticisms against "Compulsory Conciliation and Mediation" features of legislation? Has this criticism had any effect? Review the latest legislation in this regard.

(12) Explain the concept of accreditation. Why is this concept so important to the construction industry. What are some of the strengths and weaknesses of present accreditation legislation?

(13) Examine the question of wage, price, income policies with regard to the realities of the Canadian political and economic life. Do you believe that government guidelines or controls have a helpful effect on the relationship between union and management? Can such guidelines or controls be enforced?

PART 3

COLLECTIVE BARGAINING AND ADMINISTRATION OF THE AGREEMENT (PRIVATE SECTOR)

Section 1
The Bargaining Process: Structure and Strategy

INTRODUCTION

The material in this part relates to the collective bargaining process and administration of the contract in the private sector. In the preceding chapter the differences in legislative provisions between the U.S.A. and Canada were pointed out. Subject to these differences, the processes and techniques of bargaining in the private sector in both countries are essentially the same. Much of the original and excellent research concerning the process, strategy and methods of bargaining in the private sector has been done in the U.S.A. This research is directly relevant to the Canadian scene. Therefore, the material in this part includes several articles pertaining to the United States environment. Since collective bargaining by public employees is a developing trend of major significance in Canada as well as in the U.S.A., it merits special treatment, and will be dealt with in Part 5 of this book.

The Report of the Task Force on Labour Relations defines collective bargaining as "a process by which groups of organized workers and those desiring their services seek to resolve their differences through reason, the threat of economic conflict or actual conflict." Management, unions and the public view the process of collective bargaining differently as its results affect each party's interests. Management perceives this process as one that progressively limits its unilateral decision-making power in areas which are associated with efficiency and profitability of operations. Management has found over a period of time that as a result of collective bargaining more and more issues which were traditionally management's prerogatives are now subject to joint determination with unions. The union leaders and members look upon the process as an opportunity to challenge the concept of inherent managerial rights, which is based on the principle of efficiency and profitability. They insist that the principle of humane justice be given equal weight in making operating decisions. The public views the process as a means of stabilizing industrial relations.

The articles in Section One, deal with the collective bargaining process: structure and strategy. Kerr examines the influence of the process itself, that is, the degree to which the rules of the game and their administration are likely to provide a framework for present and future relations between the parties. Collective bargaining is a power relationship. Monat examines three models of bargaining power and concludes that concessions by either party, moves and countermoves, and changes in attitudes within labour or managment groups continuously modify bargaining power. In a collective bargaining situation the parties employ a battery of tactics and strategies to influence their opponents as well as the outcome of the bargaining sessions. Walton and McKersie use a behaviourial approach in developing alternate bargaining strategies. Gunderson discusses the issue of Canada – U.S. wage parity. The last selection in this section is by Arthurs. He examines the out-right application of private-sector collective bargaining legislation in Canada to municipal employees.

One of the major issues in collective bargaining has been union and management rights and responsibilities. Unions and management both have often approached these issues emotionally rather than logically. Many of the classic battles have been fought in the arena of "management rights," the right of the company to hire, fire, promote, to contract out work, to change its operations, its organization and its technology. Unions have been able to obtain various degrees of union security by controlling the hiring of workers; the check off of union dues; work assignment and work jurisdictions; subcontracting, makework rules and policies, the way in which seniority is applied, the methods by which discipline and discharge are carried out and finally by resorting to grievance procedure and arbitration.

Unions would like to be informed in advance of any technological changes management is planning and would like to have a decisive influence over matters affecting their members. They are demanding that they should have a right to strike during the term of the contract if both parties fail to arrive at a satisfactory solution to such problems. Generally speaking, unions have resisted changes that meant a loss of jobs, a reduction of union security, a diminution of their rights and strength. To resolve problems arising from "union security" versus "management rights" issues, Professor Slichter of Harvard University, in a major research study, "The Impact of Collective Bargaining on Management," suggests the establishment of a system of industrial jurisprudence which enables both labour and management to bargain with each other on an equitable and systematic basis.

In Section Two will be found a discussion of several aspects of union and management rights. There are often conflicting arguments among the bargaining parties as to their individual rights and responsibilities. Metcalfe gives a managerial perspective of its rights while Archer discusses the union's point of view. The debate is largely centred on efficiency versus job security. Young examines pros and cons of contracting out in the next article. The challenges thrust upon unions and management by automation, technological changes and corporate mergers, not only affect the balance of power in bargaining, but threaten the very existence of the institution of collective bargaining. Jain critically examines some of the creative experiments which have taken place in North America to solve these problems. Kruger analyzes the impact of technological changes on the bargaining process. The next selection deals with the ways and means of resolving convlict when the parties experience difficulties in the administration of the contract. Dunlop and Healey describe the characteristics and problems of the grievance procedure.

It will be clear from these readings that in collective bargaining noneconomic issues are as important as the economic issues. While the institution of collective bargaining is an imperfect institution, there is no other viable alternative to it. In the final analysis, if collective bargaining has to play a greater and more constructive role, both parties must have a strong commitment to identify and solve mutual problems by developing new creative approaches to collective bargaining (Healey and Associates).

A series of discussion questions are included at the end. It is hoped that these questions will provide the students with generalizations and insight on the way in which collective bargaining works and why.

BARGAINING PROCESSES*

Clark Kerr

Kerr examines tactics which aid labour and management in arriving at a compromise. He suggests that bargaining systems go through several stages before reaching maturity.

Since organized group relationships between employers and employees have expanded, the collective-bargaining process has become important not alone to the parties but also to the public in general. Successful negotiation serves two purposes: (1) it avoids the withdrawal of performance by either side, and (2) it determines the rewards for performance and the conditions which shall prevail. The peaceful conduct of the bargaining and the conformance of the resulting terms

---

* "Bargaining Processes" by Clark Kerr is reprinted from *Unions, Management and the Public*, 3rd ed.; E. Wight Bakke, Clark Kerr and Charles W. Anrod, eds.; copyright © 1967 by Harcourt Brace Jovanouich, Inc., and reprinted with their permission.

to the requirements of the general welfare are both tests of the success of collective-bargaining processes. Peace alone is not enough in an interdependent society, although in the short run it is the more pressing consideration. The quality of the peace in the long run must also be examined.

Bargaining is an art, not a science. The problems are too complex for the slide rule. It is not, however, always one of the more delicate arts. It is often composed of almost equal parts of bluffing and bulldozing. The parties' strategy and tactics reach various levels of refinement depending on their degree of sophistication and the animosity between them. Standard tactics applicable in most types of games or conflicts are adapted to the particular setting. Efforts are made to divide the opposition and thus weaken it. Surprise is used on occasion. An effort is made to analyze in advance the goals and moves of the opposing party, without exposing one's own. Timing is of the utmost importance. Skillful bargainers usually observe most of the amenities and are expert in semantics. The "golden mean" of Aristotle must be constantly sought — for example, being publicly friendly but not intimate with representatives of the opposing party and being conciliatory without being weak.

Essentially, successful collective bargaining is an exercise in graceful retreat — retreating without seeming to retreat. The parties normally ask for more or offer less than they expect ultimately to have to accept or give. The "take it or leave it" proposition is not viewed as within the rules of the game. One of the most damaging criticisms is that a party is adamant in holding to its original position. Before retreating with as much elegance as the circumstances permit, each party seeks to withdraw as little as possible. This involves ascertaining the maximum concession of the opposing negotiator without disclosing one's own ultimate concession. In this sense all negotiations are "exploratory" until the agreement is consummated.

Implicit in the whole process is the ultimate resort to force. . . . The threat of warfare backed by both the ability and willingness to fight, is the primary bargaining weapon of each side. The alternative of no bargain at all is constantly before the parties. The final question asked is whether it is better to settle at a specific figure than to fight. The greater the relative capacity of a party to fight, the greater the relative capacity to bargain to a conclusion acceptable to that party. The results of the process depend on how iron the hand as well as how silken the glove.

The bargaining is not always solely with the opposing group, but within each group itself. The representatives must ascertain what their own clientele will accept, and resolve, so far as possible, divergent views within their own organization. Sometimes negotiations, where experienced representatives know fairly specifically what the results will be, become thereby "putting on a show" for the benefit of the principals on both sides of the table. While the solution is approximately known, it must be arrived at after a proper interval and through the expected procedures.

The resulting bargain is seldom the final and ultimate solution of all differences between the parties. It is the current compromise which is sufficiently acceptable to both parties for the ensuing contractual period. The last demand or the last concession, viewed historically, has not been made. The bargain may or may not be a just one. Abstract justice is difficult to define or attain. The parties usually are satisfied with an agreeable bargain, and are less concerned, if concerned at all, with its effects on groups and persons external to the bargain. But these private bargains often have public repercussions — both favorable and unfavorable. Union-management cooperation to increase efficiency illustrates the former; and union-management collusion to restrict production and raise prices illustrates the latter. . . .

Some bargains are the result of a dictated peace rather than any real meeting of the minds. Where power resides almost exclusively with one party, the terms of the contract may be determined unilaterally. The "price list" placed before the employer by some craft unions is an example. Effective bargaining presupposes some degree of equality between the parties.

The area covered by the one bargain has in recent times become a matter for debate. Some employers and some unions prefer to blanket the entire competitive area under a single agreement, while others prefer to deal company by company. The public becomes particularly concerned when bargaining on the larger scale is unsuccessful and all competitive sources of supply are simultaneously closed. . . . Whether rightly or not, however, historically the areas covered by single bargains have tended to expand.

A bargaining system is a complex mechanism. It comprises the parties, with their separate goals, resources, and techniques, and negotiating meetings and conferences, however informal. While the basic economic and political situations provide the general setting, whether the controversy is peacefully resolved often depends on the negotiating machinery and the way the parties approach the discussions. Good techniques do not guarantee peace, but they contribute importantly. . . .

Bargaining systems typically go through several stages in reaching full maturity. From original belligerency and warfare, they often evolve into passive acceptance, and finally into active cooperation. This cooperation may be of two types. First, cooperation may serve to increase efficiency through better use of raw materials, introduction of piece rates, encouragement of union suggestions for managerial efficiency, or through other methods. Second, cooperation may be directed toward raising prices to purchasers; restricting entrance into the trade, and generally reducing competition. Cooperation between the parties is not necessarily socially desirable in all its aspects. For either type of cooperation to develop, the parties must be on good terms with each other.

Emphasis on efficiency is more likely to be chosen when the product is sold competitively, that is when higher prices would reduce demand and therefore employment, and when lower prices would expand both. Then both parties have an interest in increased efficiency since it will contribute to more employment and produce higher wages and profits, or both. But if the demand for the product is such that higher prices can be charged without much reduction in demand, then higher profits and wages can be secured by raising prices without an offsetting loss in production and employment. . . .

To the public, collective-bargaining processes and procedures are important in so far as they contribute or fail to contribute to resolution of conflict, and, when maturity is reached, in so far as they lead to greater efficiency or to more monopoly. The public desires techniques which will aid in the reconciliation of the parties, and bargaining systems which will concentrate on increasing the flow of goods and services rather than on restriction.

THE STRUCTURE OF COLLECTIVE BARGAINING (CANADA)*

The Woods Task Force Report on Canadian Industrial Relations summarizes the main features of the structure of Collective Bargaining in Canada.

The collective bargaining system in Canada is limited in its coverage, and is fragmented and decentralized. It now only covers about one-third of the non-agricultural labour force. Even when other organized groups are included, a majority of Canadian workers remain uncovered by collective bargaining. The effects of the process, however, extend beyond those embraced by collective bargaining through both formal means, such as the decree system in Quebec, and informal means, such as non-union firms that choose to emulate union standards. Moreover, most of those who engage in collective bargaining in the traditional sense are concentrated in the major manufacturing, mining and transportation sectors of the economy, a feature which must be recognized in assessing the system's inflationary potential.

Within the organized sector of the economy, collective bargaining is anything but a consolidated and centralized process. Table 6 provides a percentage breakdown of collective agreements in 1953 and 1965 and the numbers of employees covered by type of bargaining unit in units involving 500 or more workers. Although a majority of these agreements are negotiated between a single establishment and a single

* From: *Canadian Industrial Relations*. "Report of the Task Force on Labour Relations", Queens' Printer, December, 1968, pp. 60-3. Reproduced by permission of Information Canada.

union, only about one-third of the employees included in the survey are covered by this type of agreement. There were no major changes from 1953 to 1965. Most of these agreements are to be found in relatively small and medium sized single-plant enterprises, although they are common among large multi-plant companies in the steel, aluminum, chemical and auto industries. The proportion of single-establishment single-union collective bargaining would probably be much higher if negotiating units of less than 500 employees were included in the survey, but there would likely be a much smaller increase in the percentage of employees affected by such arrangements.

Single-establishment multi-union negotiating units account for less that 4 per cent of the work force. There was a greater increase in such units than in the proportion of workers covered by them. Little significance should be attached to this development since this kind of bargaining is confined to specialized situations where unions share contiguous bargaining units, something which can happen in a wide variety of industries.

Table 6

Percentage Distribution of Collective Agreements and Number of Employees by Type of Negotiating Unit[1]
(Collective Agreements Covering 500 or more Employees)
1953 and 1965

	Agreements		Employees Covered	
Types of Negotiating Units	*1953*	*1965*	*1953*	*1965*
	%	%	%	%
Single Establishment — Single Union	55.3	56.1	30.8	34.3
Single Establishment — Multi-Union	3.4	3.7	1.1	2.9
Multi-Establishment — Single Union	21.2	18.5	19.6	22.2
Multi-Establishment — Multi-Union	1.9	2.9	1.6	3.6
Multi-Company — Single Union	3.4	6.1	1.3	5.9
Multi-Company — Multi-Union	1.9	0.7	29.9	14.1
Employer Association — Single Union	11.5	11.2	14.4	15.6
Employer Association — Multi-Union	1.4	0.7	1.2	1.5
Total	100.0	100.0	100.0	100.0

[1]Excluding the construction industry.
SOURCE: Alton W.J. Craig and Harry J. Waisglass, "Collective Bargaining Perspectives", *Relations industrielles/Industrial Relations*, Vol. 23 (1968) No. 4, p. 582.

196. In 1965, multi-establishment single-union collective agreements accounted for 18.5 per cent of the surveyed agreements and covered 22.2 per cent of the workers. This was almost a complete reversal of the corresponding proportions in 1953, but nothing special is to be inferred from this change. Such agreements may embrace two or more plants of a corporation and may cover plants in only one area, region or province, or may extend across the country. Although corporation-wide bargaining is not the dominant practice within this category, it occurs in many industries, including railways, automobiles, agricultural implements, meatpacking, electric power, communications and broadcasting.

197. There has been some change in the level of multi-establishment multi-union bargaining, but what was said with respect to single-establishment multi-union cases applies to this situation as well.

198. Despite a substantial increase in multi-company single-union bargaining, especially in terms of the number of employees covered, it still accounts for only about six per cent of the agreements and workers covered by the survey. It also tends to be limited geographically to particular cities or regions, as in the case of Ontario breweries, major retail food chains, and British Columbia pulp and paper.

199. The greatest decline has occurred in multi-company multi-union bargaining, particularly in terms of the proportion of workers involved. The decline in this percentage is explained largely by developments in the railway and pulp and paper industries. In the former there has been a marked decline in employment. In the latter there has been a breakdown of some multi-union arrangements that prevailed for many years.

200. Employer-association single-union bargaining has increased its coverage of the work force but not its percentage of agreements. Such bargaining is to be found on a community basis in clothing, printing and leather and on a broader basis in trucking, coal mining, sawmilling and shipping. The number of employees covered by this kind of bargaining would increase sharply if construction negotiations were included in the survey.

201. Employer-association multi-union bargaining continues to account for a small proportion of agreements and workers. Its strongest base is in certain parts of the pulp and paper and sawmilling industries.

202. The data presented in Table 6 show that collective bargaining in Canada is not conducted in a concentrated fashion. Multi-party bargaining is uncommon in the sense of involving more than one company or one union. For example, agreements which involve no more than one corporate entity accounted for over 80 per cent of all agreements in 1965. At the other extreme, 1.4 per cent of the agreements were negotiated in cases involving more than one company and more than one union. The structure of bargaining, however, is more cen-

tralized than these figures suggest as is revealed when the distribution of agreements by the number of employees covered is used as the basis for comparison. Instead of the proportion of 1.4 per cent, the coverage of agreements embracing more than one company and more than one union jumps to 15.6 per cent. Nonetheless, the overall agreement-making process is far from centralized.

203. What the Canadian collective bargaining system lacks in structure could be made up in practice through a series of formal or informal pattern-setting and pattern-following mechanisms. Such a phenomenon depends on the emergence of settlements in key firms which spread to other enterprises. However, the little research that has been done on this possibility in Canada shows only limited evidence to support it. As one study has indicated:

> Unfortunately, little evidence exists on this subject in Canada and therefore it is not possible to assess fully the extent, nature and influence of pattern bargaining in the Canadian economy. Negotiations resulting in similar terms of settlement have been observed among major manufacturing, mining, logging and railway companies but the patterns of such settlements are generally regional, largely because the industries affected, e.g., automobiles and rubber, are concentrated regionally. However, even in the case of such nationwide or multi-regional industries as steel, logging, pulp and paper, and mining, the spread of patterns tends to be restricted regionally. Nation-wide patterns in some terms of settlement are found at times in meatpacking and can manufacturing. Similarity of settlements across major industry lines have been more difficult to document, especially beyond the local or community level.[2]

204. This summation of the available data on pattern setting and pattern following indicates few direct links between settlements in different localities and different industries, but it suggests many links between various bargaining units on a locality and intra-industry basis. Against this evidence, however, is the fact that no existing study has ruled out the possiblity of major settlements creating a "demonstration effect" in the form of higher expectations in many other bargaining units in the same locality or industry or elsewhere, both in the collective bargaining system and in non-union situations. This possibility is not to be ignored, although there are no firm data on its significance, except perhaps in some of the larger and more dramatic collective bargaining confrontations where terms of settlement negotiated in other major enterprises sometimes loom large in the thinking of both parties.

FOOTNOTE

[2] George Saunders, *Wage Determination in Canada*, (Ottawa, Canada Department of Labour, Economics and Research Branch, Occasional Paper No. 3, 1965), pp. 14-15.

DETERMINATION OF BARGAINING POWER: THREE MODELS *

Jonathan S. Monat

The author suggests three models for determination of bargaining power. Dunlop's model is concerned with the growth of the labour movement, Smythe's deals with specific bargaining relationships, and Chamberlain's pragmatic model adds other variables, such as public opinion.

Many models to determine the bargaining power of the parties to collective bargaining relationships have been proposed. Recently proposed models tend to be general conflict models derived from psychology, game theory, and higher mathematics where collective bargaining is merely noted as a special case of a broader class of conflict models. But the three models discussed herein were developed specifically to explain collective bargaining relationships and bargaining power.

John Dunlop's model[1] places bargaining structure and bargaining power within a societal framework. C. F. Smyth's model[2], though similar to the Dunlop model in some respects, is pragmatically oriented to specific bargaining relationships. Neil Chamberlain's model[3] has applications at both societal and pragmatic levels, but is probably most useful in the analysis of ongoing collective bargaining relationships.

Bargaining power as it is used herein is defined as the ability to affect wages, hours, and working conditions in a positive manner above (or beyond) which the other party would not voluntarily move. It is the ability of A to force B to settle on A's terms. Although bargaining power is discussed below chiefly as a function of economic variables, psychological variables operate to modify significantly bargaining power. Two questions must be asked: How much bargaining power does a party have? How effectively can this bargaining power be used? Both labor and management, as well as third parties may use these models to answer these questions and to analyze any given bargaining situation or relationship.

JOHN T. DUNLOP

Dunlop's model has four elements[4].
1. Strategic technological position of the work group,
2. Strategic market position of the work group and the employer,
3. Community institutions, and
4. Ideals and beliefs.

Strategic technological position creates bargaining by virtue of location and position in the production process. This is not identical

* Jonathan S. Monat, "Determination of Bargaining Power," *Personnel Journal* Vol. 50, No. 7 (July, 1971), pp. 513-20. Reprinted with permission.

with skill, but the withdrawal of a strategic work group's skills will lead to restriction or shutdown of the production process. The greater the strategic technological position of the work group, the greater will be its bargaining power. If a work group is not strategic technologically, it must achieve bargaining power in the market structure.

On the other hand, management will have greater bargaining power if it is able to continue operations by shifting production to other plants which have not been struck. In the longer run, management might weaken work group or union bargaining power by job rotation practices, re-arrange job skills to require a greater proportion of skills outside the bargaining unit, or automation.

Strategic position in the market has two elements: 1) the labor market and 2) the product market. A work group is strategic in the labor market if the skills it encompasses are in short supply and there are few substitutes for these skills. Unions can restrict labor supplies in many ways, including strikes, picket lines, apprentice standards, control of hiring and training, and other techniques. Many work groups can limit labor supply through control of state occupational licensing procedures, a common phenomenon in medical occupations and some crafts. Management can protect or increase its labor supply through training and retraining programs, subcontracting, or reorganization of the work.

A work group is strategic in the product market if the demand for the employer's product is inelastic. If the demand for a product is inelastic, the employer can pass increased labor costs on to the consumer without product demand decreasing. Recent success in collective bargaining by registered nurses in many states suggests this to be the case for medical services.[5] If a work group is strategic in the labor or product markets, it can more readily exact a price for its services. The greater a work group's strategic position in either or both markets, the greater will be its bargaining power. Thus, strategic position in the market structure is sufficient to give a work group bargaining power.

JOCKEYING FOR BARGAINING POSITION

A work group may increase its bargaining power by becoming more strategic in the firm's technology and/or the labor or product markets. Technology and market positions are more or less independent, but are not mutually exclusive. Economic bargaining power (i.e., strategic position) determinees the limits to union organization. A union will extend its organizational boundaries until it achieves optimal strategic position(s). This requires, additionally, relatively few political problems within the work group or union and a stable work group at the strategic point. Stability can be achieved through exclusive jurisdiction.

On the other hand, management's strategy to prevent expansion of labor's organizational boundaries is to take advantage of the unstable nature of a work group. Unstable work groups are harder for unions to organize since such groups often lack the necessary leadership to control and coordinate workers in the group and are made up of heterogeneous individual interests. Technological change and job rotation are useful techniques to prevent cohesive work groups, although improperly conducted job rotation may have the latent function to inappropriately create unstable work groups in the face of union activities, for this risks costly (financially and psychologically) unfair labor practice charges.

Management may also protect its labor supply and long-run interests by expanding its product line, diversifying the product line, or decentralizing its facilities. Diversification can change the required skills needed in production. Skills may not become concentrated in any one work group, plant, or product market, and a withdrawal of any given skill will not deprive the organization of products or create for it a competitive disadvantage. Decentralization, though requiring a cost-benefit analysis before implementation, is also useful in spreading skills and placing the organization in many, often unrelated labor markets. The success of General Electric in collective bargaining is attributable in large measure to both a diversified product line and participation in many unrelated and/or unorganized labor markets.

Once a work group or management has determined its strategic technological and market positions (economic bargaining power), its ability to use this power effectively depends on two other factors: Community Institutions, and Ideals and Beliefs. Dunlop[6] includes as community institutions favorable to the development of labor organizations such things as the legal system, free public education, the labor press, and political parties and organizations. The union itself becomes a dominant political influence favoring labor organization. It changes its attitudes concerning the union's role in society and the use of such tactics as strikes. Hence, as a union gains political power, it is likely to make greater use of its bargaining power. To maintain balance, management must seek to influence those same institutions or create new institutions for this purpose.

Whether or not the work group or management uses its bargaining power also depends on ideals and beliefs held by workers and managers. Do they adhere to the Protestant Ethic or is there a strong push for increased leisure? Are the goals of management compatible with collective bargaining? The more workers and managers adhere to a leisure ethic, desire more spendable income, and demand property rights, the greater will be the expectations that bargaining power will be used against the employer.

THE NEED FOR ECONOMIC BARGAINING POWER

Thus, Dunlop's model can be viewed schematically in Figure 1. Economic bargaining power is a necessary condition to initial or-

FIGURE 1

BARGAINING POWER (ECONOMIC VARIABLES)	USE OF BARGAINING POWER	LIMITS TO LABOR ORGANIZATION
Strategic Position in: 1) Technology 2) Labor Market 3) Product Markets	1) Community Institutions 2) Ideals and Beliefs 3) Political Nature of the Union	1) Size of the bargaining unit 2) Scope of the bargaining unit

ganization of a work group or extension or constriction of a union's boundaries. The use of bargaining power to determine limits of organization then depends on favorable community institutions, favorable ideals and beliefs among workers, and political nature of the union. The degree and effectiveness of a union's use of its bargaining power to offset management's bargaining power determines the limits to organization.

The situation must be viewed as dynamic. If a union is effective in using its bargaining power, it has achieved optimal organizational limits. If it is not able to achieve its bargaining goals, the union's organizational boundaries will have to be expanded or contracted to make it more strategic. Or, it may be necessary for a strategically located union to attempt to change its members' ideals, and beliefs or community institutions. Similarly, if management is unable to limit effectively the extent of union organization and/or bargain effectively against the union, it may reorganize the production process or change the ideals and beliefs of its managers. Changing these beliefs may simply be a matter of resocializing current managers or may require bringing in new managers.

Finally, Dunlop does not assume that the parties act rationally. Specifically, the contradictory nature of men's behavior makes the assumption of rationality untenable. The attachment of professional nurses to anti-collective bargaining attitudes in the face of substandard income and working conditions was irrational, given their economic bargaining power. But Dunlop's model will operate because it separates economic and psychological-sociological factors, and does not assume rational calculation.

C. F. SMYTHE

Smythe's model may be divided into five elements:[7]
(1) Critical need
(2) Irreplaceability
(3) Cost of agreement and disagreement
(4) Perception of bargaining power
(5) Willingness to use bargaining power
As with Dunlop's model, Smythe's model bases bargaining power on economic variables of technological and market positions. Critical

need equates with Dunlop's technological factors. The employer cannot produce goods or services without the services of the striking work group. The greater the critical need for the work group in the productive process, the greater will be its bargaining power. The same techniques available to unions and management within Dunlop's framework apply here.

IRREPLACEABILITY IN THE LABOR MARKET

However, irreplaceability is not the same as Dunlop's market factors. When Smythe refers to irreplaceability, he is referring only to the labor market. Can the union effectively cut off the employer's access to the labor market? This can be achieved through general shortages of skill, exclusive jurisdiction over skills (as a craft union), picket lines, inability of employers to find substitutes, control of hiring halls, etc. The ability of a union to deprive employers of sources of labor increases the union's bargaining power. Employers, on the other hand, are limited in techniques to protect their labor supply. They may attempt to automate production to minimize reliance on skills controlled by the Union or try to use other techniques like subcontracting. Management has available very few short-run techniques to protect its labor supply.

But having economic bargaining power is not in itself sufficient to be effective in achieving collective bargaining objectives. The parties must perceive their bargaining power and be willing to use it. The inclusion of specific psychological factors — perception and willingness — is the critical distinction between the Smythe model and the Dunlop and Chamberlain models. Dunlop conceals these variables in broad, theoretical constructs of cultural and social values. Chamberlain does not consider psychological factors, except indirectly.

Cultural and social values are taken as given by Smythe. The important variables are the psychological variables arising from a specific bargaining relationship as perceived by the parties to that relationship at a given period in time. Environmental constraints, such as laws or community values, are considered only when they affect bargaining behaviors, attitudes of the parties, or the costs of agreement and disagreement. Effectiveness is achieved when the parties perceive their economic bargaining power and are willing to use the most appropriate strategies and tactics at the right time and place, and only to the degree necessary to implement bargaining objectives. The unwillingness of a party to use strategies or tactics appropriate to perceived bargaining power will result in ineffective bargaining and an inability to protect its long-run interests.

ROLE OF PSYCHOLOGICAL VARIABLES

The central role of psychological variables in the Smythe model reflects the encouraging trend toward the emphasis of the study of psychological processes in collective bargaining. The notable efforts of Walton and McKersie to derive a comprehensive model of these psychological variables and processes of conflict and conflict resolution should be continued.[8] The ability to define and measure operationally these variables has broad implications for the practice of labor relations.

Another major difference between the Dunlop and Smythe models is the assumption of rationality. Unlike Dunlop, Smythe, for predictive purposes, assumes that the parties till act in a rational manner. Given complete, accurate information, the parties should be able to accurately estimate costs of agreement and disagreement and choose the appropriate bargaining strategy and techniques. In other words, the parties ought to arrive at a certain decision, assuming they act rationally, and this decision should promote their long-run interests. However, in actual bargaining situations, parties often do not or cannot behave rationally. They will miscalculate costs of agreement and disagreement and, therefore, follow an inappropriate bargaining strategy. Thus, Smythe's model is a tool for objective analysis of a given bargaining relationship to predict the probable result of bargaining. If the actual result of bargaining differs from the predicted result, either or both of the parties have acted irrationally. The model provides a standard of comparison to determine sources of irrationality.

Management's most effective method of achieving rational decisions based on complete, accurate information is to develop sound, consistent personnel policy. Union-management relations should be an integral part of this policy and those who implement labor relations policy should be thoroughly familiar with it. Front-line supervisors should be trained to deal with union, for many of management's problems arise from inept supervisory behavior and the failure of higher personnel to support supervisory decisions. Inconsistent administration of policy merely gives the union another lever to weaken management's bargaining power.

COST OF AGREEMENT AND DISAGREEMENT

The final element of Smythe's model involves the calculation of the costs of agreement and disagreement, using Chamberlain's model. As noted above, this is a rational calculation based on economic bargaining power, perception of bargaining power, the willingness to use the appropriate bargaining strategy, and the effectiveness in use of the strategy to advance long-run interests. In practice, this is a difficult calculation because every bargaining situation is unique, relative to other bargaining relationships and changes constantly over time.

Thus, Smythe's model may be viewed schematically in Figure 2.

Bargaining power is derived from economic factors. The importance of bargaining power in calculation of costs of agreement and disagreement depends upon the perception of bargaining power by union members or management and their willingness to use it.

FIGURE 2

BARGAINING POWER (ECONOMIC VARIABLES)	USE OF BARGAINING POWER (PSYCHOLOGICAL VARIABLES)	COST OF AGREEMENT AND DISAGREEMENT
1) Critical Need	1) Perception	
2) Irreplaceability	2) Willingness	

NEIL CHAMBERLAIN

Chamberlain's definition of bargaining power, the relative costs of agreement and disagreement, has two elements: A's bargaining power and B's bargaining power.[9] A's power is the ratio of the cost to B of disagreeing on A's terms to the cost to B of agreeing on A's terms, as assessed by B. B's power is the ratio of the cost to A of disagreeing on B's terms to the cost to A of agreeing on B's terms, as assessed by A. Hence:

To facilitate calculation, Chamberlain suggests that each party convert all bargaining demands into dollar equivalents. This "standardizes" all demands and facilitates calculation of bargaining power using different sets of demands. The result of calculation is a readily comparable set of the net dollar advantage or disadvantage of various potential agreements. The costs of agreement and disagreement, i.e., each party's bargaining power, depend on the set of demands. In a given bargaining situation, each party has an upper and lower limit of power. The purpose of this model is to aid each party in achieving as much power as possible within these limits.

Achieving maximum bargaining power would seem to be a simple process of changing the other party's costs of agreement and disagreement. A union may lower its wage demand five cents an hour, thereby lowering management's costs of agreement. Management may lower its costs of disagreement by stockpiling goods, such as in the steel industry; by automation, as in utilities; or in other ways.

IRRATIONALITY AS A COST OF AGREEMENT OR DISAGREEMENT

For Chamberlain, irrationality is a significant cost of agreement or disagreement. The recent auto strike at Ford exemplifies this point. The Ford Motor Company took a long strike at a time when profits were at record levels and its products held a strong competitive edge. The strike cost the company almost $100 million dollars in revenues, its competitive position, and loss of income from after-sales parts and service. Further, the company substantially met the union's original demands. These are significant costs of disagreement. A rational calculation might have led the company to settle without the strike. Hence, irrational decision-making reflects the consequences of social and psychological gamesmanship which occurs in every collective bargaining relationship. Irrationality is a cost of agreement and disagreement.

The calculation of bargaining power for alternative sets of demands gives each party the flexibility to deal with irrationality and uncertainty. Other aspects of collective bargaining leading to uncertainty include such conditions as political conflicts within the union membership, between the union membership and union leadership, and between the union and management. Similarly, management is likely to be faced with internal political problems. But this does not exhaust the list of costs of agreement and disagreement to be calculated, for every aspect of the bargaining relationship affects bargaining power. Each party should convert into dollar terms economic, social, psychological, and environmental variables likely to affect negotiations. The dynamic nature of bargaining suggests that reevaluation of bargaining power should take place continuously, not unlike a game of chess.

SUMMARY

Bargaining power can be determined by at least three methods. Dunlop's model is a theoretical model, and the determination of bargaining power is a secondary question. His greatest concern is with the growth and development of the labor movement within the broader society.

On the other hand, Smythe's model is pragmatic. It deals with specific bargaining relationships, assuming each party to be self-serving. The welfare of society is not calculated except when it is specifically involved in negotiations.

Chamberlain's model is essentially pragmatic, although it includes some variables (such as public opinion) which often affect a collective bargaining relationship only indirectly. With the exception of the indirect variables, Smythe incorporates the Chamberlain model into his own. Smythe, however, specifically enumerates the psychological variables (perception and willingness) left undefined by Chamberlain.

Thus, the three models under discussion do overlap. They should not be viewed as static but must be used in a dynamic context. The complexion of every bargaining relationship changes throughout negotiations and contract administrations. Concessions by either party, moves and counter-moves, and changes in attitudes within labor or management groups continuously modify bargaining power. Figure 3 schematically depicts the process of determining, using, and adjusting bargaining power.

In Figure 3, the determination of a party's bargaining power leads it to identify alternative courses of action in any given situation. The course of action selected by either party reflects its assessment of both its own and the other party's bargaining power. The course of action will then be implemented, requiring the parties to evaluate the consequences of that strategy. These models again are the frameworks for assessment. How has the action modified economic, social, psychological, and output variables? Latent, as well as manifest, functions of the action should be evaluated. If the action does not result in the appropriate bargaining outcome desired by the party, adjustments should then be made in limits to the organization, economic, or psychological bargaining power.

FIGURE 3

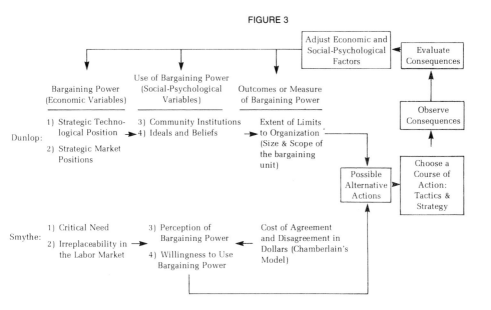

Negotiations represent a series of moves and counter-moves and each move changes the nature of the relationship, especially the social-psychological variables. The fundamental change in economic bargaining power probably does not occur as quickly or fluctuate as much as social-psychological factors moderating economic bargaining power. But any adjustments should be made with the objective of preserving, protecting, and enhancing one's long-run interests. Adjustments made with only a short-run view often are not consistent with long-run objectives. For unions, key long-run objectives include institutional strength and for management, key long-run objectives include the retention of decision-making power, i.e., management rights.

Thus, Figure 3 represents a dynamic system which has relevance for every aspect of the collective bargaining relationship, from contract negotiation to contract administration. The proper application of any of these models to a given bargaining situation should enable either or both parties to evaluate alternative bargains rationally. Most important, more accurate objective measures of each party's bargaining power can be achieved.

Two general strategies are apparent from the models discussed. Management (or labor) should attempt to lower the other party's economic bargaining power and/or psychological bargaining power and costs of agreement and disagreement. In fact, adjusting the other party's costs of agreement and disagreement can lower its economic and psychological bargaining power. The tactics suggested above are only a few of the possible tactics which might be used in implementing either strategy. The uniqueness of each collective bargaining relationship requires that tactics be tailored to that relationship and to the distribution of bargaining power in that relationship as determined through the use of one of the models outlined above.

FOOTNOTES

[1] John T. Dunlop, "The Development of Labor Organizations: A Theoretical Framework," in Lester, Richard and Joseph Shister. *Insights into Labor Issues.* New York: The Macmillan Company, 1948. pp. 163-93.

[2] C. F. Smythe. Introduction in *Teacher-Administrator*, University of Minnesota, January 1967. pp. 1-3.

[3] Neil Chamberlain and James Kuhn. *Collective Bargaining*, 2nd edition. New York: McGraw-Hill Book Co., 1965. Chapter 7.

[4] Dunlop, *ibid.* at 174-5.

[5] Jonathan Monat. *Some Factors Influencing Collective Bargaining by Professional Nurses.* Unpublished Master's Thesis. School of Business Administration, San Diego State College, September 1967.

[6] Dunlop, *op. cit.,* at 184-185.

[7] Smythe, *ibid.*

[8] Walton, Richard E. and Robert B. McKersie. *A Behavioral Theory of Labor Negotiations.* New York: McGraw-Hill Book Co., 1965. See also Stagner, Ross and Hjalmer Rose. *Psychology of Union Management Relations.* Belmont, California: Wadsworth Publishing Company, Inc., 1965.

[9] Chamberlain and Kuhn, *op. cit.,* 170-72.

BARGAINING STRATEGY: A BEHAVIORIAL APPROACH *

Richard E. Walton and Robert E. McKersie

Negotiation is comprised of four subsystems of activities, each with its own function, logic, and identifiable set of acts and tactics. The authors propose a series of hypotheses concerning the choice of strategies and the point at which negotiating parties make their maximum commitment in the sequence of bargaining.

THE ANALYTICAL FRAMEWORK

Labor negotiations, as an instance of social negotiations, is comprised of four systems of activity, each with its own function for the interacting parties, its own internal logics, and its own identifiable set of instrumental acts or tactics.

We shall refer to each of the distinguishable systems of activities as *subprocess.* The first subprocess is *distributive bargaining;* its functionss to resolve pure conflicts of interest. The second, *integrative bargaining* functions to find common or complementary interests and solve problems confronting both parties. The third subprocess is *attitudinal structuring* and its functions are to influence the attitudes of the participants toward each other and to affect the basic bonds which relate the two parties they represent. A fourth subprocess, *intraorganizational bargaining,* has the function of achieving consensus within each of the interacting groups.

Distributive Bargaining. Distributive bargaining is a hypothetical construct referring to the complex system of activities instrumental to the attainment of one party's goals when they are in basic conflict with those of the other party. It is the type of activity most familiar to students of negotiations; in fact, it is "bargaining" in the strictest sense of the word. In social negotiations, the goal conflict can relate to several values; it can involve allocation of any resources, e.g., economic, power, or status symbols. What game theorists refer to as fixed-sum games are the situations we have in mind: one person's gain is a loss to the other. The specific points at which the negotiating objectives of the two parties come in contact define the issues. Formally, an *issue* will refer to an area of common concern in which the objectives of the two parties are assumed to be in conflict. As such, it is the subject of distributive bargaining.

---

* From *A Behaviorial Theory of Labor Negotiations* by E. Walton and E. McKersie. Copyright © 1965, McGraw-Hill Book Company. Used with permission of McGraw-Hill Book company.

Integrative Bargaining.

Integrative bargaining refers to the system of activities which is instrumental to the attainment of objectives which are *not* in fundamental conflict with those of the other party and which therefore can be integrated to some degree. Such objectives are said to define an area of common concern, a *problem*. Integrative bargaining and distributive bargaining are both joint decision-making processes. However, these processes are quite dissimilar and yet are rational responses to different situations. Integrative potential exists when the nature of a problem permits solutions which benefit both parties, or at least when the gains of one party do not represent equal sacrifices by the other. This is closely related to what game theorists call the varying-sum game.

Attitudinal Structuring.

Distributive and integrative bargaining pertain to economic issues and the rights and obligations of the parties, which are the generally recognized content of labor negotiations. However, we postulate that an additional major function of negotiations is influencing the relationships between parties, in particular such attitudes as friendliness-hostility, trust, respect, and the motivational orientation of competitiveness-cooperativeness. Although the existing relationship pattern is acknowledged to be influenced by many more enduring forces (such as the technical and economic context, the basic personality dispositions of key participants, and the social belief systems which pervade the two parties), the negotiators can and do take advantage of the interaction system of negotiations to produce attitudinal change.

Attitudinal structuring is our term for the system of activities instrumental to the attainment of desired relationship patterns between the parties. Desired relationship patterns usually give content to this process in a way comparable to that of issues and problems in distributive and integrative processes. The distinction among the processes is that whereas the first two are joint decision-making processes, attitudinal structuring is a socioemotional interpersonal process designed to change attitudes and relationships.

Intraorganizational Bargaining.

The three processes discussed thus far relate to the reconciliation process that takes place between the union and the company. During the course of negotiations another system of activities, designed to achieve consensus within the union and within the company, takes place. Intraorganizational bargaining refers to the system of activities which brings the expectations of principals into alignment with those of the chief negotiator.

The chief negotiators often play important but limited roles in formulating bargaining objectives. On the union side, the local membership exerts considerable influence in determining the nature and strength of aspirations, and the international union may dictate the inclusion of certain goals in the bargaining agenda. On the company side, top management and various staff groups exert their influence on bargaining objectives. In a sense the chief negotiator is the recipient of two sets of demands — one from across the table and one from his own organization. His dilemma stems from conflict at two levels: differing aspirations about issues and differing expectations about behavior.

Intraorganizational bargaining within the union is particularly interesting. While it is true that for both parties to labor negotiations many individuals not present in negotiations are vitally concerned about what transpires at the bargaining table, the union negotiator is probably subject to more organizational constraints than his company counterpart. The union is a political organization whose representatives are elected to office and in which contract terms must be ratified by an electorate.

ISSUES IN BARGAINING STRATEGY

Commitment Strategy. Let us return to the strategy issue in distributive bargaining mentioned earlier; namely, at what point in the sequence of bargaining moves does one make his maximum commitment — one which is final and precise and which has important associated consequences?

In essence the alternate commitment strategies are as follows in their extreme formulation: (1) On the one hand, Party can state his final position at the outset, even before Opponent can indicate his own initial position. (2) On the other hand, Party can at the outset and then continuously through subsequent moves take only unclear or tentative positions along the bargaining spectrum until bargaining terminates, when Opponent indicates his own final position and leaves Party with the option of either taking it or leaving it. Strategies which approximate the first type we shall designate as strategies of "early firm commitment." Those which approximate the second type will be referred to as strategies of "gradually increasing commitment."

Some companies,[1] General Electric, for example, have adopted a strategy of "factual bargaining," in which they make their "final offer first"; while others engage in "blue-sky bargaining," taking an obviously unrealistic position at first and gradually modifying their position in subsequent bargaining moves, at the same time increasing their resolution not to make further concessions.

Why should not the party with the first move commit himself to a position near the other's resistance point and thereby settle on terms most favorable to himself? We hypothesize that the following factors will bear on the choice of commitment strategies and that they will affect the rate at which Party becomes committed to a particular point on the bargaining spectrum:[2]

Hypothesis 1

The more knowledge Party has about the resistance point of Opponent, the fewer the bargaining moves before Party commits himself to a final position. Recall that the "knowledge" is in fact usually derived from one of two sources: (a) clues from the bargaining table and (b) inferences based on information regarding Opponent's utility preferences or strike costs. When he has made these assessments, he is in a position to calculate the probability of obtaining each position within the settlement range. Then, depending upon his risk preference and general psychological orientation, he will commit himself to a particular position. Support for this proposition comes from the experimental work of Siegel and Fouraker. They found that when Party was given information about Opponent's payoffs, he tended to adjust his opening position, or gambit, closer to the final settlement point.[3] As a general matter, few negotiators obtain sufficient information in sufficient time about their own or Opponent's situations to adopt the early-firm-commitment strategy.

Hypothesis 2

The more understanding Party has about his own resistance point and the factors which combine to determine this point, the fewer the bargaining moves before Party commits himself to a final position. The point here is that Party does not always think through in advance of the first bargaining move precisely how far he can go in accommodating Opponent. He depends upon the bargaining process to either (a) stimulate explicit thinking about this problem, or (b) generate more information about exact implications of the various possible outcomes. As we shall see later Party often needs to (c) obtain more consensus within his own organization than he has at the outset of negotiations.

Hypothesis 3

The more available to Party the tactical operations for convincing Opponent that Party will not under any circumstances revive his current position, the fewer bargaining moves before Party commits himself to a final position. Devices for communicating and confirming commitments are not always equally available, and the lack of availability limits their use.

Hypothesis 4

The more prominent the expected settlement position the fewer bargaining moves before Party (and Opponent) commits himself to a final position. If a particular position possesses a focal quality because of pattern settlements, etc., it is likely that the parties will converge rapidly, and the side having the more accurate perception will reach the position in fewer moves. This proposition has been supported by experimental work.[4]

Hypothesis 5

The more available to Party the tactics for rationalizing the abandonment of a "final" commitment to Opponent, if necessary, the fewer bargaining moves before Party will make that apparently final commitment. Like confirming tactics, the situation largely determines what rationalization tactics are available.

Hypothesis 6

The greater the expectation on the part of Party that Opponent will become committed in a small number of moves, the fewer bargaining moves before Party commits himself to a final position. The value of waiting for progressively more information diminishes if the other will become committed shortly.

Hypothesis 7

The smaller the costs associated with a strike which results from mutually incompatible commitments, the fewer bargaining moves before Party commits himself to a final position. The choice of strategy depends among other factors upon a negotiator's weighting of "loss of face" versus breakdown. The early-firm-commitment strategy minimizes the descent and hence the loss of face — it establishes bargaining credibility for future negotiations — but it maximizes the possibility of miscalculation and deadlock. On the other hand the gradually increasing-commitment strategy avoids the danger of taking an untenable position, but it involves considerable descent and, in that sense, loss of face.[5]

There are other conditions which we believe affect the choice of commitment strategy; for example, the requirements of integrative bargaining, the need to preserve a certain relationship between the parties, and the internal consensus process of one or both parties which may constrain the use of an early-firm-commitment strategy.

Modifying Utilities versus Commitments.

Although we do not intend to discuss all the strategical or important tactical issues raised by our analysis of the component activities and functions of distributive bargaining, one in particular needs further exploration: What conditions influence whether Party's bargaining strategies rely upon clarifying the basic utilities and strike costs impinging on the parties or upon executing commitment tactics?

According to the analysis in Part 2, making tactical commitments and making certain points prominent play a large role in bringing about a convergence in distributive bargaining. We indicated in Part 1 that this convergence also occurs as a result of attempts to influence perceptions of underlying utilities associated with the alternate outcomes. Thus, Party has available to him two types of influence mechanisms. Sometimes they are utilized in a way supplementary to each other, and sometimes they are considered as alternatives. A major resort to the more arbitrary commitment mechanism is often made only when the other influence mechanism shows little promise of success.

The mix of tactical operations between, on the one hand, those involving persuasion to modify the other's perceptions of underlying utilities and strike costs and, on the other hand, those involving commitment mechanisms may influence the nature of the type of negotiating outcome.[6]

Hypothesis 8

Because the commitment mechanism which involves more arbitrary influence tends to create more tension, it is more likly to precipitate a breakdown in negotiations, "Breakdown" refers to a nondeliberate bolting from the bargaining situation — to be distinguished from an outcome of "no agreement" at the customary deadline, an outcome which could occur after reliance on either mechanism.

The analysis can be carried a step further. Assuming an agreement is reached, the extent to which the parties have relied upon these two mechanisms (for achieving a convergence of their expectations and explicit bargaining positions) may have important consequences for their feelings of satisfaction about the ultimate decision and their future adherence to it in spirit and letter.

Hypothesis 9

Satisfaction and compliance are greater under contracts in which reliance was relatively greater on manipulating perceptions of utilities and strike costs and less on commitment tactics.

FOOTNOTES

[1] The issue also arises in international diplomacy — in some instances a country will set forth in relatively unambiguous terms and very early in the development of a crisis, the solution or set of conditions they can tolerate, whereas in other instances the same country will be much more cautious in arriving at such a statement of what is tolerable; for example, one could probably distinguish between the strategies of the United States in the Korean, Berlin, Suez, Congo, and Vietnam crises along these lines.

[2] These propositions are being tested in a series of two person bargaining experiments being conducted by W. H. Starbuck and R. F. Walton at Purdue University.

[3] Sidney Siegel and L. E. Fouraker, *Bargaining and Group Decision Making,* New York: McGraw-Hill Book Company, 1960, p. 94.

[4] M. L. Joseph and R. H. Willis, "An Experimental Analog to Two-party Bargaining," *Behavioral Science,* Vol. 8, No. 2, 1963, pp. 117-27.

[5] G. L. Shackle, "The Nature of the Bargaining Process," in J. T. Dunlop (ed.), *The Theory of Wage Determination,* London: International Economic Association, Macmillan & Co., Ltd., 1957, pp. 292-314.

[6] An extremely significant point made by Carl Stevens in his analysis of negotiating tactics appears also to be applicable to the somewhat different distinction we make here between influence mechanisms. Stevens distinguishes between Class I tactics (those designed to induce Opponent to avoid his own position) and Class II tactics (those designed to reduce Opponent's opposition to Party's position). C. M. Stevens, *op. cit.,* p. 24.

CANADA – UNITED STATES WAGE PARITY*

Morley Gunderson

Gunderson examines the ongoing issue of wage parity with emphasis on the auto industry. He defines different types of parity, and enumerates factors which influence wage parity.

DEFINITIONS AND TERMINOLOGY

Before dealing with the parity issue itself, it is desirable to explicitly define the various concepts of wage parity. In general, there are four types of wage parity:

(A) *Nominal wage parity* — Canadian workers receive the same wage rate as their U.S. counterparts but they receive it in terms of Canadian currency.

(B) *Exchange adjusted parity* — Canadian workers receive the U.S. wage rate plus the exchange differential.

(C) *Real parity* — Canadian workers receive U.S. wages adjusted for the cost of living so as to equate the relative economic position of workers in each country.

(D) *Total parity* — Canadian workers receive the total U.S. wage package (wages, fringes, working conditions), adjusted for the cost of living and exchange rate.

In addition to the problem of defining parity, there is also the problem of determining the group with which the wage comparison is

* Morley Gunderson, "Canada – United States Wage Parity" (pp. 4-6, 20-7), Research Branch, Ontario Department of Labour, Sept. 1968. Reprinted with permission.

going to be made. Is it parity by industry, occupation, region or some combination of the three?

The concept of parity that is usually used, and the one which will be used throughout this analysis, is nominal wage parity between Canada and the U.S. by occupation in a given industry. No adjustments are made for the differences in the exchange rate, the cost of living or the fringe benefits and working conditions.

Although this paper deals explicitly with parity between industries in Canada and the U.S., the issues developed will generally be applicable to any situation involving parity within an economy (e.g. the present grain strike where grain handlers at the Lakehead are pushing for parity with their East and West Coast counterparts).[1]

PRESSURE FOR WAGE PARITY

Factors Influencing Pressure For Parity

The factors influencing the demand for parity have been dealt with at great length both by Brian Downie in his thesis and various papers on the influence of international unions on Canadian collective bargaining and by John Crispo in his book on *International Unionism*. The various interrelated factors influencing the demand for Canadian-U.S. wage parity include:

(1) The extent of integration of the product markets — Pressure for parity for the auto workers was accelerated when the auto pact brought about a greater integration of the product markets and encouraged Canadian exports to the U.S.

(2) The extent of integration of the labour market — When the labour market is fairly integrated, as in the entertainment or university teaching field, there exists high pressure for parity. Here the possibility of labour mobility is very distinct and does not stop at the political boundary.

(3) Traditional rivalry of unions — Prestige of the leaders and pride of the rank and file may be distinctly related to the extent that parity is achieved. Closing of the wage parity gap may become the measure of a successful union. In the words of one economist "there is a friendly rivalry between the United Automobile Workers and United Steel Workers over what they can accomplish for their members. The steel union has negotiated parity between the Canadian and American wage scales in our largest steel company. The Canadian officers of the prestigeous U.A.W. must feel they can hardly do less for employees of the auto manufacturing companies".[2]

(4) U.S. control of industry — Where there exists appreciable U.S. control in the Canadian industry there may exist a psychological climate favourable to parity. Also, it may be administratively more

simple to negotiate a master contract in the U.S. that will apply equally to Canadian and American workers.

(5) Geographic proximity — When plants are situated close to each other, then the psychological pressure for parity again is strengthened. It is difficult for labour to see how an artificial border can justify wage differences. Also geographic proximity may be interrelated with some of the other factors influencing the demand for parity such as integration of the labour and product market.

According to the above analysis, the pressure for wage parity is greater when the product and labour markets are well integrated, there exists a traditional rivalry amongst unions, there exists heavy U.S. control over the industry and there exists considerable geographic proximity. Although the impact of these factors on the pressure for parity has not been rigorously documented, a superficial glance at those industries striving for parity (auto, steel, pulp and paper, metal cans, university staff, entertainers) suggests that the existence of any of the above factors does encourage parity.

Internal and External Pressure for Parity

The above mentioned factors that influence the pressure for parity can operate both internally and externally. In the Canadian case the pressure for parity can come from *within*, as Canadian labour demands equal pay for equal work and it can come from *without* as U.S. industry wants to remove what it feels to be Canada's "unfair" advantage in low wage labour.

(1) Pressure from within — Canadian workers see parity both as a slogan delineating a "just wage" and as an issue that will give them more pay. They seldom regard it as a *universal* moral issue because if they did they would have to fight equally hard to have it apply to other workers who are paid *less* than they but who are doing similar work. Parity is thus sought with the highest paid reference group in mind. It is not sought with labour in less developed countries nor is it sought with labour in low wage areas in the U.S.

The leaders of Canadian labour organizations regard the parity issue as a bargaining device in that it is a target or slogan to rally around so as to get higher wages. As John Fryer, Research Director of the Canadian Labour Congress put it: "Parity is a good issue on which to get the boys steamed up".[3]

(2) Pressure from without — Pressure for wage parity can also come from *without* Canada but for very different reasons. U.S. industries and their workers may want to remove what they consider the "unfair" advantage of Canadian firms having low wage labour. U.S. firms feel they may lose a portion of their product market to Canadian firms that can sell for less because of lower labour costs. U.S. workers also may

worry about their jobs as American plants move to Canada to take advantage of low wage labour (e.g. Studebaker to Hamilton).

In the language of economics, Canada has a comparative (not "unfair") advantage in low wage labour. The most efficient way to remove this comparative advantage is for the forces of competition to allow out-mobility of labour and in-mobility of capital.[4] The first is deemed undesirable by Canadians and Americans for political reasons and both are deemed undesirable by American workers for obvious reasons of self interest.[5]

CONCLUSION

Summary and Evaluation

Wage parity is viewed by labour as an attempt for wage justice and it is viewed by labour leaders as a slogan to rally the rank and file into greater solidarity and hence bargaining power.

Competitive theory tells us that the movement towards wage parity is compatible with the efficient allocation of resources only if this movement reflects natural economic forces such as an increase in labour demand, an increase in the education, training or mobility of labour and an increase in the disutility of work associated with more difficult job assignments. Any or all of these forces *could* be at work after the auto pact, but unless they are, then the movement towards wage parity is not justified from the point of view of the efficient allocation of resources. Even if they are at work it must be remembered that such forces justify only a movement *towards* parity and not necessarily the *achievement* of parity.

Because markets are not perfectly competitive however, the parity issue must be viewed in a different light. To the extent that there exists considerable discretionary or administered pricing then the industry may be able to pay parity wages by passing the cost increase on to the consumer in the form of higher product prices. It would, of course, be *desirable* to have the discretionary pricing removed or to have certain rules of thumb (e.g. guidelines along with their exceptions) to ensure a more competitive result. If the labour market were monopsonistic in that labour was paid a wage less than the value of its marginal output, then a wage increase resulting from pressure for parity (*or for any other reason*) would be desirable from an efficient allocation of resources point of view. The increased labour costs would simply come out of reduced monopsony profits. Finally, to the extent that the firm was not maximizing its profits by operating efficiently, the increased labour costs may shock or induce it into operating efficiently and hence enable it to pay for the cost increase by saving elsewhere. Under the potential threat of unemployment resulting from parity, labour also may be induced into working harder and more efficiently or into making mobility shifts it should have made beforehand.

Again, however, it must be stressed that the existence of non-competitive markets does not justify wage parity from the point of view of the efficient allocation of resources. It may *simply enable* a firm to *pay* parity wages or in some cases it may justify a movement towards parity (i.e. simply a higher wage) rather than parity itself.

The idea of non-economic constraints was also seen to be relevant to the parity issue. Although an equitable distribution of income was suggested as a possible goal, it did not seem to be one that parity would help achieve. Other political constraints such as the preservation of the auto pact, the reduction of foreign ownership and of emigration of skilled labour were suggested as being more relevant to the parity issue. It was suggested that even though parity was not justified from the point of view of the efficient allocation of resources, it *may* be justified to satisfy the political constraints. Whether it is or not, is a political and not an economic question. It should also be remembered that there may be other economic policies that may satisfy the political objectives and which might be more effective and less harmful than wage parity.

In spite of the general adherance to the principle that parity of wages between two industries is not possible without parity of average productivity between these industries, it was suggested how such a concept, by itself, is irrelevant from the point of view of efficient allocation of resources. The relevant measure is marginal rather than average productivity and it is the value of this output that is important, not its absolute amount.

Rules of Thumb for Wage Determination

In light of the above analysis — and especially the criticism of the average productivity concept — can we devise relevant rules of thumb for wage determination at the firm or industry level that will be consistent with the achievement of our aggregate or macro-economic goals?

Since the wage-price guidelines evolved as an answer to this sort of question, the same sorts of problems associated with the guidelines are associated with the parity issue.

An increase in wages is economically justifiable if there exists a labour shortage at the existing wage rate. This increase is needed to efficiently allocate labour into its most productive use. An increase in wages may also be justified on equity grounds if the present wage is considerably below the average. Care should be taken, however, to see that the person does not become unemployed as a result of the increased wages. Also, wages should increase if they reflect a positive return to a worker investing in himself through education, training, mobility or other forms of investment in human resources. They should also increase if the contribution of the worker to efficiency increases by his accepting more difficult or undesirable job assignments.

Some of these points — especially the first two on labour shortage and inequities — were explicitly referred to by the Council of Economic Advisers in their 1962 Guidepost statement. The justification of a wage rate increase based on an increased return to investment in human resources is seldom explicitly referred to in the literature on the guideposts. The Council of Economic Advisers may have alluded to this concept in their statement: "Employees are often able to improve their performance by means within their own control. It is obviously in the public interest that incentives be preserved which would reward employees for such efforts." The idea of sanctioning a wage rate increase when this increase is specifically associated with labour accepting more difficult or undesirable job assignments is also largely ignored in the literature, although the recent emphasis on productivity bargaining in Britain is essentially a recognition of this point:

> The productivity agreement, in essence, represents a trade-off of inefficient working practices for higher pay. The term excludes general promises of greater effort or efficiency, as well as productivity gains flowing solely from technological change. The contribution of the worker must be specific and direct and involve more exacting work or a major change in working practices.

The above arguments generally point to the fact that wage increases are justified if labour is the source of a productivity increase. Such increases are necessary to reward labour fully for the productivity increase and to attract more labour into such areas. If the productivity increase is completely general (say, as the result of neutral technological change or perhaps of political agreements such as the auto pact), then the efficient allocation of resources require that the benefits be passed on to the consumer in the form of lower product prices. To the extent that discretionary pricing prevents such price flexibility then steps should be taken to remove the discretionary pricing or to force prices down by administrative ruling on the part of the government.

The auto pact may be used to show how the above mentioned rules of thumb may be applied to the wage determination process at the industry level. It also shows how the rules may have to be modified in light of political constraints.

Ways of Distributing Gains of Auto Pact

By lowering tariff barriers and rationalizing the Canadian auto industry, the auto pact has resulted in considerable gains to the Canadian auto industry. From society's point of view, the basic question then becomes: "What is the best way of distributing these gains from such an increase in productivity?" The answer from the point of view of the efficient allocation of resources is first of all to increase the returns to those factors of production that are now in short supply in the Canadian industry. If this happens to be labour or the human capital component of labour then a *movement* towards wage parity may be justified. To the extent that competitive markets operate however, supply responses will ensure a restoration of the old equilibrium wage rate.

Secondly, it would be desirable from an equity point of view to compensate (on a once and for all rather than permanent basis) those who lost from the auto pact. This may take the form of relocation or training allowances to workers who are adversely affected, and it may take the form of once-and-for-all subsidies to the auto industry to cover its "turn around costs" or "costs associated with the rationalization of the industry" over and above normal organizational investment costs.

Thirdly, it would be necessary to reward labour in accordance with any changes in its skill classification or job assignments that took place as a result of the auto pact. Specifically, if the required average level of skill (e.g. training, education) was increased, then the average wage in the industry would increase simply as a result of the change in occupational mix. Also, if the job assignments became more difficult after the rationalization of the industry, a permanent wage increase would be desirable to compensate for this change. The logic of this argument also requires increased management salaries if the rationalization of the industry requires a shift in the managerial hierarchy to hiring "better management" or if the managerial responsibility increases as a result of the industry changes. If such payments are not made, the industry will find it has a shortage of the appropriate labour skills and managerial talent.

Once, these rewards are made to compensate the losers and to ensure an efficient allocation of resources, then the benefits of the auto pact should be fully passed on to the consumer in the form of lower product prices and hence higher real wage rates for *all* labour. To the extent that competitive economic forces are not sufficiently powerful to ensure price reductions, then administered ruling may be necessary.

As mentioned previously, the existence of the political constraints of maintaining the auto pact and reducing the inflow of foreign capital and outflow of Canadian skilled labour may make the price reductions and increase in Canadian production less desirable. As such, it may be necessary to artificially raise Canadian costs by distributing more of the gains of the auto pact in the form of higher wages, salaries and managerial incomes. Whether it is desirable to do so is a political, not an economic, question.

The impact of this analysis for the wage parity issue is that the movement towards wage parity is justifiable to the extent that the skill level or job assignment is changing such that if a wage increase is not forthcoming there will be shortages of the appropriate labour. The same is true for the managerial hierarchy and management salaries. When one adds certain political constraints that may prevent the full benefits of the auto pact from being passed on to consumers in the form of lower product prices, the case for wage (and salary) parity is also strengthened on purely pragmatic grounds. It should be remembered,

NORTHWEST COMMUNITY
COLLEGE

however, that the above arguments simply imply relative wage increases, and not necessarily the exact achievement of wage parity.

Appendix A

Example Showing the Relationship Between Average Productivity, Marginal Productivity, Wages, and Changes in Productivity

Assume two firms in two countries with different production functions so that the same amounts of labour produce different amounts of output and that the change of this output with respect to different amounts of labour also differs.

Firm C in Canada				Firm U in U.S.			
Units of Labour	Output	Average Product	Marginal Product	Units of Labour	Output	Average Product	Marginal Product
1	15	15	—	1	50	50	—
2	25	$12^{1}/_{2}$	10	2	65	$32^{1}/_{2}$	15
3	33	11	8	3	76	$24^{1}/_{3}$	11
4	39	$9^{3}/_{4}$	6	4	84	21	8
5	44	$8^{4}/_{5}$	5	5	89	$17^{4}/_{5}$	5
6	$48^{1}/_{2}$	$8^{1}/_{2}$	$4^{1}/_{2}$	6	93	$15^{1}/_{2}$	4
7	52	$7^{3}/_{7}$	$3^{1}/_{2}$	7	96	$13^{5}/_{7}$	3
8	54	$6^{3}/_{4}$	2	8	98	$12^{1}/_{4}$	2
9	55	$6^{1}/_{9}$	1	9	99	11	1

The production function of the firm in the U.S. is assumed here to be such that each given unit of labour produces a higher *level* of output and hence has a higher *average* product. This could be due to differences in technology or in the uses of other factors of production.

FOOTNOTES

[1] Telegram, September 10, 1968, p. 1.

[2] Allen Porter, *The Impact of Wage Parity in Canada*, paper delivered at the Loyola College Third Annual Symposium on the Current Economic Problems of Quebec and Canada. Mimeographed paper. March 15, 1968, p. 4.

[3] Financial Post, March 16, 1968.

[4] This does not account for the "theory of factor price equalization" which under a set of *highly* unrealistic assumptions predicts factor price equalization resulting from free trade only, with no factor mobility being necessary.

[5] The long run patterns of emigration from Canada to the U.S. and the flow of capital from the U.S. to Canada, however, may be taken as evidence of the competitive forces at work.

THE PRIVATE SECTOR MODEL: MUNICIPAL EMPLOYEES*

Harry W. Arthurs

Arthurs examines the application of private sector collective bargaining legislation in Canada to municipal employees, and the practical problems such an application poses.

As indicated above, Canadian constitutional law views municipal corporations as the creatures of statute; they possess neither inherent powers nor sovereign immunities. Accordingly, in the absence of a specific exclusionary provision, municipalities will fall within the ambit of a general labor relations statute. In Ontario, for example, such an exclusion existed at one time, but by the mid-1960s municipal labor relations were brought under private sector legislation in almost every Canadian province, including Ontario.[1] However, a variety of special procedures exist which regulate the right to strike of municipal employees engaged in essential industries.[2]

In Ontario some municipal employees have apparently practiced collective bargaining at least since the 1920s.[3] When modern legislation in the style of the American Wagner Act was first introduced in the mid-1940s, municipal employees were among the early groups to claim its protection. Thus the present relationship in such large urban centers as Toronto has developed over a quarter-century or more.

In all respects, as indicated, municipal employees fall under the ordinary private sector statute: they are guaranteed the right to organize and bargain collectively; they are entitled to be represented by a union which may seek certification on the basis of majority support in an appropriate bargaining unit; following good faith bargaining and compliance with the general requirement of exhausting the statutory conciliation procedures, they may lawfully engage in strikes; and they may enter into binding collective agreements which are enforceable through conventional grievance procedures and arbitration.

Obviously, however, the working out of these procedures in the special environment of municipal government has posed certain practical problems. Thus in defining the appropriate bargaining units for civic employees, it has been necessary to establish certain tests for "community of interest" among those included. In the major Toronto area municipalities, for example, there are separate "inside" (white-collar) and "outside" (blue-collar) units.[4]

What is of particular interest is the bargaining process and the pro-

* H. W. Arthurs, *Collective Bargaining by Public Employee Unions in Canada: Five Models* pp. 15-18; Institute of Labor and Industrial Relations — The University of Michigan – Wayne State University, Ann Arbor, 1971. Reproduced with permission.

cess of dispute settlement. Unlike the private business corporation, the municipal employer operates under a variety of constraints: the limited opportunities for increasing revenues to meet increased labor costs; the absence of clear authority vested in a particular spokesman to negotiate and conclude a collective agreement; the political reaction of the public to the costs of settlement or the inconvenience of a strike. Each of these deserves review.

Usually a large Ontario municipality will be governed by an elected council with either an executive committee elected by the aldermen from among their number or a board of control elected on a municipality-wide basis. The mayor, although a member of the board of control or executive committee, has no independent executive power or, indeed, any special political power other than that derived from the force of his personality or of his municipality-wide electoral mandate. Accordingly, all decisions must ultimately be made by the council itself, although a two-thirds majority is required to overturn decisions of the executive committee or board of control. This governmental structure molds the collective bargaining procedure of the municipal employer.

Typically, the employer negotiating team comprises the mayor, some or all of the executive committee members or controllers, and senior management and financial officials of the municipality. In preparation for negotiations (which do not occur on any statutorily determined cycle) the annual municipal budget estimates will be prepared with possible increases in view. These will be concealed from the union by the nonsegregation of wage and other items in the budget finally approved by council, and by the establishment in that budget of unidentified reserves. As negotiations approach, the employer position will be determined more closely, usually by secret deliberations of council.

Negotiations proceed in the normal fashion of the private sector with no overt attempt by the union to mount direct political pressure to bear on the council. To some extent this forbearance is explained by the absence of party politics in Canadian urban governments, and by the fact that negotiations will seldom be close enough to elections to provide a convenient occasion for such pressure. On the other hand, members of council are no doubt aware that civic employees have long memories and that they might be able to tilt the electoral balance in civic elections in which voter turnout is traditionally low — about 35 percent or less. Thus, the use of political leverage cannot be altogether discounted.

Following negotiations, of course, council must ratify any agreement reached by the management team. The reasonable flexibility of municipal budgets facilitates this process of ratification. In Ontario the upper limit of the tax rate which must be struck to pay for any wage increase is not determined by statute or referendum. The only recourse of voters who must bear the heavy tax burden occasioned by over-generous wage settlements is to vote the council out of office at the next election. Indeed, even the fact that a tax rate has been struck, and the taxes collected, does not unduly inhibit the ability of the municipality to meet the costs of settlement. As indicated, there is some flexibility within the budget estimates so that funds can be shifted from nonwage to wage items; moreover, reserves and contingency funds can be tapped. Perhaps most important, municipalities may, if driven to it, engage to a limited degree in short-term deficit financing to meet current operational costs, although the practice is probably illegal.

This is not to say that Ontario municipal employers have been free-spending or over-generous. Collective bargaining is inevitably difficult, and even those members of council who are politically prolabor usually take a firm stance in negotiations. Over the years the larger centers have developed benchmarks, often by mutual agreement between the parties, which establish the framework of demands and counterproposals. These benchmarks look to rates paid both by other municipal employers and by a sample of private sector firms. Naturally they are not binding on either party, and the level of settlement reflects the relative strength of the two sides, as in the private sector.[5]

There are no inhibitions on the right of Ontario municipal employees to strike, other than the general requirement that the conciliation procedures provided by the Labour Relations Act be exhausted.[6] On several occasions in recent years this right has been exercised, as for example in 1966 and 1968 when the Toronto "outside" workers struck. Although these strikes potentially posed a serious threat to the community, since the employees involved included garbagemen and operators of the sewage and water supply systems, in fact no danger ensued. In 1966 key functions were maintained in the sewage and water plants by supervisors, in 1968 by union-arranged emergency crews. In 1966 cold weather prevented the spoilage of garbage, while in 1968 polyethylene bags were distributed to homeowners, who either retained the garbage for the one week duration of the strike or deposited it in predesignated dumps in city parks.[7]

On only one occasion has the Ontario government actually intervened, by ad hoc legislation to require compulsory arbitration of a threatened strike of municipal hydroelectric employees.[8] In this respect Ontario has acted in a much more restrained fashion than other provinces, which have enacted statutes containing permanent procedures for preventing strikes by municipal (or other) employees engaged in providing essential services.[9]

Perhaps the most impressive fact about Canadian municipal labor relations is that the system operates in a reasonably "normal" fashion. In that sense it hardly presents as interesting a picture as other areas of public employment, which are characterized by more novel statutory arrangements.

FOOTNOTES

[1] Prior to 1966 the Ontario Labour Relations Act provided that a municipal council might by by-law bring itself outside of the statute, thus leaving its relations with employees to be governed by common law principles. This privilege was abolished by Stat. Ont. 1966, c. 76, s. 37. However, an analogous provision is still in force in Prince Edward Island, see the Industrial Relations Act, Stat. P.E.I. 1966, c. 19, s. 1(j)(ii)(B), as amended. See also Frankel & Pratt, Municipal Labour Relations in Canada (1954).

[2] See generally Arthurs, *Public Interest Labour Disputes in Canada*, (1967) 17 Buff. Law Rev. 39, and Essential Industry Disputes (Task Force Study No. 8, 1969).

[3] See *Toronto Electricity Commissioners v. Snyder*, [1925] A.C. 396 (P.C.).

[4] See generally Willes, A Study of Labour Relations Law Pertaining to the Bargaining Unit (unpublished LL.M. thesis, Osgoode Hall Law School, 1967); Herman, Determination of the Appropriate Bargaining Unit by Labour Relations Board in Canada (1966).

[5] See generally Simmons, Collective Bargaining at the Municipal Government Level in Canada (Draft Study prepared for the Task Force on Labour Relations, unpublished, March, 1968).

[6] Labour Relations Act, Rev. Stat. Ont. 1960, c. 202, s.54.

[7] 1966 was a crisis year in Canadian municipal employment relations. Approximately 75,000 man days were lost as a result of 14 municipal employee strikes.

[8] The Toronto Hydro Employees Union Dispute Act, 1965, Stat. Ont. 1965, c. 131; see also the Ontario Hydro Employees Union Dispute Act, Stat. Ont. 1961-62, c. 94, which similarly withdrew the right to strike (on an ad hoc basis) of employees of the provincially owned hydro-electric generating and distribution system.

[9] *Op. cit. supra*, note 2.

PART 3

Section 2
Issues in Contract Administration

1. Employee – Union – Management: Rights and Responsibilities

EMPLOYEE RIGHTS AND UNION RESPONSIBILITIES*

The members of the Woods Task Force on Canadian Industrial Relations argue that a strong case can be made for assisting unions and their leaders to contend with membership pressures without jeopardizing their own positions, the collective bargaining process, or the welfare of society at large. But an equally strong case can be made for ensuring that labour organizations do not violate the basic democratic rights of their members either as a group or as individuals. These competing interests call for a delicate balancing of membership rights and union responsibilities.

The power that unions can exercise over present and prospective members suggests that union membership rights are a subject of legitimate concern. Labour organizations have acquired a number of important quasi-public powers since the days when they were no more than voluntary associations. The state has endowed them with one especially important prerogative and permitted them to exercise two others. First, unions are granted exclusive bargaining rights in units appropriate for collective bargaining. The rules incorporating this policy vary from jurisdiction to jurisdiction, but the effect is essentially the same. Much of the right of negotiation, particularly over terms as distinct from the fact of employment, is transferred from the individual to the collectivity. Second, having been recognized as sole bargaining agents, unions are free to negotiate any kind of union security clause they are able to extract from management. Such arrangements range

* From: *Canadian Industrial Relations*, "Report of the Task Force on Labour Relations," Queen's Printer, December 1968, pp. 101-5. Reproduced by permission of Information Canada.

from an "open union shop", where a man cannot work unless he is already a member of the union. In between lie the more common "union shop", where a worker must join the union after a specified waiting period, the "agency shop", under which there is a universal obligation to pay union dues but not to join the union, and other variations.[1] Third, many unions have acquired virtually complete control over entrance standards and a great deal of control over the rights of their members to continuing membership.

321. Given the potential power that unions can exercise over present and prospective members, one would expect that steps would have been taken to prevent abuse, limited though it may be. In fact, little has been done except for the occasional *ad hoc* measure introduced in the face of glaring abuses. Such was the situation when a government trusteeship was imposed over several maritime unions, at least in part because of the arbitrary and capricious use by the Seafarers' International Union of Canada of its infamous do-not-ship list.[2] Even in this case it is not clear that any action would have been taken had there not been other equally disturbing elements. The danger is that abuses in other unions, though apparently few and infrequent, may go unchecked in the absence of basic rights and remedies guaranteed by law.

322. A member or prospective member of a union may appeal to the courts if he feels his legal rights have been abridged. But these rights are not always clear; they can be minimal, legal costs can be great, and a decision can be long in coming. Thus, resort to the courts scarcely provides a complete answer, although it has had a salutary effect in several cases. On more limited grounds, an employee may seek recourse from a labour relations board if he feels his rights under a labour relations act have been violated. Similarly, a human rights code can provide partial protection. A few unions, notably the United Automobile Workers,[3] have created independent appeal tribunals for their members. Such tribunals have much merit, but their contribution is limited because they operate within the union's constitutional framework, something which the tribunals may or may not be able to influence if they deem the framework unfair or unjust.

323. Several basic rights deserve attention. First is the fundamental question of access to union membership, particularly where membership is a prerequisite to employment. As we discuss more fully elsewhere, there are inherent dangers in allowing any collective entity in the labour market to close or arbitrarily limit its ranks without some degree of public scrutiny and control. The public interest in this area goes beyond the protection of individual rights that may be affronted, to concern over the wider ramifications of permitting any organized group to control access to a particular segment of the labour market.

324. Related to the right of access is that of equitable treatment in the distribution of available work where a closed shop is operated in conjunction with a hiring hall. Moreover, if some minimum standard of competence is required, it would seem essential to ensure that the

means of acquiring and establishing that competence are available on a basis equal to all.

325. Equally important is the protection of a worker's civil rights as a union member. Unions cannot bring industrial democracy to the work place if they themselves operate in an autocratic fashion.[4] This does not mean that unions should be expected to exhibit all the trappings of a political democracy, including, for example, a multi-party system, but it does suggest that the basic attributes which are axiomatic to meaningful participation and protection in any organization must be present. Thus, the elementary right to express one's opinions and to seek office without fear of reprisal must be preserved. Above all, the individual member must be assured a fair trial and an appeal to a tribunal free from predisposition should he be brought under charge. Without this basic protection, all other rights are in jeopardy.

326. In the United States, many of these rights have been incorporated into a "bill of rights" for union members.[5] This legislation followed the McClellan Committee disclosures[6] of a variety of corrupt and undemocratic practices in certain unions. The legislation not only includes a bill of rights guaranteeing equal rights within unions, freedom of speech and assembly, electoral safeguards, protection against improper disciplinary action, and other basic democratic principles; it also provides for the regulation of trusteeships, full financial accounting by unions to their members, the bonding of certain union officers, other fiduciary responsibilities, and a wide variety of reports.

327. Although circumstances in Canada call for some reform in these areas, nothing as comprehensive as the United States enactment seems either necessary or desirable. Relatively few procedural and substantive safeguards appear to be in order. As quasi-public bodies, unions can hardly object to such safeguards, first because they are not merely private associations, and second because, few though the abuses may have been in this country, they are nonetheless important. Moreover, if state intervention in this area is limited to certain bare essentials, there are, according to union spokesmen, very few unions that should ever run afoul of the law.[7] Where necessary, international unions have already brought their constitutions and practices into line with the provisions of the *Landrum-Griffin Act* in the United States, and nothing enacted in Canada need be any more demanding.

328. There are more specific problem areas such as the use of union funds for political purposes, especially when they are raised through the compulsory check-off of dues. No difficulty arises as long as these funds are employed solely for legislative lobbying. But when they are used to back a political party, there are grounds for concern. Members whose political persuasions are different from those of their union may object to the expenditure of any of their dues on a party with which they do not sympathize. Yet unions should have the same right as other organizations to support the party of their choice, as long as that choice has the support of a majority of their members. A way must be found to

reconcile these competing interests without doing an injustice too any of them. Whatever is done should not put labour organizations at a disadvantage relative to other interest groups.

329. Another troublesome issue concerns the relative rights of the collectivity and of individuals in the negotiation and administration of a collective agreement. The problem can best be illustrated in relation to the individual member's right of access to the grievance procedure and to arbitration. Normally such access is controlled by the union, and this is as it must be if collective bargaining is not to be undermined. Yet the union should be expected to exercise this discretionary power in a fair and impartial manner if it is not to have arbitrary control over its members. This suggests that a union should be able to show that it acts in good faith whenever it chooses not to pursue a member's grievance or to pursue another one contrary to his interest. This must be the limit to any concept of fair representation if responsible collective decision making within and between union and management is not to be jeopardized.

330. Whatever is done to protect union membership rights must be accomplished without undermining the basic fabric of the labour movement or its ability to play a responsible role in society. With respect to the former, a union is like a country perpetually in conflict with a neighbour without which it cannot get along. As a militant organization, a union cannot afford the ultimate in democracy. Nor would this be desirable from the viewpoint of society at large, since it might preclude a union from taking unpopular but responsible positions in the face of membership restiveness. Accordingly, the challenge is to fashion a code of civil rights for union members, and machinery for administering it, that neither so weakens unions as to render them ineffective in bargaining nor so exposes them to membership pressures that they cannot act responsibly when circumstances dictate.

FOOTNOTES

[1] Canada Department of Labour, Economics and Research Branch, *Collective Agreement Provisions in Major Manufacturing Establishments*, Labour-Management Research Series No. 5 (Ottawa, Queen's Printer, 1964).

[2] The Honourable T. G. Norris, *Report of Industrial Inquiry Commission on the Disruption of Shipping*, (Ottawa, Queen's Printer, 1963).

[3] J. Stieber, W. E. Oberer, and M. Harrington, *Democracy and Public Review: An Analysis of the UAW Public Review Board*, (Santa Barbara, Center for the Study of Democratic Institutions, 1960).

[4] Gérard Dion, "La démocratie syndicale" Gérard Dion (ed.), *Le syndicalisme canadien: une réévaluation*, (Québec, Les Presses de l'Université Laval, 1968), pp. 77-99.

[5] Title 1 of the Labor-Management Reporting and Disclosure Act, Public Law 257, 86th Congress, (73 Stat. 519-546).

[6] U.S. Congress, Senate Select Committee on Improper Activities in the Labor

or Management Field, (Washington, U.S. Government Printing Office, 1960).
[7] Canadian Labour Congress, *Report of the Commission on Constitution and Structure as approved by the Executive Council of the Canadian Labour Congress*, (Toronto, May 1968), p. 10, para. 46.

MANAGEMENT AND UNION RIGHTS AND RESPONSIBILITIES *

A. M. Metcalfe

Metcalfe examines the three levels of the industrial structure – the management, the union and the employee – with reference to their specific rights and responsibilities.

He discusses the apparent interferance of unions into traditional management areas, and the advantages and disadvantages of this development from a management point of view.

What are the rights of management? There have been many attempts at defining them, and I don't profess to be any more capable than others who have tried.

The definition I like is — "Management's right to make the decisions and take the actions necessary to discharge its responsibility of conducting the enterprise."

Since we are discussing management rights as they relate to industrial relations, this must be further clarified by pointing out that we are primarily concerned with those rights which relate to the management of people, work, and those functions which affect the terms and conditions of employment.

To make an itemized list of these rights which would be complete and satisfactory for all time would be impossible because circumstances are continually changing.

In the definition we have said "necessary to discharge its responsibility of conducting the enterprise." This indicates, then, that the rights must be consistent with the responsibility, and management has three basic responsibilities:

a) *To the shareholders or owners of the business*   It is responsible for operating an efficient and profitable business. If it does not, there will not be a business to operate.

b) *To the consumer*   It is responsible for producing a useable, safe

*A. M. Metcalfe, "Management and Union Rights and Responsibilities," *Canadian Personnel and Industrial Relations*, July 1964, pp. 30-2. Mr. Metcalfe is Personnel Manager of Outboard Marine Corporation of Canada Ltd., Peterborough, Ontario. Reprinted with permission.

and realistically priced high quality product. If it does not, the product won't sell, the owners losw money and once again there will not be a business to operate.

c) *To the employees*   It is responsible for providing continued employment at safe jobs with the best possible wages and working conditions consistent with the first two responsibilities.

I don't believe that the order of importance of these can be changed, or that the dependence of (c) on (a) and (b) can be changed.

Can he be held responsible for the type of product produced or the cost or quality of same? Once again I don't believe so.

We like to think that employees are concerned about and interested in both quality and cost or efficiency, but the grievance and arbitration processes have, in my opinion, proven conclusively that we cannot hold the employee responsible beyond the specific limitations of his instructions as they relate to a given job or assignment.

If you doubt this you have only to go before a board of arbitration on a discharge for faulty work. One of the first and key questions you will have to answer is — "Was the employee properly instructed as to what was expected of him and how he was to perform the job?"

The board will leave you in no doubt, if the union has not already convinced you, that this is the supervisor's responsibility, not the employee's.

In actual fact, then, the employee can be held responsible only for adhering to the rules laid down for his conduct and for carrying out the assignments and instructions given to him. This is not to say that many employees don't have a sincere interest in their companies, or that we can't hope for more and more of this attitude among employees, but the possibility of this happening under present union philosophies is rather remote.

Getting back now to the basic reason for any discussion of this topic — the retention by management of its right to manage — I seriously doubt that anyone but management really wants this right and the responsibility it entails.

Unions want more and more of the benefits which can come to them directly or indirectly as a result of good industrial management. They feel they must also, in the interest of their own survival, introduce through collective bargaining certain provisions requiring joint discussion or mutual agreement, which are intended not as a taking over of management's rights, but rather as a guarantee that they may question or object to complete and unfettered management authority. There may be a thin line between the two objectives, but nonetheless it is there, and it is very real when you talk in terms of responsibility.

The result of these provisions is not necessarily the loss of the right to manage, but the introduction of complications, delays and hurdles which are, for the most part, completely unnecessary and which generally reduce the overall efficiency of management.

The important question is — if unions do not want management responsibilities why are they intent upon making the job more difficult for management? There are, I suggest, at least two possible answers to this question.

1. *Sales & Business Promotion*   Unions, like companies, are constantly trying to find new ways of promoting their merchandise, increasing their volume of business, and, in the end, increasing their profits. There is no doubt that unions are big business today, and if they are to continue to support the highly paid staff now involved in this business, they must continue to create a demand for their services. They have been successful in establishing the pattern for the excellent wages, benefits and working conditions which prevail on this continent today, and, in fact, it is conceivable that they have come to the end of the era of spectacular achievements in these conventional types of improvements. Thus only by making themselves a significant force in other areas can they hope to retain their present status, let alone improve it.

2. *Traditional Distrust*   I believe it is a recognized fact that Management was, to a large extent, responsible for the birth and growth of the present day union by reason of its lack of consideration for the employee as an individual, and by reason of arbitrary and discriminatory actions. However, I believe also that it is high time everybody, the unions in particular, recognized the fact that our industrial society has progressed from the early 1900's. Many of the practices followed by management at that time would not be tolerated even by management today, with or without the presence of unions. With possibly the odd exception management would not revert to the old days in the absence of union pressure or vigilance because it has found that the change has been for the better, and who knows for sure that the changes would not have been inevitable even without union pressure, though possibly slower and less painful.

At any rate, while it may add drama and sensationalism to the relationship, I cannot agree that the perpetuation of the battle for recognition is necessary or desirable in this day and age, either from the viewpoint of management or labour. Labour has proven itself as a power in industry, and having done so, it should now approach with reason and logic the real problems so vital to continued existence of the very system which permits it to live and grow.

There is no doubt that management can inspire and promote a sounder basis for the new approach, because there is no more effective way of inviting a challenge than to tell a person that something which vitally affects him is none of his business, or to refuse to discuss it with him. Likewise, there is no better way of losing a right or a privilege than by abusing it through arbitrary or inconsiderate actions, or by over-asserting the right.

Here a quotation from a speech in 1960 by P. M. Draper, President of

Pressure Pipe Ltd. and for a number of years a member of the Ontario Labour Relations Board is very appropriate. Mr. Draper said — "We cannot wish away or talk away conflict on the management rights issue. But if we must admit that conflict is inevitable, we must also acknowledge that cooperation is essential if acceptable solutions are to be found."

He also said — "And above all management and labour must always have in mind that they both seek the realization of their goals through the medium of the enterprise, and that neither will attain those goals unless the basic objective — the success of the enterprise — is recognized and achieved.

To this I can only add that if you want someone's consideration, recognition, or cooperation, you can only get it by being ready, willing and able to give the same to him. To do this does not mean the unconditional surrender of the rights or dignity of either party, and both management and labour should stop pretending that it does.

MANAGEMENT RIGHTS*

David Archer

Management rights are examined from a labour point of view. Archer suggests that many managerial abuses are derived from residual rights not covered in collective agreements. He calls for amendments in labour legislation to remedy this problem.

The introduction of collective bargaining into our economic system has drastically modified the rights of management to unilaterally do many of those things he previously did. As trade unionists, we believe this is not only right and proper but necessary if our modern industrial society is to remain truly democratic. Management must continually be reminded that property rights should not give you authority over people. Since property is a "thing," the ownership of "things" should not be a foundation for authority over people. Many managements have not fully recognized this change in our society and still operate within time-worn economic and political concepts evolved at another stage of our economic development when the factory was family-owned and operated.

Using this concept, managements argue that they hold their management rights by virtue of ownership. They seem to have forgotten that they, in most cases, do not own today's modern enterprise. In fact in many cases the employees may be owners themselves in the sense

* David Archer, "Management Rights," *Canadian Labour*, Dec., 1964, pp. 19-21. Reprinted with permission.

that they own shares in the enterprise. Thus any question of management "owning" the business and disposing of it or its employees regardless of the social consequences of their actions is an anachronism
that the trade union movement should endeavour to destroy. It is
"Goldwaterism" or oversimplification at its very worst in the labour-
management sphere.

Unfortunately most Canadian arbitrators and every Canadian court
or administrative tribunal operates on what has come to be known as a
"managements' residual rights" theory. This theory is simplicity itself.
It means that any rights not restricted by contract or prohibited by law
belong to management. Under this theory a company could fire a
staunch unionist because management did not like the colour of his
eyes. If this type of discrimination is not prohibited specifically by a
union agreement, there is nothing in law to protect the aggrieved employee. The only discrimination prohibited by law is on account of race,
creed or colour. He remains fired and there is nothing the union can do
about it, without breaking the law and engaging in illegal activity.

In the organizing stage of a union campaign where there is no
protection by agreement one is at the complete mercy of management.
This problem is compounded by the fact that in Ontario one is denied
the right to strike, slowdown or take any other effective action to redress the situation. In the Milrod vs. Steelworkers case an employee was
fired merely because he handed another employee a union leaflet on
company time. The labour board in a majority decision, somewhat
apologetically, said this was not activity protected by the statute and
the employer was within his rights in firing the offending employee.
While the discharge may have been discriminatory according to the
board, it was not discrimination prohibited by the Act. The same
lawyer, encouraged by the board's attitude, used the same technique in
the Hamilton Wire Case vs. Steelworkers. Again two workers were fired
for trying to organize a union, and the union was left without any
method of redress.

Even where there is an agreement the problem is not solved. There
are many questions not covered by agreement, some difficulties are not
even thought of at the time the agreement is signed. The Labour Act
states that final determination (arbitration) can only be made "where a
difference arises between the parties on the interpretation, application
or administration of the agreement." Most agreements spell out managements' rights by a managements' rights clause. Matters such as
speedup, introduction of new methods of manufacturing, and the introduction of automated machinery, among others, are usually outside
the scope of the agreement and management's rights in these areas are
not restricted by law. So a union finds itself in the position of watching
its bargaining unit weakened or destroyed without any effective remedy, since the right to strike has been taken away by statute. Even the
Taft-Hartley Act in the United States does not go this far. And, in every
other western democratic state in such circumstances, workers are al-

lowed to withhold their labour until a mutually-satisfactory settlement is arrived at.

One or two Ontario arbitrators have tried to modify this theory, but with little success. Professor Bora Laskin and Judge Fuller have shown some understanding of the unions' problems but most other arbitrators, particularly judges, have been completely hostile to any modification of management's exclusive and unilateral right to manage its workforce in any way it desires without interference by the union. This is an intolerable situation since the union has no way of protesting unjust or discriminatory discipline or loss of jobs.

Companies argue that they can pay whatever they wish to whom they please, claiming the union-negotiated wage scale is merely a minimum or base. So long as they do not go below this minimum they are not in violation of the agreement. It is one of their residual rights to pay more, without the union's permission, even if the recipients of the extra pay just happen to be the least enthusiastic unionists in the shop. This view is upheld by most Canadian arbitrators. In the U.S. the Supreme Court, the National Labour Relations Board and individual arbitrators have taken a much more realistic view of this situation. And in the U.S. unions can strike during an agreement on issues not covered by the agreement.

Professor Bora Laskin, in the Peterborough Lock Case, put the case very well. He stated:

> In this board's view, it is very superficial generalization to contend that a collective bargaining agreement must be read as limiting an employer's pre-collective bargaining prerogatives only to the extent expressly stipulated. Such a generalization ignores completely the climate of employer-employee relations under a collective agreement. The change from individual to collective bargaining is a change of kind and not merely a difference in degree. The introduction of a collective bargaining regime involves the acceptance by the parties of assumptions which are entirely alien to an era of individual bargaining. Hence, any attempt to measure rights and duties in employer-employee relations by reference to pre-collective bargaining standards is an attempt to re-enter a world which has ceased to exist. Just as the period of individual bargaining had its own "common law" worked out empirically over many years, so does a collective bargaining regime have a common law to be invoked to give consistency and meaning to the collective agreement on which it is based.

The more orthodox legal view has been expressed by Judge Thomas in the Studebaker-Packard case. He stated:

> (An arbitration board) is strictly limited to interpreting the written contract. The company has the right to manage its business to the best of its ability in every respect, except to the extent that its rights

are cut down by voluntary abrogation of some of these rights through contract with the union. The Reservations (not restrictions) to Management clause which appears in most agreements is nothing but a gratuitous acknowledgment by the union of this fundamental right. If the board is unable to find anything in the contract between the parties which takes away from the company's right to conduct its own business, then it cannot be concerned with the quality of the action taken by the company, or whether it results in a loss of jobs for employees of the company, or whether the action which produced such results was exercised inside the four walls of the plant.

Because the attitude of almost all Ontario arbitrators is the same as Judge Thomas's, we must make these demands on the government:

1. That all matters relating to employee-employer relationship during the terms of a collective agreement are arbitrable. Thus the Laskin view of arbitration would prevail.

2. And/or the "no strike" legislation be repealed and the union be allowed to use its economic power to redress unfair treatment of the people it represents. If we are to suffer severe penalties for protesting managements' unfair and discriminatory decisions and no satisfactory method of final settlement of those differences is open to us, then we are duty-bound as trade unionists to demand, for our own protection and survival, the repeal of the "no strike" clause in the Ontario Labour Relations Act.

The same situation holds true with regard to automation and other changes in working procudures. Government is demanding labour-management consultation before widespread and far-reaching changes are made in industry. What good is consultation if we are precluded from using our economic strength at the consultation table. Here is a situation that cries aloud for redress. The federal government through Labour Minister Allan MacEachen, has suggested that it is aware of the problem and is looking for a remedy. It is much more important that the remedy be incorporated into provincial legislation. This is where it may be much more difficult to receive a sympathetic understanding of our problem. However, it is worth the effort if we are to return industrial democracy to union-management relations.

2. Subcontracting

ISSUES IN CONTRACTING OUT*

F. Young

Young discusses the issues involved in subcontracting in industry. He examines it in terms of efficiency versus job security. He points out its impact on union structure and on management prerogatives.

There are many industrial relations issues involved in the practice of contracting out. Here, attention will be focussed on the three major issues which underlie this study: efficiency v. job security; union security and structure; and management prerogatives.

EFFICIENCY V. JOB SECURITY

While the subcontracting of work and services raises a number of industrial relations issues, the key issue is undoubtedly that of company efficiency versus job security. This is the issue which underlies many of the differences between unions and management. The issues come sharply into focus when we contrast the goals of management and unions.

The company objective, as it is traditionally stated, is to maximize profits. While this idea has been buffeted somewhat by distinctions between short-run and long-run profit maximization and emphasis on alternative, non-economic motives, we shall assume that normally a company does try to conduct its business in the most efficient way with this end in view. Union objectives, on the other hand, are not only to increase the take-home pay of its members, but also to protect existing job opportunities for its members, and to ensure that the union itself will continue to exist. If contracting out should mean that there will be fewer in-plant job opportunities and that bargaining units may be eliminated, there will clearly be a direct conflict between the company objective and these latter union objectives. How sharp is the conflict?

First, let us look at the effect of contracting out on employment. There is little doubt that in almost every case the subcontracting of work and services has the effect of reducing in-plant job opportunities. In the individual plant, however, these effects may not always be obvious. In some cases, contracting out may result in the displacement of company employees. In other instances, it may result, not in lay-offs, but in lower hiring rates and in-plant transfers. While the overall effect on company employment may be the same in each case, the actual impact may be obscured because of this different incidence. Some

---

* From F. Young, *The Contracting Out of Work*, Ottawa, Queen's Printer, 1964, pp. 10-16. Reproduced by permission of Information Canada.

companies, for example, reported that in-plant employment had actually increased as a result of contracting out. What probably occurred was that employment increased as a result of expansion in the company's activity, or that it increased in a particular department because of in-plant transfers. In fact it is unlikely that at the plant level employment could rise as a direct result of contracting out. By contrast, in looking at the broader employment effects of contracting out, it would be necessary to consider the increases which take place in the contractor's work force, and increases in employment which result from induced demand generated by greater efficiency and technological change. The effect on employment at the individual plant level, in other words, may be quite different from the broad employment effect of contracting out.

The problem of employment security takes on added significance during the downswing of the business cycle, in periods of rapid technological change, or when there is a slow-down in the rate of economic growth. During full-employment conditions, trade unions can afford to devote their energies to increasing the take-home pay of their members, leaving the problem of employment security more or less to take care of itself. When unemployment rises, however, these priorities are reversed. Employment security becomes the over-riding goal, and such items as separation pay, supplementary unemployment benefits, portable pensions, retraining plans and a guaranteed annual wage become the key bargaining issues. Unions are also likely to demand that clauses be inserted in the collective agreement limiting management's right to take unilateral action in such matters as the introduction of machinery, plant relocation, work assignment, and subcontracting.

In view of the persistent high unemployment which we have experienced during the last five or six years, it is hardly surprising that contracting out has become a key industrial relations issue. Concern with greater productive efficiency during this period to meet growing domestic and international competition has simply accentuated the gravity of the issue.

UNION SECURITY AND STRUCTURE

A second important issue arising from the practice of contracting out lies in its implications for the labour movement. There are two aspects to this issue: first, its implications with respect to union security, and secondly, its implications in regard to union jurisdictions and structure.

It was stated earlier that union objectives include not only improvements in the wages and working conditions of its members, along with protection of job opportunities for these members, but also the survival of the union as an entity in itself. While these objectives generally reflect those of the union's individual members, in some cases they may clash with the interests of those whom the union represents.

For example, one authority cites a case where employees in the circulation department of a newspaper asked that their status be changed to that of independent contractors. While it was reported that the employees themselves preferred the change, the union was obliged to protest this action since it had cost the union 58 members. In this case, then, the interests of the employees ran counter to the institutional interests of the union.[1] While this is a good illustration of how the survival of the union may be threatened by the subcontracting of work and services, the issue is not always so clear-cut. There are really three aspects which must be considered: first, the effect on the bargaining unit at the local union level; secondly, the effect on the individual national or international union; and thirdly, the effect on the union movement as a whole.

If work which was previously done in the plant is contracted out, the union is likely to view the move as a threat to the existence of the bargaining unit. Whether the work is contracted out to non-union employees, to another local of the union, or to another union altogether, union officials in the plant will oppose the change. As far as they are concerned, the move involves a loss of membership and the possible destruction of the bargaining unit.

While union officials in the plant may oppose the change, the parent union may be quite neutral about the matter if the work is simply contracted out to another of its locals or units. No overall loss of membership occurs. The survival of the union itself is threatened only if the work is contracted out to a group of non-union workers or to another union.

Where the work is contracted out to another local of the union or to another union, the issue of survival is not likely to be of concern to the union movement as a whole, even though it may affect particular unions or locals. However, if it should mean that work previously done by union members is now done by non-union workers, the issue could well become a major one. It would mean that unions as a whole were losing members. At a time when the growth in union membership has almost come to a halt, any loss of membership as a result of contracting out is likely to be of great concern to the union movement.

In fact, it appears that the subcontracting of work generally involves the transfer of work from one union to another union, or from one local to another local of the same union. As far as the union movement is concerned, therefore, the major problem is not that of overall loss of membership but rather of structures and internal jurisdictions.

Since contracting out frequently results in one union increasing its membership at the expense of another, the practice inevitably touches off sharp inter-union disputes. The subcontracting of maintenance work from an industrial union to a craft union, for example, is likely to spark jurisdictional disputes which at the same time aggravate the various other problems caused by contracting out. These jurisdictional problems are themselves complicated by the present structure of the labour movement. In North America the traditional union structure has been on a narrow craft and industrial basis. With the rapid technological, industrial and occupational change of recent years, however, this clear-cut industry and occupational distinction has become blurred. Some industries have broadened and crept over into closely related ones; many job classifications have broadened and have bunched together into related families. The result is that, in many cases, the traditional lines of union structure are no longer appropriate to today's occupational and industrial complex.

MANAGEMENT PREROGATIVES

The third major issue, that which receives the most detailed attention in this study, revolves around the various legal aspects of contracting out. This involves the question of management prerogatives. Over the years, trade unions have been successful in having clauses inserted in collective agreements which have the effect of limiting management's control over its work force. Examples of these are management rights clauses, recognition clauses, union security clauses, seniority clauses, and more recently, subcontracting clauses. In this study, the specific issue is whether management prerogatives have been limited to the extent where the company cannot freely contract out any work or service performed in the plant.

There are two opposing theories of management rights. The residual rights theory put forward by management asserts that all the pre-existing rights and privileges of an employer are reserved to him except when they have been specifically surrendered or limited in the agreement. The bargaining theory or limited view of management rights put forward by the trade unions, holds that the establishment of collective bargaining eliminates earlier rights, practices and precedents. If a matter arises which is not covered by the collective agreement, it must be dealt with by mutual agreement, or by following practices established since collective bargaining began, or by exercising an exclusive management right found in the agreement.

Where a collective agreement is silent on the subject of contracting out, a management decision to let out work is challenged by the trade union which is a party to the agreement. In many cases, this challenge takes the form of a grievance which eventually results in a case before an arbitration board. The awards of arbitrators are thus a fruitful source of information with respect to management rights, particularly as they relate to contracting out. The different views of arbitrators on management's right to contract out, and the sharp difference between Canadian and United States arbitrators on this subject will be analysed in subsequent chapters of this study.

SUMMARY

1. The practice of contracting out is extensive in Canadian industry and has become increasingly prevalent in recent years. While it is extensive in the private sector of industry, particularly in manufacturing, it is also common in federal, provincial and municipal governments.

2. Heavy reliance upon subcontractors was indicated for the performance of work and services in areas peripheral to the main business of the company. On the other hand, there was little subcontracting of the actual processing and manufacturing of the company's products, where its own employees were generally capable of carrying out the main business of the enterprise without outside assistance.

3. The crafts and occupations most frequently affected by contracting out were construction crafts, such as painting, masonry, electrical, carpentry, plumbing, sheet metal and iron work trades; and service occupations, such as trucking, janitorial, cafeteria and security services. Reliance upon outside help was greatest in the case of cafeteria operations and frequent in the cases of masonry, sheet metal, trucking, and security occupations.

4. The major attraction of contracting out lies in its cost advantage to the employer. Specifically, this includes various reductions in labour costs, the facilitating of technological change, and the streamlining of administrative and accounting procedures. Against this must be set possible offsetting factors — the contractor's profit margin, the cost of work stoppages and slowdowns, and unfavourable effects on the company image.

5. Both management and unions view the technique of contracting out chiefly in terms of cost. Management generally appears to use the term broadly as a synonym for overall company cost considerations. Unions seem to construe the same term more narrowly, concentrating upon labour costs rather than overall costs. This semantic problem suggests that justification of contracting out in terms of cost, or opposition to it on these grounds, may prove to be a dangerous error for its proponents.

6. Contracting out raises a number of industrial relations issues. The issue which underlies many of the differences between unions and management is the question of efficiency versus job security. The problem of job security takes on added significance during the downswing of the business cycle, in periods of rapid technological change, or when there is a slowdown in the rate of economic growth. Because of the persistent high unemployment which we have experienced in recent years, contracting out, and the associated issue of efficiency versus job security, have acquired increasingly greater significance.

7. A second key industrial relations issue in contracting out relates to union security and structure. There is no evidence that contracting out poses a threat to the union movement as a whole although it may result in a loss of membership for particular unions or locals. This loss of membership often gives rise to sharp inter-union disputes which aggravate many of the problems caused by contracting out. The issues are further complicated by the fact that the traditional lines of union structure are no longer appropriate to today's occupational and industrial complex.

8. A third major issue is whether management prerogatives have been limited to the extent where the company cannot freely contract out any work or service performed in the plant. Over the years, unions have been successful in having clauses inserted in collective agreements which have the effect of limiting management's control over its work force. The remainder of this study examines the extent to which management's right to contract out has been limited by trade unions and looks at the broad legal and industrial relations implications of this issue.

FOOTNOTE

[1] Slichter, Healy, Livernash, *The Impact of Collective Bargaining on Management*, The Brookings Institution, Washington, 1960, pp. 289-90.

3. Technological Change and Collective Bargaining

CONTINUOUS BARGAINING: RECENT DEVELOPMENTS IN THE U.S.A. AND CANADA*

Hem C. Jain

In the last decade some creative experiments within the framework of collective bargaining have taken place in the U.S.A. and Canada. The author examines some of these. He points out limitations of collective bargaining with reference to long-range developments such as the implementation of technological change, and suggests ways in which collective bargaining may be made more effective.

Since the 1930's the process of free collective bargaining on the North

* Hem C. Jain, "Continuous Bargaining: Recent Developments in the U.S.A. and Canada," *Indian Journal of Industrial Relations*, Vol. 6, No. 2 (Oct. 1970), pp. 133-47.

American Continent has gone through three different stages: (*i*) Organisational stage, (*ii*) Containment stage, and (*iii*) Accommodation stage.

Prior to 1935 the union movement faced opposition and hostility in the efforts to organise workers, and to seek the right to be recognised by management as the workers' representatives in collective bargaining. It was management's belief that unions, by their very nature, interfered with managerial authority. The second stage involved containment of the union movement. In the late 1930's and the early 1940's, when political, economic, and social events made the acceptance of unions necessary, management's philosophy of industrial relations had to change. When collective bargaining became mandatory, management tried to circumvent the power and influence of unions by establishing direct management – employee communication, and by pursuing policies which would guarantee the maximum amount of managerial authority and control. The third stage may be called the stage of growing accommodation between labour and management. After the Second World War, that is in the 1950's, as union and management became more experienced in the process of collective bargaining, their relationship became more stable. This is especially true of large industries where negotiations between labour and management were carried out on an industry basis. Unions obtained institutional protection through the union shop in large industries. High level of employment and continually rising standards of living brought about a significant change in the attitudes of top union leaders. The leaders became less militant, more mature, and sophisticated. They developed a high degree of social skill in dealing with management and showed moderation and good sense in collective bargaining. Management's philosophy of industrial relations has also changed in recent years. Management has recognised that unions are here to stay, and it is in its best interest to develop a reasonable working relationship with them.

AMERICAN EXPERIMENTS

The Armour Automation Committee

Armour & Co., the second largest meat packing company in the U.S.A., closed several meat packing plants between 1956 and 1958. The plants employed 25 per cent of its production workers. Loss of jobs created frustration among union members and brought about intentional slow-downs and "wild-cat" strikes. Unions demanded, in the negotiations, a short work week, limitations on sub-contracting, guaranteed employment, advance notice of plant shut-downs, and the right to reopen the entire contract in the event of another plant closing.

However, guaranteed employment was the main issue in bargaining. The company was afraid that a costly strike would ensue if something was not done to assist the displaced workers. It agreed to the establishment of a committee having equal representatives from union and management, chaired by a neutral executive director, to study the problems and make recommendations. The six main recommendations of the committee, which were accepted by unions and management, can be summarised as follows:

(i) The company must give 90 days' notice before closing plants.
(ii) Transfer seniority rights were established. Included herein was a clause relating to "replacement plants" which was to loom very large in the future of the committee. Employees transferred to a replacement plant were to be "credited with all continuous service and seniority rights held at the closed plant".
(iii) The fund was to pay relocation costs.
(iv) Technological adjustment pay was established which was to provide funds for displaced workers awaiting transfer.
(v) Severance pay was improved.
(vi) Provision was made for early retirement at age 55 at one and one-half times full retirement pay.[1]

Pacific Maritime Association Plan

Another example of the establishment of a fund to cushion the effect of technological changes is found in the agreement reached in 1960 between the Pacific Maritime Association and the International Longshoremen's and Warehousemen's Union. The management of the shipping industry was greatly concerned with rising costs and was interested in mechanising cargo handling and loading methods. The union, as a matter of policy, viewed mechanisation and modernisation of operations as a threat to their jobs and would not readily agree to such changes. However, in 1957 the union realised that, though it had succeeded so far in protecting jobs by the so-called "system of work rules", management went ahead anyway with the technological changes. The union felt these changes would affect the job security in the long run, and decided on a change in tactics. The union demanded "a share of the machine in return for the employers' demand for full freedom to modernise". In other words, the union would agree to permit the introduction of labour-saving devices and methods on the docks if workers were allowed to share in the benefits from mechanisation. Finally, in 1961, both parties signed an agreement under which:

> The shipowners and stevedoring contractors are freed of restrictions on the introduction of labour-saving devices, relieved of the use of unnecessary men and assured of the elimination of work practices which impede the free flow of cargo or ship turnaround. These guarantees to industry are in exchange for a series of benefits for the workers to protect them against the impact of the machine on their daily work and on their job security.[2]

Under this agreement, a fund called "The Mechanisation and Modernisation Fund" was created to provide security for the workers. The fund, which will amount to five million dollars, is to be financed on an annual basis from the contribution of the members of the Pacific Maritime Association.

As a result of this agreement, the labour relations of the industry on the west coast became highly centralised. The Joint Coast Labour-Relations Committee, which was originally set up to settle grievances at the top, became a forum for exchange of ideas and mutual problems on a continuing basis. The greater centralisation of authority on both sides has resulted in greater uniformity in contract administration.

The Pacific Maritime Association agreement is different from the Armour Automation Committee in that the Pacific Maritime agreement was reached without the participation of neutrals. Both parties were committed from the beginning to work out the solutions of their problems among themselves. They had faith in each other which helped reach an eventual agreement.

Kaiser Plan

Another unique plan called the Kaiser Plan has been widely discussed and publicised all across the continent. The plan was developed in 1959 when the Kaiser Steel Company broke away from the other companies during a one hundred and sixteen day, industry-wise steel strike, and established a tripartite committee, consisting of union and management representatives and third party neutrals. Kaiser, who took the initiative in forming this committee, hoped that it would develop a plan for equitable sharing between the stockholders, the employees, and the public of the fruits of the company's economic progress.[3]

The committee agreed upon a plan which divides savings resulting from cost reductions through increased efficiency. The plan also provides job security. In substance, it protects jobs and income against technological changes. It guarantees wages and benefits equal to or better than the rest of the steel industry. It provides for lumpsum payments to such incentive employees who are willing to withdraw from the incentive systems.

From management's point of view the replacement of the existing incentive system for those workers who choose the plan is the most desirable feature of the plan. Management is becoming increasingly aware of the fact that wage incentive systems instituted earlier for the purpose of increasing productivity have become outmoded, and that it is the machines, not the men, that increase production. Many other large companies are seriously considering doing away with the wage incentive systems.

Under this plan, management is assured of uninterrupted production, free from the threat of strikes at least for four years. As far as the success of the plan is concerned, in the first few months of its operation in 1963, the monthly bonus for the employees averaged $100, and it dropped to $14 in April 1964. As the bonus dropped sharply in 1964, it gave rise to some concern. The committee discovered that reduction in bonus payments could be attributed to several reasons: inexperienced employees, problems in accounting and administration, etc. The committee recommended several changes in the plan to fit it to the changing circumstances. One such change was that new employees were to be barred from sharing in cost-savings until they had been on the job for six months.

The Kaiser Plan has proved to be successful and beneficial to both parties so far because union and management have demonstrated their willingness to change the cost sharing plan or even replace it with something else if the present plan does not meet the specific objective of both parties. George Taylor, Chairman of the Long-Range Committee, in assessing the success of the Kaiser Plan has this to say:

> If this plan works, it will be because the people on both sides want it to work. If there is anything transferable about it, it is not the specific arithmetic but the basic principles of progress plus security on which it is built. It grows out of the determination of both sides to get away from crises bargaining and work out realistic programmes of dealing with the human problems of technological change.[4]

The Human Relations Committee

In January 1960, the Human Relations Committee in the Basic Steel Industry was established to plan studies and recommend solutions for mutual problems. To be more specific, the committee was asked to study problems in the following areas:

(i) Guides for the determination of equitable wage and benefit adjustments.
(ii) The job classification system.
(iii) Wage incentives, including development of appropriate guides for determining fair incentive compensation.
(iv) Seniority, including maximum practicable protection for long-service employees against lay-offs.
(v) Medical care.
(vi) Such other oral problems as the parties by mutual agreement may from time to time refer to such committee.

The composition of the committee as provided in the agreement is as follows:

(i) The Human Relations Research Committee shall be composed of an equal number of representatives designated by the parties to such memorandum agreement (the number of which by agreement of the parties may be changed from time to time), and shall be under the co-chairmanship of two persons of outstanding qualifications and objectivity, one to be designated by the company parties to such memorandum agreement and the other to be designated by the union.

(ii) The Human Relations Research Committee shall be empowered to retain, by mutual agreement of the co-chairmen thereof, qualified experts and services in the various fields of study for the purpose of consultation and advice.

(iii) The expense of the Human Relations Research Committee's work shall be shared equally by the parties.[5]

In the initial stages, the Human Relations Committee worked very well. However, later on, due to the internal crises in the union, the committee had to be abolished.

Common Characteristics

In all of the above-mentioned plans and experiments there is one common characteristic: they provide for a joint continuing study of problems and issues of mutual interest to both parties. These experiments indicate that the institution of collective bargaining is adapting itself to a new climate. In some instances parties included neutrals, because these outsiders were men of skill and knowledge, who could deal with the problems at hand more objectively and might bring a different viewpoint to the bargaining table. In other cases it was felt that outsiders would not have an intimate knowledge of the problems existing in the industry, and instead of assisting the parties they might create suspicion and distrust in the initial stages of the formation of a study group, particularly, if they were brought in at the request of one party. This is true of the Pacific Maritime Association plan where union and management avoided the use of neutrals by agreeing to a well-defined set of objectives, which made the work easier later on. All these new techniques are keeping the institution of collective bargaining alive.

The American plans are tailor-made for specific situations. However, the general principles on which the above-mentioned creative experiments are based are equally applicable to the Canadian scene.

CANADIAN EXPERIMENTS

Domtar Experiment

The Dominion Tar and Chemical Company, a broadly diversified company, has pioneered in calling a series of meetings between representatives of labour and management and the local unions throughout its enterprises all across Canada to bring about a better understanding between labour and management and to create mutual trust. The company has dealings with 120 locals which are represented by some

27 national and international unions. In November 1964, the sub-committee reached an agreement on a "Plan for Reciprocal Transferable Seniority". Under the plan, an employee with a minimum of five years of company service, whose services have been terminated through no fault of his own, will be eligible to transfer his seniority to a new location to which he might be transferred. The plan will be administered by a joint labour-management committee. In the event labour and management representatives of the committee disagree as to the manner in which the plan should be implemented, an umpire will be appointed to resolve such differences. The umpire will also settle any grievances which might arise from the interpretation or administration of the plan. The award of the umpire will be binding on both parties. In 1966, the joint committee adopted an "Industrial Conversion Plan". The plan will be financed by the company but will be administered jointly by union and management. Under the plan a credit will be established by the company of one cent per hour worked by participating employees. The maximum credit accumulation will be five million dollars. This plan is designed to assist employees adversely affected by industrial conversion for such things as severance pay, income during retraining, and supplementation where necessary in the event of early retirement. The joint committee felt that the plan would provide reasonable security to employees adversely affected by technological changes and at the same time would enable the company to change its operating methods, product lines, products, etc., to meet competitive pressures.[6]

Railway Job Security Fund

In 1962, the two major railway companies signed separately a similar agreement with the unions representing non-operating employees. An important provision in this collective agreement was the establishment of a job security fund. The employers agreed to contribute one cent per employee per hour worked to the fund. The fund will be used primarily to help the displaced workers in their adjustment, that is, to provide for maintenance of wages, transportation, resettlement, and training costs or other kinds of support as agreed upon.

IMPACT OF TECHNOLOGICAL CHANGES ON EMPLOYEES

The following two case studies deal with the effects of technological changes on displaced employees in two pulp and paper companies (Bowater's Mersey Paper Company and New Brunswick International Paper Company) in the Atlantic region. The data on these two case studies were compiled by the author during personal visits to both of these companies. Both union and management officials were interviewed and some documents were made available by both parties.

Bowater's Mersey Paper Company — Nova Scotia

It was in 1955-56 that Bowater's Mersey management saw a definite need for technological changes. By 1961, it became obvious that personnel reductions would have to be made. The third shift of the machine shop would be eliminated by October 1963, displacing six men. Another 18 men would be displaced with the elimination of the third shift of the wood-handling department by May 1964.

Management approached the unions and presented them with proposed technological changes which would result in the reduction of the work force. The unions could see that the changes were necessary and agreed to sit down with management to discuss the fate of individual workers involved, so that hardships could be minimised.

Management expressed a willingness to establish a policy that when changes were made every effort would be made to maintain people in jobs rather than to lay them off. Second, the unions made an equally important decision and agreed to cooperate with management in waiving seniority rights, thereby allowing people to move from one department to another without losing seniority and agreed generally to help management in relocating people whose jobs were being eliminated or to put these men on a spare list until jobs became available.[7]

The first step towards a solution was to draw up a schedule of retirements over the next 10-year period. This retirement schedule helped unions and management in making relocation decisions. The next step was to create a labour pool from which spare workers could be drawn. When the third shift of the machine shop was eliminated, the six men who were affected were transferred to the day shift. In the day shift there was now a surplus of men. However, the company was prepared to carry this surplus for a period of three years. When day shift workers retired they were not replaced for three years. In May 1964, the third shift in the wood-handling department was dropped. Of the 18 men displaced by this action, seven with high seniority were immediately placed in jobs intentionally left vacant after retirement in the past year. The balance were placed in the labour pool.

It should be noted that none of the employees transferred to the other departments, or to the labour pool, suffered a loss in take-home pay during the changeover period. Since the mill has been operating for some time on a continuous (seven-day) basis, all the men placed in the labour pool were re-absorbed. In short, permanent lay-off was avoided.

New Brunswick International Paper Company

In 1963, the New Brunswick International Paper Company decided to mechanise the operation of finishing rolls of newsprint for reasons of efficiency and economic considerations. The unions were informed of the company's intentions four months prior to the target date for the start up of the installations, and together they solved the problems which would ordinarily have brought on a major labour-management confrontation.

Thirty-five employees were affected by this technological change. In this case, as in the previous one, a labour pool of displaced workers was set up. From the pool they were drawn as spare workers for all operating departments, provided they were capable of doing the work. Since the mill was operating on a continuous seven-day basis, all of the displaced employees were easily absorbed, with the result that there was no permanent lay-off.

It is interesting to note that in this case study both labour and management agreed to modify the plant-wide seniority clause of the agreement in order to provide equitable treatment to affected people. "We have found, in practice, that employees were not in favour of having the seniority of an employee in the finishing department used to 'bump' or have laid off, a junior employee in the ground-wood department. They feel that each department should take care of its own." This indicates that even though there was a specific provision in the collective agreement, yet when the actual problem arose, both union and management felt that it was in their interest to modify the plant-wide seniority provisions. In the former case study on the mechanisation of the wood handling department of Bowater's Mersey Paper Company Ltd., though there was no specific clause dealing with broadened seniority rights in the 1963 collective agreement, unions waived seniority rights and allowed the workers, whose jobs were eliminated, to move from one department to another without losing seniority. Local ad hoc arrangements made by both parties in finding a mutually satisfactory solution seem to be of great importance in both cases.

Technological Changes in Oil Industry in B.C.

In 1966, a research committee under the chairmanship of Montague was set up by Imperial Oil Enterprises, IOCO, B.C. and the local Oil, Chemical and Atomic Workers' International Union to investigate the impact of technological changes on the present employees and to establish a procedure to deal with reduction of employment at the IOCO Refinery. The committee found four significant issues concerning employment at the IOCO Refinery.

> First, the age of the work force at IOCO is relatively high and the workers as a result are perhaps more than usually security conscious. Second, transferring among occupations within the plant requires evidence of a minimum of a Grade XII education or equivalent. Since transfers are the obvious safety valve for workers under the pressure of change, the educational barrier has been a cause of concern. Third, the concern of the workers is primarily

about the future patterns of employment and income. The fourth point is that the company, faced with an industry which is heavily committed to technological efficiency, required an adaptable work force.[8]

The committee recommended a four-point plan (by age group) to ease the uncertainties surrounding technological changes in the petroleum industry:

(i) Workers between the ages of 57 and 65 may retain their regular wage rates till the age of retirement. They may retire early with a better than normal pension.

(ii) Employees between the ages of 47 and 56 may retain their present wage level until the wage on new job rises to previous rate or they are posted to a job carrying the previous rate.

(iii) Those between 35 and 46 are entitled to retain their wage levels for a period equivalent to one week for each year of service or for a period of training for a higher paid job in the plant. Workers have the option of taking severance pay at the end of the six months' notice period.

(iv) Employees outside these categories are protected by clauses in the general wage agreement which provides for six months' notice of job change due to change in technology, severance pay and security of position based on seniority.

This four-point plan negotiated by the Oil, Chemical and Atomic Workers' Union and the Imperial Oil Limited is expected to set the pattern for much of the oil industry in Canada.

Limitations

These creative approaches to collective bargaining have been developed in a pragmatic manner to meet certain specific situations. However, they are far from being common in Canada. It must be recognised that the institution of collective bargaining, in its present form, has certain inherent limitations in dealing with the problems caused by technological changes.[9]

Domtar was faced with the problem of implementing its industrial conversion plan in its initial stages because too many local unions involved in the company's operations would not accept it. In 1969, union representatives demanded at a bargaining session that a specific clause on severance pay be included in the collective agreement. Domtar management maintained that the principle of severance pay was already covered by the industrial conversion plan and that according to this plan, each case would be considered individually on merits. It appears that rank-and-file union members in Domtar as well as in the railways prefer that specific, clearly defined rights, such as earnings at termination of employment, relocation expenses, maintenance of basic rates, early retirement allowance, be included in the collective agreement rather than having to depend upon the union-management joint committee's judgement on such matters. This tendency towards more specificity is evident from the recent contract signed between the railways and the unions. It should be pointed out that one of the key features of industrial conversion plans is the flexibility, that is, the ability to treat each case on an individual basis rather than the development of fixed formulae. The demand by rank-and-file union members to include specific clauses in collective agreement on such issues puts a serious limitation on the effectiveness of such plans.

In the pulp and paper industry it is evident from the two case studies that problems arising from technological changes were dealt with informally by union and management and were not negotiated at the collective bargaining session. Moreover, in one case, both union and management were willing to modify a specific clause on plant-wide seniority during the term of the contract.

Technological changes in the oil refinery have served to blunt the most effective weapon of the union movement, that is, the strike. It has been proved beyond doubt that during the strike an oil refinery can be operated for a long time with technical and supervisory staff. The B.C. Oil Industry's settlement which provided for the eventual establishment of the Montague Committee was negotiated at the political level, between the B.C. Federation of Labour and the Premier of British Columbia. The purpose of the negotiated settlement was to avert a 24-hour general strike called by the B.C. Federation of Labour in support of the oil workers' dispute in November 1965. It was probably one of the few cases in Canada where a "political strike" instead of conventional strike was used to achieve union objectives.

Even with the best of intentions both parties have come to realise that collective bargaining while an important and versatile instrument in our industrial society cannot provide a solution for all the problems even in the organised sector. Some of the more pressing problems, for instance revamping of the plant seniority system for lay-off, promotion and transfer of employees from one plant to another, will continue to be with us for a long time. Furthermore, the long-term solutions with regard to problems such as geographical and occupational mobility training and retraining, relocation and income maintenance programme, naturally extend beyond the scope of traditional bargaining at a plant, corporation, and even at industry level. Wood's task force on Canadian Industrial Relations strongly recommends that there is a need to give priority to public policies to provide a solution to the above-mentioned problems. The task force recommendations are as follows:

> First, is a pressing need to place more emphasis on education for adjustment at all levels in the school system in order to ensure maximum human adaptability. Second, is a need to maintain a high level of employment so that other jobs are available for those displaced by industrial conversion. Third, is a need for an active

labour market policy designed to facilitate mobility between jobs through improved information, counselling, upgrading, retraining, relocation and income-maintenance programmes. Fourth, is a need to develop as many transferable fringe benefit plans as possible in order to minimise the sacrifice which workers have to make when they move from job to job. Fifth, is a need to expand the community dislocation programme. Within the public policy framework we recommend, collective bargaining could play a constructive supplementary role by helping to adapt public policies to particular situations and by experimenting with new approaches wherever possible.[10]

SOME SUGGESTIONS

Based on the experience of a variety of inventive devices used by union and management in the 1960's in resolving problems posed by technological changes, certain generalisations can be offered.

(i) There is a need for a continuing process of identifying problems and a steady and persistent search for solutions of such problems away from the crisis atmosphere of contract negotiations. However, the experience of the U.S. Steel Industry Human Relations Committee in this regard is not very promising. The real success of the Human Relations Committee was in becoming a permanent negotiating mechanism, but this success was obtained at a cost — that of by-passing the second echelon leadership of the union and the locals, a development that catalysed the internal crisis in the union and contributed to the defeat of McDonald. Finally, the Human Relations Committee had to be abolished. This case illustrates the fact that a mechanism which might appear to be very effective can nevertheless give rise to unforeseen problems. Therefore, in the search for solutions, the part played by the human and institutional factors must be taken into account to a greater extent than was thought before.

(ii) There is a need for information and communication. All relevant, reliable information is essential if parties have to reach sensible and just solutions to the complex problems posed by technological changes. Equally important is the development of two-way communication within the union and management organisations as well as between each level of union-management relationship. Most importantly, as J. J. Healey and his associates have pointed out,[11] union and management must have a strong commitment to identify and solve mutual problems by developing new creative approaches to collective bargaining.

Finally, if the institution of collective bargaining has to play a greater and constructive role, it must acquire new dimensions not only in its structure, but perhaps to a greater extent in the conception we have of it. It must adapt itself to the manpower and employment policies established at a higher level than at the narrowly defined bargaining units. Furthermore, not only should leaders of union and management be willing to discuss and assist government in formulating manpower and employment policies at national and provincial levels, but also they must be willing to implement such policies within politically defined economic and social priorities.[12]

FOOTNOTES

[1] James J. Healey (ed.), *Creative Collective Bargaining*, Englewood Cliffs, New Jersey, Prentice-Hall, 1965, p. 151.

[2] Louis Goldblatt (ed.), *Men & Machines*, San Francisco, International Longshoremen's and Warehousemen's Union and the Pacific Maritime Association, 1963, p. 3.

[3] *Monthly Labour Review*, March, 1959, p. 82.

[4] A.H. Ruskin, "An Approach to Automation, the Kaiser Plan", *New York Times Magazine*, No. 3, 1963, p. 116.

[5] "Agreement between the United States Steel Corporation and the United States Steel Workers of America", January 4, 1960, Pittsburgh, Pa., U.S.A., p. 86.

[6] Domtar Industrial Conversion Plan — "Information Booklet for Negotiated Employees", January, 1969.

[7] The written material and statistical data on the case study of Bowater's Mersey Paper Company was supplied by W. H. Tidmarsh, Industrial Relations Manager, Bowater's Mersey Company. Most of the facts described in the case study were discussed by this writer at a joint meeting of the I.B.P.S.P.M.W. Local union president, G. A. Webber, and W. H. Tidmarsh held in the office of Tidmarsh at Liverpool, Nova Scotia, in August 1966.

[8] J. T. Montague, Atuomation Committee Imperial Oil Enterprises and Local No. 9-601. Oil, Chemical and Atomic Workers' International Union, Report of the Chairman of the Search Committee, pp. 10-11, January 12, 1967.

[9] "The Report of the Task Force on Labour Relations", *Canadian Industrial Relations*, Ottawa. The Queen's Printer, December 1968, p. 189.

[10] *Ibid.*, pp. 194, 195. See also paragraphs 677, 679, 681-683-685.

[11] See James J. Healey (ed.), *op. cit.*, pp. 282-288.

[12] See J. R. Cardin, *Canadian Labour Relations in an Era of Technological Change*, Ottawa, Economic Council of Canada, Queen's Printer, 1967.

TECHNOLOGICAL CHANGE AND COLLECTIVE BARGAINING*

Arthur M. Kruger

Kruger examines the prospects, constraints, and limitations of collective bargaining for dealing with technological change. He gives specific examples of labour-management co-operation as well as examples of problems unlikely to be resolved through the collective bargaining process.

There are two ways that economists measure technological change. One is with what we call the macroeconomic level or the level of the total economy, where we try to see what has happened to the output of society. We try to see how that has grown relative to the amount of labour that is put into the system. We refer to the measure used in this case as output per unit of labour.

Another way of measuring technological change is at the level of the firm or the plant. We look at what has happened to unit costs of production, to see whether costs are falling.

In measuring technological change at either of these levels let me tell you what an economist can and cannot do. An economist can measure whether output per man is increasing or decreasing. D.B.S. statistics show this. An economist can go into a firm and measure whether the unit costs have decreased. In fact you do not need an economist. You can get an accountant who can show you whether your unit costs have increased or decreased.

What we cannot do, is isolate what part of the change in these measures is due to technological change, and what part may arise for other reasons. Let me illustrate briefly.

At the level of the firm, unit costs may decline not because technological change has occurred but because one of the factors of production is cheqper than it used to be. For example, raw materials are cheaper or the scale of output has changed and the plant moves to a larger scale of output. Costs fall, not because of any technological change but because of better utilization.

It is extremely difficult to untangle what part of this cost change is due to technological change and what part due to the other factors. Some of the studies that have attempted this I think have been doomed to futility. I can recall one in my own province that involved asking workers who were laid off why they were laid off. They had a scorebox and if the worker said he was laid off due to technological change, they

* Arthur Kruger, "Automation and the Individual," in *Proceedings of the Manitoba Conference on Technological Change*, 1968, published by the Department of Labour of the Province of Manitoba, 1968, pp. 39-57. Reprinted with permission.

put that down. If he said he was laid off because the demand for the product had fallen, they ticked that off. By and large the worker cannot untangle why he is laid off. If there is a technological change and the demand for a product increases, the man is not laid off. He may be simply transferred within the plant. And then six weeks later or six months later demand decreases and he may be laid off. Why is he laid off? Is it because of a technological change or because demand has decreased? Statistics do not lend themselves to separating these things.

In looking at technological change we must remember that anything that reduces costs (and technological change after all is designed to do that,) may also decrease prices and by doing so increase sales. If sales of a product go up, even though the amount of labour needed per unit has declined, more labour in total may be required. So technological change can be employment-expanding even if it means that you need less labour per unit of output.

I think this came out very well in Professor Pentland's discussion of some of the problems of Manitoba; ultimately it may be better to get technological change even though it may displace some people initially. In any case, however, I do not think we can lose sight of the fact that even if technological change in the long run is good, nonetheless at the time of change, it almost inevitably causes displacement. It causes displacement either by generating employment or it causes displacement to a different occupation, firm, industry or geographic location.

Technological change is not an abnormal condition of an industrial society. Such changes are intimately linked with economic growth and to impede them would seriously threaten our future welfare. In the long-run these changes make for a healthy, more viable economy. It is short-run consequences of these changes — temporary dislocation from jobs, skill shortages in certain occupations and the need for job changes — that make up the set of problems that a modern industrial society must face. Perhaps we should recall the comment of the late Lord Keynes who said that the long-run is very interesting but in the long-run we are all dead. The problems that we face and the problems that trouble us are the short-run problems. There is not much advantage in telling a displaced worker that in the long-run Manitoba will profit from his displacement and his grandchildren will lead a better life. In the long-run he will not be around to see this, so it does not interest him very much.

What is the source of change and what are the attitudes of the various participants to change? To the employer, technological change is initiated, for two basic reasons. First, with a given product that he is producing it is a device for cutting costs and thereby raising his profits. Second, it may permit him to produce some newly invented product which he has never produced before.

There are two key factors which strike me in this area of technological change. One of them provides, if you like, a basis of optimism and one of them provides, I think, a basis for pessimism about the ability of collective bargaining to cope with technological change.

First, let me give you the optimistic factor in the situation. In almost every case, there is for the employer a substantial period of time between the day that he becomes convinced that he will have to make a change and the time when the change itself will be implemented. There usually is a substantial period of time in which advance notice and some form of advance consultation can take place. This is so for a number of reasons. First of all, there is always a lag between invention and application. There is always a long period of study of new technological change. I am not thinking of a minor change which involves using a different sort of paper in your typewriters or something like that. I am thinking of a change which is going to be big enough to cause serious displacement in the plant. There is almost invariably a considerable period of time for study by the firm to see whether this change makes any sense. Secondly, economists have long noted that even where a firm is convinced that a new process is cheaper than an existing process, the firm will be delayed in implementing that change because the firm already has a plant that is on-going. As long as the out-of-pocket costs of operating its existing plant and existing machinery are less than the costs of implementing the new change, the firm will delay the implementation.

Many, many plants continue for years and even decades in an "absolete condition" because it does not always make sense to implement the new technology immediately. There is usually considerable time for consultation to take place and that provides an optimistic basic for hoping that collective bargaining can do something about coping with change.

What, on the other hand, is the pessimistic factor? This is one that has not been discussed adequately in the past. It is the fact that when a union and a company bargain about adjustment to change, if such adjustment is costless to the firm, there is no problem in the bargaining. Management is usually willing to give anything that does not cost money. On the other hand, if the adjustment is going to be costly, it becomes contentious.

One should remember that the union is doing a peculiar thing. It is saying to the old firm: "You are intending to make a change, which will displace 432 workers. You will have to do something to ease the adjustment for these workers." Now, simultaneously, there may be a new company which enters this market, using the latest up-to-date plants and nobody approaches this company and says: "You are making a change that involves displacement that should involve extra cost to you." Such costly expenditure on the part of an old firm is discriminatory because no similar demand is made on the newly-entering firm which is going to use the latest up-to-date machinery and equipment and does not have this problem of retraining or relocating anybody. In addition, of course, there is also the fact that imports provide another source of competition and no one in this country, can say to the firm in the other country that is doing the exporting to us: "You must make certain provisions because of technological change."

One must be careful in demanding in collective bargaining that management make these adjustments and pay for these adjustments. They may act in a very discriminatory manner and may, in fact, put firms at such a serious competitive disadvantage that they are unable to function and in the long haul this will hurt the labour force in those particular firms.

I have talked about employers contemplating technological change and I want to talk now about workers facing technological change. I have already indicated that the time horizon of most workers is not the long-run, but the immediate period — today, tomorrow. This is understandable given the situation in which most workers find themselves. The notion that productivity will rise and the country will be better off in the long haul has little appeal for them. A second factor is that the worker's horizon is also his own plant, his own locality, rather than the nation as a whole.

The union differs somewhat from the workers, and here my trade union colleague may disagree with me. Obviously, the union's horizon includes other things. It includes the survival of his institution which he heads. It includes the orientation to the craft or to the industry over which his union has jurisdiction rather than a broader sort of view of the situation. There may therefore be conflict between what the worker seeks, or what the worker would find in his own self-interest, and what the union may seek for him. Probably the clearest example of this, that I can think of in recent history, was the printers' strike in Toronto, where I would contend there was a difference between the goals of the workers and the goals of their trade union leaders.

We must remember that we have in Canada a tremendous multiplicity of unions. We have most of the American internationals and added to that we have a number of national unions of our own. Because of this, most unions or a large number of them have relatively small memberships and highly parochial interests; they have a very, narrow view of things. When you come to something like seniority, you will find that your seniority units are narrow. The steel workers' union in the United States covers many times more workers than it does here. The plumbers' union in the United States covers many times more workers than it does here. Given this, the likelihood of our achieving very much through the collective bargaining process is much less than that of our cousins south of the border. Relatively little flexibility in a union's ability to move people around and still keep them within its jurisdiction is, I think, a severe problem that we face.

Now, what about the government? The government is concerned with a numbe;of goals: full employment, stable prices, economic growth, and equitable income distribution. Lately, we have added preservation of the foreign exchange value of our dollar and I would add to the list something that the Economic Council has left off. I do not understand why they left it off, but it is the preservation of private decentralized decision-making in the economy. While that may make my trade union friend here wince a bit, as soon as I say that collective bargaining is an integral part of this private decentralized decision-making system that we have in the economy, the trade union people usually come with me a considerable way. This is a goal which we should add very explicitly to the list of economic goals that we have in this country. Because, in trying to decide policy, we will see that this soon comes into conflict with many of the other objectives that we try to achieve.

The government's policy as it concerns technological change is really tied to broader policies. Central to this is the area of monetary and fiscal policies. It is much easier to cope with technological change involving worker displacement in a situation of relatively full employment than it is in a situation with 7 or 8 per cent of the people unemployed. The whole debate on automation has diminished significantly not because there is less automation or less technological change but because of less unemployment. The other areas of government policy involve things like unemployment insurance, which is an economy-wide policy aimed at coping with the displacement of labour. At the local level, at the level of the firm or the industry or the community, governments have begun to evolve new kinds of policies. One of these is industrial location policy and there was some discussion of that this morning — Brandon versus Winnipeg versus Toronto. The other is the whole area of manpower policies. The government is interested in doing something about displacement and it is doing it partly through the traditional tools of monetary and fiscal policy and partly through the evolution of new kinds of policies on industrial location and manpower.

There have been experiments through collective bargaining and I am going to highlight briefly some of the results of recent research that I have been doing for the task force on collective bargaining and technological change. We have looked at the more interesting experiments in adjusting to technological change. Focusing on about 20 contracts which we think illustrate the most advanced ways of attempting to cope with technological change. What I have tried to do in that part of the study is to examine two things: First, I looked at the kind of contractual provisions that have been made to cope with technological change. Second, I examined the sort of industry or union that negotiated these provisions to see if I could make any connection, between a certain kind of union, industry, or economic environment which was conducive to negotiating one kind of provision but not conducive to negotiation of another.

Some of the provisions we looked at are worth describing. First, was the provision for advanced notice and consultation. Second, were ways of avoiding lay-offs. We subdivided attrition into natural attrition and induced attrition by which I mean early retirement, and retraining at company expense or at the employee's expense. We looked at transfers, with allowances and without allowances. We looked at downgrading and the role of seniority if people had to be downgraded. We looked at work-spreading provisions — shorter hours, longer vacations and so forth. We looked at income maintenance programs, severance pay, S.U.B., productivity-sharing agreements, joint committees and the establishment of funds specifically designed to deal with technological change.

On the environmental side, we looked at the environment of an industry and its product market to see whether the industry that had negotiated this kind of agreement was competitive or monopolistic. We looked at the labour market to find out the firm's position in the market; whether it was in a company-dominated community or a diversified community. We looked at employment conditions. Was employment expanding or contracting at the time this contractual provision was made? We looked at the number of employers involved. Was it a multi-employer agreement, or a single employer? We looked at the union situation. Was it one or many, craft or industrial unions? We looked at the labour force, the age of the workers, and their number. Was it a big plant or a small plant? I must emphasize that we dealt with only 20 cases. And some cases we did not cover in depth. We did not have the budget or time to permit us to travel around the continent and examine these 20 situations in great depth. Generalizations are hazardous at best and yet some things I think have already come out.

First of all, there is the area of advance notice. This provision usually includes a specific allowance of "x" days' or "x" months' notice before change. We excluded agreements calling for continuous consultation between labour and management. Those are dealt with elsewhere. Advance notice is a formal procedure and it is not surprising that it is found in all kinds of environments, with big companies and small companies, big unions and small unions, craft and industrial. It is not unique to any particular context and there is no reason really to expect that it should be.

The area of avoiding lay-off, the use of attrition, and so on, that I talked about earlier, and the use of downgrading through seniority, are found more widely in an environment of contracting employment than one of expansion. You seldom find these kinds of clauses emphasized in a community where employment is expanding. You almost invariably find them emphasized in a community where employment is contracting.

This leads me to say that the employment environment is extremely critical in determining whether people see this as a problem or not in the first place. If you have expanding employment then people are seldom concerned with negotiating these kinds of clauses. Where you have contracting employment in a community then this becomes a very central issue and it tends to get into the agreement. The technique of attrition and retraining is more feasible for the firm if it is dealing with small numbers of workers. And attrition can assume even greater pre-eminence if the labour force is relatively old. It is seldom that attrition is used with a young labour force. Attrition is more widely used when there is one industrial union dealing with a small and older work force, than when you have many unions. In an expanding employment context, provisions to avoid lay-off are less necessary, and it is usually the fact that they are not used in this kind of environment.

The number of employees does not seem to be a particularly significant factor in the area of transfer without allowances. The degree of employer domination within the market has little impact although these provisions do seem to be more widely used in markets where the company is the dominant employer. The technique of transfer without allowance is little used unless the labour market is diversified, and the overall employment picture is characterized by rising labour demands. There is no point in having a clause which allows for transfer of employees unless there is rising labour demand which offers opportunity for transfer.

Retraining is rarely undertaken other than at company expense and this did interest me. It is very rare that you have any kind of retraining agreement that involves any obligation on the part of the union or the employees to share in the retraining costs. The employee only pays for retraining after he is fired. Then he will pay the whole shot. Otherwise, if he is still employed, the agreement usually says that retraining is completely at company expense. It is more feasible when you are dealing with only one plant and there is greater impetus for its use when alternative employment opportunities are contracting. If people have other jobs that they can readily turn to, you do not find retraining provisions. If other jobs are scarce, then I think out of desperation the union usually asks for a retraining provision and, of course, at the end of the retraining it does not guarantee that there is anywhere for the displaced retrained workers to go.

Transfers are more easily undertaken with an allowance when the company dominates the labour market or in cases where employment is contracting or in cases of agreements covering many plants with many unions. Also, wider seniority systems and wider scope for collective bargaining permit you to experiment with this kind of thing. But a craft union, organized in a small one plant operation, has nowhere to transfer people and so the degree to which you can use this sort of provision is extremely limited. Our unions tend to be highly segmented, very small relative to American unions and therefore I think this sets up an inflexible framework for coping with these problems.

Workspreading devices appear to be the most rarely used of the contractual techniques uncovered in these cases. Only four plans used this approach and they are all basically similar. They were used in multi-plant operations in a diversified expanding environment with most of the labour force in a single union. These were in big oligopolistic industries with strong unions that were able to push for this technique. Income maintenance benefits, and by this I mean things like supplementary unemployment benefits, and so on, tended to go hand-in-hand in the large industrial union's operations in an overall context of expanding employment in a diversified labour market. The other provisions, severance pay, preferential hiring, and so on, tended to occur where the union was weak. So a strong union gets supplementary unemployment benefits while a weak union may get severance pay. The union is more likely to be craft in nature for something like severance pay and it is likely that the labour force will be relatively small. Productivity sharing was only employed in three plants. None of these was a multi-employer operations. All of them were single employers and generally had a small labour force organized in one union.

The joint committee can be more easily established as labour demand is expanding and if there is one employer operating in one plant. If you are dealing, in other words, not with industry bargaining but bargaining with a single employer and a single plant, it is easier to get a joint committee going. The establishment of a fund occurred in ten out of the twenty plans considered. There did not seem to be any particular environment that was conducive or not conducive.

Overall it would appear that the degree of competition has little influence in determining the approach that the parties will take. The direction in which employment opportunities are moving and the magnitude of the change that is taking place in employment opportunities appears to be significantly more important. In some cases, the degree of employer domination in the labour market also appeared to be significant. The age and size of the labour force have relevance for certain specific approaches although, for many techniques, they are of little importance.

I did not uncover any outstanding innovations through the process of collective bargaining. Partly this may be my definition of outstanding innovations. Perhaps I take a too limiting an approach to what I could consider to be a great innovation. But thus far I have not found any cases or many cases where firms and unions have sat down and really made a major break-through in coping with technological change through collective bargaining. I wonder if this is really surprising. The question I raise with you is should we really expect collective bargaining to resolve this kind of problem. To what extent can we expect management to accept the notion that labour is a fixed cost rather than a variable cost? Labour is a very flexible factor in the productive process. Unions for obvious reasons have argued that labour should have somewhat greater security in the employment relationship, that the worker has in fact a right to his job in some sense. To what extent will management agree to the notion that labour should become fixed and paid for whether it is utilized or not utilized, with something like a real guaranteed wage?

Secondly, to what extent can management and unions bargain for benefits which involve workers who will no longer be members of that firm or even members of that union? This is what a lot of the bargaining is going to be about. It will be about retraining or relocating people into some other plant, some other industry, some other locality, and some other union jurisdiction. To what extent can we expect management and labour to be seriously concerned about those who are displaced?

This morning we heard some discussion about the extent to which we can expect Manitoba to pick up the training costs for people who end up going to Ontario. There is a reluctance for any group to pick up the tab for people who will no longer belong to that particular community, whether it be a city, a province, a trade union, or a firm. I think that there the answer is that when they recognize that these people are no longer going to be in the jurisdiction of the firm or union, they are going to be much more concerned with those who remain in the union's jurisdiction or the firm's employ than with those who are about to leave.

Thirdly, how successful can collective bargaining, oriented to the very local level of the firm or the locality, be in coping with the problem that involves things like labour market forecasts? Forecasting involves not just the labour requirements of this firm because the labour requirements of this firm presumably are going down. The issue is what kind of training do you give displaced workers, or what kind of relocation do you arrange for them. To what extent can you expect a firm or an industry in one place to decide what is likely to happen to its workers after they are retrained? To ask them to engage in retraining them is really to ask them to decide what kind of training to give. Therefore, you must know what sort of events are going to occur outside the jurisdiction of the firm or the union. I suggest that no union and no company that I know of are equipped today to really go out and do this kind of study.

The evidence indicates that public policy on aggregate demand — monetary and fiscal policies and so on — per se resolves many of the adjustment problems and that it determines the degree of success or failure of collective bargaining attempts. Worker displacement occurs at the level of the firm or the industry, but the degree to which it generates adjustment problems is a function of what is going on in the total society of which that firm, industry, trade union or locality is a relatively small part. Collective bargaining, in my opinion, cannot and should not push too far in the direction of attempting to cope with these kinds of problems. We run the risk of over-taxing and destroying a valuable institution by pushing collective bargaining too far in this direction. Society is beginning to remove from collective bargaining the responsibility for these things. Medicare will replace union-bargained health plans. A better pension system at the federal level will diminish the demands and the emphasis on pension bargaining at the local level. I do not say the only reason this has been done is because collective bargaining has run out of steam. I say that collective bargaining perhaps has been saved by the fact that the state has moved in increasingly to take these things out of collective bargaining and let collective bargaining function in those areas where I think it is best designed to function.

My guess is that, if we were to insist that collective bargaining cope with problems of adjustment to technological change, we might destroy the very institution of collective bargaining. This is not to say that collective bargaining has no role in the area. Collective bargaining can, should, and does supplement government policies. We must remember the limited but important role of collective bargaining in this area. Overall government policies are designed for the average. The fact is that most of us in most situations deviate from the average and what collective bargaining can do is supplement or adapt "average" policies to the particular, peculiar needs of a given situation. Again I go back to my analogy with pensions and health plans. I think there is still room for these things; but now as minor supplements or adaptations of a national program rather than as the only way of coping with them. Similarly, in the area of adapting to change, I would argue there is room for collective bargaining, but primarily as a supplement, as a way of adapting national policies to particular situations.

The fact that employers can in most cases provide the opportunity for lots of advance notice and discussion does give us some basis for optimism. There is usually time to talk before technological change hits. But I think that an employer will not agree to utilize this period of time to provide the trade union with the discussion time that a union will demand unless the employer is assured that the discussion will not ultimately result in raising his costs. In other words, if an employer knew a year ahead of time that change was going to take place, and if I were a consultant to this employer in today's environment, I would say to him: "Don't say a word to anybody. Get the new machine all lined up, and then just make an announcement over the loud speaker or in a little yellow slip in the pay cheque that next Monday morning the new machine is coming in, 300 people are laid off, and let them fight you then. Because if you talk now, it's going to cost you a lot more money."

As long as the employer feels that there is a bargaining disadvantage in announcing this earlier, he is not going to do it. If the employer is assured that the discussion will merely be designed to find ways of utilizing instruments that the public has devised, and that this discussion itself will not lead to a bargaining disadvantage for him, then the incentive for the employer to come up and begin talking earlier in the game I think will be enhanced greatly. The fact that collective bargaining can unduly penalize existing firms to the benefit of new entrants to the industry and to the benefit of foreign competition, I have mentioned earlier. If we do not watch this, then the attempt to cope with this through collective bargaining can be discriminatory. It can serve to retard innovation. It can serve to retard economic growth and it can hit areas that have old and obsolete plants that want to make the kinds of changes that were discussed this morning and may be unable to do it, whereas other areas will simply go ahead and develop new competing plants without the cost of adapting to change.

Labour, management and local communities have a very narrow perspective on the problems of adjustment. Should management get very heavily into the business of education and training? Management focuses on the kind of training that will suit a man for its particular company and the union's focus is on that kind of training that will keep a man a member of that union. A community's horizon is what kind of training will suit people for industry in the area. It raises serious doubts about the new community colleges that John Dunlop praised so highly. The tendency across this country, in these community colleges, is to have advisory boards from labour and management — the worst place they could get them. They will be training people for jobs in these communities which are low-paying (that is why there are shortages) and which probably will disappear in eight to ten years in many cases and these people will move to other communities for which they will be terribly ill-suited. So the horizon of labour, management and local community officials is narrow, is parochial, as it should be, as you would expect it to be and this is not the ideal place for training or decisions on training to be made.

I have reservations on government policy in this area because that, it seems to me, involves two things. One is what we have called cost-benefit analysis in economics. This involves weighing five or six policies one against the other to see which one gives the greatest payoff and I think the government could profit greatly from this. Industry intuitively has done this for generations in deciding whether to make this product or that product. You take a look at what each of them will cost. You take a look at what you can sell them for. You decide which will give you the greatest profit. The government does not operate that way in general. The government simply moves in because there is a desire to push a certain kind of program and it is never weighed or very rarely weighed against alternative programs. It seems to me that one thing that the Department of Manpower failed to do was to examine the alternative ways of handling manpower problems and decide which would give the best payoff.

The second thing I think that damns manpower policies is that manpower policies are usually cited as adjusting supply to demand changes. That is what I have heard anyway. If the demand for some kind of workers goes up the idea is to simply train more for that area and if the demand for some kinds of workers in another location goes up to move them into that area. I do not have the time to develop this now, but I think that we deceive ourselves. Generally speaking, in attempting to adapt supply, we also influence the nature of demand, and if manpower policies continue to grow the way they have been growing, we are going to find the state involved in determining not only where workers work, but what gets produced, and how it gets produced.

I see a role for collective bargaining. I see a role for government action. Yet I see real dangers in each case as well. And so in the area of what collective bargaining should do or what the government should do, I am ambivalent. I am in the position of a parent who believes in sex education but does not want to see his daughter at the top of the class. I will leave it at that.

4. The Grievance Procedure

THE GRIEVANCE PROCEDURE

John T. Dunlop and James J. Healy

The authors describe the characteristics and the problems of the grievance procedure. It may serve many diverse purposes.

The grievance procedure may serve many diverse purposes in a collective bargaining relationship, depending upon the language of the agreement and the intention of both parties.

1. The grievance procedure may be used to locate problem situations in the relations between a union and management and to discern difficulties within both organizations. From this vantage point, the explicit grievance is not to be taken at its face value. The real problem may be a foreman or a shop steward. It may be evident that subordinates are not receiving proper instructions. The grievance is seen as a symbol of some maladjustment, and the skillful representative of the union or management will seek out the real and submerged difficulties.

So also in the complaints of single employees there may be little overt basis for the grievance; but the real difficulty may be a health condition, or a family situation, or a longstanding personality problem. . . . In a day when more than more than 60 per cent of the visits to the doctors' offices of the country are found to have a psychic rather than a purely physical basis, it should not be surprising that a large proportion of grievances of individual employees should also have their roots in psychic difficulties. . . .

* Reprinted with permission from John T. Dunlop and James J. Healy, *Collective Bargaining: Principles and Cases*, (rev. ed., Homewood, Ill.: Richard D. Irwin, 1955), pp. 78-81.

There is no question . . . that the grievance procedure can be made to serve the function of discovering problem situations, both of individuals and of parts of the organization, when the grievance is approached as a symbol of some maladjustment.

2. The grievance procedure may be utilized by both organizations as a device by which information is channeled both ways between the top and the bottom of the hierarchy. In language that has become popular, the grievance procedure is a channel of communication. The top-management officers and the union leaders who follow carefully the status of grievances are frequently able to keep in touch with developments at the level of the individual worker. New problems are rapidly reflected in the grievance procedure.

As a channel of information, the grievance procedure is likely to be more reliable than most chains of command in a hierarchy, since both the union and management (steward and foreman or plant manager and business agent) are aware that the grievance may go a step higher or even to arbitration. Any statement they make will be subject to check by the other side before a superior officer. In this way the grievance procedure as a channel of information may be expected to be less subject to self-serving statements of fact than most chains of command within an organization.

3. The explicit purpose of the grievance procedure is to interpret the provisions of the agreement, to apply the contract to the new and changing aspects of everyday relations between a union and a management. This procedure must translate the necessarily general language of a contract into particular decisions in specific cases. It will also be used to achieve uniformity of interpretation in various units of management and divisions of the union.

The grievance procedure is related to the periodic negotiations of a new agreement in at least three ways. First, the general policies and language agreed upon in contract negotiations as has been noted, are applied through this procedure. In this sense the grievance procedure is sometimes referred to as "collective bargaining." Second, the contract negotiations may re-examine and alter interpretations established by the grievance procedure. One side or the other may request a reconsideration of the whole problem in the light of experience. Third, the grievance procedure discovers and records many problems which one side or the other may wish to raise at the next contract negotiations period.

4. The contract language of some grievance procedures is so broad as to permit the raising of any problem or difficulty that may arise. The procedure mayy not be limited to contract interpretation. Under the circumstances the whole relationship of the parties may be shaped through the grievance procedure. Each side is committed to discuss and settle any question that may be raised during the contract period. The grievance machinery in these circumstances serves the purpose of

providing an orderly and systematic way in which problems may be studied and decided. . . .

There are undoubtedly a great many ways of classifying the types of grievances that arise. It may be helpful to consider grievances in their relation to the contract and to the two organizations, as follows: (1) Some grievances involve a conflict between two or more sections of the agreement. The union will point to one clause, and the company will refer to another. The problem may involve a reconciliation or clarification of conflicting sections of the agreement. (2) The contract may be silent on the specific problem. The issue may clearly involve a subject treated in the agreement: in this sense the grievance is within the scope of the agreement. The problem in such a grievance is to fill in the gap in the agreement. (3) The grievance may raise the question of the applicability of a general rule to a particular case. (4) Some grievances present exceptional circumstances, the type of situation no general rule or regulation can be formulated to handle. (5) At times a grievance presents no contract problems but arises as a device to "save face" for one side or the other. A union or management representative may find it expedient to pass along a grievance rather than to make an obvious settlement. . . .

QUESTIONS FOR DISCUSSION, PART 3

(1) Bargaining is an art, not a science. Discuss this statement. What are the main objectives of a successful negotiation process?

(2) It is said by some authorities that emotions must be kept out of the collective bargaining process. Do you agree with this statement? Why, or why not? Explain.

(3) Monat discusses three models for determination of bargaining power: compare these three models and point out strengths and weaknesses of each model. Can we say that in all cases a decrease in the power of one party to a bargaining relationship automatically leads to an increase in the power of the other party? Why, or why not?

(4) What are the practical problems of outright application of legislation pertaining to collective bargaining in the private sector in Canada to the employees in municipal government?

(5) Major technological changes are about to be implemented in your plant. By means of a role-playing situation, negotiate its implementation. Roles: General Manager, Union Leader and Worker.

(6) Why are the unions so concerned with union security and subcontracting? Are such issues likely to become more or less important in the future? Why?

(7) Union has argued that contracting out any existing services or products before the date of termination of collective agreement is

a breach of contract. However, management has claimed that is inherent right to contract out in good faith, to increase the efficiency of the operation, can only be limited by express stipulation in the agreement; and in the absence of any such limitation management has the right to contract out the whole operation. Discuss the pros and cons of these arguments.

(8) Unions and their members have attempted to increase their job security, through (a) seniority, (b) regulations with respect to the introduction of technological changes, (c) shorter hours with no cut in pay. Do you believe such measures promote or retard job security? Give examples to support your arguments.

(9) What are the main classifications of grievances?

(10) The grievance procedure is frequently considered to be a process distinct from the process of collective bargaining. Is this distinction justifiable or not? Give reasons.

(11) What are the different types of parity? Discuss the factors which influence wage parity.

PART 4

UNION – MANAGEMENT CONFLICT AND ITS RESOLUTION

INTRODUCTION

Strikes, lockouts and outbreaks of violence are the most visible forms of industrial conflict. The general public deplores them because of the economic loss and inconvenience they cause. Yet strikes and lockouts or the threat of such conflicts are means of stimulating collective bargaining and inducing the parties to reach agreement. Collective bargaining is an adversary system in which both parties have divergent goals with respect to the division of the economic pie. How much consideration should be given to production costs and profits as against direct human satisfaction of working people? Kornhauser, Dubin and Ross in the introduction to their book *Industrial Conflict* state that conflict regarding the relative weight assigned to these factors is seen not only in union-management disputes over economic matters, but also in the personal dissatisfactions of individual workers over job assignments, safety of working conditions, supervisory attitudes, opportunities for participation and self-expression[1]. Conflict often arises when workers feel that they are being unjustly treated or when they find work tedious and, dehumanizing, and feel that their legitimate aspirations are being thwarted. The unions share some responsibility in not correcting this situation. For example, in 1973 the United Automobile Workers, in its list of bargaining goals, assigned "job enrichment and teamwork," which are intended to alleviate boredom and job alienation, as among its lowest priorities.

Labour unrest and industrial conflict can be expressed in a variety of ways. Organized restriction of output, slowdown, rotating strikes, study sessions, boycotts, featherbedding and the complete stoppage of work are the weapons employed by organized labour in union – management conflict. Management's tactics, such as: autocratic supervision; overstrict discipline and penalties; discriminatory firing; layoff; demotions; unofficial speedups; unilateral changes of work standard; piece rates; changes and innovations in technology, product and procedures without prior consultation with unions; removal of plants; and lockouts often result in conflict and even violence.

The fact that Canada has deliberately opted for a system where conflicts plays an important role in industrial relations does not mean that other avenues of resolving labour – management differences should not be fully explored. Public dissatisfaction over strikes has generated demands for generalized compulsory arbitration. Generally speaking, in the private sector both union and management in North America have rejected compulsory arbitration for the settlement of interest disputes for a variety of reasons. Experience in North America and abroad seems to indicate that compulsory arbitration tends to undermine the willingness of the parties to bargain conscientiously over their differences. Parties either prefer to pass this responsibility on to the arbitration tribunal or they fear that any compromise they may make initially will cause the arbitrator to reach a compromise settlement less favourable to their own interest. Compulsory arbitration also affects the willingness of union and management leaders to explain, defend and implement the decision of the arbitration tribunal. An unpopular decision by the tribunal may give rise to resentment among workers, and they may refuse to implement the award. Clarification, interpretation and implementation of such awards may lead to further litigation.

With the examples of the Federal Public Service experience in Canada, and most recently of the steel industry in the U.S.A., of settling interest disputes by voluntary arbitration, it may be wise to try this idea in other industries and sectors. It has the advantage of flexibility and adaptability.

The readings in this part bring together the scholarly thinking of academics and practitioners representing a variety of approaches in dealing with the problems of industrial conflict. The search for causes and solutions of such problems should encompass broad socio-psychological and political factors rather than be limited exclusively to economic considerations.

The high incidence of strikes and labour unrest in Canada in the 1960's, and their characteristics, are analyzed in the context of broad socio-psychological forces, peculiar to our times, by Crispo and Arthurs. Megginson and Gullett develop a model of union – management conflict and isolate the variables which influence the degree of union – management conflict in a given situation. In recent years behaviorial science concepts and theories have been increasingly applied to resolving industrial conflicts. A detailed case study by Blake, Mouton and Sloma of a union – management intergroup laboratory shows how groups in conflict have worked effectively after they have dealt with tensions and frictions that have accumulated over an extended period of time.

The next three articles present the views of representatives of organized labour, management and academics on the causes and possible solutions of industrial conflict. These spokesmen discuss the pros and cons of the various proposals, in recent years, for resolving industrial strife. The last article by Jain puts into perspective the role of education in creating a stable industrial relations climate.

FOOTNOTE

[1] See Kornhauser, Dubin and Ross, *Industrial Conflict*, Ch. 1, "Problems and Viewpoints; pp. 3-22, McGraw-Hill, 1954.

DIAGNOSING INDUSTRIAL UNREST*

John H. G. Crispo and Harry W. Arthurs

Dr. John Crispo, Director, Centre for Industrial Relations, University of Toronto, and Professor Harry W. Arthurs of the Osgoode Hall Law School, diagnose the recent wave of industrial unrest in Canada. The authors believe that much of the unrest is characterized by union militancy and rank and file restlessness. They analyze in depth the legal framework within which collective bargaining and trade unionism function and the conflicting strains within the law which contribute to the labour unrest.

Labour – Management conflict seems to be the unavoidable by-product of industrialization in a free society. It would be naive to suggest that law and order would ever have the undivided respect of labour and management, if only because historically the trade union movement feels that it could not have secured many of its present rights without deliberately defying legal restraints placed upon it. But if the present difficulties are merely part of the price of prosperity, then this feature in itself is disturbing, for it suggests that a free society could not maintain a period of sustained economic advance without engendering serious industrial unrest.

To the extent that this unrest can only be relieved by round after round of generous settlements, the problem of maintaining price stability during a period of full employment can be aggravated. Thus it can be made increasingly difficult to achieve these two goals, let alone our other economic objectives at one and the same time.

Although collective bargaining might sometimes appear to result in a desperate and never-ending succession of crises, it is an essential part of industrial organization in a free society, and trade unionism is an indispensable participant in the collective bargaining process.

There are diverse, conflicting strains within the law. The older policy favours protection of entrepreneural activity against union interference, and the newer policy favours protection of collective bargaining against employer hostility. Since collective bargaining statutes accept, as legitimate, occasional "disorders" that the common law condemns, and since the quality of the bargain struck under the two systems is likely to be very different, labour and management have each acquired a vested interest in preserving and expanding those laws that reinforce their power position. Labour relations law, then, has become as much a tool of contending groups as an expression of social consensus.

* John H. G. Crispo and H. W. Arthurs, excerpts from their paper "Industrial Unrest in Canada: A Diagnosis of Recent Experience," prepared for a joint meeting of the Canadian Political Science and Canadian Law Teachers Association, The Labour Gazette (Oct. 1967), p. 624-5. Reprinted with permission.

Lawyers skilled in the use of legal techniques frequently win critical battles before boards and courts, leaving behind a residue of resentment. But lawyers could, and increasingly do, operate in a constructive and creative way. Through skill at negotiation, ability to resolve conflict by constructive compromises, and instinct for reasoned, rather than arbitrary solutions, lawyers can contribute much to good labour relations.

Six specific features of unrest are:

□ the unseating of long-time union leaders;
□ the failure to ratify collective agreements;
□ wildcat strikes;
□ inter-union raiding and breakaway movements;
□ union breakthroughs in new sectors of the economy; and
□ lost time due to strikes.

The reasons for rank and file militancy, are that society had institutionalized the business of creating discontent by having developed a whole new profession whose members might be described as "merchants of discontent." We are not implying that acquisitive instincts would disappear if not constantly bombarded by hidden and not-so-hidden persuaders. We merely point out that middle-class mores have been accepted by the organized worker . . . and that middle-class purchasing power is his immediate objective in collective bargaining. Related to this first point is the role of inflation and the rising cost of living. Once the cost of living starts to rise, the scramble for more intensifies, because it then takes more in money terms just to hold one's own in real terms. Although inflation and the rising cost of living explained much of the unrest among workers today, they are not the underlying causes; they are merely symptoms or aggravating factors that reflect general disagreement about the distribution of economic fruits. This lack of consensus, rather than inflation and the rising cost of living, is surely a more fundamental cause of difficulty. A third facet explaining "rank and file militancy" is the public's false impression of "the abnormally high level" of settlements made through government intervention — an impression aggravated by faulty reporting in the mass media as to the exact nature of the settlements. The essential point is that although government intervention might have been unavoidable, the results encouraged a wide variety of groups to adopt extravagant bargaining demands in the hope of benefiting from benevolent government intervention. Job security is another issue. The fear haunting many workers is not that of losing jobs through automation or the new technology, but having to cope with adjustment, even though it might not involve external displacement. Older and less educated workers, in particular, favour the status quo because they are constantly being reminded of their own disadvantages in an age of rising skill requirements. Many of these workers are demanding protection from their unions.

Management secretiveness also generates job insecurity. An employer's sudden unilateral action affecting employees can breed discontent, add to their anxiety, and thereby induce them to pressure their unions to win job security safeguards. When a new machine is introduced, which requires the performance of a new range of duties, the company will unilaterally fix the rates for those duties. There is nothing in the agreement that is violated by this action; probably the agreement specifically preserves management's rights to decide upon the processes and machines to be used. Consequently the union is powerless to stop this erosion of its hard-won structure. Canadian boards have yet to adopt even the minimal requirement that an employer bargain with the union over the possible effects of technological change in an effort to minimize worker dislocation. The majority of Canadian arbitrators support the "residual rights" theory that reserves to management all of the rights it enjoyed before the advent of collective bargaining, with the exception of those that are specifically surrendered in the precise language of the collective agreement — among them, the right to make technological and corporate changes, and to establish new wage scales for new jobs. In our view, this doctrine . . . has lessened the value of the arbitration process as an administrative safety valve, and has reduced the workers' faith in it. Suffice it to say that, while the prevailing practice may seem to be sound conventional legal doctrine, and to favour management, it may for those very reasons be an important factor in aggravating worker restiveness. Workers might try to win by an unlawful strike what they could not achieve through legal remedies. And a doctrine that tends to induce workers to revert to the law of the jungle is hardly in the interests of either management, labour or the public. Both sides have learned that arbitrators give a great deal of weight to past practice, at lease in the event of ambiguity in the language of the agreement. To protect its interests, and to guard against setting precedents that could prove harmful in arbitration, management has frequently stripped its first-line supervisors of the power to make any significant contract interpretations lest they concede something they should not. And under these circumstances, it doesn't take long for the union steward and ultimately the union members to discover that no one around them has the power to settle their grievances.

In large organizations, the delays that are inherent in more centralized handling of such problems can easily lead to a frustrating accumulation of unresolved issues. Both grievors awaiting an answer to their complaint and supervisors humiliated by the need to confess their lack of effective authority are thus subjected to unnecessary tension. Newly organized groups of workers possessed of unrealistic expectations about the potential of concerted action to solve their problems, can produce an unhealthy combination of naiveté and strike-happiness. Further complicating the situation is the tendency to sign two-, three-, or even four-year agreements. Many unforeseen issues could accumulate during the life of the agreement and make if difficult to satisfy the pent-up demands of members in the next round of negotiations.

Internal factors within the labour movement are other causes of unrest, such as the lack of communication between leadership and membership, the widening conflict of interest between skilled and unskilled workers, job dissatisfaction, inter-union rivalry, and ambitious "young turks" eager aspirants to full-time union office. Then there is the conflict between generations; younger workers want more in their pay cheques, and older workers favour increased pension plans and other fringe benefits. There are also young members who regard the possibility of a strike "as something of a lark." The average level of education in the labour force is steadily increasing. This produces high expectations, both in a material and in a job-satisfaction sense, and makes workers aware of their enhanced bargaining power in a period of prosperity. Increased educational opportunities might also divert intelligent and capable members of the work force away from the factory into "white collar" occupations, thus diluting the indigenous stock of potential leaders. Where, a generation ago, union office might be one of the few outlets for a bright youngster who was obliged to leave school prematurely . . . today's educational opportunities equip such persons for many other roles.

One of the most obvious reasons for the continuing militancy among union members is that it pays off. In numerous recent cases . . . workers have discovered that after they have turned down a company offer, their leaders are able to extract further concessions. The temptation to use this ploy regularly is irresistible. Even union leaders themselves have been embarrassed by the availability of alternative employment during a strike. On occasion, workers have refused a substantial increase because they were under no real pressure to see the end of the strike. In terms of expediency, it is quite understandable that management should often attempt to buy peace, especially when rank and file militancy is channelled through formal union action. But this policy of appeasement is dangerous when worker resentment is being directed as much against the union as against management.

A PREDICTIVE MODEL OF
UNION – MANAGEMENT CONFLICT*

Leon C. Megginson and C. Ray Gullett

The authors in this paper suggest that an intelligent awareness of both the costs and the gains of increasing or decreasing conflict should be a part of the tool kit of every manager and union representative, and thus provide parameters for those relationships.

We may study intergroup behavior from a number of different approaches. First, we can select the relationships (e.g., the line-staff-relationships) that exist between and among the various major departments within a company. Second, the interactions among groupings at the level of informal intergroup relationships could be investigated to show that the force of the informal work group upon the behavior of an individual affects not only his behavior with respect to the other members of his group, but also his behavior towards members of other groups. Still a third approach to intergroup behavior description would be a look into the internal workings of a union in order to describe intergroup factionalism and power struggles. Fourth, the continuing power struggle between management and labor affords an excellent laboratory for studying cooperation, competition, and conflict.

The purpose of this article is to study the last mentioned phenomenon, that of union-management relationships. The approach followed is a behavioral one which attempts to discover some basic reasons why each side behaves as it does toward the other. The study attempts to deal with the reasons for the degree of conflict which exists between the two groups and how each side can generate intensified or decreased conflict in their relationship. A model is then constructed which can be used as a predictive tool for estimating union – management conflict levels. No ethical value judgments as to the desirability of either increasing or decreasing the level of conflict between the groups are offered.

Although we find many definitions of the word "conflict," Dubin's definition seems most appropriate for this study. He defines conflict as the "actual or threatened use of force in any continuing social relationship. Force is the attempt to override opposition by an act designed to produce injury to the other party."[1] This definition is useful because it stresses action, or the threatened use of action, to override the opponent's wishes in favor of one's own.

---

* Leon C. Megginson and C. Ray Gullett, "A Predictive Model of Union–Management Conflict," in *Personnel Journal*, June 1970; pp. 495-503. Reproduced with permission.

SIMPLIFYING ASSUMPTIONS

It is well known that the more complicated a model of "real world" behavior becomes, the more closely it generally approaches reality. But we also know that the more complicated the model is, the harder it is to be understood itself and the less useful it is as a learning or predictive device. Therefore, we are taking an intermediary approach by making some simplifying assumptions which it is believed do not impair the effectiveness of the predictive model. These simplifying assumptions involve holding a number of variables in the labor – management relationship constant.

OMISSIONS

We begin by ruling out both industrial giants and the very small firms as subjects for our study. Kerr pointed out that the unions — or perhaps management itself — chooses the giant firm with which to do battle over terms of a contract that will set precedents not only for a single industry, but often for other important segments of the national business community.[2] The strategic place the large firm possesses for collective agreement pattern setting thus makes it more susceptible to industrial conflict with the unions with which it deals. Conversely, the very small firm is highly dependent on the patterns set by larger firms as it is in a relatively weak bargaining position, and usually can do little to resist the demands of a large and powerful union.

Secondly, we will assume that production patterns are not highly irregular, but follow a steady flow since a moderately stable production pattern throughout the year typifies most United States industry.

Also omitted from our list of variables is the problem of interunion rivalry. Given the fact that there are other unions attempting to sway the allegiance of the workers from the union in power, there will be a greater degree of conflict generated between management and the union. Kornhauser, Dubin, and Ross found that de facto stabilization of bargaining rights is conductive to more peaceful union – management relations, while interunion rivalry has pronounced unsettling effects.[3] As long as most unions in the United States remain members of the AFL-CIO, and as long as this federation is able to accomplish the settlement of jurisdictional disputes and to establish no-raiding agreements between its members, it is believed that this variable can be safely ignored as an important conflictual influence.

Finally, it is assumed that the union and management representatives have had some experience in dealing with each other. Sloane and Witney point out that relationships between management and union leaders tend to be less conflictual as time passes.[4] This assumption is believed to be valid because relatively experienced relationships typify most union – management associations in the United States.

CONFLICTUAL "GIVENS"

In any theoretical framework there are germane factors which must be assumed to be present and accepted as fixed factors. These then become part of the fixed environment for the resulting analysis. There are several such given factors in our analysis.

The first basic "given" is that some degree of intergroup conflict is inherent in every union – management relationship. As Chamberlain points out, "What is involved here is a power struggle, a conflict of relationships which has gone on over the years, perhaps over the centuries."[5] Indeed, it is fair to say that any relationship in which the authority of one individual or group over another is in question occasions some degree of conflict.

Although sweeping generalizations are dangerous, inasmuch as they necessarily are somewhat inaccurate in specific cases, an attempt is made in the following paragraphs to outline some of the factors which contribute to at least some minimum level of conflict between organizations.

DIFFERING GOALS AND VALUE SYSTEMS

One basic difference between the two groups lies in their goals and value systems and the methods used to reach those goals. We stress here the orientation of the groups toward the basic beliefs or values that they possess concerning the reasons why their organization exists, the objectives that they wish to attain in order to uphold these values, and the resultant techniques they employ in order to obtain these objectives.

Management tends to perceive of its task as the effective utilization of the material and human resources of the firm in order to produce a good or service for its customers and hopefully, a profit for the owners of the firm. Thus, the firm's industrial relations must contribute to, or at least not detract from, the over-all efficiency and productivity of the firm. In the view of management, demands and actions of the union often are detrimental to this over-all efficiency. In referring to this fact, Bakke states that "any manager, whatever his philosophy or degree of benovolence will 'get tough' when the productiveness and profitability of his own firm starts going down."[6]

The union tends to view itself as attempting to regulate the decisions of management in those areas of activity which affect the working force. Both legally and in terms of union interest there is no logical limit to the matters over which unions assume they might bargain with employers.

Thus, while management views its responsibilities for the long-term profitability and success of the enterprise as depending upon its freedom of action and maneuverability, union representatives see themselves as checks on this arbitrary and unilateral action necessary to maintain and increase the economic welfare of their members.

No implication is intended here that management is disinterested in the economic welfare of its employees. But management is oriented toward a philosophy which states that flexibility and change are necessary to achieve maximum economic welfare for both the firm and its employees. Further, management's responsibilities are to a number of groups, only one of which is comprised of its employees.

We have shown that differences in values, goals to be achieved, and the methods to achieve the goals exist between these two groups. Conflict is thus likely to arise because both these organizations try to achieve the differing objectives through the same medium; namely the business, the firm, the corporation. Or, in alternate phraseology, we may say that there is a competition between interested parties for the scarce resources of the firm.

QUASI-POLITICAL NATURE OF THE UNION

A second reason why some degree of hostility is a necessary "given" in these intergroup relations is the nature of union organizations themselves and the way in which solidarity within them must be built and maintained. Union organizations are not economic entities in the same sense as business organizations; instead they could better be described as a "movement." Although it can be argued with some effectiveness that unions today are not the evangelical organizations they were in the 1930's [7] the nature of unions is still basically the same: They are quasi-political organizations which must promote solidarity within their ranks in order to be effective. [8]

But what does this need to build solidarity within the union's membership have to do with intergroup conflict? Psychologists and sociologists have found through research — and union leaders would agree — that one important way to generate unanimity within the ranks of the union is to focus attention on the "unfair" and "unjust" behavior of some outside force — usually management — toward the members. For example, one research project found that heightened in-group solidarity and cooperativeness was observed at the very time when intergroup hostility was at its peak, that is, during the period when the groups asserted emphatically that they would not have anything more to do with each other. [9]

If management is acting in ways considered unjust by its employees, union leaders will likely use those actions to generate zeal within the ranks of employees for the union and its demands. But it is also true that in order to achieve and maintain in-group solidarity, it may be necessary for union leadership to look for issues where perhaps no serious ones currently exist in the minds of the workers. It may be necessary to create a degree of worker dissatisfaction with current managerial actions. [10]

While this quasi-political nature of unions and the need to promote in-group solidarity by common resistance against and out-group will vary with circumstance and with specific unions and managements, it must be accepted as a "given" in the union – management relationship.

STATUS OF THE GROUP'S REPRESENTATIVES

A closely related reason for some given level of conflict between the two groups involves the position of the representatives of each group. Since each side's representative faces a certain degree of pressure from those he represents, it is not in the representative's best interest to be too cooperative with the other side. Cooperation may be looked upon as the equivalent of capitulation which results in the representative losing both his status and his position with the group he represents.

The results of this in-group orientation are that completely cooperative associations are virtually impossible.

VARIABLES INFLUENCING THE DEGREE OF UNION – MANAGEMENT CONFLICT

In addition to the basic assumptions made and the conflictual givens, there are variable factors which influence the union — management relationship.

The relationships that have existed in the past between the two organizations can strongly color the degree of cooperation and conflict that is present in an existing industrial relations situation. The often bloody and conflictual relationships of the 1930's left scars on participants from both sides which often faded only as the individuals who participated in them passed from the scene and were replaced by others who did not personally experience those conflicts.

An example of such conflict is the famous "Battle of the Overpass" in 1937 in which Walter Reuther and a group of unionists did battle with company guards at an overpass between buildings at the Ford Motor Company's River Rouge Plant. That bloody struggle, in which 16 union leaders (indluding 6 women) were badly beaten, eventually led to the unionization of Ford.[11]

The significance of events such as these to present relationships can be expressed in terms of the attitudes they create in the minds of the other side and the tendency of these attitudes to remain fixed or at least change much more slowly than objective events do. One result of this tendency to relate to the past is that a management and union with a history of high conflict are more likely to remain hostile to one another even when some of the bases of this conflict no longer exist. It can also be concluded that conscious effort by either side to emphasize or deemphasize past relationships which were conflictual can have strong effects upon the level of conflict between the groups.

PERCEIVED LEGITIMACY OF EACH SIDE FOR THE OTHER

A significant factor which will contribute to the extent of intergroup hostility or cooperation that exists between management and labor is the degree to which each side views the other as "legitimate" as to its ends and means. This legitimacy involves recognition of the organization by those with whom it deals. It is based upon not only the acceptance of its point of view but of its right to a point of view, as well as its privilege of functioning and of its methods of operation.[12]

If the company is determined to deal with the union only to the extent imposed by law and by the power of the union itself, the degree of hostility between the two groups can be predicted as great. Management may view its dealings with the union as only a temporary phenomenon and, therefore, do everything possible to destroy the union itself. It inevitably follows that the sentiments and action of either party along these lines will generate combative reactions in the other which will result in increased intergroup hostility and anxiety. Walton and McKersie state that management and labor's dislike "for each other frequently assumes irrational proportions. Because of the prospect of irrational and extreme behavior, the relationship is marked by considerable anxiety."[13]

The relationship between the Kohler Company and the United Auto Workers Union exemplifies this truth, for although the firm is now unionized, apparently neither considers the position of the other as "legitimate," so the relationship would be classified as conflictual.[14]

Management is often not alone in viewing the interests of the opposing group as less than legitimate, for some union leaders are persuaded that the economic and class position of management is in conflict with the best interests of the working man.

It should be remembered that there is not a dichotomy existing in the perceived legitimacy of each side toward the other. Acknowledgment of the other's legitimacy might best be depicted as a continuum with many possible shadings of relationships. It is also appropriate to note that these relationships can, and probably do, change over time and can certainly move in either direction.

PERSONALITY FACTORS OF KEY LEADERS

Key leaders on both sides, including those who influence and take part in the collective bargaining process and those who administer the agreement between bargaining sessions have an important effect upon the relationship that their groups have with one another. The fact that personality plays a role in the determination of intergroup relationships may be demonstrated by referring to labor patterns adopted by management through the impact of a single individual. The bargaining tactics of General Electric have been designated "Boulwarism" because of the strong influence of Lemuel R. Boulware. From labor's side, John L. Lewis of the United Mineworkers is perhaps a good example of a strong personality's effect upon the union – management relationship. Kuhn predicted that where there is a clash of personalities between those representing each side, "Personal relations are apt to involve bickering and repeated aspersions about motives of sincerity."[15]

If personality factors of the leadership have a strong effect upon group conflict or cooperation, what type of personality attributes encourage trust and friendliness and what sort of personality inhibits this relationship? Walton and McKersie concluded that a person who rates high on authoritarianism, i.e., an individual characterized by conservatism, emotional coldness, power seeking, and hostility toward outgroups, is relatively more likely to initiate a low-trust competitive pattern in labor management relations.[16]

The amount of self esteem of key persons in a labor – management system may influence their responses to challenges in the situation. For example, Titus and Hollander found that ego-involving problems tend to produce rigidity in problem solving for those with an authoritarian personality.[17] Thus, an individual whose personality can be described as authoritarian is more likely to perceive the actions of representatives of the other group as threats and to view their actions as power moves.

In a further attempt to verify the hypothesis that personality factors do influence intergroup behavior, research evidence has indicated that a change of leadership in one of the two groups has often resulted in improved relationships.[18] Thus, either side might consciously attempt to influence its relationships with the other group by placing in positions of frequent contact with the other side individuals who tend to generate cooperative or conflictual relationships.

EMPHASIS ON CONFLICTUAL OR COOPERATIVE ASPECTS OF PROBLEMS

It was shown earlier that one cause of inevitable conflict between the two groups being discussed is each side's pursuit of opposing goals within the framework of the same organization. Thus, the relationship between the two parties tends to be a contest — in some degree — for the scarce resources of the organization.

But many issues contain at least the potential for some degree of mutual accommodation and goal achievement, and the approach of the parties to each other and to the common problems between them can determine the degree to which the issue becomes one of fixed sum relationships, or the gain of one at the expense of the other. While the question of how economic benefits will be distributed between the parties is one of inherent conflict, many questions which might be defined as power oriented problems are capable of mutually satisfying arrangements.

The approach of the parties to their common problems can, therefore, be divided into two extremes along a spectrum of approaches. The two ends of the continuum might be termed (1) a power struggle orientation and (2) a problem solving orientation. In the power struggle approach, the parties see themselves as battling for the upper hand in any dispute and any gains made by the other party as losses incurred by themselves. Those questions, described as "management prerogatives" and "union rights," could best be described as the degree of freedom to act independently of the other party. For the union, rights and authority involve the extent to which the union has a voice in the way management runs the business. While neither side can completely relinquish its views concerning questions of this sort, for there is often a redistribution of power from the settlement of issues in even the most accommodative relationship, the important consideration is the degree to which both sides emphasize the power portion of each issue that comes up.

The problem solving approach, while not ignoring the fact that power redistribution may occur from the decisions made by the parties, does not place primary emphasis on this aspect of the issues at hand. Under this approach the parties attempt to find solutions that will not involve loss for one side over the other, or at least look for solutions that will be of minimum sacrifice to the other. Whether or not mutually accommodative solutions are reached is perhaps not as important as the *desire and willingness* of both sides to reach them. In an atmosphere of mutual accommodation, the power aspects of the problem are deemphasized. As parties move away from the power orientation end of the spectrum, they are likely to find a number of new problems which may hold mutually accommodative potential. We might assume, then, as some issues are found which move the parties away from the power orientation and increase the degree of mutual accommodation, other issues would be perceived by the parties as holding mutually satisfying potential.

SUPERORDINATE GOALS

In his studies of intergroup behavior, Sherif found the most effective measure for reducing intergroup friction was the introduction of a series of superordinate goals. These have "high appeal value for both groups, which cannot be ignored by the groups in question, but whose attainment is beyond the resources and efforts of any one group alond."[19] Finding areas of cooperative endeavor between management and the union is thus believed to be a means of reducing hostility and frustration.

What are some of the problem areas that may contain potential for union – management cooperation? Although no listing of such areas could be either complete or applicable to all relationships, a few examples of specific cooperative endeavors would be helpful in understanding the phenomena.

Historically, the use of profit sharing as a means for stimulating employees to produce more efficiently has been opposed by unions, but in recent years union acceptance has become more prevalent. An indication of this shift is shown by the fact that "The coverage extends to over two million persons — 12 per cent of plant and 22 per cent of office employees — in medium sized and large establishments within all metropolitan areas. . . . In terms of worker coverage, it has doubled in importance over the past decade."[20] The success of the Kaiser Steel-United Steelworkers' sharing plan is an example of a reasonably successful plan for increasing cooperative action of both management and labor. It has resulted in such gains as cost savings, stable company-union relations, and a decrease in incentive grievances.[21]

A second example of cooperative action is the steel industry in which a human-relations committee consisting of both labor and management members has been established. It functions during the life of the contract by studying problems of technological change, revisions or eliminations of incentive methods of pay, changes in seniority districts, and stabilization of employment which cannot readily be confronted and resolved in the normal negotiation period of sixty days.

Bakke has suggested these and other possible areas for mutual accommodation such as:

> cost and waste reduction, safety promotion, technological improvement, atuomation, training programs, the improvement of standards and administration of unemployment insurance, workmen's compensation, health insurance. . . .[22]

EXTERNAL FACTORS AFFECTING CONFLICTUAL LEVEL

The labor-management relationship cannot be considered in isolation. It is affected by the ecology in which it occurs. Although the total cultural *milieu* has an impingement upon the relative position in the power struggle of the two parties, only the most cogent ones will be discussed.

It is relevant in a study of this nature to consider the effects of government activity upon the intergroup relationship. And with a trend toward more governmental control of union – management activities, an attempt should be made to predict the future effects of this trend upon conflict and cooperation between the two parties.

What has been the effect of increasing governmental influence upon the degree of conflict and cooperation between the parties? Although both sides have bitterly contested legislation which would hamper their freedom of action, once the legislation was enacted and upheld in the courts, it removed from controversy issues which formerly resulted in possible dispute. In other words, since neither party could influence the outcome of the issue in a significant way by putting pressure on its opponent, no longer was there conflict over the issue. Conversely, the return of an issue to, or the maintenance of an issue in, the hands of the interacting parties tends to allow at least greater possibility for conflict.

While we are not necessarily advocating increased government control over industrial relations, for this is an ethical value judgment, the very fact that governmental action is somewhat effective in reducing labor – management conflict seems to be influencing public opinion in the direction of additional demands for governmental action with regard to union – management relationships.[23] This action involves not only legislation, but also the "moral suasion" of the government.

In summing up, it might be said that (1) governmental activity in the industrial relations field tends to decrease conflict between the parties and (2) that the success of this activity has generated increasing public pressure for more governmental action.

The likelihood that in the advent of a strike, the firm's customers will take their business to a competitor and not return when the strike is ended will have a strong impact on the extent to which management and the union can tolerate a strike. If it is anticipated that customers not served during a strike will take their trade elsewhere permanently, the cost of strikes will be greatly enhanced and there is more pressure on the parties to maintain peace.

CONFLICTUAL MODEL

This study has attempted to identify and isolate selected variables which influence the degree of union – management conflict. Also, an effort has been made to develop a model which could be used to predict the extent of conflict under modifying assumptions and given factors. Figure 1 is a graphical summation of the significant forces assumed to affect the level of conflict between union and management which have been discussed in this paper.

INTERDEPENDENCE OF CONFLICTUAL VARIABLES

The union-management relationship is assumed to be a system in which each of the factors is interrelated and interacting.[24] Thus, the inclusion of two-directional arrows between the conflictual variables is intended as a means of showing the interrelatedness of, and interaction between, each variable. For example, a change in the perceived legitimacy of one side by the other might affect the parties' approach to problem solving and their emphasis on cooperative or conflictual relationships that have existed in the past. The change might also call for placing in positions of frequent contact with the other side those individuals who tend to generate a greater or lesser amount of conflict with their opposite number. Similar interdependencies can be imagined by manipulating any one of the variables.

FIGURE 1
CONFLICT MODEL

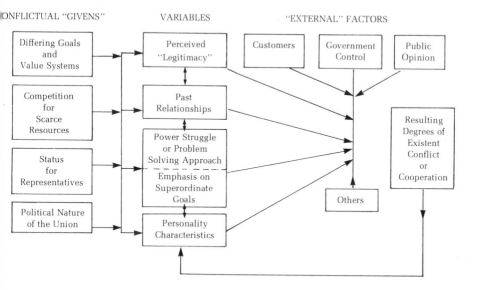

The model also depicts the resulting level of conflict as "feeding back" upon the conflictual variables and further influencing them toward the generation of a greater or lesser degree of conflict between the two groups in future relationships.

IMPLICATIONS FOR THE FUTURE

What are the implications of the present state of union-management relationships today? What does the future hold with regard to the degree of conflict between them?

Before commenting on the situation today, or making an attempt to discern trends for the future, we should again emphasize our basic point that some degree of conflict between the parties is inevitable, with at least some minimum level of controversy present in every union-management relationship. Also, on the whole, the trend in labor-management relationships has moved during the last generation away from the conflictual end of the spectrum toward the more accommodative relationship.

But the union-management relationship is not, as was briefly indicated in the beginning of this article, one of enthusiastic acceptance of the other side, but instead a relationship that Bakke has termed antagonistic cooperation.[25]

The state of the relationship between relatively mature union and management organizations seems to have stabilized into one of realistic acceptance of the other party, but certainly one of less than wholehearted cooperation. We believe that this is perhaps the most realistic relationship for the association between most unions and managements now and in the future. We are also aware that the manipulation of the variables which we have discussed, either consciously or unconsciously, by the parties in a specific relationship can determine the conflictual level between them.

The authors have thus attempted to develop a roadmap, broad in stroke though it may be, of the "territory" of union-management conflict: its causes and its cures. As pragmatists we must agree that either side in the relationship may find it quite advantageous to its aims to either raise or lower the conflictual level of the relationship. The criteria for both sides will no doubt be "what will work best" for the achievement of organization ends.

We do feel that increased awareness by both sides of what variables are involved and what a change in a variable will do to the existing relationship in terms of conflict should aid in the effectiveness of both sides in the pursuit of their particular goals.

FOOTNOTES

[1] Robert Dubin, "A Theory of Conflict and Power in Union-Management Relations." *Industrial and Labor Relations Review*, XIII (July, 1960), p. 501.

[2] Clark Kerr, *Labor and Management in Industrial Society* (Garden City, N.Y.: Doubleday and Company, Inc., 1961), pp. 150-51.

[3] Arthur W. Kornhauser, Robert Dubin, and Arthur M. Ross (eds.). *Industrial Conflict* (New York: McGraw-Hill Book Company, 1954), p. 508.

[4] Arthur A. Sloane and Fred Witney, *Labor Relations* (Englewood Cliffs, N.J.: Prentice-Hall Inc., 1967), p. 170.

[5] Neil W. Chamberlain, *The Union Challenge to Management Control* (Hamden, Connecticut: Archon Books, 1967), xi.

[6] E. Wight Bakke. *Mutual Survival; The Goal of Unions and Management* (Hamden, Conn.: Archon Books, 1966), p. 4.

[7] George Strauss, "The Shifting Power Balance in the Plant," *Industrial Relations*, I (May, 1962), p. 76.

[8] See Leon C. Megginson, *Personnel: A Behavioral Approach to Administration* (Homewood, Ill.: Richard D. Irwin, Inc. 1967), pp. 67-71 for a fuller discussion of this point.

[9] Muzafer Sherif and others (eds.). *Intergroup Conflict and Cooperation* (Norman, Okla.: University Book Exchange, 1961), p. 207.

[10] See Benjamin M. Selekman, *Labor Relations and Human Relations* (New York: McGraw-Hill Book Co., 1947), Chapter 7, "When the Union Enters," for an excellent discussion of these points.

[11] Roger Rapoport, "The Battle of the Overpass," *Wall Street Journal* (New York: May 25, 1967, p. 12).

[12] Chamberlain, *op. cit.*, p. 204.

[13] Richard E. Walton and Robert B. McKersie, *A Behavioral Theory of Labor Negotiations* (New York: McGraw-Hill Book Company, 1965), p. 186. See

Keith Davis, "Attitudes Toward the Legitimacy of Management Efforts to Influence Employees." *Academy of Management Journal*, XI (June, 1968), pp. 153-62 for an excellent article on the attitude of employees toward the legitimacy of management efforts to influence employees.

[14] See, for example, Walter H. Uphoff, *Kohler on Strike* (Boston: Beacon Press, 1966), p. 166.

[15] Alfred Kuhn, *Labor: Institutions and Economics* (New York: Harper and Brothers, 1951), pp. 173-87.

[16] Walton and McKersie, *op. cit.*, p. 193.

[17] H. Edwin Titus and E.P. Hollander, "The California F. Scale in Psychological Research: 1950-55," in Martha T. Mednick and Sarnoff A. Mednick (eds.), *Research in Personality* (New York: Holt, Rinehart and Winston, Inc., 1963), p. 462.

[18] William F. Whyte, *Pattern for Industrial Peace* (New York: Harper and Brothers, 1951), pp. 173-87.

[19] Sherif and others, *op. cit.*, p. 202.

[20] Gunnar Engen, "A New Direction and Growth in Profit Sharing." *Monthly Labor Review*, XC (July, 1967), p. 4.

[21] "New Slices for Kaiser's Melon?" *Business Week*, (March 4, 1967), p. 150.

[22] Bakke, *op. cit.*, p. 108.

[23] The American Assembly, Columbia University, *Challenges to Collective Bargaining* (Englewood Cliffs, N.J.: Prentice-Hall, Inc., 1967), pp. 4-6.

[24] See E. Wight Bakke, Clark Kerr, and Charles W. Anrod (eds.) *Union, Management and the Public* (3rd ed.: New York: Harcourt, Brace and World, 1967), pp. 1-15 for an excellent discussion of industrial relations systems.

[25] Bakke, *op. cit.*, p. 90.

THE UNION – MANAGEMENT INTERGROUP LABORATORY: STRATEGY FOR RESOLVING INTERGROUP CONFLICT *

Robert R. Blake
Jane Srygley Mouton
Richard L. Sloma

Behavioral science concepts and theories are rapidly finding increased application in business, government, and other organizations and institutions.

The following article is a description of a recent step in applying behavioral science theories and research findings to a concrete organization situation. Described is a systematic approach for confronting the intense intergroup hostility between a management

* Robert R. Blake, Jane Srygley Mouton and Richard L. Sloma, "The Union–Management Intergroup Laboratory: Strategy for Resolving Intergroup Conflict," *The Journal of Applied Behavioral Science*, Vol. 1 1965, pp. 25-57. Reproduced with permission.

and an international union and moving the relationship toward a sound problem-solving one.

Following a brief description of the setting in which this intergroup situation is embedded, a "blow-by-blow" accounting of the events that occurred during a Union-Management Intergroup Laboratory is presented. The attitudes, assumptions, values, misunderstandings, and goals of each group are brought into bold relief as they jointly examine their present relationship. Through a series of systematic steps, the two groups, working independently and jointly, examine their relationship in depth. Specific or concrete issues are set aside to focus underlying barriers that are causing eruption of conflict at the surface level.

The Intergroup Laboratory permits groups in conflict to come together to work through tensions and frictions that have built up over an extended period of time. Confrontation at this level permits group representatives to get beneath the issues separating them. Once areas of misunderstanding and sources of tension have been identified and resolved, it is possible for the two groups to more effectively deal with the day-to-day operational problems shared by them.

This is a story about conflict — raw, heated, vengeful conflict. The conflict that is the subject matter of study is the invidious, vitriolic, self-destroying kind too often found in the ongoing lives of unions and management.

How an actual management and an international union came to grips with the intense conflict that existed between them is to be described. In the first part is a sequence-by-sequence account of an actual union-management inter-group laboratory. The quality and character of the intense hostility separating the international and management gradually unfold as the description moves from one sequence of events to the next. Like a surgical instrument, the description lays bare the raw flesh of an intergroup situation that has become malignant through festering win-lose competitiveness. It is not a pretty picture. It is a true one.

The basic design of the intergroup laboratory, which is a prototype of the model used in the present application, has been tested in numerous experimental situations.[1] It is based on behavioral science research regarding intergroup win-lose conflict and cooperative intergroup problem solving. The approach has been tested in a variety of industrial and governmental intergroup conflict settings.

The background against which this intergroup laboratory took place and certain events preceding it are described before presenting the actual events of the laboratory.

The plant employs nearly 1,000 managers and over 3,000 wage and salary personnel. It is one of several locations that make up the complex of a large publicly-owned corporation.

The wage membership is represented by four major unions. The international union involved in the present application is the bargaining agent for a highly specialized and skilled group, representing approximately 10 percent of the total wage force. Membership in this local is 95 percent of those eligible. It has been the certified bargaining unit for 25 years. At present, it is one of two international unions representing wage personnel. The other unions are independent.

Chronic long-term hostility typifies the relationship between management and this international local. No one seems to know clearly today how the conflict began. At the time just prior to the introduction of the union-management laboratory, there was no inclination to seek constructive solutions in either the union organization or among managerial personnel. Grievances had been on a steady rise. A rather large number of arbitration cases were pending. Only the financial expense involved in pushing issues through to arbitration had prevented many of the pending grievances from going all the way. Day-by-day frictions between representatives of both groups became sharper and more heated. The last round of contract negotiations had been characterized by accusation and counter-accusation. The eventual contract agreement represented a "no victory" result. Strike threats had become relatively commonplace. The union seemed to be moving in this direction as the basis for trying to achieve what it regarded as its inevitable right.

Several events, but one in particular, triggered the union-management laboratory.

Local Plant Improvement Efforts. For a period of three years, the management organization had been engaged in intensive study and application of a laboratory-seminar organization development effort. The strategies and details the behavioral science laboratory-seminar methods of organization development are presented elsewhere.[2] The significance in this connection is the fact that each member of management participated in such a laboratory-seminar. The curriculum of each laboratory-seminar included an experiment concerned with intergorup conflict and cooperation. Also included was the examination of behavioral science theory regarding the conditions for achieving sound relationships between two groups in conflict.[3]

In later organization improvement steps, management has applied the concepts and methods for conflict resolution in the work situation. These application steps had brought about the restoration of problem solving between contending groups in a number of settings that involved friction between managerial components. In each of the applications substantial improvement was visible. These successes encouraged management to hope that the concepts and methods might find utility in the international union and management application.

A Decision To Experiment. Hardly a management meeting went by without the "question" of the international union coming up for discussion. Animosity toward the union was visible as management reacted to each new union "move."

An organization development specialist, who was auditing the development effort, was present at one such typical meeting. Following a review of the usual complaint, the specialist intervened with the following questions: "Why not experiment with the situation toward searching out a solution for it? Rather than continually complaining about the unsavory state of affairs, why not try to solve the basic problem rather than search for ways of defending against what you regard as inappropriate union behavior? Why not find ways to get to the root of the problem rather than engage, as you have done, in actions which appear to me to have the purpose of antagonizing the union?"

These questions took management members by surprise. Up to this point, their thinking and planning had been from a win-lose orientation. The intervention served as the basis for considering what the impact of such a union-management laboratory might be and how such consultation might be brought about.

Acting from the notion that such an effort could do no harm, though with low expectations that it would be of any substantial help, management personnel concluded that it would be worth a try.

Agreement Reached – With Reservations. The assistant general manager arranged a conference between himself and the international business representative. A proposal for the laboratory was discussed. The meeting concluded on the note that the business agent would convey the proposal to the officers of the local for their reactions and decision. He did so. An agreement was reached among union officers to the effect that the other's offer could not properly be turned down, even though they were reluctant to accept it. The reluctance to meet with management stemmed from two sources. One was in the union's conviction that management's intention was "to get them, one way or another." Thus, the question was, How could such a meeting be of any real merit?

The other reluctance on the part of the union stemmed from fear that the proposal might involve some invisible gimmick. They suspected a management strategy that could result in the union's being caught in an even more difficult position. Other sources of reservation included the possibility that the methods involved would result in some kind of brainwashing and "softening up" of the union. Nonetheless, it was agreed that a two-day laboratory should be scheduled.

Those attending the union-management laboratory to represent the union included the international's business agent; Jones, the local president; Smith, the secretary; the vice-president; and others in the union hierarchy. In all, nine union members participated.

An equal number of plant management personnel participated. The nine included the assistant general manager, the head of administrative services, the employee relations manager and his field representative, a general foreman, two union supervisors, and two first-line supervisors.

Two behavioral scientists conducted the laboratory. One met with the management group; the other with the union. Both attended all the joint sessions. The behavioral scientists familiarized themselves in advance with the situation of intergroup conflict that existed between the two participating groups.

These, then, are the conditions and background considerations against which the following description is cast. The international union and management came together — tentatively and under conditions of great mutual suspicion — for the purpose of testing each other. There was little real belief in either party's mind that the laboratory would be of any constructive help. On the other hand, there was genuine, unstated hope that they might be able to force the other over into capitulation.

The eight steps that were involved in the sequence, the content or activity involved in each step, and the amount of time allocated to it are shown in Table 1. Each step will be briefly described, its rationale discussed; and the reactions of both parties reported.[4]

Table 1

Sequence of and Time Devoted to the Phases of the Two-Day Union-Management Intergroup Laboratory

Phase	Activity	Time (Hours)
1	Orientation	$\frac{1}{2}$
2	Intragroup development of own image and its image of the other	5
3	Exchange of images across groups	1
4	Clarification of images	2
5	Intragroup diagnosis of present relationship	4
6	Exchange of diagnosis across groups	3
7	Consolidation of key issues and sources of friction	2
8	Planning next steps	1

At the outset, management and the union convened in one location for a brief orientation. The behavioral scientists in charge of the laboratory pictured the purpose, ground rules, and background considerations involved.

The senior behavioral scientist began by saying, "The last decade has seen some very important experiments in problem solving between groups that have become locked in an intergroup win-lose orientation. A great deal is now known about intergroup conflict and cooperation. The union-management situation, in particular, is very prone to becoming an intensely hostile, win-lose relationship; although its genuine purpose should be a problem-solving one.

"During these next two days, what we wish to explore are problems that are blocking the relationship — to identify them and, if possible, to plan constructive steps for their elimination.

"Therefore, we are not concerned with issues of bargaining, with specific problems of grievance handling, or with attitudes about problems that currently are under arbitration. Nor are we concerned with personalities, as such. Rather, the key concern will be with the *character* of the relationship between your two groups and with the strategies of the orientations that have characterized the two of you in the past."

It was further emphasized that this two-day intergroup laboratory might be regarded as a first activity in a sequence of events rather than as an interaction which was likely in and of itself, to bring about a resolution of the differences. Following this brief orientation, the two groups received their initial two-part task assignment. First, each group meeting separately, was asked to develop a written description — an image — of how it saw itself, particularly in its relationship with the other group. Second, management and the union were each asked to develop an image of how they saw the other group's behavior. As these images emerged, they were to be recorded on large newsprint sheets for use in reporting back when the two groups reconvened.

Organized groups do have characteristics of behavior and conduct that are visible sometimes only to members themselves. But more frequently, there are characteristics that are more celarly visible to outsiders who observe such groups. The review and exchange on an ingroup level of perceptions of how that group performs — how its behavior is motivated, what its conduct has been, what its intentions, purposes, and goals are — can do much to bring to an explicit level the assumptions, attitudes, and feelings that exist among members. It is likely that these will be areas of behavior which have never previously been exchanged and understood. The very process of doing so, indeed, frequently has been observed to result in ingroup members' coming to recognize that what they *thought* they had in common was not, in fact, widely agreed upon. Group members find it far easier to develop an image of the counter-group than to develop an image of themselves. The conduct, purposes and so on of the counter-group are seen in the minds of ingroup members in a clearer and more vivid way than are similar aspects of their own group. The development of self-image versus the development of an image of the counter-group constitutes in itself a significant learning experience. Members on either side of the group cleavage are thus made more aware of themselves and of the fact that they, many times, are not clear regarding their own behavior, conduct, intentions, purposes, and goals.

The Union's Reaction to the Task. Union members had great difficulty in understanding the assigned task. Their initial reaction was one of floundering. A false start took them into a discussion of issues surrounding a recently completed bargaining session. The session began by the business agent's exercising strong leadership, with support coming from the union secretary.

After several minutes the behavioral scientist intervened. He redefined the task for them: "The present task is aimed at describing the *character*, the quality, of the relationship — that is, typical behavior and attitudes. The task is *not* to debate technical and legalistic issues."

At the beginning, then, the union did not have the concept of examining the process of behavior — to examine and discuss actions, feelings, and attitudes. Their initial thinking pattern was so deeply ingrained on the *content* side that they, literally, did not have a process orientation. To step back from content and to take a process approach proved to be very, very tough for the union. Eventually they were able to do so.

The intervention by the behavioral scientist led to a proposal by the secretary who, addressing the business agent, said, "I think we should caucus before we go any further!"

This proposal was interrupted by the behavioral scientist. "Look, if the matters cannot be discussed in my presence, then there is little hope that anything will be achieved in the next two days."

This intervention was followed by several moments of silence. Several union members exchanged glances, but no one spoke. Finally, the business agent began again. Gradually, tediously, the discussion shifted toward a detailed picturing of the union's behavior and attitudes in their relationship with management. Participation became more widely spread among all members.

Management's Approach to the Initial Task. Management launched into this first task with a feeling of confidence. In contrast to the union, management *had* the process orientation. This is not to say that process examination came easy for them but only that after three years of laboratory-seminars they did have the concept.

Management decided to develop its own image first, and here they ran into trouble. Their antagonistic relationship with the union was of such duration and embedded with such intense feelings that discussion of their own image repeatedly slipped into a discussion of the union. They spoke of union personalities. They accused the "clique" in the next meeting-room of being the source of all their frictions. One member of management said, "Basically, the union membership is made up of good, solid citizens. It's a shame five or six power-mad guys are running things for them."

A first-line supervisor said, "I've got some of the best hard-working guys in the plant under me that are members of this union. We really work together. But I can't even talk with these guys. I just 'see red' and clam up every time I see one of them coming. Jones (the president) began stirring up trouble the day he joined the union. That was 15 years ago. I was president of the union myself at the time."

At this point, the behavioral scientist who was meeting with management intervened. "As I understand it, the plan you set for yourselves was to develop your own image first and then to develop that of the union. Obviously, you are having difficulty in doing this. Your own image is repeatedly forgotten, and union behavior and personalities keep coming into the picture. Everyone seems to have something he wants to get off his chest. Let me offer this suggestion. You might table your own image for the time being and begin on that of the union. Having done this, you may find it easier to talk about your own behavior.

"Maybe it would be best at this point to summarize what has been said so far and to post it on the newsprint. Again let me re-emphasize what we said earlier in the general session. The purpose is to identify behavior, actions, feelings and attitudes as you see them, not to place blame or to locate problems in 'personalities.' "

This intervention caused management to pause and examine how it was working. Black, the employee relations manager, spoke up. "Let's admit it. They are no damn 'angels,' but neither are we. Let's get a mirror up here where we can see ourselves, and let's put down what we see, whether we like it or not."

Someone volunteered to record. The assistant plant manager summarized key points he thought should be in their own image. Management decided to continue with its own image. This time they stuck with it.

Each group presented its self-image for examination by the other group. It also presented its image of the counter-group as the basis for enabling the counter-group to compare its own self-image with its observed characteristics, as seen from the outside.

Each group quickly recognizes that the counter-group is more readily able to picture its opposing member than itself. The images evaluated from an ingroup point of view, and from an outgroup point of view, respectively, many times are grossly different. The sheer contradictions that they contain many times identify the hidden causes for much of the surface antagonism that makes problem solving difficult. The exchange results also in the identification of those areas of behavior and conduct, intentions, purposes, and goals where group members of the two groups do see themselves accurately. These correct perceptions may be intensely negative from the standpoint of establishing sounder intergroup relations. For example, one group may be dead set to maintain warfare. This perception from an outgroup point of view, and valid recognition from an ingroup point of view, is sufficient to indicate that the approach to intergroup relationships therapy being involved here is without merit. In other words, where one or both parties are committed to continue fighting, there is then no basis for exploring how mutual problem solving might be achieved. If, on the other hand, the perceptions by the counter-group conform in many respects to those developed on the in-group plane, and they are not of the kind that insures perpetuation of the conflict, then each group is substantially encouraged that the underpinnings of an improved relationship are present.

Results. It was easier for both management and the union to discover and discuss negative aspects of the other's attitudes and behavior than of their own. On the other hand the "goodness" of one's own intentions and the "rightness of one's attitudes came out quite easily. Despite such unevenness, there were areas of agreement in the iamges and counter-images developed by the two. However, misinterpretations and misunderstandings were frequent and deep. The lists prepared by the two groups are shown in Table 2.

Table 2

**"Self" and "Other" Images Developed
by Management and the International
Union During Phase 2 of the
Union-Management Laboratory**

Management's Image

Of Itself	*By the Union*
1. Concerned with running the business effectively	1. .... (an issue not considered)
2. We show equal concern for production and people	2. Management is concerned only with production
3. Autonomous, decentralized decision-making body	3. They follow all of headquarters' policies and dictates
4. Want to learn to work better with international	4. Opposed to all organized labor
5. Prefer to deal with independent unions	5. Prefer to deal with independent unions
6. Strive continually to upgrade supervision	6. ....
7. Goal is to establish problem-solving relationship with the international	7. Their goal is to drive us out of the plant
8. Maintain flexibility in areas concerning our "rights to manage"	8. Management wants power and control over every aspect of a worker's life — they are "fatherly dictators"
9. We are inconsistent in how we treat independents and the international	9. They treat the independents one way and us another
10. Honest and aboveboard in our dealings	10. They are underhanded and they lie

The Union's Image

By Management	*Of Itself*
1. Little concern shown for the profit picture of the company	1. Concerned primarily with *people*
2. They are skillful and have intense pride	2. Proud of our craft and skills
3. Controlled by a scheming professional leader and a minority clique	3. We are governed by the will of the total membership
4. Legalistic and rigid in interpreting contract	4. Approach problems and contract with open mind
5. The union pushes every grievance to the point of arbitration. When they want to establish a precedent, they want to arbitrate	5. Do not want to have to arbitrate every grievance. We want to work them out with management
6. They want to prove they can "win" — they don't care what, just so it is something	6. We want good relations and to solve our problems with management
7. They want to co-manage. They want a say in every decision we make	7. We want a voice in those areas that directly concern us
8. The union wants the training of their people back under their control	8. We want joint control of the training and apprenticeship program
9. The union does not communicate internally. Their people don't know what is going on	9. Our people always know what is going on and what important union business is coming up
10. Union is concerned only with seniority and job security. They are not concerned with our problems	10. We want greater consideration for our skills and what we can contribute to the plant

Management's image of itself stressed especially:

1. We are running an agressive, competitive, "hard-nosed," growing business.
2. We are competent at managing.
3. We are upgrading our supervision.
4. We are willing to be more fair in dealing with the international, to treat it as well as the (previously favored) independent union; we desire to get to the bottom of this running battle we have been having over the years.
5. We need to prevent loss of power to unions, to preserve our freedom to act, our right to manage things in the best interests of the business.
6. We are fair and honest in meeting our obligations.

The local's business agent spoke for the union. Contrasted with management's self-image, the union's image of management was short, crisp, and to the point. Even then, the major points the union made could have been summed up in one simple statement: "This company is opposed to organized labor in any form, shape, or manner!"

More specifically, the union charged:

1. Management, under pressure from headquarters to cut costs, would like nothing better than to throw out the international.
2. Management gives us a "run around" with every grievance case. You try to make the union look bad by failing to settle. You try to force arbitration because you know we haven't the money to arbitrate every single case.
3. Management is a fatherly dictator. You think you are three stories taller than the worker who really makes this plant run. You want to tell us, as you do children, what is "best" for us.
4. Management took over the apprenticeship program and wrecked it.
5. Management has been chipping away at our membership for the past five years. Wherever possible, you have changed the class and scope of work that used to be under us. More and more work is contracted. You get people from the outside to do our work and pay them a dollar and a half less. You have already run one international out. We are the only sizable one left, and you are trying to starve us out.
6. Production and profits are Number One on your list. They have to be — that is your job, and headquarters won't let you forget it. That's why we have to take steps to keep you from running over our people. You're interested in a man for what you can get out of him.
7. Management is two-faced. In spite of everything headquarters and plant management have said and done, they deny publicly that they are against unions. You try to paint a different picture in the public's eye. From top to bottom, management talks out of both sides of its face at the same time.

Already it can be seen that deep differences have come to the surface. However, embedded in these differences are similarities neither party sees, particularly the union with respect to management's image. These differences and similarities will become sharper as we move through the images of the union. At this point, though, the union does not "see" or "hear" of management's interest in people. Yet, like the union, management says it *is* concerned with people. All the weight of the union's interpretation of management is given to management's *production* concerns. And the union sees much of this being "pushed" down from company headquarters. They do not see management as being autonomous — free to deal with the union in any way other than in an anti-union way. The international and management agree on management's past preference for independents. But the international sees this as meaning that management is openly against internationals.

The union's image of itself:

1. We are people-oriented. That's our job — to see that our workers get a fair shake and everything that is coming to them.
2. We do our work; we are craftsmen; we do a job in the best and most skillful way it can be done; we return a fair day's work for a fair day's

pay; we recognize our responsibility to the company and to the community.

3. We would like better relations with the company; that's why we are here today; but if you start to lean on us, we'll push back.

4. We are locally run; unlike management, we don't have to follow a "party line" from headquarters; we don't make decisions without going to our membership. (At this point, management objected that only about 10 percent of members turn out for meetings.)

"I don't know out of what hat you pulled your figures," the union secretary returned, "but our regular attendance is well above that. At the last wage discussion, over 75 percent were there. Our people are always there when something important is going on."

The behavioral scientist suggested at this point, "Both of you are banging at each other and this could go on and on, but no real understanding will come from this. Let's move ahead."

5. The business agent continued: "The union wants more recognition. Management has never given us the recognition our skills and craftsmanship merit. To you, it's just another job. You wouldn't recognize a good piece of work if it were staring you in the face. We contribute a lot to the operations of this plant. And, much more could be contributed by us with half a chance. The international should have a voice in those things that affect our work and our livelihood. We don't want co-management. We want the recognition we deserve, and a chance to contribute."

Management's image of the union:

1. The union is controlled by a small minority; it doesn't truly represent the membership; the business agent is a career man looking for a higher job in the international; he and a few rabble-rousers keep the membership stirred up; most members don't know what's going on and don't care; they are proud and skilled craftsmen, but are run by a small clique.

2. The union is a tough bargainer; you fight us every step of the way; all you really care about is winning; you don't care what is won, just so it's something; union leaders want to demonstrate to the membership that they are "successful"; you use more force and pressure on us in bargaining than any of the other unions; every point in the contract is given a rigid, legalistic interpretation; you never are willing to compromise.

3. Union rules on seniority hurt the business; we can't move up the men with the best skills.

The union spokesmen see themselves as democratic agents of the membership; management sees the membership as "sound" but misled by union leaders. The union is proud of skillful work but feels management fails to recognize this. The union wants to be more involved in the operations of the plant, and management has expressed the same desire; but neither sees this as a common interest at this point.

A wide gulf separated the union's and management's views of each other at the outset of the laboratory. At this point, there is perhaps even less confidence on both sides, than initially, that the two would be able to achieve any degree of understanding or a resolution of their differences.

There, then, were the "raw materials" participants had to work with during the night and day remaining in the laboratory.

Each group asked questions of the other to insure understanding of what had been said. The aim was to clarify rather than to belittle or attack.

The purpose of this step is to insure that there is a complete and full understanding of the impressions, attitudes, feelings, and facts presented by each group. Less than full understanding can result in continued erroneous thinking concerning the goals, attitudes, and feelings of the other. At this point, interventions by the behavioral scientist can become critical. Frequently, without an outside observer to focus what is taking place, it is easy for the discussion to slip into one of charges and countercharges as each side seeks to defend itself against attack. Such actions and reactions, however, only tend to reinforce the beliefs each holds regarding the other's "intentions."

Results. The next two hours were spent in a joint session over the images each had developed and presented. Neither side could believe the other could be so "wrong" about it. At times the discussion, designed to clarify, became heated and sharp. Each side quickly forgot its good intentions to work in a problem-solving manner. Renewed tensions and old sources of friction bubbled at the surface. Without interventions by the behavioral scientists to focus what was taking place, it is likely the discussion would have slipped onto the more typical win-lose exchange of vindictive accusations.

"Little will be gained," one of the behavioral scientists said by way of intervention, "at the present rate. All I can hear is one side 'explaining' to the other why it is 'right' and the other is 'wrong.' The purpose of this session is to *clarify* what has emerged in your images. This is to insure that both of you understand clearly the behavior, attitudes, feelings, and intentions of the other. If common understanding is not achieved at this level, then it is likely both of you will continue to misinterpret each other's intentions and actions. Rather than discovering a common basis on which to build, differences and resulting antagonism will keep you apart."

However, the need to "bang" one another was too strong. For example, the international continued to hammer at its point that management intended to slowly drive them from the plant. "Look at what you have done," the business agent said at one point. "You've taken jobs away from us and assigned them to the independents. You have gradually shifted the class and scope of our work. More and more you contract work we should be doing."

Also, the union kept returning to grievances. "You have headquarters' answers for every grievance that comes to you. And that is because you go along with their policy of no affiliated unions in the organization. You've yet to review a case solely on merit. You force us into arbitration in order to break us. You deal with us in bad faith. Regardless of what you say, you insist on a different arbitrator so it will cost us more. The only question in our minds is, What will you think of next?"

Management in turn answered with denials and counter-charges. "It is not we who are controlled from 'upstairs.' I know of no such policy, written or otherwise, that says we are to force the international out of this plant. You file a grievance over every little thing that happens. You want to show your membership how good you are. The truth is, they don't know what is going on because this little group sitting right in here makes all the decisions. Look how you raised the dues last time. You called a meeting, just you guys showed up, and you voted to raise the dues. No one else had a chance to vote otherwise.

"During the last wage issue with another international, you gave your people a bunch of bum facts to make us look bad. You people are the union, not the 170 that are supposed to be."

At this point, one of the behavioral scientists again intervened. "It still appears that little is being 'heard' because people are so preoccupied with defending what they say and denying what others are saying. Here is a suggestion. Make sure you understand what each has said up to this point. Disregard whether you agree or not. The kinds of questions you ask should be ones that will insure that you fully understand each point that both groups have made, If one of you says 'the moon is made of blue cheese,' then the other wants to be clear that he said 'blue' cheese and not Swiss or something else. Whether you agree with this description of the moon is not what we want to accomplish at this time."

Several guarded questions were asked following this intervention, and it was obvious that most were suppressing the urge to move back to the attack. Not wanting openly to resume their previous line of "questioning," yet not knowing how and not trusting themselves to seek further "clarification," members from both groups waited for the other to make the next move.

The behavioral scientist again intervened with the following suggestion. "If it is felt no further clarification is needed at this point, then for the remainder of the evening and for, let's say, the first two hours in the morning, more might be accomplished if both groups devote themselves to answering fully the following questions: One, what is it we do (the union or management) that has contributed to the image the other group has of us? Second, what is it in our own beliefs and actions that leads us to the conclusion we have reached about ourselves? To do this, take with you the images on newsprint that the other group developed. In this way, you can focus on the issues and characteristics described by the other group."

Although participants attempted to restrain themselves during the exchange of images, the clarification session ended on a note of "charges" and "countercharges." Each side sought to defend itself against the other. This only tended to reinforce the belief each held about the other's "intentions."

Phase 5, self-diagnosis, is a pivotal point in the union-management laboratory. The need at this point is for both sides to look "inside" themselves and underneath surface tensions to discover *why* the relationship has become what it is.

Both groups, meeting separately, spent the evening and part of the following morning in (1) self-analysis and (2) diagnosing the "why" of their own actions. Although still far from any real degree of mutual trust or understanding, the door at least was open for both management and the union to see what actions would need to be understood and shifted if a sound problem-solving relationship were to be achieved.

Management's Approach to the Diagnosis. Initially, upon returning to their meeting-room, the management group launched into berating the union's "gross misunderstanding" that they had just heard.

One manager remarked, "I told you! Anything he (the business agent) said, the others would back him up. Those guys don't even know what is fact and what is fiction."

"How could they be so wrong?" others chimed in.

"They have always used this tactic," said the first man. "We are always the 'scheming' ones and *they* are the 'innocent' ones. The business agent has been to the international's school. They taught him all the tricks."

This line of self-justification continued for several minutes before the behavioral scientist who was meeting with management intervened with the following: "What you are doing now is not likely to move you toward better understanding of your relationship with the union. First, you are disregarding your initial commitment to work during the laboratory in a problem-solving manner. This will defeat why you are here and any progress that may have been made up to this point. Second, working through the present task, as it is intended, can help both you and the union to move toward the 'nub' of what it is that has brought about such wide differences between you."

At this, the employee relations manager made the following proposal. "Let's take their image of us as it is on the newsprint and just start listing everything we can think of under each one of their points that could possibly lie behind how they interpret us."

The proposal was picked up and management went to work.

The Union's Reaction. Meanwhile, the union reacted in a similar fashion. Management, as far as they were concerned, had demonstrated to the union's satisfaction that they (the union) had been right all along.

"How can they honestly think that we are a clique running our organization?" the president asked.

"The whole problem," the business agent answered, "is that they are still living in the Nineteenth Century. They can't understand that unions are here to stay. They have no concept of the ideology of unions."

But gradually union members were beginning to get a feel for process examination. They moved more rapidly this time into digging into their attitudes and feelings and into their reactions to the images developed by management.

Both groups worked on this task until past ten in the evening. They picked up again at eight the next morning and completed their tasks around ten.

Following the individual diagnosis of its own behavior and its "contributions" to the relationship, management and the union came back together to exchange the results of their analyses. Most of the day was devoted to exchanging and then debating through the results of both groups' diagnoses. In its diagnosis, management had taken the seven characteristics of itself as the union had listed them.

Under each item, management had listed contributions (past events and actions) that it felt it and the company had made to this image. This list was quite full — so full, in fact, that management did not get to diagnosing the union's image of itself, except as it happened to relate to the management's image. The union, on the other hand, was more brief, but had studied both its own and management's images.

The assistant plant manager, as he had done in the earlier exchange (during Phase 3), began the interchange in this session. The first item he discussed was the Number One issue so far as the union was concerned, namely, "The company is opposed to international (affiliated) unions." Management was able to cite a number of instances where it could have left such an impression in the union's mind. However, it was pointed out that management did not see this statement to be an accurate description of its present thinking.

"We looked around," the assistant plant manager said, "in the whole organization, as well as in the plant, to see what it was in the past that could lead you to think we, here at the plant, are against affiliated unions. I'd like to cite a few instances. But before I do, let me say again, as clearly as I can, we *prefer* independent unions; but this does not mean that we are opposed to internationals.

"What are some of the examples? For one, Mr. _____, the now retired president of the company, made a public statement several years ago to the effect that we preferred company unions, and that the company would do all it could to keep internationals out. Of course, as you know, in 1959 the 'X' International was voted in. At that time, Mr. _____, the plant manager, issued a letter to all employees, stating he was sorry to see this swing, and that it was management's hope that the independent would get back in. However, he did not say that we would not cooperate with the 'X' International, as long as they were in.

"More close to home, we feel many of our own and the company's economy moves have not been seen as such. Rather, these moves have been interpreted as efforts to get rid of the international. Our recent layoff falls into this category. The closing of a nearby plant by the company is another. Most employees have the impression that headquarters would not make investments or expansions of our plant as long as the international was in."

The international's business agent interrupted to ask, "And isn't this true? The company hasn't made any investments in the plant in over four years. They have at others. We think this is a big reason why you go right along with the policy of 'no affiliated unions!' "

"But you are still saying there is no difference between what headquarters thinks and what *we* here at the plant think," the assistant plant manager returned.

"We make no distinction whatsoever," the business agent replied. "You can't afford to do anything else. It figures. Take another of our points. In order to maintain your public image, you deny opposition to affiliated unions, but that doesn't square with the facts. You said it yourself. The company has demonstrated it prefers independents."

"But this is still not to say we are opposed to internationals. We only say we prefer independents," the employee relations manager interrupted. "You are here now, have been for over 25 years, and we expect you to be here for a long time to come. We want to work with you, but it is awfully hard when you think the opposite. I think it is true that, in headquarters, in many ways there has been opposition to internationals which the company has tried to cover up. But even this is not so true at headquarters today. And it certainly isn't true here at the plant."

Maybe a couple of points we came up with can clarify what we are saying here," the assistant plant manager said. "We think you get this impression through our *omission* to support or reject internationals, particularly in the recent case of the 'X' International. You will recall that we took no stand during the certification election. We *publicly* said we were not going to support either the independent or the international. Our silence, we think, is what gives you the impression that we *deny* our opposition to unions."

"Do you deny that you were pleased when the independent won out?" the union president asked.

"No. I can't help saying that we were honestly pleased. But, had the international won, we would have continued to bargain in good faith with them and to fulfill our obligations. Right up to the election, we were still negotiating with them."

"You were just going through the motions to maintain the false image you were trying to project," the business agent said. "In the background, though, you were doing all you could to make the international appear incompetent to its membership. Your 'foot was in the aisle' all the while. This is what you are doing to us. And you were getting your orders straight from headquarters. Look at the wage issue. You offered a ridiculous amount, way below the straight rate, just to embarrass the international. We think local management would have offered them a just amount if you had been free to do so. But the whole problem is that you were not free. How can you say you work to bargain and deal with us in good faith and to cooperate with us when you cannot because of headquarters, even if you wanted to?"

"Let me answer that," the assistant plant manager continued. "At our 'Y' plant, the 'X' Union was offered the straight rate because to do so did not put plant 'Y' out of line in their area. We offered less because to do otherwise would have put us way out of line with the rates in our area. We were among the top 'five' at that time. Even then, we offered the 'X' Union an increase that would have put us above everyone. All this is to say that headquarters' position with respect to wages is that plants *should* exercise local responsibility to keep rates in line. Their policy is *not* to use wages to punish unions.

"We don't think we can answer why you feel we are, as you say, 'out to get you.' We don't know really how to answer your belief that we lack local autonomy any further except by denial and to say in the most honest way we know that we make our own decisions. And as far as this concerns this union, our decision is that we want to work with you in a sound manner."

"I wish we could believe that," the business agent said. Others nodded.

The assistant plant manager went on to cite other events the management group felt contributed to the union's belief that management had long-range designs to abolish affiliated unions. Included here were a recent reduction in rolls, the abolishment of two departments in which the employees were represented by international unions, contracting of work, and the movement of certain work performed by this union into areas represented by independents.

"That last one is a good example of why we say you do not act in good faith," the union secretary said. "Look at the change you made in the toolroom. You said you were only making some physical changes, but before we knew it the change resulted in different jobs. This was not what you led us to believe."

"We did not say there wouldn't be any changes in the jobs affected," a member of the management group returned. "You only assumed this."

"But it's always the same thing," the business agent countered. "You deal in half-truths — you don't tell the full truth. What we say is, that if you really wanted to work with us, you would not always be so evasive. We think you should face the issues squarely and operate on the table with trust. We want to be treated with respect. We can disagree and bargain and still act with trust and in good faith. But we cannot disagree with respect when management is evasive and does not act aboveboard.

"I'll give you another example," he continued, "and this probably is the biggest problem area we know. Again, it's the way in which you deal with grievances. Rather than giving us a straightforward answer to issues you take a legalistic approach. Now this is what you accused us of earlier. But I'm saying that if things are legalistic it is because you have made them this way. This kind of legal approach stifles openness and straightforward answers. But we feel this is only a minor part of the problem. What we see you doing is hiding your real motives in the language of your written grievance decisions. And getting back to the point of respect, your interpretations of our grievances are stated in such a way as to make us look childish even to have raised a grievance in the first place."

Both groups now were more openly exchanging their feelings and interpretations on a variety of events in their history. For this reason, the behavioral scientists did not intervene when the discussion slid into the union's picturing its analysis of management's counter-image. It was felt that, in this way, overlapping issues could be productively discussed as they were encountered. The interplay from this kind of interchange seemed to generate greater understanding for the moment than mechanically completing one group's presentation before moving to the next.

"While we have been talking all this time," the business agent said during a lull, "we have covered a number of the points we had to make with respect to your image of us. However, there are still a number of things we want to lay out on the table. So, unless there is more management has to add from their newsprints, I would like to summarize the remainder of our points now."

Management responded that they thought this would be good. They said, though, that they would like to keep it loose, the way it was. Management wanted to be able to interrupt and return to some point if something the union said triggered a thought in their minds.

This approach was agreeable to the union.

"There is one point," the business agent began, "that we think is a basic, fundamental, ideological breach in the thinking of our two groups. We are not sure this can ever be patched — that is, your over-riding preference for independent unions. I don't want to get into, *again*, whether this means management is 'opposed' to internationals or not. But, I don't see how we can interpret so many arrows in this direction in any other way. Anyway, here is what we see. In many companies, and especially this one, *independent* unions are set up to *deny* workers the freedom to bargain. When people do not have the freedom to select between an international or an independent, then we feel that, actually, they do not have the freedom of choice they should have. And people in *this* plant *don't* have that choice."

The plant manager reacted to this one. "People in this plant have the right, 'freedom of choice' in your words, to be represented by either an independent or an international. I don't see why you say they don't. We can't keep an international out. Employees can join an international whenever they want. If that isn't freedom, I don't know what you mean by freedom."

"And what if they did?" the business agent asked. "You prefer an independent. Would you treat them in the same way? No! You wouldn't. That's my point. People have no choice but to stay with independents."

The assistant plant manager responded, "I don't think we would be that different. Maybe we would. But they still have freedom of choice."

"That's like asking a man whether he wants to be shot or hanged."

The question of "freedom of choice" was kicked around at greater length, with neither management nor the union able to agree on whether or not employees did have a "free choice." Management and the union seemed to be sparring, each testing for an opening.

"Decentralization is another anti-international strategy of the company," the business agent said as he shifted the topic somewhat. "It serves to spread us so thin that we can't be effective. That's the whole strategy behind scattering plants from one end of the country to the other. You say we misinterpret economic moves you make. And we say that headquarters' real motive is to get rid of international, not just to 'pinch' a few of the pennies they so dearly love."

The Union Operates Democratically. "One of your points that we really can't understand is that 'the union is run by a clique.' Nothing could be further from the truth. We think management has this impression because they don't understand how we operate. You have never been to a union meeting. Well, let me change that to say only Joe and Pete, who were once in the union, have been to union meetings. You guys ought to attend one to see what really happens. And you ought to read our by-laws to learn how we operate. Our organization is more democratic than yours."

The employee relations manager interrupted to say, "What the by-laws say and what really happens can be completely different. Didn't you just recently pass a dues rise when only a minority — the usual 10 percent — were present?"

"I don't know who your 'stool-pigeon' is," the union president shot back, "but he sure gave you some bum information."

"This is a good example of how little you know about how we operate," the business manager said. "Let us tell you the procedure we have. It's in our by-laws." He went on to describe how action must be taken. "If we take a position in bargaining, it is because we have discussed it with our people and that's what they want. And don't be too sure our people wouldn't strike if you pushed us into it."

The business agent went to his last point. "You also said we were not interested in production — that we were not concerned with your problems. The truth is, you don't want us to be interested; that is, not beyond the pount of doing what management wants. This kills any incentive and any concern for management's viewpoint."

"You know what management's attitude is?" the union vice-president asked. "It is, 'Look, you are supposed to do *what* you are told *as* you are told to do it. We are not interested in your ideas.' With that kind of attitude, how can you expect us to act differently? Management at this plant still hasn't caught up with the idea that employees today want to be more autonomous and make a real work contribution. And that doesn't mean through some 'corny' coin-your-idea program."

The employee relations manager, who had been listening intently all this time, stood up with a look of disbelief on his face. He didn't seem to realize he was on his feet. "Do you mean to say you people are really interested in *production*?" He had listened to the union say this for two days, but he had just "heard" it for the first time. His next question was a simple one, but it triggered an hour-long discussion. He asked, "What could management do to use people more effectively?"

The earlier period of self-analysis and this exchange made it possible for both to "hear" better what the other was saying. In turn, being able to "hear" made it possible for both sides to communicate their attitudes and feelings more openly — more honestly. Some points of agreement and similarities in thinking came to the fore as differences were examined, put into perspective, and understood.

Progress was made and better understanding achieved during this latter exchange, yet under the surface underlying tensions still remained. Neither side was "owning up" any more than the other. Old "bargaining" habits still permeated the exchange between the two. On many points, one side was unable to see why the other felt or thought as it did. Often members yielded to the temptation to explain to the other side why they were "wrong."

Over-all, though, both sides were "listening" better to each other. Although not always agreeing, they were hearing each other out. As the session continued, questions and replies gained the quality of clarifying rather than of attacking or defending.

The remainder of the day was spent thrashing through the many points of differences that had been uncovered in the early development of images. Both the union and management were able to get many things off their chests.

Although the two sides were far from having talked out their differences, the last part of the day was devoted to identifying those issues which seemed critical in the relationship between the union and management. Working with the behavioral scientists, union and management jointly identified, as barriers, those issues that would require more examination, discussion, and resolution if relations were to be improved. They were summarized as follows:

1. *Lack of Mutual Trust and Respect.* This was tagged as a key element in the relationship by both groups. The general feeling was that once genuine trust and respect between the two were achieved, many of the other things would fall into place. Management's preference for independents, despite its position that it wanted to learn to work with the international, was cited as an issue "that needed better understanding."
2. *Ideological Differences.* Both agreed there existed wide differences in matters of purposes and principles. Common purposes would need to be identified if joint problem solving were to become a reality.
3. *Inadequate Knowledge and Understanding.* During the exchanges it became clear to both sides that many factual matters about each other

were not known. Both the union and management felt that neither of them really understood how the other operated — how decisions, regulations governing their behavior, long-range plans, traditions, and so on, were handled at either level.

4. *Attitudinal Differences*. Differences in attitudes toward each other, plant operations, and the management of business affairs, existed between the union and management. Part of this was recognized as a difference in perspective — part was seen as due to different levels of knowledge and to past experiences and relations.

5. *Need for More Effective Use of People*. Both agreed there should be more participation and involvement of wage people in the operations of the plant. "We don't want to co-manage," the union said, for example, "but there are some areas where we have high stakes. In these matters we want to be consulted. We think we can contribute to the effectiveness of operations if management will involve us more."

6. *Better Understanding of Rights and Obligations*. Union and management, they felt, need to understand better and to respect the rights and obligations each has toward the other. There existed a need for better understanding and acceptance of each party's role in the bargaining process. Included here was the feeling that a better understanding of the mutual expectations each held for the other was needed.

7. *Better Communications*. It was also felt that management and the union need to communicate more openly, more freely, and more honestly with each other. Both felt that communication barriers precipitated many of their problems.

8. *Better Listening*. Along with a need for better communications, it was felt that both sides needed to listen more and "better" to the other. For example, the union pointed out that employees were concerned with and wanted their views heard on the economic health of the plant. One union member had remarked, "I know right now how to save the plant $10,000, but I haven't found anyone who will listen to me yet. I gave up trying a long time ago."

Based on the above summation, the final period of time was devoted to debating what follow-up steps, if any, should be taken to the two-day laboratory. It was agreed that many tensions and a residue of hostility still existed. Much remained to be talked out. It was felt that the two groups were not yet ready to tackle their operational problems. It was concluded that a lot of "air still needs to be cleared" before the two sides would be able to sit down together and work in an effective manner.

It was proposed and accepted that the two groups spend some time in considering what they had learned during the laboratory. Both wanted to talk among themselves about what had come out of the session and to consider what the next best step would be. Each wanted to report to its other group members the progress that had been made, to get their reactions, and then to make a tentative proposal of what they felt needed to be done next. With this, the union-management laboratory ended.

Summary of Issues. The union showed great concern for and tested, throughout the two days, the degree of local autonomy in management. There was a considerable amount of anxiety over what they saw as corporate ideology and implementation of an anti-international objective. The real question to the union, although they were not able to focus it, was not whether or not management had local autonomy, but the *degree* of autonomy management had.

The union was convinced that management was "dollar-oriented" all the way, without values with respect to people. Therefore, the union felt bound to counteract this "inhumanity" they saw in management.

Management again and again demonstrated extreme suspicion regarding the anti-democracy of the union and the "clique" qualities of the union leadership. Management genuinely felt that the union leaders did not represent the people.

Management's attitude was that the union was an institution with intrinsic goals of protecting and building itself. Management felt strongly on two points: (1) that the union had no concern for productivity and (2) that actually they had only an administrative concern for people, *i.e.*, wage rates, seniority, class and scope of work, security, and the like. In other words, management saw the union's concern for people to be an institutional one.

Similarities Not Seen. Several points of similarity were not observed by either management or the union because of their concern for the *differences* between them. For example, management saw itself as *production-oriented.* The union also saw this. But management also had a *human* interest which the union did not recognize.

On the other hand, the union saw itself as having a *people* obligation. This, in turn, management recognized in the union. The disparity here was that management did not see the same weight being attached to productivity by the union.

What the two groups shared in common, then, they were not able to recognize. More importantly, what they shared in common they saw as differences.

Intergroup conflict undergirds much of modern, complex organization life. More than ever, there is greater interdependence among the functions of groups. This interdependence can aid organizations to take giant strides forward toward the accomplishment of mutual goals. Or, this same interdependence can breed the most hostile and disruptive of conflicts. Once conflict erupts, it is difficult to bring it under control. It can consume everything and everyone it touches.

We have presented a view of the misunderstandings and misperceptions generated out of a long history of antagonism between an international union and the management of a large industrial plant. Both sides were weary from "battle," but neither knew how to alter the course of the conflict.

Based on behavioral sciences concepts, an educational-laboratory approach to the resolutions of the conflict was proposed. Leaders of the international and management met for a two-day period to confront the conflict between them. The differences between them, uncovered by the two groups, were presented in detail. These differences became the foundation on which the two groups began tediously to work toward a more healthy relationship. Through self-analysis and an exchange of views, management and the union moved slowly toward a better understanding of the relationship between them.

After the laboratory, much tension and distrust still existed and remained to be worked through. But by confronting each other squarely with the issues involved, the way was opened for building a more cooperative and productive relationship for the future.[5]

One should not expect that a single, brief confrontation such as that described will cause a repeal of the past. It is unlikely that well-established conditions will be greatly influenced, if at all.

The greatest impact will become evident when *new* issues and different problems arise in the relationship. At that time, the parties will be able to apply themselves in a more problem-solving manner. In other words, the background of conflict does not dissolve. Rather, it remains to color and influence old issues born in that era. However, new issues, with no anchorage in the past, do not have the same "tug" in the directions of old norms and past practices. Members in both groups are not "bound" by old expectations. Instead, they are now free to explore jointly for new solutions with the other group under the more collaborative conditions produced by the laboratory sequence.

Correcting a situation of long-term, chronic hostility requires continuous and diligent follow-up efforts. As much as a five-year span may be needed before the root system that produced the original animosities can be replaced by a new and healthier root system — one that can cause the relationship to flourish.

FOOTNOTES

[1] For a review of relevant experimental work, see Blake, R.R., & Mouton, J.S. Overevaluation of own group's product in intergroup competition. *J. abnorm. soc. Psychol.*, 1962, 64, 237-283; Blake, R.R. & Mouton, J.S. Comprehension of points of communality in competing solutions. *Sociometry*, 1962, 25, 56-63; Blake, R.R., & Mouton, J.S. Comprehension of own and outgroup positions under intergroup competition. *J. conflict Resolution*, 1961, 5, 304-310; Blake, R.R., & Mouton, J.S. Loyalty of representatives to ingroup positions during intergroup competition. *Sociometry*, 1961, 24, 171-183; Blake, R.R., & Mouton, J.S. Perceived characteristics of elected representatives. *J. abnorm. soc. Psychol.*, 1961, 62, 693-695; and Blake, R.R., & Mouton, J.S. Reactions to intergroup competition under win-lose conditions, *Mgmt Science*, 1961, 7, 420-425.

Also, for a review and discussion of the prototype intergroup experiments, see Sherif, M., Harvey, O.J., White, B.J., Hood, W.R. & Sherif, C. *Intergroup Conflict and Cooperation: The Robber Cave Experiment.* Instituté of Group Relations: Norman, Oklahoma, 1961; Sherif, M. Superordinate goals in the reduction of intergroup conflict. *Amer. J. Sociol.*, 1958, 43, 349-356; Sherif, M., & Sherif, C. *Outline of Social Psychology* (rev. ed.). New York: Harper, 1956, and Sherif, M., & Sherif, C. *Groups in Harmony and Tension*. New York: Harper, 1953.

2 Blake, R.R., & Mouton, J.S. *The Managerial Grid*. Houston: Gulf, 1964, Chapter 12.

3 Blake, R.R., Shepard, H.A., & Mouton, J.S. *Managing Intergroup Conflict in Industry*. Houston: Gulf, 1964; Blake, R.R. & Mouton, S. The intergroup dynamics of win-lose conflict and problem-solving collaboration in union-management relations. In M. Sherif (ed.), *Intergroup Relations and Leadership*. New York: Wiley, 1962, 94-13, Blake, R.R., & Mouton, J.S. Union-management relations: From conflict to collaboration. *Personnel*, 1961, 38; and Blake, R.R. & Mouton, J.S. *Group Dynamics – Key to Decision Making*. Houston: Gulf, 1961.

4 For a review of intergroup laboratory applications in other than union-management relations, see Blake, R.R., Shepard, H.A., Mouton, J.S., *op. cit.*, 1964; Blake, R.R., & Mouton, J.S. Headquarters-field team training for organizational improvement. *AST J.*, 1962, 16, 3-11; Blansfield, M.G., Blake, R.R., & Mouton, J.S. The merger laboratory: A new strategy for bringing one corporation into another. *Train. Directors J.*, 1964, 18, in press. Additional relevant discussions contained in Blake, R.R. Psychology and the crisis of statesmanship. *Amer. Psychologist*, 1959, 14, 78-94. Also see W.G. Bennis, K.D. Benne, & R. Chin (eds.), *The Planning of Change*. New York: Holt, Rinehart, & Winston, 1961, 466-477; and Blake, R.R., & Mouton, J.S. Intergroup therapy. *Int. J. soc. Psychiat.*, 1962, 8, 196-198.

5 For a description of another format for reducing tension between a union and management, see Muench, G.A. A clinical psychologist's treatment of labor-management conflicts. *Personnel Psychol.*, 1960, 12, 165-172; and Muench, G.A. A clinical psychologist's treatment of labor-management conflicts: A four-year study. *J. humanistic Psychol.*, 1963, 3, 92-97.

RESOLVING INDUSTRIAL STRIFE: IS THERE "A BETTER WAY"?*

Ed Finn

Ed Finn, a noted labour columnist, advocates the use of preventive mediation as a workable method of resolving contract disputes.

In Arthurian legend, one of the Knights of the Round Table, Sir Galahad, devoted his life to a search for the Holy Grail. The modern version of his quest has been undertaken by some "knights of the bargaining table" — the search for the ideal system of labour relations, one that contains no flaws, no conflict, and, above all, no strikes.

Conflict is inherent in the present adversary system of labour relations. Inevitably this conflict occasionally culminates in strikes, caus-

* Ed Finn, "Resolving Industrial Strife: Is There a Better Way"? *The Labour Gazette*, December 1971, pp. 774-83. Reproduced with permission.

ing economic loss and public inconvenience. Nevertheless, the federal Task Force on Labour Relations, after a detailed study of Canada's collective bargaining system, concluded that its benefits far outweigh its defects. "Although this system may seem constly," the task force report declared, "it may well be more healthy and less expensive in resolving labour–management disputes than any other method".

This judgment of the task force is not universally shared. Many Canadians in all walks of life — journalists, politicians, jurists, academics and even some trade unionists — have become disenchanged with the disruptive aspects of industrial warfare. The Financial Times articulated their exasperation in an editorial deploring "the obsolete rules of collective bargaining" and calling for the discovery or invention of "a more civilized way of regulating labour relations."

This refrain — the insistence on a better way of resolving disputes between labour and management — runs through most of the current complaints against the adversary system. Although most of the critics fail to offer alternatives, a dozen or more proposals for improving or replacing the present system have been suggested in recent years. They range from a slight tinkering to an elaborate reconstruction of collective bargaining from a more permissive to a more repressive approach, from the most fanciful to the most hard-headed reforms. These proposals may be divided into five categories: Utopian, Repressive, Radical, Innovative, and Mediative.

THE UTOPIAN PROPOSALS

The utopian suggestions usually start from the premise that labour and management have common goals and interests — they should therefore consider themselves partners in industry rather than opponents. It follows from this roseate view that sane, sensible representatives of both sides should be able to reach an accommodation without resorting to threats or coercion.

A leading exponent of the cooperative approach is T.G. Norris, who retired from the bench of the British Columbia Court of Appeal in 1968. The eminent ex-jurist conducted an inquiry into labour strife on the Great Lakes ten years ago and was the author of the Norris Report that led to the imposition of a government trusteeship over the Seafarers' International Union. "All that is needed to bring about industrial peace", Norris contends, "is a proper measure of good-will and tolerance".

He believes that labour–management accord can best be achieved at summit meetings of top union and business leaders. Instead of using their brains to destroy each other, such men should be capable of using them in the public interest . . . in a real effort to bring about that which they say, possibly with tongue in cheek, is their ultimate aim: industrial peace.

When it comes to specific techniques, Norris speaks in rather nebulous terms of "a system of formula-pricing for labour that would lead to the salvation of our industrial economy. But he does not flesh out this system, other than to suggest that it could be devised by a three-man commission made up of businessman J.V. Clyne, CLC Secretary-Treasurer Bill Doge, and Labour Economist Kenneth Strand. He says he knows what he has suggested is purely visionary, but vision has been the basis of the success of our country and its democratic institutions.

Unfortunately, the Norris vision is much too vaguely defined to serve as a workable substitute for the prevailing system. It also has the flaw of being an élitist approach — one that assumes that an accord reached at the summit can somehow be implemented at all levels of labour relations in Canada. This, to put it mildly, is a very dubious assumption.

Some of the more extreme proposals of the advocates of industrial democracy must also be regarded as Utopian, at least in the short-term outlook. These ideas go beyond the co-management principle to envisage "workers' control" of industry. Andre Bekerman, education and publicity officer of Local 1000, Canadian Union of Public Employees, Toronto, defines the objective of workers' control: "To obtain direct control by workers over the scheduling of work, the speed of production, work methods, and the selection of supervisors. It is also essential to establish veto rights over layoffs, discipline and other managerial prerogatives . . . and control can be extended over all significant decisions such as pricing, technological change, expansion plans, plant shutdowns, and relocation and investment policies".

From a union standpoint, these may be desirable goals. But their attainment would call for nothing short of a sweeping reform — if not the destruction — of the entire capitalist system. It would also entail drastic changes in the philosophy of Canadian labour unions, most of which are now as committed as the most conservative employer to the tenets of "free enterprise" and the separation of labour and management functions. Prospects for such a revolution are exceedingly dim.

Another series of proposals that must be labelled utopian are those calling for the transplanting of foreign labour relations systems to Canada. The most favoured model is the Swedish system, which has produced the lowest incidence of strikes and disputes of any western industrialized nation. Other countries' methods however — for example, those of Japan, the Netherlands, Yugoslavia, West Germany and Switzerland — also have their local supporters.

What the foreign-model enthusiasts usually overlook is that these labour relations systems flow out of, and reflect, the indigenous and often unique social, political, cultural and economic conditions of those countries. They cannot be uprooted from their native soil and grafted successfully onto an entirely different socio-economic structure. The effectiveness of the Swedish system, for example, stems largely from the exceptionally high degree of union and management organization; more than 90 per cent of all workers and business firms are represented by unions or employer associations. The nation-wide bargaining this framework permits is unattainable in Canada as long as two-thirds of the workforce remains unorganized.

The tranquility obtained by The Netherlands' system has come from an extensive array of state planning and regulation, including rigid wage and price controls, of a magnitude that neither unions nor employers in Canada show any inclination to accept. The Japanese system is anchored to an all-embracing industrial paternalism in which employers assume lifelong responsibility for virtually all the material needs of workers and their dependants. This approach is clearly alien to Western thinking.

It should be noted, too, that most of these foreign systems have been experiencing some difficulties in recent years. Even Sweden's labour relations Eden has been infested by the serpent of strikes and lockouts. As Labour Minister Bryce Mackasey observed in *The Labour Gazette* of January 1971, "The Fact of the matter is that, in all parts of the world, systems of industrial relations are feeling the pressures of rapid economic and social change, and are responding with only limited success."

THE REPRESSIVE PROPOSALS

Most of the repressive proposals start from the premise that the main cause of industrial conflict is the exercise of undue power and freedom by one or both of the participants. (Labour is cast as the villain more often than management.) If this premise is accepted, the obvious solution is to impose restraints on excessive use of power by either unions or business firms.

These proposed curbs usually take some form of compulsory arbitration. The most popular seems to be the establishment of labour courts, vested with the authority to impose a settlement in the event that a union and employer cannot reach voluntary agreement. Morris C. Shumiatcher, a Regina lawyer, is one of the most outspoken advocates of labour courts. He argues that such courts are as necessary to protect the public from industrial warfare as the civil courts are to guard the public interest in other areas. He sees labour tribunals also as a corollary of the present custom of referring to compulsory arbitration those disputes that arise during the contract term.

"A labour court," says Shumiatcher, "would be a natural outgrowth of the practices that unions and companies have acknowledged ought to be vested in a third party — namely, an impartial abitrator — where irreconcilable differences arise out of an already existing agreement".

This analogy is not nearly as valid as Shumiatcher and other labour court supporters seem to think. An arbitrator called upon to rule on a grievance involving interpretation of a collective agreement has a written set of rules to guide him — the terms of the contract itself. An arbitrator empowered to rule on the justification of a union's demands for improved wages and working conditions has no such objective criteria on which to base a decision. No such criteria exist. Under these circumstances, arbitration becomes a chancy and imprecise procedure.

Shumiatcher refers approvingly also to the system of labour courts that have existed in Australia since the turn of the century, seeming to ignore their dismal record. For, as Frances Bairstow, Director of McGill University's Industrial Relations Centre, has observed: "After 60 years of compulsory arbitration, Australia has the unenviable record of five times the annual number of strikes as does Canada."

The Woods Report listed several other defects of compulsory arbitration. It has a potentially corrosive effect on the decision-making process, both within and between unions and management. It serves also as a crutch for weak leadership, to the extent that it enables union and company officials to take all politically embarrassing disputes to the arbitrator and let him make the unpopular decisions. . . . In the long run, the effect would be to undermine both the leadership in question and the collective bargaining process itself.

Most of the vocal champions of repressive measures are to be found among the ranks of senior company executives — men like R.P. Riggin, Vice President of Noranda, Harold Clawson, Vice President of Stelco, and Lloyd Hemsworth, Vice President of Kimberly-Clark Limited. These management spokesmen argue that unions have become too powerful, and that major legislative controls over their power are needed to restore the alleged imbalance that has occurred. "Union monopolies should be curtailed", says Riggin. "All our labour legislation and administration is significantly canted in favour of the unions," charges Clawson.

There is no empirical evidence to support these contentions. Powerful unions are still far less numerous than weak unions. More strikes continue to be lost than won. The image of huge labour bullies buldgeoning helpless employers into submission hardly squares with the actuality of the union-management relationship. Besides, an imbalance of power is often an essential ingredient in arriving at an accommodation. As Professor Roy Brookbank of Dalhousie University has pointed out, settlement often occurs because one side or the other doesn't feel it has adequate power to back up further agrument. There is always, in the democratic system, some kind of imbalance — but the democratic system makes constant adjustment the main issue, not perfection, or peace at any price.

The unions probably could argue more persuasively that labour legislation is slanted against them. In any event, the businessmen's clamour for more curbs on unions evidently failed to impress federal Department of Labour officials, judging from the proposed amendments to the IRDI Act tabled in Parliament last June. "The bill provides no comfort for those who look to restrictive legislation for solutions to the problems of industrial relations," Labour Minister Mackasey said bluntly when he introduced the amendments.

The defects of restrictive laws and compulsory arbitration have been graphically demonstrated in British Columbia, where a Mediation Commission empowered to impose settlements has floundered ineffectually for the past three years. Instead of cooling off industrial conflict, the Commission's first three years of operation have seen more man-days lost in strikes and lockouts than had been lost in British Columbia in the entire preceding decade.

THE INNOVATIVE PROPOSALS

A more appropriate label for the innovative proposals might be "gimmicky," because most of them involve a clever twist in the customary bargaining process. Their ingenuity, however, is no guarantee that they are practicable.

One of the most intriguing proposals in this category is "forced choice" arbitration, more commonly known as "final offer selection" (FOS). It differs from conventional arbitration in that the arbitrator, instead of devising a compromise between two extreme positions, decides wholly in favour of one of the final offers submitted by the two sides. The assumption is that both union and management will be compelled to present realistic positions for fear of having their opponent's terms imposed on them.

This concept has been advanced as a dispute-settling formula by Val Scott, General Manager of the Ontario Hydro Professional Engineers and Associates. He points out that, although the FOS method is new to Canada, it has been adopted in the United States by the Tennessee Valley Authority for its engineers, and was a central feature of President Nixon's proposed bill to regulate bargaining by the railway unions.

"In practice," says Scott, "FOS would bring sufficient pressure to bear to encourage reasonableness, and greatly reduce the number of unresolved issues that might require recourse to arbitration." His advocacy of the FOS technique is forceful, but it overlooks some obvious shortcomings. First of all, the system would put into the hands of one man awesome power over the wages and working conditions of large numbers of people. Not many groups of workers would willingly yield such power to a single individual, regardless of how great a paragon he might be. They certainly would balk at surrendering their right to ratify final contract terms.

The biggest hitch in the FOS concept centres on the definition of the word reasonable. The selection officer, we are told, will consider each submission as a package, and will decide totally in favour of the one he considers the most reasonable. But in the absence of objective criteria, reasonableness is purely subjective. How does an officer decide whether the union's demand or the employer's counter-offer is reasonable when much of the relevant background information is denied him, or, if available, is too abstruse to be properly evaluated.

Then there is the not unlikely possibility that the selection officer will find both the union's and the company's final positions equally reasonable. That is, each of them will be as reasonable as their conflicting interests will permit, and still be poles apart. What does the selector do then, toss a coin?

These are some of the more obvious flaws in the FOS proposal. It may nevertheless be a feasible method for professional groups such as engineers, and perhaps for other employees in essential services who eschew the strike weapon, either on ethical or practical grounds. But it should be used only when the employees themselves freely ask for it. Any attempt to impose it on all workers through legislation would be as fiercely resisted as compulsory arbitration.

Another gimmicky proposal is the "non-stoppage strike," in which workers remain on the job, but forego their wages, while managers and owners correspondingly forfeit salaries and profits. The theory behind this bright idea is that it enables the parties to apply economic pressure on each other while protecting the interests of innocent third parties. A variation of this proposal, advanced by an American professor of business, J.H. Foegan, calls for both the union and the company to make regular daily or weekly deposits into a fund held by a mutually agreed-upon trustee. Both production and bargaining continue, with less of these funds returnable as settlement is delayed. Beyond an agreed-upon point, none is returnable, and all the money is assigned to some acceptable charity.

The U.S. Labor Law Journal has dismissed this brainstorm as being "of questionable legality and doubtful usefulness." Looking at it from a labour standpoint, its chief drawback is that it assumes fiscal equality between workers and employers. No such equality exists. The ability of management to sustain loss of income and profits is infinitely greater than the capacity of their employees to forego their wages. Endurance contests based on cessation of income would thus be heavily weighted in favour of the employer.

Less innovative, but still a startling departure from the conventional wisdom, is the proposal of voluntary arbitration. It is especially surprising when espoused by unionists who had hitherto been stalwart champions of the strike weapon. These converts to arbitrated settlements include such prominent U.S. labour leaders as AFL-CIO President George Meany, Steelworkers President I.W. Abel, and Communications Workers President Joseph A. Beirne. Meany has been saying for the past year or so that we are getting to the point where a strike doesn't make sense in many situations. They don't settle a thing. As early as 1959, Beirne referred to the need to re-evaluate the union's ultimate weapon, the strike. When fewer and fewer people are actually engaged in providing the direct service to the customers, and more and more are involved in auxiliary functions, how effectively can you halt production?

The American Arbitration Association has appointed a two-man committee to discuss with union leaders the possibilities of using arbitration as an alternative to strikes in deadlocked negotiations. The two men — David L. Cole, a veteran arbitrator, and David A. Morse, former head of the ILO in Geneva — have received sympathetic hearings from most labour officials they have so far met. Meany stated openly that voluntary arbitration is worth exploring. It's something highly desirable if it can be accomplished.

The response to voluntary arbitration from the rank-and-file has not been so favourable. Already the Steelworkers' chief, I.W. Abel, rebuked by a militant membership, has had to back off from his flirtation with arbitrated settlements. It may well be adopted by certain unions and employers in large key industries where strike confrontations in the past have proved mutually calamitous. But the prospect for any wide-scale adoption of third-party awards in Canadian collective bargaining must be considered remote. It has even fallen into disrepute in the Federal Public Service, the only sector where it has been extensively used in Canada.

A more attractive and feasible method of settling contract disputes — at least in essential industries — has been proposed by Leland Hazard of the Carnegie Institute of Technology. His proposal is based on a simple assumption: that public service employees will not strike if their wages and working conditions approximate those of similar workers in private industry. The reasoning is that strikes against the public can be avoided only if the public, through its elected representatives, decides to remunerate its employees adequately. Otherwise the public has no more right to claim immunity from labour troubles than do stingy employers in the private sector.

The problem is how to determine objectively what constitutes a fair wage for workers in the public service. Hazard's scheme offers a possible modus operandi. He suggests establishment of a permanent industrial peace commission whose function would be to review working agreements in essential industries and to propose equitable terms of settlement in each set of negotiations.

The commission members, selected for their impartiality, would be drawn from labour, industry, the professions and the universities, and appointed on a long-term basis to free them from political influence. They would be supplied with a secretariat and a staff of statisticians, economists, reserachers and other specialists. Periodically, the commission would hold public hearings at which unions, employers and other interested parties could make representations.

The commission and its technicians would continually evaluate all factors bearing on employment standards in the public service. It would ascertain and study information on such subjects as job skills, living costs, and comparative rates of pay in private industry. Basing its recommendations on this analysis, it would issue annual or biennial proposals for adjustments in wages and other benefits for all workers in the public sector. The recommendations, or course, would not be legally binding; but they would carry such moral weight that any union or employer failing to prove their inequity beyond doubt would incur great public disfavour if it were to ignore them. Hazard does not advance the IPC as a fool-proof formula. He admits that its adoption would not entirely eliminate public service strikes. Nevertheless, he believes it would reduce strikes to a tolerable minimum, which is perhaps the best that can be hoped for in a democratic society.

Hazard's plan merits a trial. Even if it proved effective, however, its limited application to essential services would still leave most of the private sector untouched. Perhaps that is as it should be, but others who seek the Shangri-la of labour relations might not agree.

THE RADICAL PROPOSALS

One factor common to all the foregoing schemes is that they presume a continuation of the standard bargaining methods, at least up to the point of an impasse. They also avoid tampering with union and employer structures. Not so the radical proposals. They are based on the premise that the inadequacies of collective bargaining derive from the allegedly cumbersome and outmoded character of our industrial institutions.

"The existing structure must be remodelled completely to give freedom of action a chance to work", declares Vancouver labour lawyer John Laxton. "All efforts in the past to improve labour-management relations have amounted only to piecemeal reforms. We must now recognize that this kind of tinkering is not working. It is time to give earnest consideration to a radical restructuring of the whole system".

Laxton's proposal is the most radical of all those made in recent years. He calls for the enforced merger of all labour organizations in Canada into ten or twelve giant unions, and the allocation of the entire workforce, organized or not, among these groups. Employers would be similarly lumped together into units corresponding to the unions. Contracts for all employers would be for a two-year period and would all terminate on the same date. Bargaining would be continuous, and the right to strike and lockout would be preserved.

Laxton argues that this "radical restructuring" would take away from labour and management the weapons that now enable them to wage limited but harmful battles, and arm them instead with the equivalent of atomic bombs. "Thus it will be all-out war or nothing. A strike or lockout would put hundreds of thousands of people out of work at the same time, and severely endanger the economy. The chances are that, given such powers both sides would refrain from using them. Yet the basic freedoms to withdraw one's labour or close down one's business would still be preserved."

The Vancouver lawyer cites several additional benefits to be gained from his proposed overhaul: it would eliminate unfair competition between unionized employers and those paying nonunion wages; it would do away with jurisdictional disputes between unions, and eliminate the waste and duplication that now result from the labour movement's fragmentation; it would stop all picket-line violence, for picketing would be unnecessary in a system that precludes the hiring of strikebreakers; and it would virtually remove the courts from the labour scene, injunctions and appeals being associated mainly with picketing, organizing and secondary boycotts, all of which would have disappeared.

Unquestionably, the kind of highly centralized system that Laxton suggests would live up to most of the claims he makes for it. One may have qualms about the creation of vast union and employer monopolies and the threat to individual freedoms that might ensue; and one might also fear that the "atomic bomb" of wide-scale strikes would occasionally be dropped. These risks aside, however, Laxton's radically restructured system would certainly prove much more orderly and efficient than the present one.

The trouble is that a system like this one calls for state intervention on such a massive scale — requiring the close cooperation of the federal and provincial goverments — that it simply isn't feasible. Laxton suggests that it could be tackled by any one province individually, but the odds are against any province voluntarily getting that far out of step with the rest of the country. If it were only the unions that objected, perhaps one or more of the provinces might be tempted. But the employers would be even more opposed — especially to the enforced unionization of all workers; and no government is going to plunge into a major reform that both labour and management are certain to resist.

The same drawback applies to a similar scheme that was proposed a few years ago by the then deputy minister of labour in Quebec, Robert Sauvé. His plan called for "sectorial bargaining," and, like Laxton's, required that all workers be unionized and that all employers participate in joint negotiations on an industry-wide basis.

According to Sauvé, it would lead to rationalization of the province's "small-time beaneries and two-bit factories," an upgrading of the unorganized working poor, and the new era of industrial peace.

Initially Sauvé's plan was supported by both of Quebec's central labour federations, the CNTU and the QFL, by top government officials including Premier Bourassa, and even by the larger, unionized business firms that saw the advantage of removing low-wage competition. But then the objections came rolling in from nonunion employers (still in the majority in Quebec) and from unions that foresaw possible extinction in the province; so the Sauvé plan was quietly dropped.

Most other radical proposals are variations of the Laxton-Sauvé models, involving rearrangement of existing labour and management structures as if they were so many toy building blocks. An interesting twist has been offered by a Toronto lawyer, Robert D. Perkins, who suggests that wage disputes be settled by a special bench of judges with the power to call "citizens' juries." His reasoning is that the public — the supposedly unrepresented third party at the bargaining table — should be the arbiter in labour–management conflicts, and that this could best be done through the jury system.

The public, of course, is already represented in labour disputes by government conciliators and by the whole system of labour legislation. If government doesn't act on behalf of the public when it imposes compulsory conciliation in all industrial disputes, then whose interests is it protecting? Citizens' juries, with no special competence in the field of labour relations, would create much more trouble than they could possibly avert.

THE MEDIATIVE PROPOSALS

The people most closely associated with the practice of industrial relations are, generally speaking, the ones who are least inclined toward drastic changes in the present system. They see its defects, but they are also deeply conscious of its merits. They understandably lean toward the mediative approach in the event of bargaining deadlocks.

The foremost advocate of mediation is, of course, the federal Minister of Labour, Bryce Mackasey. His "preventive mediation" technique — unlike most of the others previously cited — has the clear advantage of having been translated successfully from theory into practice. During the past few years, Mackasey's trouble-shooting specialists have racked up a near-perfect record of peaceful settlements and averted or abbreviated strikes.

The mediative approach is premised on the belief that a highly skilled "referee" can work out the face-saving compromises necessary for an agreement between two mistrustful antagonists. Each of Mackasey's trained industry specialists is an expert in his own field, and personally acquainted with union and company officials. Their task is to get involved in incipient disputes and probe for strike-avoiding formulas. Because they have the confidence of both sides, they are able to cut through the bluff and bluster and find out where the settlement range really lies.

Mackasey devised his mediation approach because he is, above all, a pragmatist. He realizes that no two confrontations between unions and employers are alike; that each has its own peculiar blend of contending forces. There is no magic formula for equalizing the power of union and employer in every set of negotiations. Even if there were, it would be no guarantee of industrial peace. It might, on the contrary, produce longer bloodier, and more frequent conflicts. Neither is there any conceivable labour code that could be applied, Procrustean-like, to all labour disputes. That is why Mackasey opted for the flexibility and expertise of mediation, rather than the legalistic restraints urged on him by many businessmen and editorial writers. He decided that what was needed was a workable method of resolving each dispute as it occurs, within its own particular framework.

Mackasey was denounced in some quarters as being "too permissive," but he soon confounded his critics. In 1970, the first full year of his mediative policy, his trouble-shooters settled 92 per cent of the disputes referred to them from industries in the federal jurisdiction. This feat didn't impress some critics, who pointed out that most of the squabbles involved small groups of workers. They predicted he would come a cropper in 1971 when half a dozen crucial negotiations were scheduled in major industries, all of them potentially explosive. But once again they were forced to eat their words as, one by one, Mackasey's mediators — and, as a last resort, Mackasey himself — calmly and methodically defused the bombs of labour unrest. Their settlement record for 1971 may be even higher than it was in 1970.

This is not to imply that the mediative approach is idyllic, that it has surmounted all obstacles. It is still being attacked — not on the basis that it won't work, but on the basis that it sometimes produces peace at an unacceptable price. Several of the settlements devised by Mackasey and his mediators in 1961 were denounced by the press, and even by some of his political colleagues, as "inflationary." This charge was made despite the fact that most of the mediated wage increases were at or below the average percentage rise recorded in the entire private sector.

A few grumbles were heard also from union spokesmen to the effect that the mediators were really "enforcers" of official or unofficial wage guidelines set by the federal Government. They complained, too, that the mediators, in their zeal to get a settlement, sometimes displayed no concern for the fairness or adequacy of the proposed terms.

As no set of contract terms will ever please everyone, such carping is perhaps inescapable. More disturbing is the threat posed to the mediative approach by growing rank-and-file distrust. Mediation, by its very nature, involves only the union and management negotiators. Secrecy is a key component of its effectiveness. But the union members, unless they have complete faith in their negotiating team — a rarity these days — tend to be suspicious of agreements arrived at through a system they cannot perceive or understand. In this kind of situation, the mediators are powerless. It avails them nothing to propose a settlement package acceptable to union leaders if the rank and file then refuse to ratify it. Rejection by union members of mediated terms has occurred several times, and accounts for most of the relatively few failures on Mackasey's performance chart.

On balance, however, the mediative approach has been remarkably successful. It is by no means perfect; but then, perfection and democracy are by definition incompatible. The proponents of the other labour relations reforms previously discussed might argue, with some justification, that their ideas would produce even better results if they were given the same test as the mediation method. That may be so. Some of them are attractive, and a few may even be feasible. But until some government decides to experiment with them, the technique of preventive mediation must be accorded top honours. It has been proved effective. It promotes industrial peace. It sharply reduces the incidence of strikes. And all without tampering unduly with the traditional process of collective bargaining.

Preventive mediation may not be the Holy Grail the perfection-seekers yearn for. But it does offer a workable method of improving labour–management relations and resolving disputes. To that extent, at least, the search for "a better way" has been worthwhile.

ARBITRATION VERSUS THE STRIKE WEAPON: A MANAGEMENT VIEW*

H. J. Clawson

Mr. Clawson, Vice President of the Steel Company of Canada, predicts that growing public resentment toward strikes will lead to their demise and ultimately will result in the use of a system of voluntary or compulsory arbitration for settlement of contract disputes.

We are being inexorably driven in the direction of a revolutionary change in our methods of collective bargaining. The general public is fed up with strikes and even generally pro-labour newspapers like the Toronto Star are increasingly calling for legislation to prohibit them in essential industries. The area of permissible strike activity will be drastically reduced within the next ten years because people are fast losing faith in collective bargaining as a means of achieving reasonable settlements. Governments, too, are being forced to acknowledge that it is increasingly the public that must bear the brunt of a growing number of work stoppages. Almost eight million man-days were lost in 1972 through strikes and lockouts — a clear indication that the collective bargaining system is working poorly, particularly in the public sector. It was also Canada's worst year from the standpoint of relations between governments and their employees. To mention only a few areas of strike activity: Canada's three largest cities — Toronto, Montreal and Vancouver — did without garbage collection for a month last year; the entire public service of Quebec walked out for a couple of weeks last spring; and electric utilities in Ontario and Quebec were shut down last fall by labour disputes.

Though the federal Government has not yet modified its own legislation on work stoppages in the Public Service, a number of provinces have been compelled to end strikes in sensitive areas through ad hoc legislation or compulsory arbitration. The recent seven-month strike by elevator technicians is a case in point. It was the first time in Ontario that compulsory arbitration was imposed to settle a dispute in private industry. In Quebec, the strike was declared illegal. Ad hoc legislation also brought an end to the public service strike in that province. Recent stoppages by Hydro employees, dock workers and air traffic controllers were also subject to government intervention. The arbitration process does have pitfalls and inherent risks for both management and unions, but we must keep in mind the realities of collective bargaining. With the increasing specialization of functions in the economy, and with the growing interdependence of its units, the power of small groups of

---

* Excerpts from Mr. Clawson's speech to an Industrial Relations Seminar at Queens University. Reprinted with permission.

employees to paralyze the community is frightening. The risks of arbitration, including its inhibiting effects on collective bargaining, are of minor importance compared with the great damage that can be inflicted on all parties — including the general public — by the tendency of many unions to strike automatically as soon as the legal opportunity arises. Coercion rather than free collective bargaining is the name of the game in the public service and in some parts of the private sector. When a union strikes or threatens to strike in an essential service, the settlement is more likely to be designed to avoid the hardship of a strike than to be the result of rational analysis. Force thus replaces reason in such areas. Is there any reason to believe that imposed arbitral solutions would be less rational and reasonable than those induced by coercion? If accepting some frustration of collective bargaining is the price we must pay in order to avoid strikes that hold the public to ransom, then I am convinced we must pay it.

Too much bargaining power for the unions results not only in inflationary settlements that are greatly in excess of any equitable or reasonable standard, but also in other administrative concessions that can result in reduced efficiency and lower productivity. Employees, too, are beginning to be disenchanted with strikes. The elementary arithmetic that can conclusively show the futility of striking seems to be slowly sinking in. It is, of course, well known that the gains from strikes are usually minimal. Many union leaders (including Leonard Woodcock and George Meany) realize this; others, for some strange reason, seem to think that they have to permit, or even promote, periodic strikes in order to maintain an appropriate militancy and solidarity among their members. Workers are sometimes dragged into strikes merely because of the personal intransigence and irresponsibility of individual leaders. The Troonto Western Hospital strike is a case in point. Another example of the trivial issues that frequently bring on strikes was the threatened Toronto transit strike last summer. The main issue in the close ratification vote was the union's opposition to management's proposal that it be permitted to hire 25 temporary drivers each summer in order to provide summer vacations for as many of its regular drivers as possible. There is also the increasing tendency of unions to call strikes over political issues — some political in the broad sense, as in the overt announcements by Messrs. Pepin, Charbonneau and Laberge in Quebec — and some involving internal union politics, inter-union rivalry, or even competition among union leaders.

Unfortunately, the plausible and symmetrical models of collective bargaining that so intrigue academic analysts completely ignore or naively underestimate the costs and other effects of strikes as the final step in the collective bargaining process. It is quite possible that the fear that every aspect of collective bargaining would disappear with arbitration as the terminal process is grossly exaggerated — in other words, strikes may not be an indispensable condition to the successful functioning of the collective bargaining system. Where arbitration has been practised, the evidence is mixed. In some negotiations, the parties have indeed been inclined to let everything go to the arbitrator; but there are just as many cases, if not more, where only the basic and substantial issues have reached the arbitrator. The others were settled during the negotiations. We should be devoting our energies to improving arbitration procedures rather than indulging in endless debates about theoretical objections. It may well be that the only way the arbitration process can be refined is as a result of further trial-and-error experience. Maybe through adequate planning and research we can minimize many of its pitfalls. The Ontario Government has started a review of arbitration procedures. Ontario was the first province in Canada to prohibit strikes in certain parts of the public service, and to set up a permanent arbitration tribunal.

What often passes for voluntary arbitration is not really voluntary at all. The terms imposed by an arbitrator to whom the parties have submitted voluntarily are as much of an interference with free collective bargaining as terms imposed by compulsory arbitration. In both instances, the arbitrator wields just as much power — and the outcome is just as unpredictable. It is true that the use of ad hoc voluntary arbitration after negotiations break down would not stifle collective bargaining; but unions would only agree to it if they thought their bargaining position was weak. Yet another fallacy is the argument that arbitration should be imposed only in areas in which a strike would be intolerable to the public. This would mean, in effect, that relatively weak bargaining units whose services were not essential to the community could strike as often and for as long as they liked. What kind of a right to strike is this? It is inconceivable that governments, for instance, would grant their nonessential employees wages or benefits in excess of those awarded by arbitration to public employees performing essential services. Such a practice would run counter to the notion that taxpaying citizens have a right to continuity in all public services, not merely essential ones. If any service can be allowed to shut down, then it probably should not exist in the first place.

We need to give thought to arbitration as an alternative to strikes. If we do not, we may throw away a good chance to avoid the disorder and economic waste that only too often result from our present collective bargaining system. The first step toward improving arbitration techniques should be to establish statutory criteria. The absence of such criteria saddles the arbitrator with an impossible responsibility. It also places too much power in the hands of the most ingenious and persuasive counsel or spokesman. An impartial fact-finding body is equally necessary — something along the lines of the federal Pay Research Bureau. The arbitrator should not have to rely solely on the often haphazard and self-serving wage and benefit data supplied by the parties. Probably the most essential requirement is that we try to avoid ad hoc arbitration. Though It may not be feasible in all cases, arbitration should normally be handled by a permanent tribunal. Only through some type of continuity can appropriate jurisprudence be developed. The chairman and members need not be appointed for life, however. Nor do they need to serve on a full-time basis. It is important, moreover, to minimize the consequences of personal biases implicit in a system of ad hoc arbitration. If separate tribunals or arbitrators are to be used for various occupational groups, there must be some form of coordinating authority or tribunal. Arbitration awards covering firemen or policemen, for instance, cannot be inconsistent with general jurisprudence governing the public service as a whole. Such special awards would require the approval of a super tribunal. There should be no general right of appeal or review, except possibly in the foregoing circumstances. It is conceivable that, with the growth of arbitration, special panels of the tribunal would be assigned to make a tentative award requiring the approval of the full tribunal to come into effect. Arbitration tribunals could benefit from bipartite advisory councils. The latter would meet with the tribunal periodically (though not on specific cases) to discuss broad policies. Though arbitration of compensation and other issues may be an intrusion upon the sovereign right of the Legislature to budget and to levy taxes, this formidable problem could be solved by giving special veto power to the Governor in Council, Parliament or the Legislature. This would, of course, evoke cries of dissent and charges of unilateral imposition of wages by the employer. The problem would not arise unless the veto was exercised however; and presumably this would be a rare occurrence.

Some people objected to governments' unilateral imposition of salaries on their employees but had no constitutional objections to the taxes levied, or other restraints imposed, on all citizens by these same governments. Another condition essential to any system of adjudication for the public service is the specific exclusion, by law, of certain issues from the arbitrator's jurisdiction. This requirement has been satisfied, to some extent, by the federal and Ontario Governments. We continue the almost universal practice of three-man or tripartite boards, even in cases where the chairman holds a permanent appointment. These (sidesmen as they are called) could continue to be partisan appointments on an ad hoc basis. Most arbitrators in negotiation disputes would welcome the benefits of the sidesmen's counsel and advice. Greater understanding of the issues would assist them in achieving the art of the possible. I favour the retention of the sidesmen's voting rights, although the chairman's award would have to be the decisive one. This could make for a greater degree of accommodation in the award. I recommend also the retention of a pre-arbitration mediation or conciliation procedure, though this should be employed discreetly, depending on the circumstances of each set of negotiations. The arbitration tribunal itself should use mediation techniques to encourage the greatest possible degree of mutual agreement. For these to be successful, the chairman must have the experience and perception to be able to distinguish clearly between his role as a mediator and as an arbitrator.

I am disturbed at the excessive zeal displayed in some quarters for Final Offer Selection. FOS as an overly simplistic approach to a very complex problem, a new form of gimmickry, and a sort of arbitration roulette. Under this system, designed to improve arbitration procedures, the unsettled items of a dispute are referred to an arbitrator. Following further discussions, each party places a final offer of settlement in a sealed envelope and hands it to the arbitrator. The latter then opens the envelopes and makes his award. He must select either the employer's offer or the union's, and he has no jurisdiction to modify either of them in any way. The rationale for FOS is: 1) the arbitrator's discretion is reduced, thus making the award acdeptable to at least one of the parties; and 2) The parties would have to be realistic in their proposals. If one of them is too far out of line with reason, it risks rejection of its own offer and acceptance of the other party's offer. Many complicated issues arise in negotiations, making it virtually impossible at times to accept all of one party's proposals. A union proposal of twenty-five cents an hour, for example, might be acceptable to the arbitrator if he could attach conditions to it or offset the wage increase by a modification in the benefit package. The FOS system would not allow him to do this, however. Many of our concepts, strategies and practices must undergo change. The trend toward arbitration as a substitute for strikes will continue, because the public will demand it; and no political reincarnation of a Canute will be able to stem the tide.

FREEDOM TO STRIKE IS IN THE PUBLIC INTEREST*

Thomas Kennedy

Professor Kennedy suggests that costly strikes make compulsory arbitration look like an easy way out, but that way leads to the end of our business system.

It has often been proposed that strikes in the private sector be made illegal. The managements of the railroads and the maritime industry openly advocate compulsory arbitration as a desirable alternative to free collective bargaining. There is reason to believe that unions in industries where automation has reduced the strike power will also move to that position. Suppliers and customers hurt by a strike are likely to mutter, "It should be outlawed."

Unfortunately, it is not a matter of eliminating strikes by devices which have no costs. The various compulsory settlement methods also

* Excerpted from Thomas Kennedy, "Freedom to Strike Is in the Public Interest," *Harvard Business Review*, July-August 1970. Reprinted with permission.

are expensive, and it may be that managements, unions and the public would find such costs more onerous than the costs of strikes. We should be fully aware of these costs before abandoning the present free collective bargaining system in the private sector.

SPECTER OF MORE FAILURES

The costliness of a strike to management and labor is in itself a strong incentive for them to reach agreement. What happens if that incentive is removed? There is reason to believe that the number of failures to reach agreement would increase greatly. This was our experience during World War II, when the strike was replaced with compulsory settlement by a government agency. It was also our experience in the late 1940's, when a number of states replaced free collective bargaining in public utilities with compulsory arbitration.

There are two reasons that the companies and unions find it more difficult to reach agreement when the possibility of the strike has been removed:

1. The parties are not under so much pressure to work out a contract because, while the compulsory settlement may be less desirable than the contract that could have been negotiated, it does not carry a threat of immediate loss of production and wages.

2. If the compulsory settlement authority — whether it be a government board, a court, or an arbitrator — has the right to decide on what it thinks is a fair settlement, then the company and the union may well hesitate to make a move toward a settlement, fearing that the other party will hold at its old position and that the board, court, or arbitrator will split the difference. If, for example, the company is offering a $.10-per-hour increase, why should the company move to $.12 and $.16 instead of between $.10 and $.16? For like reasons, the union hesitates to move down from $.16 to $.14. Thus, compulsory settlement interferes with the process of voluntary settlement.

In order to avoid the effect just described, the Nixon Administration now proposes that when strikes are threatened in the transportation industries, the President be permitted to order arbitration proceedings in which the arbitrator is required to decide only which of the two final offers of the parties is the more reasonable. It is believed that this method would remove one of the undesirable effects of the usual type of arbitration — that is, the hesitancy of the parties to improve their offers for fear that the arbitrator will split the difference. However, the new proposal has the disadvantage of forcing the arbitrator to choose between two proposals, both of which may seem unfair to him.

While the type of arbitration now proposed by the Administration would probably be less harmful than ordinary compulsory arbitration in terms of hampering efforts to reach a voluntary settlement, it would still have some such effect, for management and labor would not be prodded by fears of strike costs. I believe it is erroneous to expect that the number of disputes which would go to an arbitrator would be the same as the number of strikes which would occur without compulsory settlement. The removal of the strong incentive to settle would result in a great many more failures to reach agreement voluntarily. It would therefore be necessary to establish a sizable government bureaucracy to handle the increased volume of unsettled contract disputes.

MORE FEDERAL INTERVENTION

The size of the bureaucracy could be lessened by using private arbitrators (with the parties given an opportunity to choose the men they like) instead of a labor board or a labor court. However, the government would have to become involved when the parties were unable to agree on an arbitrator. Moreover, while the Federal Mediation and Conciliation Service has been free from political bias in placing arbitrators' names on its lists for selection by the parties in grievance arbitrations, there can be no guarantee that politics would not play a role in the selection process if the stakes were high enough — as they would be in the compulsory arbitration of new contract terms in the steel, coal, automobile, and other major industries.

If a board or labor court were used to settle disputes, it would have the possible advantage of being able to establish continuing policies. Nevertheless, appointment of at least some of the members would be made by the Administration. (A board could be tripartite, in which case some members would be appointed by labor and some by management.) One of the costs of compulsory settlement, therefore, would be to move management – labor disputes — to some degree at least — from the economic to the political arena.

WILL FORCE REALLY WORK?

Under the free collective bargaining system, the government has no problem of enforcement. For instance, while both the company and the employees suffered serious losses during the fourteen-week GE strike, once it was over both the management and the workers returned to their jobs voluntarily. This illustrates an important advantage of the present system which is often overlooked — that no use of force by the government is required. Moreover, since the agreement is one which the parties themselves have negotiated, the day-to-day operations under it are likely to be more cooperative. The company representatives sell it to management, and the union representatives sell it to the employees. Since the contract is the negotiators' own handiwork, they make a real effort to get it to work — a greater effort, I believe, than they would make if the agreement were the work of some authority appointed by the government.

This country's experience with legislation that has prohibited strikes on the part of the public employees indicates that such legislation does not automatically put an end to the strikes. The Condon-Wadlin Act, which prohibited strikes by state and local government employees in New York State from 1947 to 1967, was violated often, but on only a few occasions were its penalties actually enforced. Since 1967 the Taylor Act, which also prohibits strikes by public employees in New York State, has been subject to numerous violations. Likewise, the illegality of strikes by federal employees has not prevented them from leaving the job.

What would happen, under compulsory settlement, if workers in the coal, steel, automobile, trucking, or some other major industry decided that they did not wish to accept the terms prescribed by the arbitrator or labor court and refused to work? How does a democratic government force 100,000 coal miners, 400,000 steel workers, 700,000 automobile workers, or 450,000 truckers to perform their tasks effectively when they elect not to do so? Perhaps it can be done — but I suggest that this is a question which it is well not to have to answer. It is unwise to run the risk of placing government in a position where the government may reveal its impotence unless it is absolutely necessary to do so.

THREAT TO CAPITALISM

Finally, if government becomes involved in the determination of labor contract terms in order to avoid strikes, it may not be able to stop there. With our democratic political structure it would be impossible, I believe, to prevent compulsory settlement of wages for union members from leading to compulsory determination of all wages; that, in turn, would lead to government decisions concerning salaries, professional fees and, finally, prices and profits.

So long as free collective bargaining is permitted, it forms an outer perimeter of defense against government regulation in other areas. If it falls, the possibility of more regulation in the other areas becomes much greater. It is worth noting that George Meany, the president of the AFL-CIO, stated several months ago that he would not be opposed to wage controls if similar controls were placed on salaries, prices, and profits. Meany's view of these relationships is one that many people might share.

CONCLUSION

As the public becomes more and more irritated and frustrated by the inconveniences and hardships strikes cause and by the increases in prices and taxes which follow the settlements, political pressure will probably develop, as it has on similar occasions in the past, to replace free collective bargaining with some method of compulsory settlement. How do the costs of the right to strike compare with the costs of the alternative, compulsory settlement? Taking strike costs first, my analysis indicates that:

- It is easy to overemphasize the costs of strikes.
- Much progress has already been made in replacing organizational strikes, jurisdictional strikes, and grievance strikes with peaceful alternatives.
- Strikes — even the big industrywide ones — have a minimal effect on the company.
- Some strikes, such as those in public utilities, which once were very critical, are no longer so because of automation.
- The number of man-days lost because of strikes is a very small part of the total (only 0.23 per cent in 1969), and the trend has been definitely downward.

On the other hand, my analysis indicates that compulsory settlement involves major costs like these:

- The elimination from collective bargaining of the strongest incentive to reach agreement which management and labor now have.
- A great increase in the number of failures to reach agreement.
- The development of a large government bureaucracy to adjudicate the larger number of unsettled disputes.
- An increase in political aspects of collective bargaining.
- The difficulty of enforcement of compulsory orders, with the attendant danger of divulging the impotence of government.
- The likely development of other wage, salary, price, and profit controls by government.

I conclude that the right to strike is preferable to a compulsory settlement system. It does not follow that the government should never move to protect the public against strikes which create serious hardships, but it does follow that any move to prohibit the use of the strike in the private sector should be made cautiously and only to the extent which is clearly required. Any broad prohibition of strike freedom would prove to be very costly in itself and also lead to major government controls over other parts of the economy. Free collective bargaining, which includes the right to strike and the right to lock out, constitutes the outer defense of the private enterprise system.

THE VALUE OF EDUCATION FOR STABLE INDUSTRIAL RELATIONS

Hem C. Jain

The author discusses the role of education as a contributor to a stable industrial relations climate.

It appears that unions and their leaders particularly at middle and lower echelon in the union hierarchy are ambivalent toward labour education. This writer taught at the Labour College of Canada for two years. The Labour College is sponsored by the Canadian Labour Congress, McGill University and the University of Montreal. In its 1969 annual report, the Principal of the College pointed out that "year after year the number and union status of applicants is diminishing." Partly, it may be due to the fact that the programme offered at the college is too academic and broad and partly because some union leaders fear that if they send other members of their union to the College, these members, upon graduation, might pose a threat to their leadership and might eventually replace them.

To put the role of education as a contributor to stable industrial relations in proper perspective one ought to ask a few questions. Do we need stable industrial relations? Is industrial peace in the interest of all parties? Will the government become the new power figure if labour and management do not accept their responsibility for regulation of their own affairs. The answer to these questions is "Yes".

I welcome the opportunity to share my thoughts through this article with the delegates of the New Brunswick Federation of Labour on the ways the labour movement, government, employers and educational institutions can help in creating a stable labour relations climate.

In the province of New Brunswick, the educational programme for labour functionaries appears to be limited to occasional workshops, seminars or tool courses. One cannot help but assume that either members and local labour leaders are not sufficiently conversant or not convinced of the necessity of labour education. Labour education includes such items as (1) grievance handling; (2) effective communication within the hierarchy of labour unions as well as between labour and management; (3) developing competence among bargaining agents.

In my opinion the labour movement in New Brunswick needs workshops, courses and programmes where special emphasis is placed on the pressing need for improving the communication skills of labour representatives so that they may increase their effectiveness in internal labour union administration; in dealing with management and treasury department officials at the bargaining table; and in carrying out public relations activities. It is hoped that at the 1973 Annual Convention of the New Brunswick Federation of Labour, there will be helpful discussion and dialogue among the delegates on this subject.

WHAT CAN THE UNIONS DO?

Union leaders at various union meetings could educate members about the necessity and importance of education and inform them how educational opportunities would further the goals of individual members and the union movement. Each local union or council of unions in a trade, industry or profession could conduct a survey of the educational needs of their members with the assistance of the local director of education of their unions or C.L.C., or an outsider. Courses in subject areas such as stewardship-training, grievance procedure, arbitration, contract negotiations, can be held in various local areas on the premises of technical institutes, high schools or university campuses. As an example of how such courses can be organized, let me illustrate how such a course was taught at UNBSJ.

In December 1972, the Saint John Building Trades Council approached the University of New Brunswick in Saint John to design a course for shop stewards. After an initial meeting with leaders from five unions in the Building Trades Council, a programme-planning Conference was held. This conference was attended by four shop stewards from each of the five unions interested in taking the course. It was a very productive meeting because most of the ideas for the programme and speakers came from these people. My experience tells me that unless people can identify their problems and concerns and are eager to learn and improve their knowledge and skills the success of any educational effort is very much in doubt.

THE ROLE OF THE GOVERNMENT

In keeping with past traditions and practices, the government role primarily lies in the regulatory and conciliatory domain. The government of New Brunswick must be congratulated for enacting progressive legislation, such as the new Industrial Relations Act, and the Lorneville Projects Authority Legislation. This new legislation recognizes the rights and obligations of both union and management. However, many laymen and labour representatives find it difficult to fully understand the legal implications of both statutes. One astute, highly respected observer of the Labour scene in the province of New Brunswick puts it this way:

> Both statutes are bonanzas for lawyers; as I understand, it rarely happens that either labour or management appear before the labour-relations board in even the simplest cases without a solicitor. Labor legislation should be more an enunciation of broad principles rather than rigid formulas as, when a real crunch de-

velops both labour and management, being mere humans, will lean on a legal crutch rather than face up to their problems.

I believe, it is highly desirable to keep new legislation to a minimum, leaving the parties, to the greatest extent possible, to work out their own problems by mutual agreement.

As far as conciliation and arbitration of industrial disputes are concerned most governments in Canada have relied almost exclusively on the services of judges and lawyers. Professor H. W. Arthurs of Osgoode Hall Law School evaluates the role of lawyers in industrial relations in the following words:

> It is true that many lawyers have contributed to the exacerbation of labour-management tension by violent partisanship; their capacity for mischief is part of the folklore of labour relations. Since lawyers are skilled in the use of legal techniques they frequently win critical battles before boards and courts and leave behind a residue of resentment. This resentment is directed not only at law, but at those who administer it — judges, board members and lawyers.

I believe that the labour movement has suffered to a large degree from the legalistic approach taken by lawyers and judges in arbitration. It would be in the interest of the union movement to suggest to the provincial government that it should sponsor educational workshops on the arbitration process and the impact of arbitration awards on labour – management relations. The government should invite lawyers, who have shown the ability to resolve conflicts by constructing compromises, university professors who have expertise in labour relations and behavioural sciences, enlightened union and management leaders, and government conciliation officers to attend such a workshop. By bringing these selected people together for an exchange of ideas and experiences, and by involving them in the actual decision making process through simulation exercises, the government could ensure an adequate supply of talented and experienced arbitrators. Such conferences could minimize the antagonism between labour and management and contribute to an overall better labour-relations climate.

It appears that the educational and training efforts of the department of labour are limited to offering tool courses for its staff and occasional conferences, and providing financial assistance to a few management and/or union personnel to attend courses sponsored by organizations outside the province. These efforts are commendable to the degree that they provide valuable knowledge of industrial relations. Since most of these conferences are open to the general public and are formal affairs, they do little in creating a better labour – management climate and understanding between union and management in the province. It is equally doubtful whether such conferences bring about any changes in behaviour among the individuals sitting across the bargaining table.

Furthermore there is a tendency on the part of labour, management and government officers to become so much involved in day-to-day administrative (fire fighting) matters that it becomes increasingly difficult for them to step back and look at things in perspective.

The Department of Business Administration at the University of New Brunswick in Saint John, Saint John District Labour Council and Saint John Board of Trade have jointly submitted a proposal to the provincial government to remedy this situation. The proposal is designed to bring together individuals who formulate or influence the formulations of policy in the field of labour – management relations and to expose them to a total immersion educational experience spread over a week. Hopefully at the end of this educational experience participants will become aware that the problems of labour policy are so complex and various that there are no magic formulas for their solution. They will develop their own capacities to analyze such problems and to work cooperatively with other parties. If this educational experience can prevent even one strike or reduce the number of grievances, this effort is worth every cent that the government and parties may invest in it.

In the final analysis, stable industrial relations depend upon the parties themselves. Better relationship can only prevail if union and management can trust or at least respect, one another to deal fairly with each other. It is also apparent that both parties can influence public policy by putting pressure on the government to scrap much of the restrictive legislation, if they are able to communicate openly and aboveboard in an atmosphere of mutual respect and toleration.

QUESTIONS FOR DISCUSSION, PART 4

(1) Crispo and Arthurs examine the militancy and increased defiance of the law in their article, "Industrial Unrest in Canada: A Diagnosis of Recent Experience." Discuss the underlying causes for this militancy and increased defiance of the law.

(2) Megginson and Gullett identify and isolate variables which influence the degree of union – management conflict in their article, "A Predictive Model of Union – Management Conflict." What are these variables? Explain each of these variables. What affect may each have on a dispute?

(3) How important is the political function of a union leader in a conflict?

(4) Assess the contribution of behavioural sciences and the role of education for union – management functionaries in creating a stable industrial relations climate.

(5) Researchers claim that the monotonous, unrewarding and dehumanizing aspects of work lead to discontent among employees and result in industrial strife. Discuss the attitude of union leaders toward behavioural science concepts, such as job enrichment

and teamwork which are intended to alleviate boredom and job alienation.

(6) It has been suggested that Government policies and legislation tend to decrease conflict between the parties in a dispute. Discuss the validity of this statement. Use the following quote to help you in your discussion: "Compulsory arbitration does not eliminate, or even reduce strikes; it only makes them illegal."

(7) Management contends that unions are responsible for the majority of strikes; that the union's primary function is to breed discontent among its members which in turn leads to unnecessary strikes. Discuss the validity of the above statements.

(8) Develop cases for and against strikes and lockouts. In developing your cases, draw upon the arguments presented by union – management and academic representatives in your readings.

(9) Do you agree with Mr. Clawson's prediction that growing public resentment toward strikes will lead to their demise and ultimately will result in the use of compulsory arbitration for settlement of interest disputes? Why, or why not?

(10) Discuss the pros and cons of the various proposals for resolving industrial strife, presented by Ed Finn in his article "Resolving Industrial Strife: Is There a Better Way"?

PART 5

EMERGING SECTORS IN INDUSTRIAL RELATIONS

The Growth of White Collar, Professional and Public Service Unionism, and Collective Bargaining for Public Employees

INTRODUCTION

During the decade 1959–69 the proportion of workers employed in service industries in Canada increased from 50 per cent of the total employed in all occupations in 1959 to 60 per cent in 1969. Because service industries employ a large number of white collar workers, there has been a substantial increase in the white collar occupations. During the same period, white collar workers increased at nearly twice the rate of blue collar workers. The fastest rate of increase was seen among professional, technical and clerical workers. Mrs. Bairstow, in a study of white collar workers and collective bargaining,[1] divided white collar employees into five separate and distinct categories: (1) those in the white collar industry of finance, (2) those in public service, either as public servants or as employees of government agencies and crown corporations, (3) those in retail trade, (4) those in offices directly associated with production facilities, (5) those who work side by side with production workers.

The organization of white collar workers has met with a number of complex problems since its inception, and lags behind that of blue collar workers both in numbers and in bargaining power. To a large extent the white collar organization has taken place in the public sector, that is among Federal Government employees as well as employees of provincial and municipal government. Leading public service unions in Canada are: the Canadian Union of Public Employees (C.L.C.), the National Federation of Services (CNTU) and the Public Service Alliance of Canada (CLC).

The newness of collective bargaining in the public sector gives rise to certain problems but it provides the parties with a unique opportunity to innovate. Since there is no precedent or history of early bitter struggle between the employers and the unions in the public sector, both parties can create a stable industrial relations climate by providing white collar employees with opportunities for participation in broad decision making at their work place.

The readings in this part describe and analyze the opportunities and problems parties face in white collar employee bargaining. In the first section, Dr. Wood suggests that the future of white collar unionism in Canada depends primarily on three factors. Long run external influences, management policies and practices and the willingness of the labour movement to modify its philosophy, structure, policies and approaches to accommodate the interest and needs of the rapidly expanding white collar labour force.

Professor Goldenberg analyzes the problems faced by professional workers in adapting to collective bargaining. Some of these problems are: determination of the bargaining unit, recognition of individual initiative and merit, compatibility of collective bargaining with professional ethics. Her second article deals with a comparison of public service legislation in various provinces with special reference to the machinery provided for handling an impasse in negotiations.

A paper by J. Finkelman reviews the progress made by both parties in bargaining for federal employees since the passage of the Public Service Staff Relations Act in 1967 and explains the procedures for dispute settlement in the Federal Public Service.

Mr. Finkelman suggests that under the provisions of this Act it is possible to give public employees the right to strike and still ensure the maintenance of essential services. Defining "Essential Employees" poses serious problems. "Essential Employees" in the federal public service are termed "Designated Employees" under the Act. The decision as to who the "Designated Employees" are is taken before negotiations start and the unions are involved in making this decision.

The brief by the Public Service Alliance of Canada brings into focus the inequities and weaknesses of the present collective bargaining system for federal employees. The Alliance suggests several amendments to the Public Service Staff Relations Act to remedy the situation. It suggests that the following issues, which are now excluded from the scope of collective bargaining, should be made negotiable — standards of work; work procedures; promotion; transfer; redundance; reassignment; layoff and recall. Unions also demand the right to negotiate classification standards. They feel that all negotiable matters should be arbitrable and that all grievances should be allowed to reach the adjudication stage.

The Canadian experience suggests that by and large collective bargaining for public employees has worked fairly well so far. However, it must be recognized that this is an ongoing process and that with the passage of time, both sides will develop new internal structures and new responses.

It is hoped that the questions at the end of this part will provide food for thought and stimulate the discussion among students.

FOOTNOTE

[1] See F. Bairstow's study, "White Collar Workers and Collective Bargaining," which she undertook for the Prime Minister's Task Force in Labour Relations in 1966/67.

WHITE-COLLAR ORGANIZING CHALLENGES*

W. Donald Wood

Dr. Wood discusses recent developments in the area of white-collar organization and the challenges the labour movement faces in future in organizing the rapidly growing numbers of white-collar employees in the labour force.

INTRODUCTION

The rapidly expanding field of white-collar employment today forms the major new frontier for trade unionism in Canada.

In its more traditional form, collective bargaining in the past has been found mainly among the blue-collar work force. But times are changing! Developments in recent years suggest that this may be in the process of change. Although white-collar organization is still on a relatively smaller scale than plant worker coverage, its significance lies in the fact that its potential is so great and that it has recently been expanding at a more rapid rate.

One of the problems of discussing this area is the very heterogeneous nature of the white-collar field which covers so many varied occupations and groups. Consequently, generalizations about the "white-collar" field are impractical. Attention must be focused on particular groups within this area. My remarks will be directed mianly to the office, clerical, and technician groups, although I also will make passing references to various professional categories.

THE OVERALL CHALLENGE

The postwar period has seen an explosive growth in white-collar employment — both in absolute terms and relative to blue-collar employment. The two underlying forces behind this trend have been:

(1)   The dramatic shift from goods (e.g. manufacturing) industry to service industry employment with a much higher proportion of white-collar occupations.

(2)   The significant shift within the "goods" industry from "blue-" to "white-collar" employment, which is intimately related to the revolutionary changes in industrial technology.

Consequently, the future of white-collar unionism as a fundamental issue for the Canadian labour movement is obvious:

(1)   In terms of membership growth, power, and influence, the

---

* Address to Ontario White-Collar Union Conference at Toronto Ontario, February 13, 1971. Reprinted with permission.

"key" determinant will be the ability of the labour movement to expand organization in the white-collar field.

(2)   Organization of this field will also be important in maintaining union "bargaining power," especially in blue-collar bargaining units.

(3)   It will also have an impact on
  □ the nature of union leadership,
  □ the organizational structure of the labour movement,
  □ its objectives and methods of operation
  □ and its idealistic outlook.

(4)   Finally, and probably most important, if the labour movement does not extend organization more broadly in these most dynamic growth areas of the economy, it is bound to lose much of its vitality which has been an important factor in past union growth and influence.

THE CURRENT BALANCE SHEET RE WHITE-COLLAR ORGANIZATION

Because of the serious inadequacies of our statistical series in this field, it is impossible to give a precise figure of the extent of white-collar organization. One very rough estimate indicates that:

  □ Approximately 1.5 per cent of the non-agricultural white-collar labour force is unionized.

  □ Approximately 8 per cent of the white-collar workers are organized in the private sector, reflecting the relatively greater white-collar organization in the public sector.

These figures compare with roughly 60 per cent of the manual workers organized. In an analysis of certifications in Ontario (1950 – 69), shortly to be published by the Centre, we found that of a total of 11,496 certifications for the period, only 573 (6.9 per cent of total) were white-collar units. Viewing the extent of white-collar organization on a broader general front, we can say there is fairly extensive organization in transportation, communications, and public employment, significant but scattered organization in the manufacturing industries, and practically no organization in the purely white-collar industries — banking, insurance, finance, etc.

We may conclude, then, that although white-collar unionism has established a sound base in a number of areas, it is still on a much lesser scale than blue-collar organization and has not maintained its pace in the rapidly expanding white-collar industries and organizations.

FACTORS INFLUENCING THE FUTURE OF WHITE-COLLAR UNIONISM

In viewing the future of white-collar unionism, three groups of factors must be assessed: (1) longer-run external influences; (2) management policies and practices; and (3) union activities and approaches in the white-collar field.

Longer-Run External Influences

Since World War II, there has been a series of economic, social, and technological changes which have tended to create a somewhat more favourable environment for unionizing efforts among white-collar employees. A clear understanding of these various long-run forces is important not only in analyzing white-collar unionism, but also in assessing the adequacy of personnel policies and practices for white-collar people. Let me list a few of these long-term trends.

□ The explosive growth in white-collar employment — providing a greatly expanded potential for unionism as well as creating some personnel problems commonly associated with large numbers of employees working together.

□ The decline in relative economic status (wages and fringes) of the salaried employee in relation to blue-collar workers even though his absolute position has steadily improved. Recent developments have also indicated some decline in the traditional employment security of white-collar employees.

□ The development of the "new office" with its increased scale of operations, mechanization of work, and grouping of jobs into homogeneous specialized groups. The result: concern about reduction in prestige, job satisfaction, and job security; a weakening of the traditionally strong ties with senior management; and the development of a greater community group interest in group action to solve these common problems.

□ The decline in the number of job opportunities in management for office workers as a new layer of professional employees (university graduates) has developed in between the office staff and senior management.

□ A decline in the traditional "stigma" attached to unionism as second-generation office workers, many with relatives and parents who are union members, enter the office labour force.

□ More permissive legislation and public policy concerning white-collar unionism, e.g. legislation for civil servants.

Although these long-run changes have been a "necessary" condition for "white-collar unionism," they have not always been "sufficient" reason for organization. Quite often the real "sparking" factors in generating office organization have been inadequate management personnel policies and practices resulting in grievances and poor morale. In many cases, too, these grievances are often surface phenomena concealing the long-run changes just outlined and reflecting the fact that office personnel policies and approaches have not been adjusted to meet current needs in the "new office."

Management Policies and Practices

Management seriously overlooked many of the problems of white-collar employees in the early postwar period. In retrospect, unions may have missed a most important organizing opportunity during this period. However, since the early '50s, management, at least in a number of more enlightened companies, have directed much more attention to the needs of these workers and have developed more sophisticated approaches in their policies and practices in this field.

Nevertheless, there still remain a number of personnel gaps and problems in a number of organizations. I will just note a few of these:

□ Absence of senior management and personnel management involvement in office affairs.
□ Lack of a "businesslike" approach to office personnel matters.
□ Absence of written and publicized personnel and work policies.
□ Inadequate mechanisms for bringing the grievances and suggestions of office employees to the attention of management.
□ Poor supervision — often due to the absence of policy guideposts for supervisors and the absence of formal supervisory training programmes.
□ Poor internal salary structure. Even in some cases where there has been a good salary program, there still have been complaints because it has been administered in such a confidential manner that office employees have no way of knowing that they had a good plan.

Union Activities and Approaches in the White-Collar Field.

The third set of factors in assessing the growth of white-collar unionism is the activities and approaches of unions in this field. Although there have been many union statements of intent, and although there have been significant achievements by some unions, the fact is that the union movement in general has never really attempted to organize this field on a broad front with the financial and manpower resources or appropriate approaches needed for the task at hand. In this respect we must remember that it is much easier for an employee, especially a white-collar employee, to join an available union that is actively soliciting his membership, than to set out on the arduous task of forming a new union.

The overall challenge, therefore, is whether the labour movement, geared historically mainly to blue-collar workers, can modify its philosophy, structure, policies, and approaches to accommodate the interests and needs of the rapidly expanding white-collar labour force. I will conclude by listing a few examples of these more specific challenges facing the labour movement.

The Will or Determination to Organize
White-Collar Employees

▢ As I have indicated, except in a few areas, this "will" to organize this field on a broad front has not been evident to date. One gets the impression that the labour movement in general feels a bit frustrated in the white-collar area, possibly related to the fact that it has not had much experience with the technical aspects of work in this area or a good "feel" of the interests, attitudes, and general psychology of the white-collar worker.

▢ I also detect a sort of "blue-collar" snobbery by some blue-collar unions toward white-collar employees. (The reverse of the popular idea of white-collar snobbery). If this is true, it could be a real barrier to the organization of white-collar groups, particularly in industries such as manufacturing where it has been shown that the initiative, cooperation, and support of the blue-collar union is an important factor in organizing success.

The Need for Greater Flexibility in Traditional
Union Structures, Philosophy, Policies, and
Approaches

▢ Also, there will be a need for a much greater flexibility in traditional union structures, philosophy, policies, and approaches. This is going to be a very difficult task because these have a long tradition and have been important in past union achievements. However, the union movement made these sorts of adjustments with the development of industrial unionism and it must adjust now to the era of the white-collar economy. Let me cite a few examples.

Types of Organizations

There will be a whole spectrum of organizations in the white-collar field running from traditional unions at one end of the scale to traditional professional associations at the other, taking on some bargaining functions as well as their traditional roles. Some of the latter groups will be keen competitors with traditional unions, others may be affiliated or have some sort of cooperative arrangements with the traditional labour movement.

Union Structures

The appropriate union structure for white-collar organization has been a difficult and controversial issue in all industrialized nations. In addition to the present organizations in this field — the industrial unions, and the purely white-collar unions — it seems to me that the labour movement will have to consider other arrangements in this area.

For example, more cooperation between these two types of unions, strategic organizing alliances in some areas, in others, the crossing of traditional jurisdictional lines, and possibly some organizing by, or coordination by, the Congress itself. In addition, within the labour movement, and within these unions covering both blue and white-collar workers, there must be some meaningful white-collar autonomy and visibility in policy and related matters.

Flexibility in Policies and Policy Decision Making

There also will be a need to reassess, and modify, many traditional union policies to gear them more closely to the needs and interests of white-collar employees. For example, traditional views of seniority may have to be modified for the more individualistic, promotion-oriented white-collar worker who also is often very interested in job enrichment, which often means crossing traditional occupational boundaries. Another example, is the matter of political affiliation. There are a great variety of white-collar groups differing greatly politically and ideologically. They may be interested in political action but not political affiliation. This has been a very controversial issue among white-collar unionis in Great Britain and Sweden.

Another most important factor which unions, as well as management, will have to take into account, is the interests and activities of the flood of youth entering our labour force. They have value systems markedly different from many traditional ones, they will question the purpose and objectives of their organization, they will sharply criticize policies and objectives with which they differ, they will have less regard for traditional authority or discipline, and they will demand a meaningful involvement in the policy decision-making processes. As we have learned in academia, it is a most challenging task to make these accommodations and still keep affairs generally on the "reservation" — and get the work done.

More Sophisticated Union Organizing Strategies and Approaches Needed

Another important task for the labour movement is to assess their organizing approaches and appeals, bargaining methods, servicing activities (all geared in the past mainly to the blue-collar workers) to assure they are appropriate for the needs, interests, and attitudes of white-collar workers. As other speakers on your program will be discussing these, I will only say that I imagine you could learn a lot from Claude Edwards and the Alliance, based on their experience with white-collar workers in the Federal public service.

More Emphasis on Purpose, Goals, and Objectives

Finally, it seems to me that one of the characteristics of the '60s was that companies, unions, collective bargaining, even some of our academic disciplines, tended to make systems, policies, processes, etc., an end in themselves rather than a means to solve social and economic problems. The emphasis will have to be shifted and much more sharply in the '70s to "ends," that is, to purpose and goals! As noted earlier, today's large number of young white-collar workers are particularly interested in this "purpose" emphasis.

CONCLUSION

In conclusion, then, the labour movement faces a big challenge in organizing on a much larger scale the rapidly expanding number of white-collar workers if it is to maintain its power, influence, and vitality. As I have indicated, this will involve many difficult problems of modifying traditional union structures, philosophy, policies, and approaches to accommodate the needs, interests, and characteristics of white-collar employees. Although I do not anticipate a great surge of organization comparable to that which occurred earlier in the blue-collar field, I do expect steadily increasing white-collar union activity in both the private and public sectors of the economy. The precise form of this expanded organization is more difficult to predict. Some will be in the traditional labour movement — the extent depending greatly on how successful it is in making the modifications and adjustments outlined earlier. Running parallel to these activities, there will be further development of new types of collective action in the white-collar field, differing somewhat in form, structure, and approach, from traditional and conventional unionism.

PROFESSIONAL WORKERS AND COLLECTIVE BARGAINING

Shirley B. Goldenberg

Professor Goldenberg reviews the issues involved in collective bargaining by professional workers and considers major policy implications of such issues. She also discusses the problems peculiar to professional employees in the collective bargaining relationship, such as conflict between professional participation in decision-making and traditional management rights as well as the problem of recognizing individual merit in the context of a collective relationship.

With a growing number of professional workers[1] in the labour force, and a significant proportion of these in paid employment, the issue of collective bargaining for the professional segment has become a topic of considerable current interest. So far, however, it has been marked more by controversy than by consensus.

ATTITUDES TOWARD COLLECTIVE BARGAINING

While some labour organizations are presently looking to white collar and professional groups as a potential source from which to bolster sagging union membership, many professional workers as well as their professional associations, employers, and the general public continue to regard trade union affiliation — or collective bargaining of any sort — as incompatible with the professional position. This negative attitude toward collective bargaining by salaried professionals has persisted in spite of the fact that it has long been an accepted practice for professional associations to engage in a form of *collective economic action*, fee-setting, on behalf of their members who are private practitioners.

The management orientation of the traditional professional groups in particular and the generally responsible nature of professional functions and duties have, by and large, precluded the identification of the professional segment with non-professional workers in the labour force. At the same time though, some of the problems faced by professionals working as salaried employees in large scale organizations are similar to those of their non-professional confreres. There are also some problems that are peculiar to professional employees, such as the loss of control over standards of professional performance. The inability of many professional workers to solve their employment problems on an individual basis has been stimulating the recent pressure for collective action, at least in some professional groups.

THE EXTENT OF COLLECTIVE BARGAINING

It is important to note, however, that the propensity to bargain collectively — and the actual experience with collective bargaining — varies both between and within professional groups and in different parts of the country. For example, while almost all Canadian school teachers bargain collectively, right across the country, collective bargaining by professional engineers is virtually limited to Ontario and Quebec. Moreover the experience of the engineers in these two provinces has been significantly different. Less than 10 per cent of the salaried professional engineers in Ontario bargain collectively and even those who do are opposed to trade union affiliation or the strike. But at least 50 per cent of the salaried professional engineers in Quebec now bargain collectively; they also belong to the CNTU and have gone on strike on a number of occasions.

If we were to construct a continuum of collective bargaining practice by salaried professional workers in Canada, we might put the teachers at one end of the scale of those who bargain collectively and the engineers at the other. Nurses, professionals in the civil service and other groups would fall somewhere in between. However, many professional groups would have no place on such a continuum. Although the traditional resistance to professional bargaining has been eroded considerablt in recent years, the majority of professional workers in Canada, particularly in the so-called traditional professions, still do not bargain at all.

PROFESSIONAL RIGHTS UNDER LABOUR LEGISLATION

In addition to the resistance of the interested parties, collective bargaining by professional employees has frequently been inhibited by provisions of the law. Because of the constitutional division of powers under our federal system, there is no uniform Canadian legislation in this area. The legal status of collective bargaining for these workers is determined separately by legislation in each of the provinces and at the federal level. With a few notable exceptions, however, there has been a fairly consistent policy of excluding the traditional or "closed" professional groups such as medicine, dentistry, law, engineering and architecture from the coverage of labour relations acts and consequently from legal bargaining rights.

Saskatchewan was the first province to grant collective bargaining rights to members of all professional groups; the Trade Union Act of 1944 had no professional exclusions. It took twenty years before another province eliminated the professional exclusions from its labour legislation. When Quebec enacted its new Labour Code in 1964 it granted full collective bargaining rights to all professional groups. All professional exclusions were removed in New Brunswick in 1971 and in Manitoba and the federal jurisdiction in 1972. Ontario granted collective bargaining rights to professional engineers in 1970 but has continued to exclude the rest of the traditional professions from the coverage of their labour legislation, certain changes may be anticipated. In British Columbia, for example, comprehensive amendments to the labour legislation are imminent; these may well include professional bargaining rights.

In addition to the exclusion of the traditional or "closed" professional groups, other groups such as teachers or nurses are subject to particular restrictions in certain jurisdictions. These restrictions seldom prevent them from bargaining collectively but they frequently limit their right to strike.[2]

While experience has shown that the exclusion of a professional group from labour legislation does not necessarily preclude *voluntary* recognition procedures and bargaining relationships — the case of the Ontario teachers is frequently cited as an example — there can be little doubt that an adverse public policy can reinforce employer resistance.

Thus there is continued pressure by interested groups to abolish the remaining professional exclusions.

Just as restrictive legislation does not preclude voluntary bargaining relationships, permissive legislation will not in itself guarantee the adoption of collective action or determine the form it will take. The fact that the majority of professional workers have not availed themselves of bargaining rights even where these exist must be explained apart from the legal context. The psychological resistance to collective bargaining dies hard in certain professional groups. Failure to bargain collectively can therefore not always be blamed on legal prohibitions.

But even when professional workers wish to bargain collectively, and are covered by labour legislation, certain limitations on their bargaining position are implicit in the law. Let us now look at some of the problems that professional workers and their employers face when they decide to adopt a collective bargaining relationship and consider the implications of these problems for the makers of public policy.

ESTABLISHING THE BARGAINING RELATIONSHIP

While the establishment of an appropriate bargaining unit and the choice of an acceptable bargaining agent are necessary preliminaries to collective bargaining, they present problems in the case of professional workers that do not exist for other categories of employees.

Choice of a Bargaining Agent

Three alternatives are available to professionals choosing a bargaining agent:

1. The professional association as bargaining agent
2. An independent structure for the purpose of bargaining
3. Trade union affiliation

Although some jurisdictions have legalized historical precedent by permitting nurses' and teachers' associations to act as bargaining agents for their employee members, the general practice is to rule out professional associations with licensing authority on the ground that it is undesirable to combine in one body the public interest function of licensing with the private interest function of bargaining. Professional associations may also be disqualified as bargaining agents because they include self-employed and supervisory personnel among their members as well as the salaried employees who bargain collectively.

These conflicts of interest are avoided if the professional association confines itself to the licensing function and a separate negotiating body, with or without trade union affiliation, is designated as bargaining agent. Although some professional groups in Canada have achieved considerable success in establishing collective bargaining relationships with their employers, it has been without trade union affiliation outside of Quebec.

Much of the professional resistance to trade union organization seems to be based on psychological factors, notably considerations of status, but the policy makers see other complicating factors. For example, where an organized group of salaried professionals has supervisory or managerial authority over an organized group of non-professional workers employed in the same enterprise — and where each group forms a separate bargaining unit — the desirability of both being affiliated with the same central labour organization is open to serious question. The Task Force on Labour Relations recommended that unions representing supervisory employees "not be permitted to affiliate with other unions or labour organizations except those composed exclusively of similar types of employees."[3] However, when the new Canada Labour Code (1972) extended collective bargaining rights to professional and supervisory employees it did not include this restriction on their freedom of association. Neither has any other jurisdiction that allows collective bargaining for professional and supervisory employees.

Determining the Appropriate Bargaining Unit

Whatever their decision on a bargaining agent, professional workers face particular difficulties in defining their bargaining units. Two distinct problems may be noted. One involves the professional composition of the bargaining unit — in other words, the question of craft versus industrial organization. The other relates to the demarcation line between labour and management functions.

The issue of craft versus industrial organization has been an important consideration in the determination of bargaining units for professional employees as well as for other categories of workers. The principle of craft unionism is maintained when negotiating groups are confined to members of a single profession or to specialized categories within a profession. The pattern of industrial unionism, on the other hand, is reflected when two or more professional groups bargain together and, a less frequent occurrence, when professional and non-professional employees are represented in a common bargaining unit.

The professional basis of organizing bargaining units rests on a number of factors and evokes conflicting views. In some cases, such as Quebec, and also in the Federal and New Brunswick civil service, the professional composition of the bargaining unit is rigidly determined by law;[4] in other jurisdictions there is an element of choice by professional groups and some discretion by labour relations boards as well.[5]

For groups covered by a particular code of ethics, organization on the basis of professional exclusiveness is frequently felt to be the only structure compatible with their professional position. In some of the more formally organized professions, moreover, social status is so closely related to an exclusive professional identity that bargaining in concert with other professional groups would be unthinkable.

Experience shows that the protection of craft rights is to a significant extent a function of size. The large number of professional employees in the federal civil service, for example, makes it feasible to respect professional distinctions. On the other hand, where there are many classes of professionals, generally in small numbers, as in a provincial civil service or separate institutions such as hospitals, exclusive bargaining units may be more difficult to maintain. In such cases it is not unusual for several professional groups to form a common bargaining unit if the legislation permits (as in the Quebec civil service). But the experience of professionals and non-professionals bargaining together is less frequent and less happy. While some professionals may be divided on the merits of exclusive or multi-professional bargaining units, they are all agreed on the undesirability of professional employees being included, against their will, in bargaining units with non-professional workers. Jacob Finkelman, as Chairman of the Ontario Labour Relations Board, noted that Board decisions had sometimes "swept" a small number of professional employees into a predominatly non-professional unit, but that this usually occurred where the few professionals involved had not raised any objections.[6] The implication would seem to be that the practice is undesirable. It is not surprising then that most jurisdictions that grant collective bargaining rights to professional employees protect salaried professionals from involuntary inclusion in larger bargaining units of non-professional workers.[7]

The second major criterion of eligibility for the bargaining unit is employment status. The establishment of a demarcartion line between labour and management functions has presented more serious problems for professional workers than for the mass of non-professional functions, a relatively high proportion of salaried professionals find themselves excluded from the definition of "employee" — consequently from legal collective bargaining rights — under present legislation. While professional workers claim that a rigid definition of "employee" status restricts their bargaining unit and weakens their bargaining strength, management spokesmen point out the conflicts of interest that would result if professional workers with supervisory functions sat on the employee side of the bargaining table.

The dilemma is that of assuring certain fundamental rights of association to a particular category of employees without unduly undermining the division of authority on which the administration of large scale enterprise depends. While it is evident that some demarcation line must be maintained between supervisors and supervised in defining bargaining units, a more flexible definition of "employee" status might set this line at a higher managerial level than is presently the case. Some people feel that this could be done at the discretion of labour relations boards; others feel that amendments to the legislation are necessary.

It has been suggested that a logical dividing line would exclude from a bargaining unit those professionals exercising managerial or supervisory functions that could affect the hiring, firing, promotion or discipline — in other words the career opportunities — of other professional workers. This principle has actually been put into practice in a number of cases in Quebec. Under the agreement between the Quebec government and its professional employees, for example, a civil servant may exercise supervisory functions, even over other professionals, and still be eligible for membership in the bargaining unit of his professional group. However, if his position is such that his recommendation could affect the hiring, firing, discipline, promotion, etc. of other professional personnel, or if he is employed in a confidential capacity, he is excluded as a management type. Similar criteria for management exclusions formed the basis of a settlement between Hydro-Quebec and its engineering union after two bitter recognition strikes (1965-1966) to determine the limits of the bargaining unit. The interesting point here is that the professional engineers' union, affiliated with the CNTU, preferred to rely on the use of force (an illegal strike) to define their bargaining unit, rather than risk a narrow interpretation of "employee" status in certification proceedings before the Labour Relations Board.

"APPROPRIATE PROFESSIONAL BEHAVIOUR" AND THE SETTLEMENT OF INTEREST DISPUTES

Once the psychological resistance has been overcome and the bargaining structure established, professional workers still face particular problems in the conduct of the collective relationship. Given the general concern with "appropriate professional behaviour," the problem of dispute settlement is probably the most serious dilemma facing professional workers when they decide to bargain collectively. While some professionals, the Ontario engineers for example, would voluntarily renounce the strike weapon as "unprofessional" under any circumstances, the Quebec engineers, as well as other professional groups such as nurses and teachers, maintain — and indeed have shown by their actions — that the sanction of the work stoppage is an essential ingredient of their bargaining strength.

The method of dispute settlement is also a major issue in the area of public policy where, it should be noted, the enforceability as well as the desirability of intervention must always be considered. While formal public policy on the right to strike differs between jurisdictions, there is a considerable degree of similarity in underlying philosophy. Indeed, one can generalize by saying that official concern with and intervention in dispute settlement in all jurisdictions varies directly with the degree of public interest in a particular professional service. When the nature of the professional function is such that a withdrawal of service would seem to jeopardize a "vital public interest,"[8] the problem transcends the ordinary considerations of "professionalism" and, from the public point of view at least, may take on the character of a moral issue. The moral issue is complicated, however, when professional workers withdraw their services to protest the erosion of professional standards rather than for financial reasons. Nurses at Ste. Justine's Hospital in Montreal, for example, insisted that their strike (1963) was *in the public interest* because it was called to protest unmanageable patient loads and the administration of medication by unqualified supporting staff.

Because of the high component of public interest in a number of professional services, health and education for example, sensitivity to public pressure, by both parties to a dispute, may often be sufficient to produce a settlement. It remains a central problem of public policy, however, to determine the extent and nature of intervention in the event that negotiations reach an impasse.

Legal restrictions on strike action for professional workers have taken three main forms in Canada:

1. By virtue of their formal *exclusion* from labour relations legislation, some professionals are, in fact, automatically precluded from the legal right to strike, whether or not their particular professional role is related to a vital public interest.
2. Even in jurisdictions where collective bargaining is permitted by law, public policy may restrict the right to strike in the case of specific professional groups, such as teachers and nurses, on the grounds of public interest. In such cases, compulsory binding arbitration is provided as an alternative to the strike weapon when negotiations reach an impasse.
3. Finally, even where the law itself provides a general right to strike, ad hoc measures, in the form of injunctions or emergency legislation, have been used to end particular labour disputes.

While public policy limitations on the right to strike are commonly justified in terms of *vital public interest*, a number of reservations have been noted. For example:

1. Some observers note the inconsistency of a public policy which purports to grant full collective bargaining rights to a group of workers but removes their most powerful bargaining weapon. Thus they insist that it is incumbent on the public authority to provide a satisfactory alternative for dispute settlement, if and when the public interest seems to demand a restriction on the right to strike. No guidelines presently exist to assure that compulsory arbitration will do justice to professionals, or others defined as "essential" workers, when the strike weapon is removed. The problem is currently the subject of much debate but the question is easier posed than answered.
2. Some experts feel that arbitration provisions, by their very nature, inhibit negotiated settlements. They note that ultimate re-

course to an arbitral authority can result in an abdication of responsibility by the parties to the dispute, a reduction in their efforts to achieve a negotiated settlement, and a total frustration of the bargaining process.

3. Finally, it should be noted, as a practical matter, that the effectiveness of a strike prohibition is directly related to the *possibility of its implementation.* Experience proves that legal provisions do not necessarily determine actual practice. Study sessions, coincidental resignations, black-listing of employers are a few of the mechanisms that have been used by professionals to circumvent legal prohibitions on strike action. In some cases, mass resignations of teachers for example, it has been suggested that the alternative mechanism may be more permanently damaging than the strike itself.

PROFESSIONAL ISSUES IN COLLECTIVE BARGAINING

So far we have emphasized the problems involved in professional bargaining that bear most directly on public policy. There are problems that do not directly concern the public authority, however, that are of considerable concern to the parties to the bargaining relationship. These problems must be resolved in the negotiation process. For example:

When professional workers and their employers engage in a collective bargaining relationship, the issues that arise include, but may go far beyond, the wages and fringe benefits that are the main concern of other categories of employees. The problem of handling particular professional needs within a collective bargaining relationship is complicated by the following factors:

1. The conflict between "professional prerogatives" and "management rights."
2. The problem of recognizing individual achievement in the framework of a collective agreement.

Not all professional demands constitute a threat to management rights. Provisions for continuing education, sabbatical leave and paid attendance at professional conferences, for example, have been amenable to discussion as simple cost items. Other demands, however, emphasize normative rather than monetary issues. By posing the issue of employee participation in policy decisions, these demands, by definition, would place limitations on management prerogatives and discretion.

Some normative demands, by nurses and engineers for example, have been concerned with protecting the professional role from the incursions of para-professional types (nurses aides, engineering technicians, etc.). Other demands concern the right of professionals to control the conditions and standards of their professional performance. Thus we find teachers demanding a voice in curriculum planning, classroom size, disciplinary procedure; nurses concerned with patient load, supporting staff, etc.; engineers insisting not only on the right to sign their own work but — the ultimate in professional protection — the right to withhold their signature from documents that do not meet professional standards.[9] Teachers' and nurses' disputes in particular, as well as the radiologists' strike in Quebec (1967), have shown that normative demands by professional workers are frequently less amenable to compromise — by either party to the bargaining relationship — than are accompanying monetary issues. With a growing conviction on one side that participation in policy decisions is the essence of professionalism, and a strong resistance on the other to any incursion on management discretion, professional negotiations on normative issues have frequently ended in stalemate.

While the problem of recognizing individual differences will always exist when large numbers of people are employed together — with or withour collective bargaining — some professionals are particularly concerned that they will be "frozen" into categories if wage scales are written into collective agreements. One suggestion, by the Ontario Steering Committee on Professional Negotiations, seeks to obviate this problem by providing for the negotiation of individual contracts within the framework of a basic collective agreement. This could, in theory at least, provide for substantial variation around the norm on the basis of individual ability and performance.

While it is theoretically desirable that professional agreements provide for the recognition of individual merit, it is important to note that the issue is not of equal significance for all professional groups. For the majority of professional workers in large scale organizations (e.g. engineers, teachers, nurses) a pay determination policy based on senority and academic qualifications — with some form of performance assessment for promotion purposes — has usually been considered acceptable. In other cases, research scientists for example, there is more scope for the impact of the individual on the job.

Where it is understood that differences in performance by professional workers will be reflected in financial rewards and career pattern, the method of performance appraisal becomes an issue in itself. While a number of alternatives for performance appraisal have been tried by various professional groups, one of them claims to have found the ideal solution to the problem.

NEGOTIATIONS BY NON-SALARIED PROFESSIONAL WORKERS

Most discussions of professional bargaining have focused on the problems of professional workers who, by virtue of their status as salaried employees, could conceivably be covered by labour legislation. Some notice must be taken, however, of a significant group of non-salaried professionals for whom collective bargaining is becoming increasingly important but who, because they do not qualify as "employees" under the law, lack a legal framework to define their bargaining rights and guide their bargaining practice. This is the position of doctors participating in medicare programs and will undoubtedly be the position of many lawyers when judicare is introduced. Although these professionals retain their formal status as private practitioners, they find themselves in a form of employment relationship with the provincial government. So far, however, the negotiation of professional fees and other conditions of the doctors' participation in medicare plans delays that normally govern collective bargaining. There is generally no legal time limit on doctors' negotiations and no provision for the final settlement of disputed issues if negotiations reach an impasse. It is clearly incumbent on the policy makers to elaborate suitable mechanisms to regulate the conduct of negotiations and the settlement of disputes for this new group on the collective bargaining scene. The doctors' experience has shown that the lack of such mechanisms can have serious consequences for the public, the government and the professionals alike.

FOOTNOTES

[1] With new categories of trained people recently claiming professional status (nurses, teachers, social workers, librarians, economists, statisticians, psychologists, physicists, chemists, etc.) the rigid exclusiveness of the more traditional professional occupations (medicine, dentistry, law, engineering, architecture) has given way to a broader concept of the professions. In considering the policy implications of professional bargaining we shall include teachers, nurses and university graduates with specialized degrees, as well as members of the traditional professions, in the definition of professional workers.

[2] Teachers are specifically excluded from the coverage of labour legislation and consequently from the right to strike in Prince Edward Island, British Columbia, Manitoba and Ontario. The Public Schools Acts of British Columbia and Manitoba provide for collective bargaining with binding arbitration of unresolved disputes as do recent regulations under the School Act of Prince Edward Island. While there is no statutory provision for teacher bargaining in Ontario, the teachers negotiate under a system of voluntary recognition by their employers. Teachers in Saskatchewan are not excluded from the Trade Union Act but they bargain under different legislation, the Teacher Salary Agreement Act which, as amended in 1971, gives the Minister discretion to impose arbitration if conciliation efforts fail to produce a negotiated agreement. Teachers in Quebec have the right to strike under the Labour Code but Section 99 prohibits a strike without eight days' prior written notice. This section also gives the government discretionary power to delay a strike for up to 80 days by appointing a board of inquiry into the dispute and taking an injunction to prevent or terminate the strike.

Hospital workers other than doctors are generally included in labour legislation but are subject to particular restrictions in some of the provinces. Section 99 of the Alberta Labour Relations Act gives the government discretion to forbid a strike or lockout in the hospital sector. Section 44 of the Labour Relations Act of Prince Edward Island substitutes binding arbitration for the right to strike in disputes involving hospital workers. While Ontario and Newfoundland do not exclude hospital employees from their general labour legislation, the Hospital Labour Disputes Arbitration Act (1965) in Ontario and the Hospital Employees Employment Act (1966-67) in Newfoundland both prohibit strikes and lockouts in the hospital sector and provide for arbitration as a substitute. As in the case of the teachers, Section 99 of the Quebec Labour Code may delay the exercise of the strike by hospital workers but does not prohibit it indefinitely.

3 *Canadian Industrial Relations*. Report of the Task Force on Labour Relations (Ottawa, Queen's Printer, 1968), p. 139.

4 The Quebec Labour Code (1964) confines the members of most incorporated professional groups (lawyers, notaries, physicians and surgeons, inspectors of anatomy, homeopathic physicians, pharmacists, dental surgeons, engineers, land surveyors, architects, forestry engineers, optometrists and opticians) to bargaining units of their own profession. However the Civil Service Act (1965) has more flexible provisions for professionals in government employment in Quebec. Like the Labour Code, it requires professional workers to bargain apart from non-professionals but in contrast to the Labour Code it does not restrict the bargaining unit to members of a single profession.

The federal Public Service Staff Relations Act (1967) and the New Brunswick Public Service Labour Relations Act (1968) specify separate professional classifications (published in the *Official Gazette*) for the purpose of establishing bargaining units, at least for the first round of negotiations. While the legislation permits professional classifications to be merged after the initial certification, they may not be merged with non-professional bargaining units.

5 In Ontario, for example, the Labour Relations Act (1970) provides that a bargaining unit consisting solely of professional engineers shall be deemed by the Board to be a unit of employees appropriate for collective bargaining, but the board may include professional engineers in a bargaining unit with other employees *if the Board is satisfied that a majority of such professional engineers wish to be included* in such a bargaining unit.

The federal Labour Code (1972) gives the Canada Labour Relations Board discretion to certify a unit composed only of professionals or composed of employees of more than one profession; it may also include employees performing the functions, but lacking the qualifications, of a professional employee.

Other jurisdictions that grant legal bargaining rights to professional employees, e.g. Saskatchewan, Manitoba and New Brunswick, make no special provision for separate professional units — apart from the general provision that gives the Labour Board discretion to certify in a separate bargaining unit any group of employees who exercise particular skills or are members of a craft by reason of which they are distinct from other employees.

6 Jacob Finkelman, Q.C. Paper delivered to the University of Toronto Industrial Relations Centre Conference, December 15/16, 1965. (Finkelman is at present Chairman of the federal Public Service Staff Relations Board.)

7 See footnotes Nos. 4 and 5.

[8] The crucial question of "public interest" defies a clear cut definition and is not confined to the professional category. In the case of professional workers, it should be noted, the potential impact of a withdrawal of services varies not only between but within professional groups. Compare, for example, the public interest function of the operating room nurse and the nurse-receptionist in a doctor's office, the engineer responsible for the distribution of power and the engineer producing outboard motors. There is also the question of timing. It is generally agreed that a withdrawal of teacher service at the beginning of the school year is less damaging than one on the eve of final exams. The examples could be multiplied *ad infinitum.*

[9] Contracts negotiated by unions of professional engineers (CNTU) with the city of Montreal, Hydro-Quebec and the Government of Quebec protect an engineer against disciplinary action for refusal to sign a technical document which he cannot approve for reasons of professional conscience.

DISPUTE SETTLEMENT LEGISLATION IN THE PUBLIC SECTOR: AN INTERPROVINCIAL COMPARISON

Shirley B. Goldenberg

The author presents a comprehensive up-to-date interprovincial comparison of dispute settlement legislation in Canada for employees in the public sector.

Although collective bargaining rights have now been granted to employees at all levels of government in Canada there are still considerable differences between jurisdictions, in policy and practice, on the procedure to be adopted when negotiations break down. The following discussion will compare the statutory provisions for the settlement of labour disputes in the provincial public services, that is, in those areas of public employment that are subject to special public service legislation and/or in which a provincial government is a party to the bargaining relationship.[1]

PROVISIONS FOR FINALITY IN THE PROVINCIAL PUBLIC SERVICES

Apart from Saskatchewan where government employees have been covered by general labour legislation since 1944,[2] real collective bargaining for federal or provincial civil servants has existed for less than a decade. In 1965 the government of Quebec took the lead over the other provinces and the Federal government in granting full collective bargaining rights, including the right to strike, to employees in the civil service.[3] The Federal government followed in 1967[4] and New

Brunswick in 1968.[5] Saskatchewan, Quebec and New Brunswick are still the only provinces in which governments permit their employees to strike. However all the other provincial governments have relinquished their power to impose a settlement in case of deadlocked negotiations and one or two may be on the verge of granting the right to strike. Public policy in Alberta,[6] Manitoba,[7] Ontario,[8] Nova Scotia[9] and Prince Edward Island[10] presently provides for third party arbitration of unresolved negotiation disputes.[11]

The Manitoba government intends to amend its legislation governing labour relations in the civil service but it is not certain yet how far it will go. The Minister of Labour made a public commitment last summer to give civil servants the right to strike within the coming year. More recently, however, the Manitoba Government Employees' Union has come out against this policy, indicating its preference for compulsory arbitration as a substitute for the right to strike.

While the Newfoundland statute[12] provides for collective bargaining in the civil service, including the right to strike, the Cabinet can make regulations exempting any class or classification of employers or employees from the provisions of the act; it can also forbid or terminate any strike by declaring that an emergency exists. However changes may be expected soon. A recent inquiry into labour relations in Newfoundland recommended compulsory arbitration for the first two rounds of negotiations in the civil service with the strike option on the Federal pattern after this preliminary experience with bargaining.[13]

British Columbia should also be an interesting province to watch in the coming months. Restrictive labour legislation and arbitrary decision making by the government as employer[14] seemed firmly entrenched under the Social Credit regime that had been in power since 1952. But the election of an NDP government (June 1972) brought significant changes. After repealing the most restrictive aspects of the labour legislation,[15] the new government appointed a commission of inquiry to investigate employer – employee relations in the civil service. The commission recommended full collective bargaining rights (on the federal model) including the right to strike. Legislation to implement these recommendations has just been introduced (April 1973) and will be debated in the fall.

IMPASSE PROCEDURES WITH THE RIGHT TO STRIKE

While three provinces and the Federal government grant the right to strike to their own employees, each requires a different procedure before a legal strike may take place. Let us look at the Provincial procedures.

Saskatchewan. Saskatchewan is the only jurisdiction that has no statutory distinction between labour relations in the private and public sectors. The Trade Union Act covers all areas of employment, including the civil service. There is no provision for compulsory arbitration. However, the act does allow for voluntary arbitration and provides machinery for conciliation. The conciliation machinery itself contains a germ of conflict although no serious problem has ever resulted from it. The unions note that the Minister of Labour appoints the conciliation board whether a dispute is in the private or public sector. They feel that a conflict of interest may exist when the government of which the Minister is a member is a party to the dispute. There have only been four instances of conciliation over the years and the government has implemented the recommendations of the conciliation board each time. Although the legislation permits conciliation boards to function as arbitration boards by written consent of the parties before the hearing commences, this has never been done. The emphasis in Saskatchewan has been on negotiation between the parties and public service labour relations have been remarkably peaceful.

Quebec. The Quebec Labour Code of 1964[16] gave the right to strike to all employees under its jurisdiction apart from police and firemen. A year later the Civil Service Act extended most of the provisions of the Labour Code, including the right to strike, to employees of the provincial government. However the Quebec legislation, in contrast to Saskatchewan, makes certain distinctions between the private and public sectors.

In addition to the conciliation delays required of all workers under the Labour Code, Article 99 requires eight days' notice of intention to strike by public employees and provides for an eighty-day suspension of the right to strike when, in the opinion of the Lieutenant Governor in Council, "a threatened or actual strike in a public service endangers public health or safety" or "interferes with the education of a group of students." This delay is achieved by the appointment of a board of inquiry which must report its findings within sixty days. The board has no power to make recommendations. Upon the establishment of a board of inquiry, the Attorney-General may petition a Superior Court judge for an injunction to prevent or terminate a strike if he (the judge) finds that it imperils public health and safety or the education of a group of students. The injunction may continue for twenty days after the sixty-day period in which the board of inquiry is required to report. The union then acquires the legal right to strike; no further injunction is permitted.

In addition to the above delays on strike action by all employees in public services, government employees are also forbidden to strike, under Article 70 of the Civil Service Act, unless the "essential services" and the manner of maintaining them are determined by prior agreement between the parties or by decision of the Labour Court.

Finally it should be noted that the Quebec legislation differs from that in the other jurisdictions by making no provision for arbitration. The omission is deliberate. Quebec will not permit a third party to decide on the wage bill in the public sector. The government of this province bargains simultaneously with the employees of hospitals, school boards, community colleges and government agencies as well as the civil service; their combined wage bill involves approximately half the provincial budget.

One important lesson to be learned from the Quebec experience is that the provisions of a law are only effective to the extent that they can be enforced. For example:

A strike by civil service professionals in 1966 was technically illegal as the unions did not go through the prescribed conciliation delays. They questioned the legitimacy of a procedure in which the Minister charged with appointing a conciliator was, in effect, also a party to the dispute. Hospital employees ignored court orders to return to work during a general public service strike in April 1972. They had been bargaining with the provincial government through a Common Front of public sector unions.

It is important to realize that the negotiations that culminated in the general public service strike had a political dimension that went beyond the conventional issues, and tactics, of a labour — management dispute. Thus caution should be used in generalizing from this experience. While the formal union demands were based on wages, working conditions and job security, the bargaining from the outset took the form of a political confrontation between the union leaders and the government. Still, the strike was legal, as the unions had observed the compulsory delays and given the required notice. On the other hand, their failure to agree on the maintenance of essential services, and the ignoring of the injunctions to assure these services were clearly in defiance of the law. Special legislation was passed to force the public service unions back to work.[17] This legislation suspended the right to strike rather than revoke it permanently. It provided for a contract imposed by government decree if negotiations did not produce a settlement within a two-month period. The original deadline for a negotiated settlement was subsequently extended and a four-year agreement was eventually signed by all but the teachers and Liquor Board employees. The government imposed a decree on the latter groups in the absence of a negotiated agreement.

This is not the first time that ad hoc measures have been used in Quebec in the case of a public interest dispute. A hospital strike was brought to an end in 1966 by placing the hospitals under trusteeship. Special legislation a year later ended legal strikes in the schools and established the government as a party to the bargaining relationship for future negotiations.[18] Ad hoc legislation has also ended other strikes which are beyond the scope of this disucssion — strikes by bus drivers, construction workers, doctors, policemen, firemen, etc. But still the basic right to strike in most of these services was left on the statute books.

Since the last public sector negotiations, however, the Quebec government has decided to introduce new legislation which, while not

entirely removing the right to strike, would contain much stricter provisions than presently exist for the maintenance of "essential
services."[19] It is ironic that the province that began the trend in recent
years toward the right to strike in the public services should now feel
compelled to write restrictive provisions into its general labour legislation.

New Brunswick. The Province of New Brunswick granted the right
to strike to employees in public services in 1968 a year after similar
action by the Federal government. Prior to this, it had assumed full
financial responsibility for health and education services, becoming
the effective employer, from the financial point of view, of all hospital
and school employees.[20] Thus New Brunswick's Public Service Labour
Relations Act (PSLRA) has the broadest scope of any public service
legislation in Canada, covering all hospital and school employees
along with the civil service as traditionally defined and the employees
of government agencies and boards.

The New Brunswick statute reflects to a substantial degree the legislation that had previously been implemented at the Federal level but it
also contains some interesting modifications, particularly in the provisions for the settlement of disputes. In contrast to Saskatchewan, but
like Quebec and the Federal government, public policy in New Brunswick recognizes certain differences between private and public sector
bargaining. Like the Federal statute, the New Brunswick Act provides
separate machinery, the Public Service Labour Relations Board
(PSLRB), to administer labour relations in the public services. In addition to certifying bargaining units, this Board in New Brunswick, like
its counterpart at the Federal level, plays an important role in the area
of dispute settlement. New Brunswick has removed the decisions with
respect to conciliation and arbitration from the political arena by as-
signing them to the Board. This avoids the conflict of interest situations
of which unions have complained in some of the other provinces.

Although public service employees in New Brunswick have the
right to strike, the procedures by which this right is acquired differ
from those in the private sector. The Public Service Labour Relations
Act, like the Federal Act, provides public service employees with the
alternative of conciliation or arbitration when negotiations reach an
impass: the first alternative contains the possibility of a strike, the
second involves a compulsory settlement. However, whereas the Federal act requires the bargaining agent to choose between conciliation
and arbitration prior to commencing negotiations, this decision may be
taken at any time in New Brunswick and may actually be changed as
negotiations proceed. There have been some occasions, in practice,
where after the completion of conciliation procedures the union has
indicated its willingness to accept binding arbitration.

There is a forty-five day statutory time limit on public sector negotiations — unless the parties agree otherwise. The Chairman of the
PSLRB *may* appoint a conciliator to assist in the negotiations if asked

to do so by either of the parties. However, if it appears to the Chairman that the parties are not likely to reach agreement he must appoint a conciliation board within fifteen days of the statutory, or agreed upon, time limit on the bargaining. A conciliation board consists of a member named by each of the parties who in turn select a chairman. As is the case at the Federal level, the establishment of a conciliation board, though compulsory in New Brunswick, cannot take place before the parties have agreed on, or the PSLRB has determined, a list of "designated" employees whose jobs are "necessary in the interest of health, safety or security of the public" and who shall not take part in a strike. This is in contrast to Quebec, where the determination of essential services and the manner of maintaining them does not take place until after the conciliation procedure.

A conciliation board in New Brunswick must submit a report to the Chairman of the PSLRB if it fails to effect a settlement but if the parties do not settle following the report they are still not free to strike. At this stage, either party may request the Chairman of the PSLRB to declare that a "deadlock" exists. If he is satisfied that the required conciliation procedures have been observed, the Chairman declares a deadlock and asks the parties if they are prepared to submit the dispute to arbitration. The Act provides for an Arbitration Tribunal consisting of a chairman appointed by the government and two other members, representative of the interests of the parties. The latter are selected by the Chairman of the PSLRB from two permanent panels of arbitrators, originally named by the Board. The award of the Tribunal is binding, should the parties accept the "arbitration route." If either party rejects arbitration, the union is free to conduct a vote among its members to determine whether they desire to take strike action." A majority vote in the affirmative gives the union the legal right to strike. Should a majority vote against a strike the Chairman of the PSLRB orders the parties to resume negotiations for a period of twenty-one days after which, if agreement has not been reached, either party may again request the Chairman to declare that a deadlock exists. The process continues to repeat itself until the parties either reach a negotiated settlement, agree to submit to arbitration, or the bargaining agent secures a majority strike vote after which a legal work stoppage may take place.

There has only been one instance in practice in which a deadlock has been declared but the machinery for taking a strike vote was not employed. The parties agreed to delay such action and returned to the bargaining table where an agreement was reached.

It should be noted that New Brunswick differs from the other jurisdictions in which a strike is permitted by requiring a strike vote after all the other legal delays have been exhausted. A noted Canadian expert on labour relations made the following comment on this particular feature of the New Brunswick legislation:

The compulsory strike-authorization vote in New Brunswick introduces an element of realism in that province's procedure. It is the membership of the unit of employees, acting after an impasse has been reached and at least one party has rejected arbitration, who really make the strike decision. On balance, the option of voting for a strike or for further negotiations can probably be expected to have a conservative effect since the voter will be concerned with an imminent strike situation, whereas in the federal procedure the decision has been taken when those who take it are protected by a very considerable period of time from the strike itself. Also in New Brunswick a vote against a strike does not carry with it a repudiation of the strike procedure, but only an instruction from the membership to their bargaining agent to have another try. If this leads to failure the membership may revise their vote after a relatively short period of time.[21]

SOME POLICY CONSIDERATIONS

The major peculiarity of public service bargaining flows from the fact that the government is the employer. A government, by virtue of its legislative and executive functions, its obligation to protect the public purse and to ensure the protection of essential services is clearly a very different kind of employer than one finds in the private sector. But although multiple government functions and particular public pressures place inevitable constraints on the bargaining relationship, experience has shown that certain problems can be minimized. One of these is the conflict of interest that can arise when a government, which is itself a party to a dispute, administers the machinery for conciliation and arbitration. By establishing an independent body for this purpose the New Brunswick statute, like the federal act that preceded it, removes the decisions on these procedures from all political influence. This has eliminated a major source of criticism to which governments have been subject as employers and consequently a major source of tension as negotiations approach finality.

With collective bargaining being a relatively recent phenomenon at senior levels of government, the lack of experienced negotiators, particularly on the government side, has sometimes presented serious problems at the bargaining table. The bargaining process has also been complicated by the nature of political decision. Lacking a precise mandate to effect a settlement, particularly on monetary issues, government negotiating committees in some of the provinces have required constant recourse to the political authority for which they are simply the spokesmen. Frequently when it comes to the "crunch", decisions may be made at the Cabinet level rather than at the bargaining table. The consequences for "good faith" bargaining are self evident and may be a partial explanation, at least, for the slow pace of negotiations, with the consequent build-up of frustration and tension, in a lot of public sector bargaining. This has been a particular problem where governments have established a bargaining relationship before defining a clear-cut policy on the issues that are likely to arise. If policy decisions are made on an ad hoc basis as bargaining proceeds, the union soon realizes that it must look to the political authority rather than to the negotiators at the bargaining table. Resort to a strike to pressure the public authorities by arousing public opinion may be tempting in such circumstances.

Saskatchewan, with the longest bargaining experience in the provincial public services, seems to have had the greatest success with the use of delegated authority. The Chairman of the Public Service Commission acts as the sole spokesman for the provincial government in bargaining with the public employees. The Cabinet gives him full authority to conclude an agreement, in accordance with pre-defined instructions and limitations, using whatever strategy he can command. Other governments would do well, if they have not already done so, to delegate sufficient authority to *experienced negotiators*, not only to make a deal but equally important, to inspire confidence in the union negotiators that they have the power to do so.

While the trend in the private sector in Canada is now to minimize conciliation delays, if not to eliminate them entirely, the high level of public interest in the settlement of disputes in the public services, the essential nature of many of the services involved, and the limited bargaining experience of the parties concerned, have been cited as a good reason for the continuation, or even the extension, of conciliation procedures in this area. It has already been noted that conciliation procedures can be more acceptable to the union, and consequently more effective, if administered by a quasi-judicial board rather than by a government which is itself a party to the dispute.

But what if the bargaining breaks down after all the available procedures for a negotiated settlement have been exhausted? There have been two major suggestions to make the arbitration route more acceptable to the unions. The first would provide for the administration of arbitration procedures by an independent board, as we described in considering the case of New Brunswick. The second would broaden the scope of the issues on which an arbitrator may rule under public service legislation. Otherwise unions may be tempted to use the right to strike on issues that are not subject to arbitration.

While the right to strike remains the most contentious issue in public sector labour relations, experience shows that strikes can and will occur even when forbidden by law. The problem of enforceability must never be forgotten when legislation is being considered.

As it may be difficult, or even unfair, to deprive a majority of workers in public services of rights that are available in the private sector, the most crucial question facing the policy makers becomes the definition of "essential services" and the guarantee that these will be maintained. Although provisions already exist in the provinces of Quebec and New Brunswick (as well as at the federal level) to assure that essential services will be maintained in the event of a legal strike, the defiance of these provisions during the public sector strike in Quebec (and also by electronic technicians in the federal service) show that present statutory penalties for non-compliance are not a deterrent if workers are sufficiently determined to defy them. On the basis of this experience it has been suggested that the penalties for non-compliance be strengthened. But unless the problem of the enforceability of the law can be satisfactorily resolved, and it is unlikely that it can be entirely, ad hoc legislative measures, appropriate to particular circumstances, always remain a possibility. The elected representatives of the people have the ultimate power, and responsibility, to respond to a threat to the public welfare.

FOOTNOTES

[1] The scope of such services varies between jurisdictions. In a few provinces it is limited almost entirely to workers employed in government departments — the traditional definition of the civil service. Other provinces include the employees of government agencies, provincially operated vocational schools and mental institutions in the coverage of their civil service acts. New Brunswick and Quebec are the only jurisdictions, however, in which the government is directly involved in collective bargaining in hospitals and schools as well as in the civil service Crown enterprises, and government commissions and boards. Thus the scope of the provincial public services, as defined in this paper, is broadest in these two provinces.

[2] Trade Union Act, R.S.S. 1965, c. 287.

[3] Civil Service Act, S.Q. 1965, c. 14.

[4] The Public Service Staff Relations Act, S.C. 1967, c. 72.

[5] Public Service Labour Relations Act, S.N.B. 1968, c. 88.

[6] The Public Service Act, R.S.A. 1970 c. 298.

[7] Civil Service Act, R.S.M. 1970 c. 110.

[8] Crown Employees Collective Bargaining Act, Bill 105, Ontario 1972.

[9] Civil Service Joint Council Act, R.S.N.S. 1967, c. 35.

[10] The Civil Service Act (S.P.E.I. 1962, c. 5) provides for a consultative relationship between the government and its employees. In November 1972 the government issued new *regulations* under the Act, granting collective bargaining rights to civil servants, with compulsory arbitration of unresolved disputes.

[11] Ontario has provided for arbitration since 1963, Nova Scotia since 1967. The government of Manitoba only relinquished its right to impose a settlement in 1969, Alberta in 1972 and, as noted in the footnote above, Prince Edward Island in 1972.

[12] Public Service (Collective Bargaining) Act, S. Nfld. 1970, c. 85.

[13] The Public Service Staff Relations Act (S.C. 1967, c. 72) established an innovative system of voluntary arbitration in the federal public service. Under this statute, an employee organization must specify its choice of dispute resolution procedure before serving notice to bargain. Two options are available: (1) referral of a dispute to arbitration; (2) referral of a dispute to a conciliation board with the ultimate right to strike. Where a bargaining agent chooses the second option, negotiations cannot begin until the parties have agreed on a list of "designated employees" to maintain essential services in

the event of a legal strike. In the absence of such an agreement, the determination is made by the Public Service Staff Relations Board.

[14] The Civil Service Act (R.S.B.C. 1960, c. 56, consolidated 1971, c. 56) provided for a consultative relationship between the government and its employees but left the final decision-making authority clearly in the hands of the government. The government also had sole discretion, under the Mediation Commission Act (S.B.C. 1968, c. 26) to refer a public (or private) sector dispute to the Mediation Commission for final and binding arbitration.

[15] One of the first acts of the new government was to repeal the Mediation Commission Act.

[16] R.S.Q. 1964, c. 141.

[17] Bill 19, April 21, 1972. An Act to ensure resumption of Services in the Public Sector.

[18] This was the famous "Bill 25," an Act to ensure for children the right to education and to institute a new schooling collective agreement plan, S.Q. 1967, c. 63.

[19] Bill 89, an Act to ensure public well-being in case of labour conflict, is currently before the National Assembly. This Bill would make it possible for the government to forbid or terminate a strike in virtually any public (or private) service that it may consider essential. Although it is generally agreed that Bill 89 will never pass in its present form, some new statutory provisions for the protection of essential services can certainly be expected in Quebec.

[20] When the government of New Brunswick adopted its Equal Opportunities Program in 1967, it assumed financial responsibility for services, including health and education, that were formerly administered by the municipalities. New Brunswick is the only province in which hospitals and schools are financed entirely at the provincial level.

[21] Professor H. D. Woods, McGill University, unpublished manuscript, 1972.

FINALITY IN PUBLIC SECTOR BARGAINING: THE CANADIAN EXPERIENCE*

J. Finkelman

The author describes the provisions of the Public Service Staff Relations Act (1967) which allowed collective bargaining for federal public employees in Canada. He also explains the role of the Public Service Staff Relations Board in the settlement of disputes between employer and employees in the federal public sector.

The Public Service Staff Relations Act, the statute enacted by Parliament in 1967 which established a system of collective bargaining for

* Address prepared for delivery by J. Finkelman, Q.C., Chairman Public Service Staff Relations Board, Ottawa, Canada, to the International Conference on Trends in Industrial and Labour Relations, at Tel Aviv, Israel, January 1972. Reprinted with permission.

federal public servants in Canada, has been described as a bold experiment. The phase "bold experiment" suggests a degree of innovativeness that may be misleading to observers in other countries. True, it made collective bargaining available to federal public servants[1] in Canada for the first time. However, although the Act does contain a number of unique features, particularly certain of its impasse resolution provisions, many of its other provisions are rooted in and adapted from practices and legislative enactments that had been in existence in Canada over many years in the non-governmental sector. Since one of the purposes of an international conference such as the one in which we are participating is to enable scholars and administrators, employers and employees, to ascertain whether they can learn anything from the experience of countries other than their own, a proper assessment of that experience can only be made in the context of a rather exhaustive account of historical antecedents of the legislation in each country. Obviously, time does not permit me to give such an account and I shall therefore confine myself by way of introduction to a brief summary of some of the principles that have emerged in Canada.

The topic of this session is "Finality in Public Sector Bargaining: the Canadian Experience." It is implicit in the title that impasses may arise in the course of the relationship between the public employer and its employees that the parties are unable to resolve through their own efforts, and third-party intervention becomes necessary to assist the principals in the resolution of such impasses. In the scheme of things that has been developed in Canada for industry generally over the last three decades, disputes between employers and employees have been divided into three main categories, for each of which special procedures have been devised. The three categories are: (i) disputes concerning the entitlement of a trade union to require the employer to bargain with it on behalf of a group of employees — what might be referred to as representational disputes; (ii) disputes concerning the terms or conditions that are to be included in a collective agreement — negotiation disputes; and (iii) disputes alleging misinterpretation or misapplication of the terms of a collective agreement that has been entered into between an employer and a trade union — grievance disputes.

Authority to deal with the first of these categories — representational issues — is vested in most jurisdictions in Canada in an independent, government-appointed, board — a tri-partite permanent tribunal on which both employers and labour are equally represented, operating under a neutral chairman. Such a board exercises quasi-judicial functions and its decisions are final and binding. In so far as the third category is concerned — grievance disputes — the applicable legislation in Canada provides that disputes arising during the lifetime of a collective agreement concerning its application or interpretation which are not settled by discussion between the parties must be referred to final and binding determination by an arbitrator or board of arbitration selected by the parties. An arbitrator or arbitration board may be selected for one grievance or the parties may select a person or persons who will serve for some period of time and will deal with all grievances that may arise under an agreement. Incidentally, I should point out that in Canada, once a collective agreement has been entered into, the agreement is binding for its duration and no strike or lockout can lawfully take place during its lifetime.

The legislative provisions relating to the second category, which I mentioned earlier (negotiation disputes — the category that is probably of the greatest interest to this session), have had a history in Canada that goes back to the early years of this century. A bare outline of the scheme that has emerged in the last three decades will have to suffice. Since 1944, the parties — the employer and the trade union — have been under a legal obligation to bargain in good faith and make every reasonable effort to make a collective agreement. If they cannot resolve their differences through their own efforts, they must request the appropriate Minister of Labour — Canada is a federal jurisdiction with legislative authority in labour relations being divided between the federal Parliament and the legislatures of the provinces — to appoint a neutral third party to mediate the dispute. Up until the last decade, the pattern that was generally in vogue was that the Minister appointed one of his permanent officials to act as conciliator. This was the first step and, if this official failed in his efforts, the Minister appointed a tri-partite ad hoc conciliation board consisting of a nominee of each of the parties together with a neutral chairman. Parenthetically, I would say that, in recent years, Ministers of Labour have tended to rely more on mediation by the permanent officials of their departments and to appoint conciliation boards only in rare instances. Neither a conciliator nor a conciliation board is empowered to make decisions that are final and binding unless both parties consent to be bound. They are limited to making recommendations. The applicable legislation sets relatively short time limits within which a conciliator or a conciliation board may continue his or its efforts to effect a settlement. The right to conduct a lawful strike or to institute a lawful lockout accrues at the end of a fixed statutory period, usually seven days after the conciliation process is exhausted. In some jurisdictions in Canada, the right to strike has been abrogated for some employees, chiefly policemen, firemen and hospital employees, and negotiation disputes are settled, by final and binding arbitration.

The Public Service Staff Relations Act which, as I said earlier, applies to federal public servants, adopted the three-fold approach to dealing with impasses that had evolved in earlier legislation in Canada. Authority to deal with representation disputes and related matters was vested in the Public Service Staff Relations Board, a permanent and independent tri-partite board appointed by the government and consisting of an equal number of reqresentatives of the employer and of the employees, serving under the chairmanship of a neutral chairman and vice-chairman. All members of the Board are appointed for a fixed term of years; the chairman and the vice-chairman have been given what amounts to judicial tenure for a term of ten years, thus assuring their independence of government, i.e., management, influence. For the disposition of grievance disputes, a permanent corps of adjudicators — grievance arbitrators, to give them the title by which such persons are generally known in Canada — has been established under the supervision of a chief adjudicator, all adjudicators having tenure for a fixed term of years. The independence of the adjudicators is assured through a two-tier system of appointment. The appointment of adjudicators rests with the Government, but appointments can only be made on the recommendation of the Public Service Staff Relations Board and you will recall the tri-partite composition and independent status of that Board. Neither can act without the concurrence of the other.

It may be of interest to draw to your attention one unique feature of the Public Service Staff Relations Act. Under other labour relations legislation in Canada an employee can process a grievance to final determination by a third party only where it is alleged that an employee has been prejudicially affected by the misapplication or misinterpretation with respect to him of some provision of a collective agreement; in other words, there must first be a collective agreement before an employee acquires the right to arbitration of his grievance. The Public Service Staff Relations Act, on the other hand, gives to all employees — irrespective of, and in addition to, any right they may have under a collective agreement — the basic right to process to adjudication any grievance in respect of disciplinary action by the employer resulting in discharge, suspension or the imposition of a financial penalty. The decision of an adjudicator is final and binding, whether it be on a grievance arising under a collective agreement or a grievance relating to disciplinary action having the consequences just indicated. In the latter instance the decision of the adjudicator may include a directive that an employee who has been dismissed be reinstated and compensated for loss of earnings resulting from the improper discharge.

This brings us to the provisions of the Public Service Staff Relations Act that deal with negotiation disputes and it is here that we find one of the most innovative features of the legislation. I must begin my comments on this aspect of the topic by telling you that, in the course of the inquiries that were conducted and the discussions that took place before the legislation was introduced, some employee organizations maintained that they ought to have the same right to strike as is accorded to other employees, that there could be no effective collective bargaining without the right to strike and that to deprive them of the right to strike would relegate public servants to the status of second class citizens in their employment relations. Other employee organizations declared their abhorrence for the use by public servants of the strike weapon and favoured instead compulsory arbitration. Still other organizations suggested that their right to strike should be recognized but that arbitration should be made available to them as an alternative.

The legislation, as it was finally enacted, accommodated the diverse views of the employee organizations in a most interesting fashion. The bargaining agent, i.e., the employee organization certified by the Public Service Staff Relations Board as being entitled to require the employer to bargain with it on behalf of the employees in an appropriate constituency of employees, called a bargaining unit, has the right to opt for one of two types of dispute resolution process. It can choose to go to arbitration or it can choose the conciliation board process. If it picks the first alternative, it gives up the right to strike; if it selects the conciliation board route, it will ultimately be entitled to go on strike if it cannot arrive at an agreement with the employer. The choice between the two processes must be made before the bargaining agent gives notice to the employer of its desire to bargain and, once exercised, the option is binding upon it for the immediately ensuing set of negotiations. A bargaining agent can alter its option by giving notice to that effect not earlier than one month before it becomes entitled to give notice to the employer of its desire to renegotiate the collective agreement applicable to a particular bargaining unit. The right to specify an option is a prerogative of the bargaining agent and cannot be vetoed by the employer, although, as I shall point out later, the employer may influence indirectly the decision of the bargaining agent as to the option it specifies. Let us now examine the legislative provisions relating to each of these options and then go on to see how they have worked out in practice since the Act came into force.

Where the bargaining agent has opted for arbitration and the parties reach an impasse in their negotiations for a new agreement or in the renegotiation of the previous agreement, either party may refer the items in dispute to arbitration. The reference is made to the Public Service Arbitration Tribunal, a permanent tri-partite tribunal consisting to two panels of members representative of the interest of the employer and of the employees, respectively, under the chairmanship of a neutral chairman. The representative members of the Tribunal are appointed by the Public Service Staff Relations Board; the chairman is nominated by the Public Service Staff Relations Board and appointed by the Government, as is the case with the adjudicators of whom I spoke earlier. The chairman of the Public Service Arbitration Tribunal has tenure for a term, specified in his instrument of appointment, not to exceed five years, but a retiring chairman may be reappointed for a further term. On each reference to arbitration, the Tribunal consists of the chairman and one member representative of the interests of the employer and one member representative of the interests of the employees, the representative members being selected in each case by the Chairman of the Public Service Staff Relations Board from the members of the respective panels appointed by the Public Service Staff Relations Board. The Public Service Arbitration Tribunal is a quasi-judicial body and makes its award after entertaining the representations of the parties. The award is final and binding. The Act spells out terms of reference for the Tribunal and they are as follows:

> In the conduct of proceedings before it and in rendering an arbitral award in respect of a matter in dispute, the Arbitration Tribunal shall consider
>
> (a) the needs of the Public Service for qualified employees;
> (b) the conditions of employment in similar occupations outside the Public Service, including such geographic, industrial or other variations as the Arbitration Tribunal may consider relevant;
> (c) the need to maintain appropriate relationships in the conditions of employment as between different grade levels within an occupation and as between occupations in the Public Service;
> (d) the need to establish terms and conditions of employment that are fair and reasonable in relation to the qualifications required, the work performed, the responsibility assumed and the nature of the services rendered; and
> (e) any other factor that to it appears to be relevant to the matter in dispute.

Where the option specified for the resolution of bargaining impasses for a bargaining unit is the reference of the matters in dispute to a conciliation board and there is a breakdown in the negotiations, either party may request that a conciliation board be established. As I pointed out earlier, authority to establish a conciliation board is vested under other labour relations legislation in Canada in the appropriate Minister of Labour. In so far as the federal Public Service is concerned, since the federal Minister of Labour is part of management, it was necessary to vest in other hands the powers with regard to the conciliation process usually vested under the general labour relations legislation in the Minister of Labour. Under the Public Service Staff Relations Act, these powers are vested in myself as Chairman of the Public Service Staff Relations Board. Here again is an illustration of the way in which Parliament has sought to guarantee that the administration of the collective bargaining scheme for federal public servants in Canada will be completely independent of the Government, which is the employer.

A conciliation board is a tri-partite, ad hoc tribunal consisting of one nominee of each of the parties and a third member who acts as chairman, appointed on the nomination of the two representative members or, if they fail to agree, by the Chairman of the Public Service Staff Relations Board. A conciliation board is charged with the duty of entertaining the representations of the parties and endeavouring to bring about agreement between them in relation to the matters in dispute. The primary function of the Board is to bring about a settlement of the dispute. If it fails in its efforts, the conciliation board is required to present a report setting out its findings and recommendations. Because of the relatively short period of time within which a conciliation board must complete its work under the Public Service Staff Relations Act — usually two to four weeks from the day the board enters upon its duties — the reports of such boards usually consist, in the main, of recommendations. There is little opportunity for the preparation of the more elaborate reports that are sometimes produced by what are known in the United States as fact-finding boards.

Where the bargaining agent has opted for the conciliation board route for the resolution of negotiation impasses, the bargaining agent acquires the right to call a lawful strike and the employees become entitled to engage in a lawful strike at the expiration of seven days from the day on which the report of the conciliation board is submitted. That the right of federal public servants to engage in a strike should be recognized by statute has been regarded by some as an act of sheer folly. However here again we have to look at the Public Service Staff Relations Act in the historical context. In most jurisdictions in Canada, municipal public servants have had the right to strike since 1944. Prior to 1967, provincial public servants have had this right in only two provinces — since 1945 in Saskatchewan and in Quebec since 1966. In addition, in many jurisdictions in Canada, the employees of quite a number of Crown corporations, such as the Canadian National Railway, the Canadian Broadcasting Corporation and the Ontario Hydro Electric Power Commission, have also had the statutory right to strike since 1944. The provisions of the Public Service Staff Relations Act which accorded a similar right to federal public servants, while highly innovative, was not quite the radical departure from the traditions of the past that some appear to see in it.

Because of the nature of the services that government renders to the public — and I am sure that I need not elaborate on this point for this audience — there are some services so essential to the public welfare that no civilized community could look with equanimity on the public being deprived of them. Though the government was prepared in 1967 to accept the principle that federal public servants should have the right to strike, it was not prepared to run the risk of having certain essential services disrupted by a strike. The Public Service Staff Relations Act therefore declares that, even though a bargaining agent opts for the conciliation board route to resolve negotiation disputes for a particular bargaining unit, certain employees in such a bargaining unit may not go on strike despite the fact that their fellow employees in the same bargaining unit may do so lawfully. The employees who are thus denied the right to strike are those engaged in duties the performance of which is, or will be, necessary in the interest of the safety or security of the public. I repeat, duties necessary in the interest of the safety or security of the public. The relevant provision does not comtemplate that, in the event of a lawful strike, government will be able to carry on business as usual and make available to the public other services which are usually available.

The identification of the employees who are engaged in the performance of these necessary duties is not left to unilateral determination by the employer. The legislation declares that the employer shall provide to the bargaining agent at an appropriate time a list of the employees in a particular bargaining unit whom it regards as performing the requisite essential services. If the bargaining agent challenges the list or any part of it, the final determination as to what employees fall into the class is made by the Public Service Staff Relations Board, after hearing evidence and considering the representations of the parties. The employees whom the Board finds to be performing the stipulated essential duties are referred to in the legislation as designated employees.[2]

I said earlier that, although the specification of the impasse resolution process is a prerogative of the bargaining agent, nevertheless, the employer may influence indirectly the decision of the bargaining agent as to the option it chooses. What I had in mind is that, if the employer's proposals as to the employees who are to be designated for any bargaining unit are very extensive or, if on objection by the bargaining agent the Board does designate a substantial number of employees in any unit, the capacity of a bargaining agent to conduct an effective strike in respect of that unit may be so weakened that the bargaining agent may come to the conclusion that it is not realistic for it to proceed by the conciliation board route. Tangentially, it may be noted that a bargaining agent is likely to prefer the arbitration route where it has doubts as to whether the employees in a particular bargaining unit have the stomach to engage in a strike or if the services rendered by the employees in a particular bargaining unit are of such a peripheral nature that a strike of such employees may have little impact on the public.

The Act also safeguards the public interest in another way. There is an overriding authority vested in the employer to make orders necessary in the interest of the safety or security of Canada or any state allied or associated with Canada. Orders made under this provision are not subject to review by any of the agencies established under the Public Service Staff Relations Act.

So much for the provisions of the Act itself on the right to strike. However, so that you may have the full picture, I must refer to a statement by the Honourable E. J. Benson, at the time President of the Treasury Board, on second reading of the Public Service Staff Relations Bill in the House of Commons. He said:

> I have already indicated that, where a bargaining agent rejects arbitration in favor of the process involving conciliation and the right to strike, provision is made for the designation of employees whose services are necessary in the interests of the safety and security of the public.
>
> In relation to this aspect of the proposed legislation, however, it is not necessary for me to remind honourable members of the ulti-

mate sovereignty of parliament and its authority to protect and safeguard the public interest. It is, I believe, our duty in dealing with issues of this kind to legislate in such a way as to deny no man the ordinary rights and privileges of Canadian citizens unless in the public interest it is absolutely necessary to do so. On the other hand, no one should doubt the capacity or willingness of Parliament to qualify such rights and privileges where they are being used in gross disregard for the well-being of the community.

What I have said so far really gives you no more than the bare bones of the legislation. Time does not permit a detailed account of how the processes for the resolution of negotiation impasses under the Public Service Staff Relations Act have worked in practice. I shall be happy to provide on request to those of you who may be interested comprehensive statistics and information on what has occurred since 1967. For present purposes, I shall content myself with a few highlights.

As was expected when the legislation was introduced, the vast majority of bargaining agents representing the vast majority of employees in the Canadian federal public service — bargaining agents for 101 units comprising 160,000 employees — opted in the initial stage for arbitration. Bargaining agents for 14 units comprising 38,000 employees opted for the reference of their disputes to a conciliation board. Since then, bargaining agents for two units (60 employees) have specified an alteration of the process from conciliation to arbitration and bargaining agents for 9 units (30,000 employees) have switched from arbitration to conciliation. The score thus stands at this time as follows: arbitration 130,000, conciliation board 68,000. Arbitration is still the preferred process for dealing with negotiation disputes by a wide, though narrowing, margin. I firmly believe that, what may appear to be a growing disenchantment with arbitration may be attributed in large degree, not to disillusionment with the process itself, but with statutory limitations on the type of matters that may be referred to the Arbitration Tribunal. Some of the matters that cannot be dealt with by the Arbitration Tribunal nevertheless fall within the scope of bargaining under the legislation and may be attainable by those bargaining agents that choose the conciliation board route. The attractiveness of arbitration as an alternative to the strike will, over the long run, depend to a great extent on whether bargaining agents who rely on arbitration can legitimately expect to achieve thereby as much as they would if they were to resort to the conciliation board route. Unless there is a reasonable relationship between the benefits gained under both schemes, there is a danger that, in the not too distant future, bargaining agents that have opted for arbitration may alter their specification of a dispute resolution process. There is reason to hope that a review of the legislation that is now under way will reduce or eliminate the differences between the matters that are bargainable and those that are arbitrable.

It is a commonly accepted article of faith among trade unionists that collective bargaining and arbitration of negotiation disputes are incompatible; that, once the parties know beforehand that issues in dispute can be resolved by a binding decision made by a third party, the incentive to bargain and make every reasonable effort to make a collective agreement is destroyed. My assessment of the situation is that these fears are not supported by experience under the Public Service Staff Relations Act.

I said earlier that bargaining agents for 101 bargaining units had specified arbitration as the dispute resolution process in the early days following the coming into operation of the legislation. Settlements were arrived at without reference to arbitration for about 94 per cent of these bargaining units and, even in the very small percentage of cases in which there was a formal reference to the Arbitration Tribunal, there was, in some instances, a settlement of the dispute before the reference was heard. As a matter of fact, in several cases the reference was heard and a settlement was reached before the Tribunal had an opportunity of making its award. In short, the experience in the first series of negotiations was that bargaining was carried on effectively notwithstanding the availability of binding arbitration as a dispute resolution process.

Since one may attribute this successful experience to the euphoria that prevailed in the early days of the history of the legislation, one may legitimately ask, did the situation change after the honeymoon was over? Our records show that there has been a sharp increase in the number of cases formally referred to arbitration. In fact, in second-round negotiations, excluding a relatively small number of cases that had not yet progressed to agreement or impasse, there was a formal reference to arbitration with respect to about 45 per cent of the units. I said there was a formal referral in this high percentage of negotiations — that is to say the bargaining agent filed the necessary documents to place the arbitration process in motion. Nevertheless, almost 50 per cent of the cases formally referred were settled by the parties subsequent to the referral and, indeed, in several instances after the hearing before the Arbitration Tribunal was completed but before the Tribunal rendered its award.

It is obvious that there has been a greater tendency recently for the parties to leave the final settlement of their disputes to the Arbitration Tribunal than was the case in the first few years. However, the figures I have given you do not tell the whole story and require some explanation. To my mind, they reflect, not so much a breakdown of the normal bargaining process, as a resort to arbitration in order to meet a number of unique problems that lay outside the day-to-day field of collective bargaining. Thus, a review of the Public Service Staff Relations Act is under way at the present time and bargaining agents are testing the scope-of-bargaining provisions of the legislation so that they will be in a position to make appropriate representations for the amendment of the legislation in this regard. Again, there was the proposal by our

Prices and Incomes Commission setting certain guidelines limiting the amount of increases in wages, salaries and fringe benefits that, in the opinion of the Commission, could be granted without contributing to the inflationary cycle in Canada. It must be recognized that, where arbitration is available, there will always be some cases in which one or other of the parties feels that it has no alternative but to resort to arbitration as was the case in the situations I just mentioned. The state of affairs that I described cannot be regarded as the norm and I suggest that we ought not to draw final conclusions from what has occurred during the last few months as to the capability and the desire of the parties to reach agreement under a regime of arbitration operating in normal circumstances.

Let us now turn to examine briefly the experience with the conciliation board process. Since the advent of collective bargaining, including a first and second round of bargaining, agreements for about one-half of the bargaining units for which the conciliation board route was specified as the dispute resolution process, were concluded without any reference being made to a conciliation board. In several instances in the first round, an agreement was arrived at after a formal reference to a conciliation board was made but before the board entered upon its duties; in most of the others the conciliation board was successful in its efforts to resolve the disputes. In two successive sets of negotiations involving postal employees, the conciliation board did not effect a settlement and strikes occurred which were ultimately settled through the intervention of a mediator whom I appointed with the concurrence of the parties. In one other instance, some of the employees in a bargaining unit of dockyard workers engaged in a week-long strike and the dispute was finally resolved through the efforts of the parties themselves without further third party intervention.

I believe even the most prejudiced observer would be prepared to concede that the incidence of negotiation — dispute strikes in the Public Service of Canada during the last four and a half years has been remarkably low. On the other hand, it cannot be denied that the two strikes in the Post Office caused the public a great deal of inconvenience and the economic cost to some sections of the public has been considerable. Would Canada have been better off if Parliament had not conceded the right to strike to public employees? I doubt it. Within the last two years strikes have occurred in the Post Office and among air traffic controllers in the United States despite a legislative prohibition against such strikes and despite the fact that the employees who engaged in such strikes were subject to heavy penalties. In my opinion, government is in a much happier situation when it sits across the table from leaders of unions who are acting within the law than it would be if it is called upon to deal with a band of outlaws.

The account of strikes in the federal Public Service of Canada that I have just given you is confined to strikes to resolve negotiation impasses. In addition to the strikes I have mentioned, there have been, since

1967, a number of unlawful strikes of short duration — strikes during the lifetime of a collective agreement. These strikes occurred, not directly because of the legislation, but indeed in the face of legislative provisions prohibiting such strikes. The cure for this malaise does not lie in the prohibition, but must be found elsewhere — so far as the federal Public Service of Canada is concerned in an improvement in managerial skills, in an increased discipline among union members as union members and in a more ready acceptance by employees of the adequacy of the legal system that has been established under the Act to protect their rights.

One of the key elements in the bargaining process that has been established in the federal Public Service in Canada is one that is not even mentioned in the legislation itself, that is, the Pay Research Bureau. The Bureau was established in 1957 as part of what was then known as the Civil Service Commission, at a time when the Commission was charged with certain responsibilities in the setting of wage rates for federal public servants. When the Public Service Staff Relations Act came into force, the Bureau was transferred from the Civil Service Commission to the administrative jurisdiction of the Public Service Staff Relations Board. The Bureau is an independent research organization whose function it is to assemble, analyze and make available to the employer and to the bargaining agents, as its terms of reference provide, "information on rates of pay, employee earnings, conditions of employment and related practices prevailing both inside the outside the Public Service to meet the needs of the parties to bargaining." The terms of reference instruct the Director of the Bureau to "consult regularly with employer representatives and certified bargaining agents to insure that, as far as possible within the limits of the Bureau's resources, their requirements are reflected in the Bureau's program." In furtherance of the Director's consultation responsibility, there has been established, under the chairmanship of the Vice Chairman of the Public Service Staff Relations Board, an Advisory Committee to advise the Chairman of the Public Service Staff Relations Board and, more particularly, the Pay Research Bureau "on matters of pay research such as appropriate priorities of studies, the selection of areas of studies and classes of employment on which research will be undertaken. . . . Sub-committees may be established to study in greater depth such specific problems as methods and techniques used, employees to be covered in surveys, specifications of classes to be surveyed, statistical measures to be used in presenting data, geographic and industrial details to be presented."

As the Director of Pay Research Bureau, Mr. T. J. Wilkins, has pointed out [*Civil Service Review*, September 1967]:

> In contrast to the practice prevailing even now in industry and other governments in Canada, the Pay Research Bureau has divorced from the pay determination process in order to enhance the

objectivity of the Bureau's findings and its operational independence. This point . . . cannot be overemphasized. The Bureau provides factual, objective and impartial information; it does not actually set rates of pay or recommend changes in existing rates. Whether or not compensation for the Public Service is adjusted when differences with private employers are demonstrated by Pay Research Bureau data is a matter for employer and employee representatives to resolve at the bargaining table.

What so often occurs in bargaining and in third-party intervention for the resolution of negotiation disputes in the private sector is that each side presents its own statistical and related information and much time is consumed in reconciling the discrepencies in the information that is thrown on the bargaining table or presented to the conciliator, the conciliation board or the arbitrator, if indeed reconciliation is possible at all. In the federal Public Service of Canada, the studies produced by the Pay Research Bureau, under the watchful eye of the Advisory Committee on which both sides are represented, make it possible for the parties to start from a common accepted base. They are not precluded from drawing inferences as to the significance the studies may have for their bargaining proposals or from submitting additional information. However, reliance on the studies removes from the bargaining table to a great degree the heat that is often engendered where each of two parties insists that its information and its information alone gives the correct picture, the implication being that the information presented by the other side is fiction or worse. It is of course obvious that, at a later stage, if the dispute reaches that stage, where a third party is called upon to mediate or arbitrate negotiation disputes, the fact that the third party can rely on authentic, objective information not only contributes to speedier disposition by the third party of the issues in dispute, but also eliminates the feeling that mediators and arbitrators often have that, in the limited time at their disposal, they have to make decisions at times based on nothing more than an intelligent guess as to what the true facts may be.

FOOTNOTES

[1] Throughout this address, the term "public servant" *does not* include employees of publicly owned enterprises, generally known in Canada as "Crown corporations." Most of these corporations and their employees are subject to the general labour relations legislation in Canada.

[2] For a discussion of the principles delineated by the Board in determining the classes of designated employees, see *Third Annual Report of the Public Service Staff Relations Board*, 1969/70, pp. 58 *ff*.

COLLECTIVE BARGAINING EXPERIENCE IN THE PUBLIC SERVICE OF CANADA*

The Public Service Alliance of Canada claims that the Public Service Staff Relations Act has failed in all its objectives except one, that is representation. The Act is viewed by the union as a hindrance to meaningful bargaining in the major areas of concern to employees. The authors deplore the use of a highly legalistic approach and the lack of human considerations in employer – employee relations and recommend amendments to rectify the situation.

On March 13, 1967, a landmark was established in the history of collective bargaining in Canada when, along with the Public Service Employment Act and amendments to the Financial Administration Act, the Public Service Staff Relations Act was proclaimed in force. These Acts introduced into the Public Service of Canada an employer – employee relations framework having a number of unique features.

As expected, fundamental changes in employer – employee relations have occurred in the last few years. To take an accurate inventory of the debit and credit sides of the staff relations ledger is not possible. However, it might be useful to enumerate the achievements and the failures of the bargaining system in order to evaluate whether the legislation has been conducive to producing the intended results.

Speaking firstly of achievements, an important test of the efficacy of any legislation for collective bargaining is "the extent to which there is a ready and willing acceptance by those who are subject to it of the fundamental right of employees to organize. . . ."[1] Applying this test to the PSSRA, it can be said that the legislation has been highly successful, because over 92 per cent of the eligible employees in the Public Service are now represented by certified bargaining agents.[2] Thus, most public servants today have opportunities to participate in decision-making processes which affect their work, career, aspirations and personal development.

A large number of public servants were organized prior to 1967, but the extent of their present organization and their acceptance by the employer are due mainly to the PSSRA. This perhaps is the only major achievement that can be attributed to the legislation. In most other area of the operation of the collective bargaining system, the Act has failed to achieve its objectives.

One of the major sources of the failures of the PSSRA is its clear bias against bargaining agents. Rather than establishing broad parameters within which the parties can work out arrangements to deal with questions of mutual interest, the government of the day attempted to foresee

* Extracts from the brief by the Public Service Alliance of Canada, April 1971, submitted to Bryden Commission. Reprinted with permission.

every conceivable situation, and then tried to provide answers even before the employer and the bargaining agents had a chance to assess their respective rights, responsibilities and changed roles. Throughout this process of devising solutions for expected problems, the makers of the law focused attention on the interests of the employer, and introduced safeguards in the legislation which protect the employer at the expense of the employee. That this is a natural phenomenon is explained by Mr. J. Finkelman, Chairman of the Public Service Staff Relations Board, in an address to the Second National Convention of our Organization:

> You must bear in mind that your employer has a character quite different from that of other employers. The persons who determine how the employer is to act in bargaining with your representative are at one and the same time the manager of the government enterprise and the persons who determine in large measure the form and content of the legislation under which collective bargaining takes place. When they are determining what provisions should be included in legislation applicable to other employers and their employees, they are making laws for others and they can adopt an objective stance. *When they are dealing with what should be included in public service bargaining legislation, they are in effect bargaining away privileges that they had previously enjoyed.* (Italics added.)

Similar observations were made by employee organizations including the Canadian Labour Congress which even expressed its concern that "the legislation itself will be more the shadow than the substance of genuine collective bargaining and of a sound employer – employee relationship"[3]

The experience of the last four years has borne out these fears and our participation in the bargaining process under the present legislation has conclusively shown that the cards are clearly stacked against the bargaining agent, and against employees. Every step in the process is regulated in favour of the employer to the point of turning the bargaining process into a farce.

The process works generally along these lines: After certification but before giving notice to bargain, the bargaining agent must specify the process for the resolution of a dispute (Sections 36(1) and 49(1)). The employer, therefore, knows in advance the rules of the game, even before bargaining commences. The employer, thus, is placed in a commanding position in which his bargaining strategy dictates the tactics of the bargaining agent.

Having told the employer in advance the route to follow in the event of an impasse, the bargaining agent faces another barrier which further tilts the balance in the employer's favour. The bargaining agent cannot effectively bargain a number of subjects because they are enshrined as employer's rights (Section 7), or because they fall within the jurisdiction of the Public Service Commission, or because they are covered under other legislation (Section 56(2)). This eliminates, among other things, job security, classification and superannuation as subjects of negotiations. On these vital matters, therefore, the employer's decision is the last word even though consultations may be held on any of these issues. The result is a severe handicap to the bargaining agent's ability not only to negotiate issues involving matters of crucial importance but also to engage in meaningful trade-offs to arrive at mutual accommodations.

The direction and the course of negotiations depend on whether the bargaining agent opts for arbitration or conciliation board. If the bargaining agent chooses the former, often it faces an adamant and non-flexible employer who gains a marked advantage from prolonging negotiations and shifting the burden of decision-making to a third party rather than become involved in the give-and-take process of resolving differences by meaningful collective bargaining. The Employer is aided and encouraged in pursuing such a course because the Arbitration Tribunal can deal only with the rates of pay, hours of work, leave entitlement, standards of discipline and other terms and conditions of employment directly related thereto (Section 70(1)). Such vital issues as job security, check-off, grievance procedure and others (Appendix G) are not arbitrable. The bargaining agent, therefore, has no alternative but to accept whatever the employer offers and efforts to negotiate meaningfully on such matters are completely frustrated.

If, instead of selecting arbitration, the bargaining agent opts for the conciliation board route, the chances are that the employer's tactics will change from those of delaying and of persisting in an unbending attitude, to those of limiting and even eliminating the effectiveness of the dispute settlement process. The employer has the power to designate an entire bargaining unit under the guise of the "safety and security of the Public" (Section 79(2)). If the bargaining agent decides to object to such designations, it is confronted with a lengthy process of representations and hearings at the PSSRB. Because no conciliation board can be established before designations are determined by the Board (Section 79(1)), the bargaining agent must endure months of wrangling. The bargaining agent loses much in such a situation, while the employer is left in an even stronger position.

More often than not, the negotiating process under the PSSRA is a succession of disappointments for bargaining agents, and every stage in this process adds to inevitable frustrations. The fact that a large number of collective agreement have been signed in the Public Service in the last four years is not indicative of the success of the machinery provided in the legislation. The employer is well aware that every bargaining agent is under pressure from its membership and that bargaining agents themselves recognize the futility of the exercise. The employer is able to exploit this situation. Many agreements are eventually concluded in spite, rather than because, of the Act.

Apart from the negotiating machinery, other aspects of employer – employee relations as provided in the legislation are equally unjust to bargaining agents. For example, a bargaining agent cannot file a grievance (Section 90) and, unless the bargaining agent is seeking to enforce an obligation arising out of a collective agreement or an arbitral award which cannot be a subject of an employee's grievance (Section 98), it cannot make reference to adjudication. What is more disturbing is the fact that only certain kinds of grievances can be referred to adjudication even by an employee (Section 91(1)). This leaves a large number of cases on which justice is not available. The employee must accept the employer's decisions at the final level of the grievance process however unsatisfactory such decisions may be.

Similarly, with regard to complaints to the PSSRB (Section 20), a bargaining agent has no relief in situations where the employer either alters a term or condition of employment during the bargaining process (Section 51), or fails to implement within statutory time limits the provisions of a collective agreement (Section 56(1)) or of an arbitral award (Section 74). Even where relief is available for certain complaints, it is inadequate (Section 21). The result is more frustration and despair for the bargaining agent, a weakening of the bargaining relationship, and perpetuation of the employer's unjust actions.

On the matters of managerial and confidential exclusions (Section 2(u)), the Act again damns the union and its members and favours the employer. An employee can be excluded as a grievance officer at a post where there may be no other employee for him to supervise (Section 2(u) (v)). Furthermore, in the face of objections to exclusions by a bargaining agent, the employer can change the sub-head under which designations were initially made. When confronted with challenges to exclusions, the employer can even unilaterally declare employees as exclusions while the PSSRB processes the objections. Once again, it is the bargaining agent who suffers.

In short, the machinery established by the PSSRA is grossly inequitable because it has created an imbalance of bargaining strength. A true collective bargaining relationship cannot develop within such a framework.

In addition to its inequity, the legislation has produced a system which is inefficient, rigid and difficult to comprehend. At the hearings of the Special Committee (of the House of Commons and of the Senate on employer – employee relations in the Public Service of Canada), the Honourable E. J. Benson took great pains to show that the PSSRA (Bill C-170) was not much longer than other similar legislation. He did this by comparing the number of clauses in Bill C-170 to those in other labour relations acts in Canada.[4] But it is not the number of clauses that determines the complexity or the rigidity of a legislation. It is the substance, or a lack of it, which reflects the nature of the law.

This is what makes the PSSRA a rigid legislation, because there are a number of unnecessary clauses which hamper employer – employee relations. For instance, parts of the Act dealing with the specification and alteration of the process for resolution of disputes (Sections 36, 37 and 38) make it impossible for the parties to be flexible in situations which merit flexibility. We do not feel that there was any necessity to incorporate such an elaborate a procedure.

At the same time, there are certain other matters which are omitted from the legislation notwithstanding the appropriateness of their inclusion in collective bargaining legislation. Restrictions on the adjudication process, for example, do not permit referral to adjudication of classification grievances and complaints with respect to appointments. There are, thus, three administrative bodies with quasi-judicial processes to dispense justice in the Public Service; (i) Adjudication under the PSSRA; (ii) classification grievance procedure under the Treasury Board (Employer); and (iii) appeal boards under the Public Service Commission. The existence of different judicial processes under separate administrative jurisdictions complicates matters considerably and produces inefficiency and inconsistency. Moreover, in the case of the classification grievance procedure and appeal boards, the Employer and the Public Service Commission, respectively are called upon to judge their own decisions. This is sheer mockery of justice and equity. No wonder many public servants have lost faith and confidence in the processes designed to right the wrongs.

A smooth conduct of the bargaining relationship is hampered further by the time-consuming nature of the administrative and quasi-judicial tribunals created under the PSSRB by the Act. We have the highest regard for the Chairman and other members of the Public Service Staff Relations Board, and our comments are not a reflection on their ability and qualifications to administer the bargaining machinery. We are merely stating the fact that whether a decision on a complaint made to the PSSRB (Appendix E) or an Arbitral Award (Appendix H) or an adjudication decision (Appendix I) was involved, in several instances, months had elapsed before decisions were rendered. Time taken to render arbitral awards has been particularly long and this further aggravates feelings of insecurity and instability. To be effective, wrongs should not only be redressed, but should be redressed promptly. Delayed justice, often, is equivalent to no justice at all.

What we have said above is not what *could* happen under the present legislation, but what *has* often happened in the last four years. Our experience compels us to conclude that the bargaining system in the Public Service is inequitable, inefficient, rigid and unnecessarily complex. Too much importance has been given to legalism and very little attention paid to the human aspects of employer – employee relations. Such a bargaining process does not fulfil the aims and aspirations of thousands of public servants subject to it, it does not respond to changes which are constantly taking place around us, and it does not permit employee organizations to fulfil their role of meaningfully representing their members. In other words, the Public Service bargaining system, as established by the 1967 legislation, is collective bargaining in name only. It does not permit the exercise of rights and freedoms so essential to the survival and growth of a bargaining system.

We believe that collective bargaining is part and parcel of the liberal democratic political system of the confederation of Canada. It is a "mechanism through which labour and management seek to accommodate their differences, frequently without strife, sometimes through it, and occasionally without success. As imperfect an instrument as it may be, there is no viable substitute in a free society."[5]

A commitment to these principles underlying the Canadian bargaining system is not enough if the legislative framework within which it has to operate does not permit the system to function to its maximum potential. If the parties are to operate freely to develop sound employer – employee relationships, they must enjoy a degree of flexibility which will allow for initiative, innovation, and imagination to evolve a mutually satisfactory relationship. Under the collective bargaining legislation in the Public Service, both sides are compelled to conduct their affairs within a narrow and a restricted frame of reference, which inhibits development of a sound bargaining relationship.

The restrictions in the PSSRA are the results of a belief that the Government as Employer is unique. This distinction was emphasized time and again by Government representatives at the Special Committee hearings. We feel that the uniqueness of the Public Service has been exaggerated beyond reason, and the experience of four years has shown that public servants are people with desires, hopes, aspirations and problems like employees in any other organization. The experience has also shown that the government as an employer is not very different from other employers. We feel that the government's role as an employer should be viewed in proper perspective because the myth that the government should have special prerogatives has been dispelled in the last few years.

Government's role as a government should be divorced from its role as an employer. There has been considerable confusion between these two roles. Government as the government of the country has made decisions and policy guidelines which have been imposed on public servants by the government in its capacity as the employer. Many public servants are convinced, for example, that this is precisely what has happened with respect to the government's pronounced wage guidelines. Public servants as captive employees are used by the government as the sacrificial goat. What is more alarming is the fact that in the minds of a number of our members even decisions of the Arbitration Tribunal seem to have been influenced by government pressures and policies. If public servants are to consider the bargaining process and various tribunals under the legislation as equitable means of resolving disputes, this situation must be improved.

We believe, therefore, that the collective bargaining legislation in the Public Service should approximate similar legislation governing bargaining relationships for other employers in Canada. At the same time, certain features incorporated in the legislation in 1967 should be retained, because, with improvements, these features can contribute a great deal towards a better bargaining machinery.

One such feature is the option of arbitration. Present restrictions on the jurisdiction of the Arbitration Tribunal tend to drive bargaining agents who have opted for arbitration in the past to the other route. The Education group in the Scientific and Professional category, for example, has decided to opt for the conciliation strike route in the current round of negotiations. A number of other groups are similarly inclined. It is our firm belief that were the restrictions on the matters that can be dealt with by the Tribunal removed, this tendency could be checked, because "the attractiveness of arbitration as an alternative to the strike will, over the long run, depend to a great extent on whether bargaining agents who select the arbitration route can legitimately expect to attain through that route as much as they would if they were to resort to the other route."[6] All matters which are negotiable should be arbitrable, if those who select arbitration are to be treated equitably.

Limitations of arbitration create horrible dilemmas for employees in certain groups in which substantial portions of bargaining units have been designated under the "safety and security" provisions, i.e. Firefighters, Lightkeepers and Correctional units in the Operational category (Appendix K), where 100 per cent of the employees, we repeat, 100 per cent are designated. If these employees opt for arbitration, they cannot resolve disputes on more than a handful of subjects because of the limitations on matters within arbitration's jurisdiction. If they choose conciliation, they cannot strike because of 100 per cent designation. Where are these employees to turn to for justice? Under the PSSRA, nowhere, unless the Act is revised to extend the arbitration process to all matters which are negotiable.

But there are severe limitations in the legislation with respect to matters which can even be negotiated. Job security, for instance, cannot be subject to bargaining at present. Our experience with the layoffs over the last couple of years clearly indicates that public servants cannot tolerate this situation. We must have the right to negotiate provisions with respect to job security if we are to represent public servants meaningfully. Similarly, classification standards must be brought within the confines of collective bargaining. As long as classification is an employer's prerogative, we are going to encounter severe handicaps in effectively dealing with one of the most important aspects of employment which determines employees' jobs, careers and earnings. The problems created by the inability of bargaining agents to negotiate matters related to classification multiply because, by virtue of the authority vested in the employer, employees' classifications can be changed at the employer's whim. This may negate improvements achieved through bargaining. If bargaining agents cannot negotiate job security and classification matters, they cannot deal with crucial aspects of employer – employee relations.

The other major area of considerable concern is the limitations on the grievance and classification process. This is the process which is available to employees through which personal grievances and violations of collective agreements and arbitral awards are to be dealt with. But restrictions imposed on the process render it useless in many situations. A large number of wrongs, therefore, cannot be righted. We feel that revision to the grievance and adjudication machinery is an absolute necessity if the cause of justice is to be served. All grievances should be permitted to be referred to adjudication, and bargaining agents should be entitled to file a grievance or present it to adjudication.

We now come to the dispute settlement processes. The right to strike is as fundamental to a collective bargaining system as the right to free speech in a free democratic society. The right of public servants to strike has been recognized in the PSSRA, but the exercise of this right is made so difficult through cumbersome and rigid regulations, that it almost denies this freedom. We see no necessity for the requirement that bargaining agents must specify, in advance of negotiations, which of the two processes they wish to follow in case of an impasse. If collective bargaining in the Public Service is to be freed from barriers imposed by artificial restrictions, this requirement should be removed. Until that happens, the process will only be a shadow rather than the substance of true collective bargaining.

Another source of concern is the absence of any redress procedure when the employer fails to observe certain provisions of the Act. We believe that no violation should go unredressed, and that the present deficiency of the legislation should be removed by providing the enforcement of PSSRB's orders through the Federal Court of Canada and by empowering the Board to examine complaints alleging non-observance of any of the provisions of the Act or regulations made thereunder.

No brief on collective bargaining in the Public Service can be complete without a mention of the Public Service Commission, because its operation affects a number of matters which, in turn, relate to employee – employer relations. We are dissatisfied with the way the Public Service Commission is operating and its failure in providing adequate protection for the merit system worries us. We believe that the delegation of staffing authority to departments defeats the very premises on which the merit system was founded. We have dealt in Part II of Volume I with those areas of the Public Service Employment Act which, insofar as they affect collective bargaining, need revision. In short, we feel that these matters should be dealt with through the bargaining process.

Last, but not the least important, is the matter of union security. Under the present legislation, dues check-off can be negotiated but cannot be dealt with by the Arbitration Tribunal. Bargaining agents are often placed in the most miserable position in which they find that their very bread and butter are used by the employer in order to achieve certain advantages. We believe that not only should union security be arbitrable but that it should not also be subject to any tampering by the employer at the negotiating table. In our opinion, therefore, union security should be granted to a certified bargaining agent as of a right and should be enshrined in the legislation.

But our concern is not only for employees who have already been granted collective bargaining rights, however limited these rights may be. We are just as much concerned with those public servants who do not have the fundamental rights of organization and association. We are speaking here of the Canadian Armed Forces, the Royal Canadian Mounted Police, the employees of the House of Commons and of the Senate, the household staff of the Governor General and employees locally engaged at Canadian posts abroad. If collective bargaining is accepted as an institution basic to our democratic system, there should be no discrimination in granting bargaining rights between these and other employees.

Not all developments must be painted negatively since the introduction of collective bargaining in the Public Service. To be sure, first round collective agreements have been secured on behalf of employees in a wide variety of occupational groups, and these agreements have included notable ameliorations in conditions of employment. However, in our opinion, the apparent genuine interest of the employer displayed at the outset of the new relationship is gradually being eroded by a toughening stand on so many critical issues. Negotiations over the past year have been protracted over several months without real progress being made. The restrictions imposed by the present collective bargaining legislation are used increasingly more forcefully by an employer who appears to be leaning and deviating more and more heavily on the real letter of these restrictions as opposed to being primarily concerned in continuing the original course of good-will labour – management relations which existed two or more years ago.

We wish to conclude by emphasizing that no system which entails human elements to any significant degree can be perfect. Collective bargaining is one such system which involves certain risks. But risks inherent in a system that allows the parties wide latitude and freedom are less serious than the disadvantages and frustrations that flow from elaborate restrictions and prohibitions.

FOOTNOTES

[1] Finkelman, J., Chairman, Public Service Staff Relations Board, Convention of the Public Service Alliance of Canada, Toronto, January 27, 1970.

[2] *PSSRB*: Third Annual Report 1969/70, p. 8. About 99 per cent of eligible employees are represented, but slightly over 6 per cent of public servants are excluded.

[3] *Canadian Labour Congress*. Submission to the Joint Committee of the House and the Senate in the Public Service of Canada, July 25, 1966, pp. 2-3.

[4] *Benson, E. J.*, Minister of National Revenue, Preparatory Committee on Collective Bargaining in the Public Service before the Special Joint Committee of the Senate and of the House of Commons on Employer – Employee Relations in the Public Service of Canada. Minutes of Proceedings and Evidence No. 6, p. 202.

[5] *Task Force on Labour Relations*, Canadian Industrial Relations, Queen's Printer, 1969, p. 138.

[6] *Finkelman, J.*, Chairman, PSSRB. An address to the Second National Convention of the Public Service Alliance of Canada, Toronto, January 27, 1970.

QUESTIONS FOR DISCUSSION, PART 5

(1)   What are external and internal forces which have a restraining influence on the organization of white collar workers?

(2)   Will the white-collar workers' self-image, as being employees distinct from the blue collar ones, handicap them psychologically and prevent them from achieving the same benefits from collective bargaining that the blue collar workers have achieved?

(3)   What are the ramifications of having technical, clerical and professional employees in the same bargaining unit?

(4)   Compare and contrast the public service employees legislation in Nova Scotia, Ontario, New Brunswick and Saskatchewan.

(5)   Discuss the various approaches used for settling disputes for federal public servants.

(6)   What are the main differences between grievance settlement procedures for employees in the private sector and for federal civil servants?

(7)   Define the "Designated Employees" within the context of the Public Staff Service Relations Act (1967). Why is it that more employees in the federal service have chosen the compulsory arbitration option over the strike option for settling negotiation disputes?

(8)   What are some of the subjects which are bargainable in the private sector but excluded from the federal sector? What is the rationale for such exclusion?

(9)   In what manner do the two authors (Finkelman and Public Service Alliance of Canada) in the last section differ in their opinions on the workability and fairness of the Canadian Public Service Staff Relations Act (1967)?

(10)   Is it correct to say that a definition of "essential service" not only varies from one sector to another (private, municipal, provincial or federal sectors) but also from one party to another (unions, management, public) depending upon their perception and self-interest? How could this dilemma be resolved?

SELECTED BIBLIOGRAPHY
LABOUR RELATIONS IN CANADA
Books

Abella, Irving. *The Struggle For Industrial Unionism In Canada*. Toronto: University of Toronto Press, 1972.

————.*Nationalism, Communism, and Canadian Labour: The CIO, Communist Party, and the Canadian Congress of Labour 1935-1956*. Toronto: University of Toronto Press, 1973.

Adell, B. L. and D. D. Carter. *Collective Bargaining for University Faculty in Canada*. Kingston: Industrial Relations Centre, Queen's University, 1972.

Anton. F. R. *Government Supervised Strike Votes: A Study Prepared for the Department of Labour*. Don Mills, Ontario: CCH Canadian Limited, 1961.

————.*The Role Of Government in the Settlement of Industrial Disputes*. Toronto: Commerce Clearing House, 1962.

Archambault, J. P. and S. J. *Les Syndicats catholiques du Canada*. Montreal: Ecole Sociale Populaire, 1936.

Arthurs, H. W. *Collective Bargaining by Public Employees in Canada: Five Models*. Ann Arbor: Institute of Labour and Industrial Relations, University of Michigan – Wayne State University, 1971.

Bennett, W. *Builders Of British Columbia*. Vancouver: Broadway, 1937.

Cameron and Young. *The Status of Trade Unions in Canada*. Kingston: Queen's University, 1960.

Carrothers, A. W. R. *Collective Bargaining Law in Canada*. Toronto: Butterworth, 1965.

————.*Labour Arbitration In Canada*. Toronto: Butterworth, 1961.

Confederation of National Trade Unions. *Quebec Labour — The Confederation of National Trade Unions Yesterday and Today*. Montreal: Black Rose Books, 1972.

La Confédération des Syndicats Nationaux. *En Grève*. Montreal: Editions du jour inc. 1963).

Crispo, John G. *International Unionism — A Study in Canadian – American Relations*. Toronto: McGraw-Hill, 1967.

Crysler, A. C. *Handbook of Employer – Employee Relations in Canada*. Don Mills, Ontario: CCH Canadian Limited, 1969.

Cunningham, W. B. *Compulsory Conciliation and Collective Bargaining: The New Brunswick Experience*. New Brunswick Department of Labour, jointly with Industrial Relations Centre, McGill University, Montreal, 1958.

Curtis, The Development and Enforcement of the Collective Agreement. Kingston: Queen's University, 1966.

Dion, Gerard, ed. *La Fusion CTCC-CCT*. (Quebec: Les presses de l'Université Laval, 1957).

Downie, Brian. Relationships Between Canadian – American Wage Settlements: An Empirical Study of Five Industries. Kingston: Industrial Relations Centre, Queen's University, 1970.

Frankel, S. J. and R. C. Pratt. *Municipal Labour Relations in Canada*. Montreal: Canadian Federation of Mayors and Municipalities, 1954.

French, Doris. *Faith, Sweat And Politics: The Early Trade Union Years in Canada*. Toronto: McClelland And Stewart, 1962.

Goldenberg, H. C. and John Crispo, eds. *Construction Labour Relations.* Ottawa: Canadian Construction Association, 1968.

Horowitz, Gad. *Canadian Labour in Politics.* Toronto: University of Toronto Press, 1968.

Isbester, A. F., D. Coates, and C. B. Williams. *Industrial and Labour Relations in Canada: A Bibliography.* Kingston: Queen's University, 1965.

Jain, Hem C., *Canadian Cases in Labour Relations and Collective Bargaining.* Don Mills, Ontario: Longman Canada Limited, 1973.

Jamieson, Stuart. *Industrial Relations in Canada.* Toronto: Macmillan, 2nd. ed., 1973.

Kovacs, A. E., ed. *Readings in Canadian Labour Economics.* Toronto: McGraw-Hill, 1961.

Kruger, A., and N. M. Metz. *The Canadian Labour Market: Readings in Manpower Economics.* Toronto: Centre for Industrial Relations, University of Toronto, 1968.

Latham, A. B. *The Catholic and National Unions of Canada.* Toronto: Macmillan of Canada, 1930.

Lipton, Charles. *The Trade Union Movement of Canada 1827-1959.* (Montreal: Canadian Social Publications, 1966).

Logan, H. A., N. J. Ware, and H. A. Innis. *Labour in Canadian – American Relations.* Toronto: Ryerson Press, 1937.

Logan, H. A. *Trade Unions in Canada, Their Development and Functioning,* Toronto: Macmillan, 1948.

Masters, D. C. *The Winnipeg General Strike.* Toronto: University of Toronto Press, 1950.

McHenty, Neil. *Mitch Hepburn.* Toronto: McClelland and Stewart, 1967.

Miller, R. U., and Fraser Isbester, eds. *Canadian Labour in Transition* Scarborough, Ontario, Prentice-Hall of Canada, 1970.

Ostry, S., and M. A. Zaidi. *Labour Economics in Canada.* Toronto: Macmillan of Canada, 2nd. ed., 1972.

Porter, John, *The Vertical Mosaic, an Analysis of Social Class and Power in Canada.* Toronto: University of Toronto Press, 1965.

Robin, Martin. *Radical Politics and Canadian Labour.* Kingston: Industrial Relations Centre, Queen's University, 1968.

Schneider, B. V. H. *Canadian Trailblazer: The New Collective Bargaining Law.* Chicago: Public Personnel Association, 1968.

Tremblay, L. M., and F. Panet-Raymond, *Bibliographie des relations du travail du Canada.* Montreal: Les presses de l'Université de Montréal, 1969.

Trudeau, Pierre-Elliott, ed. *La Grève de l'amiante.* Montreal: Cité Libre, 1956.

Wade, Mason and J. C. Falardean, eds. *Canadian Dualism: La Dualité canadienne.* (Toronto and Quebec: Universities of Toronto and Laval Presses, 1960).

Woods, H. D., and Sylvia Ostry. *Labour Policy and Labour Economics in Canada.* Toronto: Macmillan of Canada, 1962.

Woods, H. D., ed. *Patterns of Industrial Dispute Settlement in Five Canadian Industries.* Montreal: Industrial Relations Centre, McGill University, 1958.

————.*Labour Policy in Canada.* New York: St. Martin's Press, 1973.

Young, W. D. *Anatomy of a Party: The National CCF, 1932-1961.* Toronto: University of Toronto Press, 1969.

————.*The Contracting Out of Work.* Kingston: Queen's University, 1964.

Zakuta, Leo. *A Protest Movement Becalmed: A Study of Change in the CCF.* Toronto: University of Toronto Press, 1964.

Canadian Task Force Reports
Government Documents and Monographs

Arthurs, H. W. "Labour Disputes In Essential Industries," a Study for the Task Force on Labour Relations." Ottawa, 1970.

Atlantic Provinces Economic Council. "Collective Bargaining And Regional Development in the Atlantic Provinces." Halifax, 1973.

Bairstow, Frances, ed. "Winds of Change from the Provinces, and New Priorities in Labour Relations." Montreal: McGill Industrial Relations Centre, 22nd Annual Conference Proceeding, 1973.

——."White Collar Workers and Collective Bargaining." A Study for the Task Force on Labour Relations. Ottawa, 1968.

Belec, Paul. "Les Organisations syndicales au Québec." A Study for the Task Force on Labour Relations. Ottawa, November 1967.

Bernard, Paul. "Structures et pouvoirs de la Fédération des Travailleurs du Québec." Study No. 13 for the Task Force on Labour Relations. Ottawa, 1968.

Black, J. M. "Successful Labour Relations for Small Business." Toronto: McGraw-Hill, 1953.

Boyd, John D. "The Industrial Relations System of the Fishing Industry." A Study for the Task Force on Labour Relations. Ottawa, 1970.

Brown, D. "Interest Arbitration." A Study for the Task Force on Labour Relations. Ottawa, 1970.

Byleveld, H., "Management – Labour Cooperation from the Executive Viewpoint: A Survey of Executive Opinion and Experience." Montreal: National Industrial Conference Board, 1963.

Canada, Department of Labour, Economics and Research Branch. "Working Conditions in Canadian Industry." Ottawa: Queen's Printer, 1966-1971.

Canada, Department of Labour, Legislation Branch. "Labour Relations Legislation in Canada." Ottawa: Queen's Printer, 1970.

Canadian Industrial Relations, "Report of The Prime Minister's Task Force on Labour Relations." Ottawa: Queen's Printer, 1968.

Commerce Clearing House. "Canadian Law Reporter: Federal and Provincial Labour Legislation, Topical Outline on Unemployment Insurance, Court and Labour Board Decisions, Case Outline." Ottawa: CCH Canadian Limited, 1968.

Commerce Clearing House. "Solutions for Today's Personnel Problems." (Chicago, Illinois: Commerce Clearing House, 1969).

Christie, Innis, and Morley Gorsky. "Unfair Labour Practices." Task Force Study No. 10. Ottawa: 1968.

Coates, Norman. "Collective Bargaining in the Automobile Manufacturing Industry." A Study for the Task Force on Labour Relations. Ottawa, 1970.

Crispo, John, ed. "Industrial Relations — Challenges and Responses." Toronto: University of Toronto Press, 1966.

Dofny, J., and P. Bernard. "Le Syndicalisme au Québec: Structure et mouvement." A Study for the Task Force on Labour Relations. Ottawa, 1968.

Eaton, George E. "Collective Bargaining in the Canadian Chemical Industry." A Study for the Task Force on Labour Relations. Ottawa, 1970.

Economic Council of Canada, "National Conference on Labour – Management Relations." (March 20-22, 1967, convened by the Economic Council of Canada.) Ottawa: Queen's Printer, 1967.

Elliott, Howard J. C. "A Study of Industrial Relations in the Electrical Products Industry." A Study for the Task Force on Labour Relations. Ottawa, 1970.

Flood, Maxwell. "Wildcat Strike in Lake City." A Study for the Task Force on Labour Relations, No. 15. Ottawa, 1968.

Frankel, Saul J. "Report of the Royal Commission on Employer – Employee Relations in the Public Service of New Brunswick. Frederiction: New Brunswick Department of Labour, 1967.

Freedman, Justice Samuel. "Report of the Industrial Inquiry Commission on Canadian National Railway Run-throughs." Ottawa: Queen's Printer, 1965.

Goldenberg, S. B. "Professional Workers and Collective Bargaining." A Study for the Task Force on Labour Relations. Ottawa, 1968.

Heeney, A.D.P. "Report of the Preparatory Committee on Collective Bargaining in the Public Service," Ottawa: Queen's Printer, 1965.

Herman, E. E. "Determination of the Appropriate Bargaining Unit by Labour Relations Boards in Canada." Ottawa: Canada Department of Labour, 1967.

Herman, E. "The Size And Composition of Bargaining Units." A Study for the Task Force on Labour Relations. Ottawa, 1970.

Issac, J. E. "Compulsory Arbitration in Australia." A Study for the Task Force on Labour Relations. Ottawa, 1970.

Jain, Harish, C. "A Study Of Managerial Recruitment in the Canadian Manufacturing Industry, Ontario." Hamilton: Faculty of Business, McMaster University, 1972.

Jain, Harish, C., and R. I. Hines. "Current Objectives of Canadian Manpower Programs." Hamilton: McMaster University, 1972).

Jain, Harish, C., and Hem C. Jain. "Staffing and Organization." Montreal: Sir George Williams University, 1973.

Jain, Hem, C. "Continuous Bargaining for Technological Changes — Some Developments in the U.S.A. and Canada." A chapter from a book, *Technological Change and Industry*. New Delhi: Shri Ram Centre for Industrial Relations, 1971.

Jamieson, Stuart. "Times of Trouble: Labour Unrest and Industrial Conflict in Canada, 1900-66." A Study for the Task Force on Labour Relations, No. 22. Ottawa, 1968.

Kehoe, Mary. "Labour Unions — An Introductory Course." Ottawa, Extension Department, St. Patrick College, 1962.

Kovacs, Aranka. "A Study of Joint Labour – Management Committees at the Provincial Level in the Provinces of Canada." A Study of the Task Force on Labour Relations. Ottawa, 1970.

Kruger, Arthur. "Human Adjustment to Industrial Conversion." A Study for the Task Force on Labour Relations. Ottawa, 1970.

MacDonald, Bruce, M. "The Industrial Relations System in the Printing Industry, Canada." A Study for the Task Force on Labour Relations. Ottawa, 1970.

McKechnie, Graham. "The Trucking Industry." A Study for the Task Force on Labour Relations. Ottawa, 1970.

McLeod, Keith, and G. Starr. "Collective Bargaining in Ontario, 1971. Toronto: Research Branch, Ontario Department of Labour, March, 1971.

Malles, Paul. "Trends in Industrial Relations Systems of Continental Europe." A Study for the Task Force on Labour Relations. Ottawa, 1970.

March, R. R. "Public Opinion and Industrial Relations." A Study for the Task Force On Labour Relations. Ottawa, 1970.

Montague, J. T., and S. M. Jamieson, (eds). "British Columbia Labour – Management Conference, 1963." Vancouver: Institute of Industrial Relations, University of British Columbia, 1963.

Morin, Fernand. "Procédure de decision utiliseé par le syndicat pour accepter l'offre patronale ou faire grève." A Study for the Task Force on Labour Relations, Ottawa, 1970.

Muir, J. D. "Collective Bargaining by Canadian Public School Teachers." A Study for the Task Force on Labour Relations, No. 21. Ottawa, 1968.

New Brunswick. "Industrial Inquiry Commission on Labour – Management Relations in the Saint John Construction Industry." Fredericton: New Brunswick Department of Labour, 1969.

Palmer, E. E. "Preliminary Report on Constitutional Law Facing the Labour Task Force." A Study for the Task Force on Labour Relations. Ottawa, 1970.

Peitchinis, S.G. "Labour – Management Relations in the Railway Industry." A Study for the Task Force on Labour Relations, No. 20. Ottawa, 1968.

Pentland, H. C. "A Study of the Changing Social, Economic, Political Background of the Canadian System of Industrial Relations." A Study for the Task Force on Labour Relations. Ottawa, 1968.

Phillips, Paul. "No Power Greater — A Century of Labour in British Columbia." Vancouver: Federation of Labour, 1967.

Public Service Alliance of Canada. Brief Submitted to the Committee on Legislation Review, "Collective Bargaining in the Federal Public Service," Vols. 1 and 2. Ottawa: Public Service Alliance of Canada, April, 1971.

Quinet, F. "The Content and Role of Collective Agreements in Canada," Don Mills, Ontario: CCH Canadian Limited, 1969.

Rand, Hon. Ivan C. "Ontario Royal Commission Inquiry into Labour Disputes — The Rand Report." Toronto: CCH Limited, 1968.

Rogow, R. "Supervisors and Collective Bargaining." A Study for the Task Force on Labour Relations. Ottawa: 1970.

Rovet, E. "Employer – Employee Rights." Layman's Guide to Ontario Labour Law. Vancouver: Self Counsel Press, 1973.

Samlaisingh, Ruby. "Broadcasting — An Industry Study." A Study for the Task Force on Labour Relations, No. 1. Ottawa, 1968.

Schieff, Stanley. "Labour Arbitration Procedures." A Study for the Task Force on Labour Relations. Ottawa, 1970.

Simmons, C. Gordon. "Collective Bargaining at the Municipal Government Level in Canada." A Study for the Task Force on Labour Relations. Ottawa, 1970.

———."Coordinated Bargaining by Unions and Employers." A Study for the Task Force on Labour Relations. Ottawa: 1970.

Solasse, Bernard. "Syndicalisme, consommation et société de consommation." A Study for the Task Force on Labour Relations. Ottawa, 1970.

Swartz, Gerald. "Industrial Relations in the Canadian Shipping Industry." A Study for the Task Force on Labour Relations. Ottawa, 1970.

Vanderkamp, John. "The Time Patter of Industrial Conflict in Canada, 1901-1966." A Study for the Task Force on Labour Relations. Ottawa: 1970.

Wace, Stephen, T. "The Longshoring Industry: Strikes and Their Impact." A Study for the Task Force on Labour Relations. Ottawa, 1970.

Weiler, Paul C. "Labour Arbitration and Industrial Change." A Study for the Task Force on Labour Relations. Ottawa, 1970.

Wener, Normand. "Les Organisations syndicales au Québec." A Study for the Task Force on Labour Relations. Ottawa, 1970.

Westley, W. A. and W. Margaret. "Work and Industrial Relations in a Mass Consumption Society." Canada, A Study for the Task Force on Labour Relations. Ottawa, 1970.

Wonnacott, Paul, and Wonnacott R. "The Wage Parity Question", A Study for the Task Force on Labour Relations, a Special Report. Ottawa, 1969.

Wood, W. D. "The Current Status of Labour – Management Cooperation in Canada." Kingston: Queens University, Industrial Relations Centre, 1964.

Woods, H. D. (ed.) "Industrial Conflict and Disputes Settlement." 7th Annual Conference, Industrial Relations Centre, McGill University, April 18 and 19, 1955. Montreal: Quality Press, 1955.

Journals

1. *Relations Industrielles – Industrial Relations.* Laval University.
2. *Labour Gazette.* Canada, Department of Labour, Ottawa.
3. *Canadian Personnel and Industrial Relations Journal.* Toronto.
4. *Industrial and Labor Relations Review.* Cornell University, Ithace, New York.
5. *Industrial Relations.* University of California, Berkeley, California.

Other Useful Publications

1. Industrial Relations Research Association (U.S.). Annual Conference, Proceedings and other publications. University of Wisconsin, Madison, Wisconsin.
2. American Management Association publications.
3. Laval University. Department of Industrial Relations, Proceedings of Annual Conference.
4. McGill University. Industrial Relations Centre, Proceedings of Annual Conference.
5. Queen's University. Industrial Relations Centre's publications.
6. University of Illinois. Labor and Industrial Relations Center, publications.
7. University of California. Labor and Industrial Relations Center, publications.
8. University of Toronto. Labour and Industrial Relations Centre, publications.
9. National Industrial Conference Board's publications, Montreal.
10. National Academy of Arbitrators. Annual Conference Proceedings, Bureau of National Affairs, Inc., Washington, D. C. 20037.